D1103872

j

U.S. Race Relations in the 1980s and 1990s

U.S. Race Relations in the 1980s and 1990s: Challenges and Alternatives

Edited by

Gail E. Thomas
Department of Sociology
Texas A&M University
College Station, Texas

⊙HEMISPHERE PUBLISHING CORPORATION
A member of the Taylor & Francis Group

New York   Washington   Philadelphia   London

U.S. RACE RELATIONS IN THE 1980s AND 1990s: Challenges and Alternatives

Copyright © 1990 by Hemisphere Publishing Corporation. All rights reserved. Printed in the United States of America. Except as permitted under the United States Copyright Act of 1976, no part of this publication may be reproduced or distributed in any form or by any means, or stored in a data base or retrieval system, without the prior written permission of the publisher.

2 3 4 5 6 7 8 9   E B E B   9 8 7 6 5 4 3 2 1

This book was set in Times Roman by Hemisphere Publishing Corporation. The editors were Amy Lyles Wilson and Shelley Klein; the production supervisor was Peggy M. Rote; and the typesetters were Linda Andros, Lori Knoernschild, Bonnie Sciano, and Laurie Strickland.
Cover design by Sharon M. DePass
Printing and binding by Edwards Brothers, Inc.

A CIP catalog record for this book is available from the British Library.

Library of Congress Cataloging-in-Publication Data

U.S. race relations in the 1980s and 1990s.

   Includes bibliographical references.
   1. United States—Race relations.   2. Minorities—United States.   I. Thomas, Gail E.   II. Title: United States race relations in the 1980s and 1990s.   III. Title : US race relations in the 1980s and 1990s.
E184.A1U16 1990   305.8'00973'09048   89-24704

ISBN 0-89116-915-6

This work is dedicated to my mother, Miriam E. Thomas, and to all of the black and brown mothers and surrogate mothers (Ruby Parker, Malilu Person, Gloria Scott) who paid their dues and paved the way so that I might become a caring and competent individual who could make a meaningful contribution to the causes of freedom and justice for all.

Contents

Contributors *xiii*
Foreword *xvii*
Preface *xix*
Acknowledgments *xxiii*

PART I
EDUCATION AND RACE

1 **Racial Stratification and Education** **3**
  John U. Ogbu

  Understanding the Persistence of Inequality **3**
  The Case of Black Americans **6**
  The Future of Racial Stratification and Education **30**
  References **31**

2 **Current Issues Affecting Blacks and Hispanics**
  in the Educational Pipeline **35**
  James E. Blackwell

  The Current Status of Blacks and Hispanics in Education **38**
  Policy Implications **46**
  Implications for Race Relations **48**
  References **51**

3 **Issues of Race and Education Affecting Blacks and Hispanics:**
  Commentary on Ogbu and Blackwell **53**
  Grace L. Butler

  References **62**

4 Inner-City Schools—Poverty and Segregation: Has the Picture
   Changed Since 1967?   65
   James L. Parsons

   The Situation in 1967   67
   The Situation in the 1980s   71
   Conclusion and Recommendations   75
   References   76

5 Black Teachers: An Endangered Species in the 1990s   79
   Patricia J. Larke

   Contributions to the Shortage   80
   Effects of the Shortage   84
   Decreasing the Shortage   85
   Conclusion   90
   References   91

6 The Current Status of America's Inner-City Schools and Black
   Teachers: Commentary on Parsons and Larke   95
   Wanda E. Ward

   References   102

                                    PART II
       OCCUPATIONAL MOBILITY, ECONOMICS, AND CULTURAL PLURALISM

7 Sports and Race Relations in American Society   105
   Jomills Henry Braddock II

   Black Participation in American Sports   105
   Institutional Discrimination in the NFL: A Case Example   107
   Discussion and Implications   116
   References   119

8 Race Relations and Sports: Commentary on Braddock   121
   Lodis Rhodes

   References   126

9 *E Pluribus Unum:* The Impossible Dream?   127
   Charles B. Keely

   The Problem with Pluralism   128
   What is "Out of Control"?   130
   The Unum   133
   References   136

10 **Race, Ethnicity, and the Portrait of Inequality: Approaching the 1990s** 137
Marta Tienda

Minority Family Well-Being, 1970–1985 138
Income Packaging and Labor Market Position 149
Discussion and Conclusions 155
References 158

11 **Issues in Ethnic Diversity and the Politics of Inequality in the 1990s: Commentary on Keely and Tienda** 161
David Alvirez

References 166

12 **Economic Progress for Black Americans in the Post–Civil–Rights Era** 167
David H. Swinton

Trends in Racial Inequality in Economic Life 169
Trends in Black Participation in Economic Activity 173
Explanations for the Post-1970 Persistence of Racial Inequality 179
Conclusions and Implications for Future Race Relations 183
References 185

13 **Inequality in America: The Failure of the American System for People of Color** 187
Edna Bonacich

Inequality in America 189
Capitalism and Racism 197
Facing the 1990s 205
References 208

14 **The Significance of Race in U.S. Economic and Occupational Life: Commentary on Bonacich and Swinton** 209
Walter R. Allen

Reflections and Conclusions 213
References 215

PART III
AMERICAN INDIANS: A SPECIAL AND NEGLECTED CASE

15 **Wounding the Spirit: Discrimination and Traditional American Indian Belief Systems**   219
   Carol Locust

   Discussion   229
   References   231

16 **Healing the Spirit: Commentary on Locust**   233
   Charmaine Bradley

   Looking to the Future   235
   References   238

17 **The Foster Children of American Education**   239
   Grayson Noley

   A Short History of Indian Education   240
   The Present Reality   244
   References   246

18 **American Indians: Education, Demographics, and the 1990s**   249
   John W. Tippeconnic III

   Demographic, Economic, and Social Data   249
   The Education of American Indians   252
   Observations: Approaching the 1990s   255
   References   257

19 **Indian Education and the 1990s: Commentary on Noley and Tippeconnic**   259
   G. Mike Charleston

   An Overview of the Socioeconomic Status of Indians   259
   The Federal Relationship   260
   Comments on Present and Future Conditions for Indians   261
   References   263

20 **Postscript—The Road Ahead in American Race Relations:**
    Challenges for the 1990s   **265**
    Gail E. Thomas

    Challenges for the 1990s   **267**
    References   **270**

Index   **273**

Contributors

About the Editor

Gail E. Thomas is professor of sociology at Texas A&M University. She obtained her undergraduate degree in sociology in 1970 from A&T State University at Greensboro, North Carolina. She received her master's and doctoral degrees from the University of North Carolina at Chapel Hill in 1973 and 1975. Her main research interests and areas of concentration are the educational and occupational attainment and achievement of underrepresented racial minorities and women, and racial and social stratification and inequality. Thomas is currently conducting a national study of major U.S. doctoral institutions to investigate their policies and practices in recruiting, enrolling, and retaining U.S. black and Hispanic students. She serves on a variety of national committees and task forces aimed at enhancing the educational and economic achievement and attainment of underrepresented minorities. Thomas has published extensively in national and international journals in the social sciences and higher education, including *The Sociological Quarterly, Harvard Educational Review, Science Education,* and *The International Journal of Higher Education.*

About the Authors

John U. Ogbu is professor of anthropology at the University of California, Berkeley. He is noted for his research on the nature and structure of American education for blacks, Mexican Americans, and other Hispanic populations. Among his works are *The Next Generation, Minority Education and Caste,* and "The Consequence of the American Caste System" in *The School Achievement of Minority Children,* edited by U. Neisser.

James E. Blackwell is professor of sociology at the University of Massachusetts in Boston. He has published extensively on minorities in higher education with a focus on graduate and professional education. Among his noted works are *Mainstreaming Outsiders: The Production of Black Professionals; The Black Community: Diversity and Unity;* and *Mentoring and Networking: Experiences of Black Professionals.*

Grace L. Butler is associate vice president for faculty affairs at the University of Houston. Her research interests are in higher education administration, organizational theory, and educational equity. She is author of "Opportunities for Career Advancement as Perceived by Teachers and Administrators" in *National Forum of Educational Administration and Supervision Journal* and coauthor of "The Technical Tools of Decision Making" in Boyan's (Ed.), *The Handbook of Research in Educational Administration.*

James L. Parsons is a doctoral candidate in the School of Education at Texas A&M University. He is project director of the Texas A&M School/University Research Collaborative and senior author of *An Aggregate Report of Nine Collaborative School Districts.*

Patricia J. Larke is assistant professor in the Department of Educational Curriculum and Instruction at Texas A&M University. She is codirector of the Minority Mentorship Project at Texas A&M. She has published in the *Journal of Law and Education, Arithmetic Teacher,* and *Education and Urban Society.* Her areas of research include multicultural education, teacher education, and school law.

Wanda E. Ward is associate professor of psychology and founder and director of the Center for Research on Minority Education at the University of Oklahoma. She is author of "The Effect of Social Comparison Processes on Self-Evaluation Reactions" in *Resources in Education* and coeditor of *Key Issues in Minority Education.*

Jomills Henry Braddock II is principal research scientist at Johns Hopkins University's Center for Social Organization of Schools/Center for Research on Elementary and Middle Schools. He is also director of the Center for Research on Effective Schools of the Disadvantaged Student. His research interests encompass issues of inequality and social justice. Among journals where his work appears are *Harvard Educational Review, Sociology of Education,* and *International Journal of Sociology and Social Policy.*

Lodis Rhodes is associate dean for Academic Affairs and Research at the Lyndon B. Johnson School of Public Affairs of the University of Texas at Austin. He is interested in public management, human services, and international trade. His most recent publication is *Housing Low Income Austinites: New Roles for the Austin Housing Authority in Meeting Changing Needs and New Community Demands* (University of Texas at Austin Press).

Charles B. Keely is professor of sociology and Herzberg Chair of Migration Policy in the Department of Demography at Georgetown University. He is nationally and internationally known for his work on migration and immigration policies and policy analysis and evaluation on immigration. He has published extensively and is author of *Global Refugee Policy: The Case for a Development Approach* and *U.S. Immigration: A Policy Analysis.*

Marta Tienda is professor of sociology at the University of Chicago and associate director of the Population Research Center. She is coauthor of the *Hispanic Population of the United States* (Russell Sage) and coeditor of *Divided Opportunities: Poverty, Minority and Social Policy* (Plenum) and *Hispanics in the U.S. Economy* (Academic Press). Her current research interests include the work and welfare consequences of amnesty, the migration and employment patterns of Puerto Ricans, and the intergenerational welfare behavior of inner-city minority populations.

David Alvirez is professor of sociology at University of Texas–Pan American. His research interest is in the educational problems of Mexican Americans. He is coauthor of *Assessing the Dropout Problems: Students' and School Personnel's Perceptions.*

David H. Swinton is an economist and dean of the School of Business at Jackson State University. He is noted for his work on poverty, labor, and income. He is author of "Economic Status of Blacks, 1987" in Janet Dewart's (Ed.), "Economics and Theories of Poverty" in *American Economic Review.*

Edna Bonacich is professor of sociology at the University of California, Riverside. She is well known for her work on dual labor markets. She is also author of *Asian Immigration Under Labor Capitalism* and *Immigrant Entrepreneurs.* Her present concern is to find a way to transform academia from an elitist institution to one that increases equality and social justice.

Walter R. Allen is professor of sociology at the University of California, Los Angeles. He is well known for his work on black students in higher education, black families and child socialization, and the demography of black America. He is coeditor of *Beginnings: The Social and Affective Development of Black Children* and more recently of *The Color Line and the Quality of Life in America.* He has published in numerous social science and education journals.

Carol Locust is a research associate at the Native American Research and Training Center, College of Medicine, University of Arizona, where she works closely with Indian people to establish culturally appropriate education programs for handicapped Indian youth. She has written monographs and produced a video about the cultural aspects of handicaps. She conducts workshops for educational, medical, and rehabilitation service providers who work with disabled American Indians.

Charmaine Bradley is a doctoral candidate in the Department of Educational Psychology at Texas A&M University. She is an assistant on the Minority Mentorship

Project at Texas A&M and coauthor of *The Impact of A Crosscultural Mentoring Relationship on Attitudinal Charges of Preservice Teachers.*

Grayson Noley is Education Department Director at the Cherokee Nation Education Department. His current interest is in facilitating a comprehensive understanding of the educational needs of Cherokee people. He is presently building a data base for this purpose. In addition, he is involved in parent intervention and community leadership programs to foster greater support for the education of American Indian children.

John W. Tippeconnic III is associate professor of educational leadership and policy at Arizona State University. He was previously director of the Center for Indian Education at Arizona State University and the Associate Deputy Commissioner of Indian Education for the U.S. Department of Education, Washington, D.C. He has also served two terms as president of the Board of Directors of the National Indian Education Association.

G. Mike Charleston is associate professor of education in the College of Education and director of the American Indian Education Policy Center at Pennsylvania State University. His areas of interest are educational administration and evaluation and computer applications. He is author of *Tradition and Education: Towards a Vision of Our Future—Volumes I–III* (Ottawa: Assembly of First Nations).

Foreword

With persistence, even tenacity, race lingers in American life, seeming to mock us like a disquieting riddle. It is our longest running unresolved issue.

The continuity of a single problem of such magnitude is curiously at odds with the American experience. This is a country that in important ways has actualized the idea of progress. Particularly striking is the speed with which the American economy created a majority middle class out of an overwhelmingly poor immigrant population, originally bereft of skills. The eager poor of every racial and ethnic origin, open land, and bountiful resources created a breathlessly expanding economy. It was difficult not to rise with the economic tide.

Ultimately this sweeping tide rejected only those who were conspicuously different. The economy's voracious appetite for labor overcame all prejudice save one. The color line survived and often thrived when ethnicity, language, and old world customs did not. This volume looks in new ways at this old subject.

The mutations that race issues assume from decade to decade warrant the fresh look that the authors give it in this unusual collection. It defines race broadly, as this country has, to include not only black Americans, the country's most visible racial group, but also two other groups of Americans who remain outsiders. American Indians and Hispanics are outsiders because of the way that their uniqueness has been viewed; but their cultural distinctiveness has acquired accentuated meaning in a country in which, in the common mind, they often also are viewed as nonwhites. This collection, therefore, is appropriately organized around color to include those for whom visible distinctiveness has helped define place, opportunity, and life itself.

However, if the color anchor of these essays is appropriate, it is not because the experience of African Americans, Hispanics and American Indians is of a piece. It is not, and these essays show the unique development and divergent problems of each population. Nevertheless, unprecedented circumstances confronting the country today make a book on race that includes all three groups useful. It alerts us to the increasing proportions of these groups in our population. And it helps us to understand the urgency of putting color behind us so that disadvantages among our people do not translate into a weakening of our position in the world.

Not only are these essays multiethnic. They are multidisciplinary. They bring to bear education, sociology, economics, and psychology on problems that cannot be resolved unless they are approached in all their dimensions. The writers in this collection bring differences in perspective and in racial and ethnic backgrounds as well. But together they update an old racial story, filling it in with the most recent data and issues of today and of the future. Theirs is an important contribution to the continuing effort to unravel the riddle of race.

In this country, however, race is not simply another problem in search of a solution. The racial riddle has defied American logic. Though labor hungry until well into the twentieth century, we refused to make use of a labor supply at our fingertips. Though animated by self-sufficiency as a central ideology, we used color to pervert law and custom in order to deny initiative. Though eloquent in the poetry of freedom and equality with which we lined our official doctrine, we began only 35 years ago to put it to use.

The consequence of this is legacy. Not surprisingly, the sometimes remarkable improvements of the last generation have not wiped away the residue of two centuries. It will take more time and more effort. The more we probe and learn about race and its shadowing effects, the greater the likelihood of illumination that will finally put us at peace with our diversity. As this collection shows, the riddle of race is not beyond our grasp. Like any hard puzzle, it will yield to unrelenting attention, intelligence, and will.

Eleanor Holmes Norton
Georgetown University Law Center
Washington, D.C.

Preface

This volume is designed to assess the nature and progress of American race relations in the 1980s and to make projections about trends and proposals for the 1990s. The volume originated from a national conference in 1988 on Race and Ethnic Relations in the 1990s, which was held at Texas A&M University. A select group of experts from around the country gave insightful presentations on this topic; these individuals were members of both majority and minority populations. Their written work from the conference constitutes a major portion of this volume.

The topic that this book addresses is both timely and relevant in view of the 20-year anniversary of the Kerner Commission Report and the increasing racial diversity in American society projected for the 1990s and beyond. In discussing the nature of race relations in contemporary society, the volume reflects a social-structural rather than a psychological or social-psychological approach. The latter approach is largely micro, with a primary focus on individual-level behavior and attributes in explaining race relations. Racial attitudes, prejudice, scapegoating, and frustration-aggression are variables that often have been associated with this perspective. This micro-level, social-psychological approach maintained a dominant influence on the study of U.S. race relations until the 1950s.[1]

The social-structural approach is more macro; it focuses on institutional and structural-level variables and on the broader societal context in which race relations occur. More specifically, proponents of this approach maintain that collective institutional components of social institutions operate in a manner that imposes objectively different statuses and positions on individuals affiliated with various groups.[2] It is further argued that these status differentials permit the dominant group to exploit subordinate groups to the former's advantage, particularly regarding economic and material gains.[3,4] Thus, race and race relations are generally viewed in this volume as an outcome of stratification and subsequent conflict over scarce resources and rewards. Variables such as racial stratification, differential power and resources, technology, and institutional discrimination are of primary importance in this regard as well as to the social-structural approach.

The current status of U.S. race relations is examined here in terms of (a) the educational, social, and economic progress of racial minorities in contrast to that of the majority group and (b) the extent to which desegregation and ethnic diversity have

---

[1]Rex J. (1970). *Race relations in sociological theory.* New York: Shocken.

[2]Rothman, J. (1977). *Issues in race and ethnic relations: Theory, research and action.* Itasca, IL: Peacock.

[3]Cox, O. C. (1970). *Caste, class, and race.* New York: Monthly Review Press.

[4]Marden, C. F. & Meyer, G. (1978). *Minorities in American society* (5th ed). New York: Van Nostrand.

been achieved in present-day U.S. society. Again, our focus is quite different from that of earlier studies, which concentrated on racial attitudes rather than on racial behavior and racial progress. Most of the chapters assume a power-conflict perspective that emphasizes structural relations and power dynamics between majority and minority groups.

The volume focuses on the three most underrepresented racial minorities in the United States: blacks, Hispanics, and American Indians. Most of the earlier studies and anthologies on race relations were restricted primarily to black–white relations. Thus we view as an asset our extended focus on other racial groups. The contributions to the volume by scholars who are themselves members of diverse racial groups is an additional strength. Such a racial array of intellectual contributions and perspectives provides extended depth and critical insight, which are necessary given the complexity of the topic and the increasing racial diversity of American society.

The volume is divided into three parts, with commentary chapters interspersed throughout by individuals who view the issues from their own unique and informed perspectives. By design the chapters vary in length and style. The intent is to assure diversity and freedom of input in an area that requires both objectivity and creativity.

Part I, "Education and Race," addresses the educational progress of blacks and Hispanics in secondary and postsecondary education and the implication of the current shortage of black teachers for the future education of black students. The first chapter, by John Ogbu, examines the persistence of low school performance and educational attainment of blacks within the context of racial stratification in America. The next chapter, by James Blackwell, addresses the extent to which blacks and Hispanics have been incorporated into the educational mainstream of American society, provided opportunities for equal education, and achieved educational progress. Chapter 3, by Grace Butler, is a commentary on the previous two chapters. In the fourth chapter, James Parsons examines the extent to which the status of low-income, inner-city minority schools have improved in quality and been desegregated since publication of the Kerner Report. In the fifth chapter, Patricia Larke examines the status of the minority teaching pool in public education and its implications for minority students and the future of American race relations. In the final chapter of Part I, Wanda Ward provides a commentary on the chapters by Parsons and Larke.

Part II, "Occupational Mobility, Economics, and Cultural Pluralism," assesses the extent of racial inequality in the 1980s in employment and income. In addition, the stance of the United States on the issue of cultural pluralism is examined. In the first chapter, Jomills Braddock II portrays the National Football League (NFL) as a major profit-producing institution and viable source of employment for Americans. He then assesses black–white differences in access and opportunities to coaching and management positions in the NFL. Lodis Rhodes offers a commentary in the succeeding chapter.

In the chapter that follows, Charles Keely examines the recent response of the federal government to immigration in light of basic American values versus the political reality of ethnic relations in the United States. He further discusses the implications of America's posture toward immigration for the future of race and ethnic relations. Next, Marta Tienda demonstrates the nature of socioeconomic inequality along racial and ethnic lines since 1960. She concludes with speculations about the political implications of changes in minority family economic inequality during the last intercensal decade. David Alvirez provides a perspective on Keely's and Tienda's chapters in his commentary. In the next two chapters, David Swinton and Edna

Bonacich document the persistence of racial and economic inequality in America. Bonacich argues that the "minor tinkering" that has been attempted in the past to eliminate poverty and inequality does not offer an adequate remedy. She therefore makes an appeal for major change in America's economic system. Part II concludes with Walter Allen's commentary on the previous two chapters.

The third and final section of the volume, "American Indians: A Special and Neglected Case," addresses important issues for an underrepresented sector of the population that is often neglected. For most American Indians, having the right to pursue and achieve adequate education in America remains a critical basic issue. Thus the authors in this section of the volume, who are themselves American Indians, devote most of their attention to this issue. In the first chapter, Carol Locust argues that American educators seldom consider how differences in belief systems impact the educational achievement of American Indians. Locust concludes by noting that American educators must understand and respect American Indian belief systems before they can begin to improve the present and future educational experiences of American Indian children. In her commentary on this chapter, Charmaine Bradley offers suggestions for such improvements.

In the next chapter Grayson Noley argues that the education of American Indians is a challenge that has been forced upon American schools and that consequently, American teachers and administrators have not readily accepted this challenge. Noley discusses the condition and needs of American Indian youth within this context.

In his chapter, John Tippeconnic III argues that the educational and social plights of American Indians are generally unknown, misunderstood, or ignored. He therefore attempts to educate the reader by portraying the demographic, educational, and economic status of American Indians. He concludes with a discussion of the implications of the data for the future of Native Americans in the 1990s. G. Mike Charleston comments on the chapters by Noley and Tippeconnic, and then I conclude the section and the book with a postscript addressing the future of American race relations.

Gail E. Thomas

Acknowledgments

I have benefitted from and greatly appreciate the assistance of the following people in preparing this volume: Mary Zey, Head of the Department of Sociology at Texas A&M University, for financially assisting this project from start to finish; members of the Department of Sociology's Race and Ethnic Relations Study Group (Ben Aguirre, James Copp, Cedric Herring, Verna Keith, William Kuvlesky, Ramdas Menon, and Rogelio Saenz) for initiating the conference and for their moral support; Karen Feinberg for her editorial assistance; Ella M. Hoover for her dedication, efficiency, and persistence in handling all technical and administrative aspects of this project; the contributing authors for their participation and commitment; and last, to my spouse and my son—Emmett and Bradford Amos—for their confidence, love, and support, which greatly facilitate my getting the job done every time!

PART I

EDUCATION AND RACE

1

Racial Stratification and Education

John U. Ogbu
Department of Anthropology and Survey Research Center
University of California, Berkeley

UNDERSTANDING THE PERSISTENCE OF INEQUALITY

On a number of occasions I have heard Americans, white and black, ask why black Americans continue to lag in school performance and educational attainment and why inequality persists after all the improvements in race relations in the last two or three decades. They point to new employment opportunities in the private and public sectors for blacks who have a good education, as well as to the growing number of middle-class blacks. I suggest that to understand the persistence of these problems we need to change our conceptual framework from one of *race relations* to one of *racial stratification*. In this chapter it is my intention to examine the twin problems of poorer school performance and lesser educational attainment by black Americans in the context of American racial stratification, but first I will explain why the concept of racial stratification is a better tool for my analysis.

Several years ago (Ogbu, 1978, pp. 101–102) I noted that most Americans prefer to think in terms of race relations or behavioral manifestations of racial stratification when they deal with such issues as education and jobs, even though such a perspective does not shed much light on the problem at hand. For example, American social scientists focus their analysis on such issues as labor market and economic discrimination, segregation in public schools and public facilities, and the like. They do not seem to recognize that these are manifestations of a common, underlying structural principle, not explainable in terms of racial prejudice. Racial prejudice, as they present it, is a psychodynamic phenomenon characteristic of individuals, rather than a function of social structure. As they themselves note, racial prejudice is caused by errors in socialization and by faulty personality development (Lyman, 1973, p. 81). In this mode of thinking, the educational problems of black Americans and similar minorities are rarely analyzed as a consequence of racial stratification; this concept does not appear in most of the influential works dealing with the education of these minorities.

In my earlier work (Ogbu, 1978), I also noted two possible sources of resistance to the recognition of racial or castelike stratification in America. One is the conscious or unconscious extension of certain European immigrant groups' experience into a universally applicable variable. The other is the prevailing ideology of egalitarianism, based primarily on white American experience and on the mythology of individualism. Maquet (1971) noted correctly that such an ideology and such a mythology tend to form a screen that prevents their adherents from seeing the system that underlies their own behaviors in conforming to superior and inferior roles.

For decades some black social scientists have taken the lead in informing us that the significance of race in determining black Americans' life chances has declined and that class differences now reign supreme (Wilson, 1978). They emphasize the emergence of an "underclass" as the fountainhead of blacks' current problems in education, employment, housing, and the like. This shift of analysis from racial to class differences is attractive not only to white Americans but also to some middle-class black Americans, who seem eager to distance themselves from the so-called underclass. One reason to reject this view is that its proponents present only a partial understanding of racial stratification. They think of racial stratification as consisting primarily of *instrumental* barriers, such as those blocking access to jobs, education, housing, and political office. Racial stratification, however, implies more than instrumental barriers. It also rests on the *expressive* barriers erected by the dominant group as well as on the minorities' instrumental and expressive responses.

Expressive barriers and expressive exploitation refer to conscious or unconscious treatment of racial minorities that satisfies the psychological needs of the members of the dominant group—namely, white Americans. It includes scapegoating and derogation of minorities. Expressive responses refer to the conscious or unconscious responses by minorities to this treatment; these responses satisfy their own psychological needs, such as the need to maintain their sense of self-worth and integrity. In a racially stratified society, both expressive exploitation and expressive responses are usually institutionalized as emotionally held beliefs that justify attitudes and behaviors toward the outgroup. According to DeVos (1984), racial stratification is distinguished from class stratification by the presence of the institutionalized expressive exploitation and responses in the social hierarchy.

As shown in Figure 1, racial stratification has four components. Therefore racial stratification is maintained by the persistence of occupational and other instrumental barriers (A in Figure 1) and by the instrumental responses of the minorities (C), as well as by the persistence of what DeVos (1984) called "socialized feelings of aversion, revulsion and disgust" toward the minorities (B) and by the minorities' socialized distrust and opposition or ambivalence toward the dominant group (D). The important point is that the expressive dimension of racial stratification may persist after formal instrumental barriers have been eliminated or after more opportunities to hold traditional, white middle-class positions have been made available to members of a racial minority group.

One reason for the persistence of inequality is that reformers and policymakers often are not fully aware of the expressive components of racial stratification and do not address them adequately. Another reason is that the minorities who are demanding change do not recognize their own oppositional or ambivalent tendencies and the functions and consequences of these tendencies. In fact, many minority spokespersons are likely to resist analysis, pointing instead to the oppositional or ambivalent processes as well as to the nature of the collective identity and the cultural frame of reference through which the opposition and ambivalence are expressed. A third reason for the persistence of inequality is that some vestiges of discriminatory treatment of minorities remain. Furthermore, DeVos (1984) noted that the expressive elements are more resistant to change because usually they have taken on a life of their own as "cultural solutions" to recurring psychological problems facing dominant-group members; they are learned early in life in the family and in peer groups.

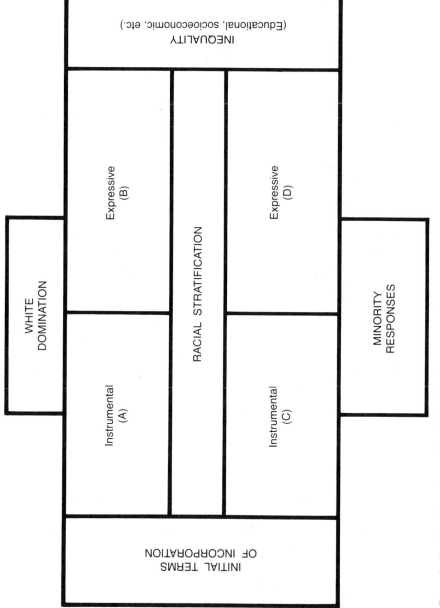

Figure 1 The Four Dimensions of Racial Stratification.

5

Racial Stratification and Minority Status

Having suggested that the framework of racial stratification is more useful than that of race relations for my purpose, I also must point out that the educational consequences of racial stratification depend on the type of minority status possessed by the subordinate racial group involved—namely, whether it is a voluntary immigrant group or an involuntary, nonimmigrant group. The two types of minorities, immigrants and nonimmigrants, differ both in their initial incorporation into U.S. society and in the pattern of their responses to subsequent treatment by white Americans.

Immigrant minorities are minorities who came to the United States voluntarily because they believed that immigration would lead to more economic well-being, better overall opportunities, or greater political freedom. These expectations continue to influence the way in which the immigrants perceive and respond to their treatment by white Americans and to the societal institutions that the latter group controls. The Chinese in Stockton, California, and the Punjabi Indians in Yuba City, California, are examples of immigrant minorities.

In contrast, *involuntary (or castelike) minorities* are those who were brought into U.S. society involuntarily through slavery, conquest, or colonization. Such minorities resent the loss of their freedom, their displacement from power, and the deprivation of property; they tend to perceive present barriers against them as institutionalized and have difficulty in seeing future improvements without a collective struggle against their "white oppressors." American Indians, black Americans, Mexican-Americans in the Southwest, and native Hawaiians fall into the category of involuntary minorities.

Both immigrant and involuntary minorities experience prejudice and discrimination at the hands of white Americans. Both groups, for example, may be relegated to menial jobs and may be denied true assimilation into the mainstream society, but they perceive and interpret these experiences differently and respond differently. In this chapter I am concerned with the involuntary minorities, and within this category, with black Americans: their treatment by whites, their own perceptions and responses to this treatment, and the consequences of their treatment and responses for their education.

THE CASE OF BLACK AMERICANS

In order to understand the present situation I must begin with the past. In surveying the past I conclude that black Americans have occupied the position of a racial caste for most of their history. Initially they were brought to America against their will as slaves; after emancipation they were kept subordinated and in menial roles by legal and extralegal devices (Berreman, 1960). Their distinctive and inferior status was and is reinforced by rules of affiliation and by white caste thinking. The affiliation rule compels anyone known to be an offspring of a black–white mating to affiliate with the black stratum. That is, anyone who is known to be born of a white and a black parent is classified automatically as black (Berreman, 1967). White caste thinking refers to whites' beliefs that blacks are biologically, culturally, and socially inferior to whites.

Whites' Treatment of Blacks

Figure 2 shows the dimensions of whites' treatment of blacks after the latter's emancipation from slavery. I will discuss first the instrumental and then the expressive aspects of that treatment. Although education falls within the instrumental domain, I discuss it separately in a later section on the educational consequences of racial stratification.

Instrumental Treatment or Exploitation

Instrumental exploitation of blacks by white Americans takes many forms, including economic, political, social, and educational. Because there is no space to deal with each of these issues I will focus on economic treatment and examine it historically in connection with blacks' educational experience. I will use the concept of a job ceiling to show how this economic exploitation works.

A *job ceiling* consists of both formal statutes and informal practices followed by white Americans to limit blacks' access to desirable occupations, to truncate their opportunities, and to channel narrowly the potential returns they can expect from their education and abilities (Mickelson, 1984; Ogbu, 1978). Specifically, the job ceiling has been used to deny *qualified blacks* free and equal competition for the jobs they desire and to exclude them from certain highly desirable jobs that require education and in which education pays off; these treatments do not permit blacks to obtain their proportional share of such jobs because of their subordinate racial status. The job ceiling also confines a disproportionate portion of the black population to menial jobs below the job ceiling. In contrast, the job ceiling benefits white individuals because it permits even less qualified whites to obtain jobs and wages to which they would not have been entitled if blacks were allowed free and fair competition. Similarly, white business establishments gain from the job ceiling. Consider, for example, that in the early 1970s a U.S. Office of Equal Employment Practices commission found that AT&T "saved" $362 million a year by not paying black, Hispanic, and female workers what it paid white males (DeWare, 1978; P. A. Wallace, 1976).

In looking at the past, I found that the job ceiling was low at first. Until the beginning of the twentieth century, blacks could hold jobs above the job ceiling only in the segregated black communities and in public institutions serving blacks exclusively, such as hospitals and schools. The segregated communities provided blacks with the few opportunities to assume entrepreneurial, religious, literary, and entertainment roles at a higher level than was open to them in the wider society. The growth of urban ghettos in northern and southern cities functioned similarly to increase the pool of jobs available to blacks above the job ceiling. A. M. Ross (1967) reported, for example, that the small gains made by blacks in the north in professional, managerial, proprietary, clerical, and sales positions at the end of the 1940s were due in part to the growth of urban ghettos, where blacks had the best chances of filling such positions.

Specifically, before the 1960s the segregated institutions and communities presented the only major avenues for occupational differentiation among blacks on the basis of formal education and ability as reflected in educational credentials. It was there that blacks gained the greatest access to professional and other jobs above the job ceiling. Even in the segregated institutions, however, blacks usually were not admitted to the highest level positions; those were filled by whites (Frazier, 1957; Greene & Woodson, 1930; Johnson, 1943; Marshall, 1968; A. M. Ross, 1967).

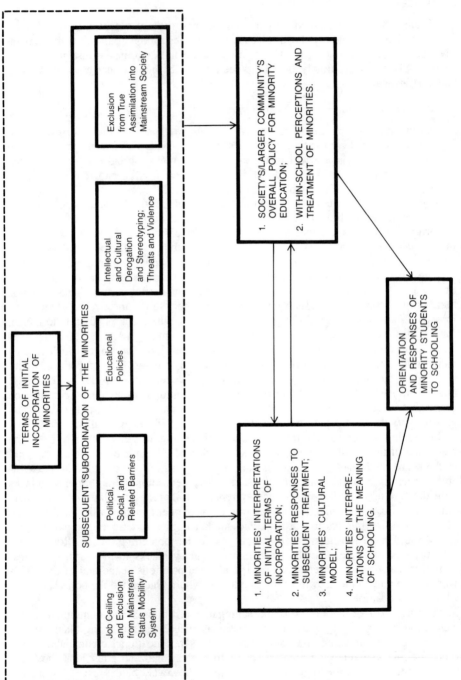

Figure 2 Whites' Treatment of Blacks and Some of the Ways in Which It Affects Blacks' Education.

These institutions still represented the major avenues to high-status jobs for blacks in the south during the 1960s and early 1970s, as shown by studies conducted by Henderson (1967) and by A. R. Ross (1973).

On the whole, before the 1960s blacks made some progress in some employment above the job ceiling, but their progress did not parallel their educational attainment. That is, their underrepresentation above the job ceiling was not proportionate to their level of educational qualification, nor was their overrepresentation below the job ceiling due to lack of educational qualification for higher level jobs. In general, black advances in mainstream industrial employment, especially above the job ceiling, occurred mainly in periods of national crisis. As Myrdal (1944) put it, black occupational progress has been the result of a unique series of happenings in isolated periods of national emergencies and labor shortages, such as those that occurred during the period of economic growth from 1900 to 1908, World War I, the immigrant labor restrictions of 1922, World War II, the Korean War, the Vietnam War, and the social reforms of the 1960s. Each of these events led to more blacks' being employed in mainstream jobs; more blacks then made their way into middle-class jobs above the job ceiling. At least until the 1960s, blacks' employment opportunities were increased largely by these events rather than by their meeting requirements for technological changes in the U.S. economy. As I will show below, the increase since the 1960s in blacks' opportunities for employment above the job ceiling is due to unique events similar to those of which Myrdal wrote.

The pattern of black employment changed in the 1960s: Employment opportunities above the job ceiling increased significantly and, for some time, more or less continuously. This change was due to deliberate government policies, backed by legislation and civil rights pressures. This new development altered the relationship between education and employment among blacks: It tended to establish an appropriate link between level of schooling and employment opportunities and remuneration by making blacks' jobs and earnings commensurate with their education. Let me summarize this development briefly.

During the Kennedy and Johnson administrations, pressures from civil rights groups and fear of urban violence led the U.S. government to develop policies designed to increase the number of blacks employed above the job ceiling in both government and the private sector. Title VII of the Civil Rights Act of 1964 and an affirmative action program were two principal mechanisms for increasing black employment in middle-class jobs. Title VII, which became law in 1966, forbids employers from discriminating on the basis of race, sex, and other such factors. Affirmative action encourages employers and institutions of higher education to give preference to qualified members of minorities and to women and, when necessary, to seek out such persons (Burkey, 1971; Ogbu, 1978, p. 347). These strategies appear to have changed employers' hiring practices significantly, especially in regard to young college-educated blacks. Wilson (1979, pp. 166–167) reported that the average number of recruitment visits by representatives of corporations to predominantly black colleges rose from 4 in 1960, to 50 in 1965, to 297 in 1970. Furthermore, black colleges that had not been visited at all in 1960, such as Clark College, Atlanta University, and Southern University, received, respectively, 350, 510, and 600 representatives of corporations in 1970.

The number of blacks who entered high-level jobs above the job ceiling rose dramatically in the second half of the 1960s as a result of affirmative action and Title VII. Brimmer (1974, p. 160) reported that between 1960 and 1970 the number of blacks in the two top-level occupational categories nearly doubled. The number of blacks in the top category, consisting of professional and technical jobs, rose by 128%, although the increase for the general population was only 49%. In the second highest category, made up of managers, officials, and proprietors, the number of blacks increased by 100%, whereas the increase for the general population was only 23%. Brimmer's report is supported by a study sponsored by the Manpower Administration (A. R. Ross, 1973).

These figures show clearly that the opportunity structure for college-educated blacks has changed. The change, however, was not caused simply by the fact that blacks met the educational requirements of jobs in a technologically changing economy; it occurred because of the political and social pressures of the 1960s. Since the 1960s the job ceiling has been raised continuously. Analysts generally agree, however, that these favorable changes have affected mainly middle-class blacks, especially college-educated blacks. It is also agreed that among college-educated blacks the appropriate link has been established between school credentials on the one hand and jobs and earnings on the other, much as it exists among whites.

No such significant changes have taken place in the employment opportunities of lower class or non-college-educated blacks. There has been no comparable official policy to increase their employability, as in the case of the college-educated; no affirmative action program of equal strength has been established to assist their social mobility. In the 1960s the increase in the pool of jobs caused by the Vietnam War and by social programs led to increased employment of blacks on all levels of the occupational ladder. The decrease in the pool of jobs in the early 1970s not only slowed the employment of non-college-educated blacks but also caused a loss of jobs among those already employed, partly because they were the last to be hired and therefore the first to be fired.

The loss of jobs among non-college-educated blacks has continued into the late 1980s; under the economic policy of the previous Reagan administration, black unemployment reached twice the national level. Thus these blacks have not been helped by determined official employment policies comparable to those developed for the college-educated; no affirmative action programs have been established for them. They continue their traditional marginal participation in the labor force, in which the link between schooling and work/earnings is weak (Newman, 1979; Newman, Amidei, Carter, Kruvant, & Russell, 1978; Ogbu, 1978, 1981a; Willie, 1979; Wilson, 1978, 1979). This marginality, however, also affects college-educated middle-class blacks, many of whom have been recruited to administer welfare and remedial programs for the non-college-educated or for those they call "the underclass." Such programs "serving" the underclass have no guaranteed future (Darity, 1983).

Expressive Exploitation: Intellectual and Cultural Derogation

White castelike thinking was based initially on biblical doctrines, according to Myrdal (1944). After the eighteenth century, however, when it was generally accepted that human beings belonged to the biological universe, it came to be believed that blacks were biologically inferior to whites. Although many whites no longer openly admit that they believe in the biological inferiority of black people, Gallup polls indicate that such beliefs have not disappeared entirely.

This caste thinking takes many forms, all of which serve important emotional functions for white people. One way in which whites express their belief that blacks are inferior is to deny them public recognition for intellectual and other accomplishments. An important clue to this tendency can be found in a report that during World War I a French military mission stationed with the American Expeditionary Army circulated the following notice, which later was withdrawn: "The merits of Negro soldiers should not be warmly praised, especially in the presence of [white] Americans" (Myrdal, 1944, p. 105). This reluctance to recognize blacks' accomplishments continued through the 1950s, even in college sports. Thus Dick Gregory (1965) reported in his autobiography that in the 84-year history of his college "the outstanding athlete had never been a black." The situation changed only in 1953, when he himself demanded the honor and made a deal with the college authorities (Gregory, 1965, p. 187):

> I walked up to the coach and told him that if I wasn't elected Outstanding Athlete for 1953, I was going to quit. I threatened them so cool that they couldn't even give it to another Negro—I went to them as an individual, make them think it had to do with me, not race. I made it. Outstanding Athlete of the Year, and all I could do was run track . . . the next year another Negro, Leo Wilson, made it, and we've been making it ever since. But someone had to break the ice; with a threat.

Another form of expressive exploitation is whites' attribution to blacks of traits that they regard as undesirable in themselves. In an article titled "What Every White Man Thinks He Knows About Negroes," Johnson (1938, p. 3) provided a detailed summary of negative stereotypes of blacks in books and articles written by whites until the late 1930s. A few years later Myrdal (1944) provided an even more elaborate and more incisive account of ordinary white people's beliefs about the "in-born indelible inferiority of blacks" (p. 100). He noted that blacks were believed to be a "contrast conception," "the opposite of the white race," and "an antithesis of character and properties of the white man." Myrdal went on to say that in white people's belief, black, in contrast to white, "stands for dirt, sin, and the devil . . . It becomes understandable, [and] natural on a deeper magical plane of reasoning that the Negro is believed to be stupid, immoral, diseased, lazy, incompetent and dangerous to the white man's virtue and social order" (p. 100). These projections were institutionalized in white people's behavior toward blacks, in their jokes, and in their oral and written tales about blacks. According to Myrdal (1944), the aversion that these projections aroused accounts in part for white people's belief that blacks are unassimiable, by which whites mean that *it is undesirable to assimilate blacks* (p. 54). Thus the long history of social and physical segregation of blacks was an attempt to "quarantine what is evil, shameful and feared in society" (p. 100).

Finally, throughout much of the history of black–white relations in the United States, white people have used blacks as scapegoats. In one common pattern whites tend to make blacks collectively responsible for the offense of a single black person. For example, after Nat Turner's "insurrection" in Southampton, Virginia, in 1831, blacks' geographical mobility throughout the country was restricted. Moreover, black children in Washington, DC, who normally attended Sunday school with white children were stopped from doing so, even though they had had no part in the insurrection (Fordham, 1984; Haley, 1976; Styron, 1966). Another example is the incident that took place in Rosewood, Florida, in January 1923. According to CBS Television Network's (1984) *60 Minutes*, a black man was alleged to have raped a white woman there. The next day some 1,500 white men from nearby towns marched into Rosewood and killed 40 black men, women, and children who apparently had no personal involvement in the matter.

Whites also have punished blacks for their own political and economic hardships. In 1934, for example, during the Great Depression, antiblack violence occurred throughout the United States. It is reported that in the same year, in Columbia, Pennsylvania, "a crowd of whites assaulted the black district, breaking up houses and beating blacks" (M. Wallace, 1970, p. 84). A few days later, white workers met and passed a resolution urging that employers not hire blacks. When white workers did not get their way with employers they rioted twice, destroying blacks' homes and beating up blacks. Even as recently as the early 1980s, white violence against blacks and other minorities increased in California during the recession. Blacks also have been blamed by whites faced with political crisis or threatened with loss of political power, as during Reconstruction (M. Wallace, 1970, p. 85), and blacks were visited with violence during the Populist movement in the 1890s (M. Wallace, 1970, p. 87). Frazier (1957, pp. 155–156) reported that the economic problems of poor whites during the 1890s were blamed on blacks and were used as the basis for disenfranchising southern blacks and enacting Jim Crow laws. Making blacks responsible for whites' economic and political problems also resulted in violence and lynching against blacks during most of the first half of the twentieth century.

To summarize, the debate about the inferiority of blacks has continued to date in one form or another. In the early 1940s, Johnson (1943) interviewed white Americans in all regions of the country and found that the belief in the inferiority of blacks was widespread. It was used to justify the segregation of blacks in public institutions such as the schools, to segregate them residentially, to limit their social contacts, to confine them to jobs below the job ceiling, and, most important, to prohibit intermarriage between blacks and whites. A poll conducted by *Newsweek* in 1978 revealed that although whites' beliefs in the racial inferiority of blacks had been decreasing significantly since the 1960s, a significant proportion of whites interviewed still held such beliefs. About 25% of the whites polled said that blacks had less intelligence than whites; about 15% thought that blacks were inferior to white people ("How Whites and Blacks Feel," 1979, p. 48).

Responses by Blacks

Black Americans have not accepted quietly their denigration or the rationales for their subordination and exploitation by white Americans. Yet they have not been entirely immune from the effects of these treatments. In order to cope with their subordination and exploitation, blacks developed their own rationale for their situation; they also developed both instrumental and expressive responses, represented in Figure 3.

Instrumental Responses

Under the economic and related subordination described earlier, black Americans appear to have evolved a worldview that, among other things, explains how American society "works" and specifies blacks' place in that working order. Thus in the economic sphere many blacks believe to this day that institutionalized discrimination exists against blacks, so that a black person cannot advance as far as a white person nor get ahead merely by acting like a white person. On the basis of generations of shared knowledge and experience of discrimination, black Americans appear to have analyzed their economic realities consciously and unconsciously and to have concluded that they cannot "make it" simply by following the rules of behavior for

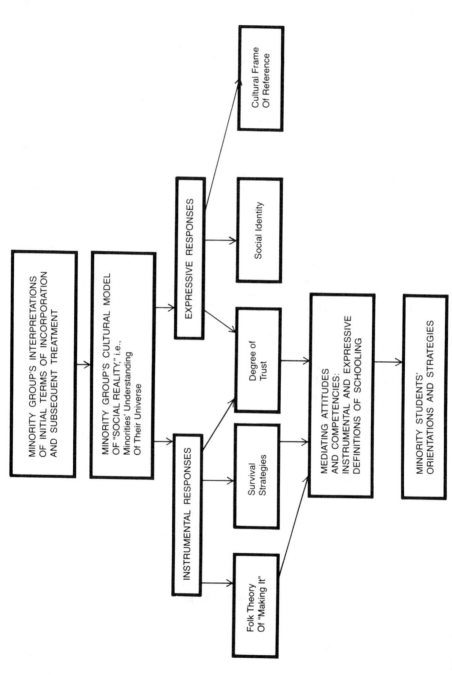

Figure 3 Black Americans' Responses to Treatment by Whites: How the Responses May Affect Schooling.

achievement or the cultural practices that work for white Americans. Consequently they have developed a folk theory of "making it" that has resulted in the adoption of several survival strategies to meet their economic needs.

The survival strategies include *pursuing mainstream employment* even in the face of a job ceiling, underemployment, and other barriers (Ferman, Kornbluh, & Miller, 1968; Harrison, 1972). Another survival strategy is *collective struggle,* one of the oldest and most effective methods from the viewpoint of blacks. They have used this strategy to raise or eliminate the job ceiling and to improve their general status in American society for as long as they can remember (Newman et al., 1978, p. 10; Scott, 1976). Collective struggle includes activities legitimated by white Americans as civil rights (e.g., demonstration for jobs, lobbying, and lawsuits) as well as other activities not legitimated in this way (e.g., rioting). It is common knowledge in the black community that collective struggle made it possible for individual blacks to advance above the job ceiling, to find jobs paying "living wages," and to live in good neighborhoods.

Another common strategy is *clientship,* or "Uncle Tomming." Black Americans learned long ago that favoritism, not merit, is a key to survival and self-betterment even in that part of the universe that is open to them. They also learned that the way to solicit that favoritism is by being dependent, compliant, and manipulative. White Americans, both as individuals and collectively, serve as patrons to individual blacks and to black groups and organizations. White organizations also serve as patrons. Clientship is not confined to blacks; it also exists among whites. Clientship among whites functions differently, however: It tends to raise the client's status to that of the patron. Until recently, practice of black clientship did not raise blacks to the status of their white patrons. Moreover, blacks are always clients, never patrons.

Another aspect of clientship involves blacks and the government. For several decades in this century, the federal government has tended especially to assume the patron role. The importance of the federal government as a patron can be seen in its role as an employer, as a sponsor of educational and other training programs, as an advisor and protector of civil rights, and as a distributor of subsistence aid or welfare. Blacks also depend on the government for raising the job ceiling and for enhancing their employment and social mobility generally.

Entertainment and *sports* are other avenues of survival of particular importance to blacks. Entertainment included the activities of a wide range of performers, such as singers, musicians, preachers, comedians, disc jockeys, and writers (Keil, 1977, p. 70). This is a traditional strategy for exploiting social and economic resources within the black community, where it both satisfies people's needs for entertainment and serves as a therapeutic technique to enable them to cope with problems arising from their subordination. In recent decades entertainment and sports have become increasingly important in exploiting conventional resources in the wider society.

Hustling and *pimping* are yet other traditional strategies, used mainly for nonconventional resources or the street economy. They are used to manipulate interpersonal relations for material gains. Selling drugs also may be a part of the "hustle" (Foster, 1974; Hammon, 1965; McCord, Howard, Friedberg, & Harwood, 1969).

Over the course of generations, the survival strategies became institutionalized and integrated as a part of black culture. They have contributed to shaping the norms, values, and competencies of black Americans. With the raising of the job ceiling since the 1960s, however, some survival strategies have changed or are changing. For example, mainstream employment has assumed a greater role, especially among the more highly educated. Entertainment and sports are directed increasingly at tapping the resources of the mainstream.

Expressive Responses

Black Americans also have responded expressively to their treatment at the hands of white Americans by forging *a collective social identity* that is oppositional or ambivalent toward the white American identity and *a cultural frame of reference* that is oppositional or ambivalent toward the white American cultural frame of reference. The oppositional identity and the oppositional cultural frame of reference are also survival strategies.

Black's collective ambivalent or oppositional identity, their sense of peoplehood, grew out of their treatment by white Americans and out of their own responses to that treatment. Enslavement was the first and foremost of the treatments promoting the formation of oppositional identity. During slavery even "free" blacks were denied the equality and justice enjoyed and valued by white citizens. Blacks were treated as property to be bought and sold; their separate and denigrated identity was institutionalized and symbolized in numerous "black codes" and customary practices. "Racial etiquettes" were established during and after slavery and continued almost to the middle of the twentieth century (Johnson, 1943; Myrdal, 1944). Other events that dramatized separate identity for blacks included political disenfranchisement, Jim Crow statutes and contemporaneous widespread lynching in the post-Reconstruction period, the use of blacks as scapegoats during economic and political crises, denial of equal opportunity by means of the job ceiling, and physical and social segregation. These events and situations informed black Americans of the permanence of their separate identity; unlike white ethnic immigrants, they would not be allowed to assimilate into mainstream society. This message was reinforced by the practice of classifying as black all known offspring of mixed black and white parentage.

Beginning in the period of slavery, blacks themselves recognized that they were different because of their color and that they had little chance of assimilating into the mainstream society because of their denigration by whites. Although they rejected the white doctrine of racial superiority and although they fought against denial of equal opportunity, justice, and freedom, nevertheless they recognized the reality of their identity as a separate people. Under this circumstance they resorted to collective struggle to achieve equality with whites while maintaining their separate identity. The collective struggle, both covert and overt, increased their sense of collective identity and, to some degree, their perceptions and interpretations of that identity in opposition to white American identity.

Although they recognized the reality of their separate identity, not all black Americans adopted the same strategy to achieve justice, freedom, and equality of opportunity. Followers of Booker T. Washington, for instance, advocated *accommodation,* a mutually separate but not necessarily oppositional stance. Thus in his Atlanta Compromise speech, Washington stated, "In all things that are purely social we can be as separate as the fingers, yet one as the hand in all things essential for mutual progress" (Hall, 1979, p. 44). Followers of W. E. B. DuBois opted for *integration,* which may lead to ambivalent identity. Ambivalence is evident in DuBois's (1903/1961) description of the "double consciousness" of black Americans at the turn of the century (pp. 145–146). The integrationists demanded more from white Americans: more access to jobs, votes, political office, public school education, and choice of residence. They met with more white resistance, racial tension, and distrust, all of which further increased their sense of collective identity.

Other black Americans favored neither Washington's accommodative approach nor the integrationist approach of DuBois. Instead they adopted a *separatist strategy* because they did not believe that there could be any satisfactory solution to whites' treatment of blacks within American society. For these black Americans the solution lay in withdrawal from American society, both physically and spiritually. Emigration to Africa, Mexico, Latin America, or some designated part of the United States was proposed and in some cases was tried, from the days of slavery to the mid-twentieth century.

The separatist strategy is represented best by the Garvey movement between the two world wars, even though this movement did not actually settle any blacks outside the United States. It is represented as well by the Black Muslim movement under Elijah Muhammed and by the Republic of New Africa movement of the 1960s. All three movements emphasized the collective oppositional identity of black Americans in relation to white Americans; their ideological contents appealed to a large segment of blacks, including nonmembers of the movements. The oppositional nature of these movements and the identity that they embodied can be illustrated by the Garvey movement.

The civil rights mobilization of the 1960s added further to both the ambivalent and the oppositional qualities of black collective identity. For blacks the civil rights mobilization helped to remove the stigma of being black, to increase racial pride, and to provide the shared ideology that black is beautiful; this ideology minimized fear and other social costs for those who wanted to express overtly what they always believed covertly. This public expression of oppositional identity was not limited to activists or to the grassroots; it touched every segment of the black community. It permeated the works of black artists and scholars. In the theater, as Baker (1984) reported, there was a replay of some events that had occurred during the Harlem Renaissance in the 1920s. At that time black dramatists had stopped trying to please white audiences: Instead they directed their attention to Afro-American folk tradition and to contemporary issues of black life. Similarly, during the second half of the 1960s, a significant portion of black Americans became totally disillusioned with goals of integration, abandoned time-honored middle-class values, and instead adopted black power as a vehicle for spiritual liberation (Baker, 1984, p. 130). Black historians began to revise black history and to reinterpret the role and contributions of the African and black American heritage to American culture. This revision can be seen in the differences between the interpretations of Elkins (1959) and Blassingame (1972) of the life and character of black slaves.

Cultural Frame of Reference

Historical and comparative studies suggest that populations that become "persistent" or "enduring" within nations usually have developed boundary-maintaining mechanisms that are both cultural and oppositional (Castile & Kushner, 1981; DeVos, 1967; Spicer, 1966, 1971). Black Americans are no exception. Before turning to the cultural consequences of black–white stratification, however, I wish to note that I will not describe the totality of black American culture as a product of racial stratification. Further, I am all too aware of the debates about the origins of the content of black American culture. My focus here is more limited; it concerns one qualitative aspect of black American culture which, I believe, derives from black experience under racial stratification and which differentiates black culture from mainstream culture, even where the two cultures have similar contents. I refer to the oppositional or ambivalent cultural frame of reference of black Americans in relation to the cultural frame of reference of white Americans *as perceived by blacks.*

Of course, there are differences in content, which I believe arose from two sources. First, as I have suggested elsewhere (Ogbu, 1978, 1986), the exclusion of blacks from certain cultural, economic, and sociopolitical activities for generations could effectively have denied blacks the opportunity to develop certain know-how and values associated with such activities. Second, I also have suggested that the survival strategies developed by blacks to cope with their economic and other realities could have resulted in cultural contents not necessarily found in white American culture.

More germane to my present task, however, is the expressive aspect of black culture. Cross-cultural observations suggest that instrumental aspects of minority cultures, including their folk theories of "making it," change except when they assume expressive qualities, that is, when they become part of an oppositional process between the minority and the dominant group, as seems to be the case with black–white stratification in the United States.

Therefore, I suggest that along with the formation of an oppositional social identity, black Americans developed an oppositional cultural frame of reference. This frame of reference includes devices to protect and maintain blacks' social identity or sense of self-worth in the face of white treatment and to maintain boundaries between themselves and white people. A key device in the oppositional cultural frame of reference is *cultural inversion* (Holt, 1972; Ogbu, 1982b). Cultural inversion in the present context has two meanings. In the broad sense it refers to the various culturally approved ways in which black Americans express their opposition to white Americans. In a narrower sense it refers to specific behaviors, events, symbols, and meanings that blacks regard as not appropriate for themselves because they are characteristic of white Americans. At the same time, blacks approve and emphasize other forms of behavior and other events, symbols, and meanings as more appropriate for themselves because these are not a part of the white American way of life. That is, what black Americans consider appropriate or even legitimate for themselves in terms of attitudes, beliefs, preferences, and behaviors or practices is defined sometimes in opposition to the attitudes, beliefs, preferences, and behaviors or practices of white Americans, who are their "enemies" or "oppressors."

I want to emphasize that from the viewpoint of black Americans, cultural inversion results in the coexistence of two opposing cultural frames of reference, guiding behaviors *in selected areas of life.* One cultural frame of reference is viewed as appropriate for whites but not for blacks; the other is accepted as appropriate for blacks but not necessarily for whites. Furthermore, the definition of what is appropriate or not appropriate for blacks is emotionally charged because it is bound up intimately with blacks' sense of social identity, self-worth, and security. Therefore individuals who try to behave in the nonappropriate way or who try to behave like whites (i.e., to "cross cultural boundaries" into *forbidden domains*) may face opposition from other blacks. Their behaviors tend to be interpreted not only as "acting white" but also as betraying black people, as "trying to join the enemy." Individuals who try to cross cultural boundaries or to "pass" culturally also may themselves experience psychological conflict or what DeVos (1967) called "affective dissonance," partly because their sense of social identity may lead them to feel that they are, indeed, abandoning or betraying their people and partly because such individuals may not be sure that they would be accepted by white people even if they succeeded in learning to "act white."

The oppositional cultural frame of reference, or cultural inversion, appears to have originated from black responses to three kinds of white treatment, dating back to slavery: collective blame and punishment, as well as denial of individuality; denigration of black culture; and inadequate rewards for rehabilitation and linear acculturation.

Both during and after slavery, whites did not limit punishment to individual blacks who violated codes of conduct or who "got out of hand." Instead, punishment usually was extended to other blacks, as in Nat Turner's "insurrection" and in the Rosewood incident described earlier. Repeated experiences of such collective blame and punishment could have led blacks to devalue and avoid certain behaviors thought to be white or to offend whites, to maintain or invent the opposite as more appropriate and safer for themselves, and to develop a strong sense of community whose members would feel responsible for one another in the face of a common enemy (Fordham, 1984; Rawick, 1972).

In such circumstances the attitudes, behaviors, and speech styles that black Americans would adopt and value would be denigrated by the whites. Blacks no doubt resented the denigration of their culture, behavior, and manner of speech. At the same time, whites held that if blacks were to be accepted and/or to succeed in societal institutions controlled by whites, such as the public schools and the mainstream economy, they must abandon their own cultural norms, behaviors, and speech styles and embrace those of the white community. Whites even set up special programs to enable some blacks to undergo this linear acculturation.

I speculate that blacks probably accepted the rehabilitation at first, believing that in order to succeed in the domains controlled by white Americans they had to abandon their own cultural norms, behaviors, and speech styles and to assume those of whites. Yet eventually they came to realize that replacing their cultural frame or "acting white" did not necessarily help them to succeed in those institutions. They might have resented the fact that acquiring white cultural norms, behaviors, and speech styles, as evidenced by success in school, did not make them acceptable to whites; it did not lead to equal opportunity with whites in the economic, political, or other domains controlled by whites (Rock, 1862; Rowan, 1975). Furthermore, blacks might have begun to perceive and interpret the rehabilitation process, including some aspects of schooling, as an attack or a threat to their own culture and identity (DuBois, 1921). This interpretation probably made them invest positive values in the very cultural norms, behaviors, and speech styles denigrated by white people.

Evidence for the oppositional cultural frame of reference, or cultural inversion, can be found in black language and speech, cultural beliefs and practices, notions of time, styles of thought or cognitive style, and folklore, art, and literature. With regard to language and speech, Holt (1972) suggested that inversion began with black people's reaction to slavery. She said that black slaves recognized that their mastery of white English meant subordination to white English because it would mean their acceptance of the white definition of the caste system. Black slaves therefore resorted to inversion as a defensive mechanism that allowed them to fight linguistic and psychological entrapment. The slaves gave words and phrases reversed meanings and thereby changed their functions. As Holt (1972) put it,

> *White interpretation of the communication events was quite different from that made by the other person in the interaction, enabling blacks to deceive and manipulate whites without penalty . . . This form of linguistic guerilla warfare protected the subordinated, permitted the masking and disguising of true feeling, allowed the subtle assertion of self and promoted group solidarity.* (p. 154)

According to Boykin (1986, p. 58), linguistic studies show that black culture stands in almost dialectical opposition to the culture of mainstream America; this observation seems to be corroborated by findings in Folb's (1980) study of contemporary inner-city youths. Folb found many instances in which these teenagers inverted the meanings that whites give to conventional English words. For example, for the teenagers "bad" means "good," "nigger" is a term of endearment, "cock" refers to female genitalia, "stallion" is an attractive or lusty female (as opposed to a sexually attractive male in white speech), "ragged" means exceptionally well-dressed, and "wicked" and "mean" are used to signify outstanding, satisfying, formidable, and stylish (Folb, 1980, pp. 230–260).

In the realm of behavior, Haskins (1976) related that in the neighborhood where he grew up, the males upheld norms that were in opposition to the norms of the law enforcement officers who represented the wider society. Recognizing that they lived in a hostile environment created by white Americans, these blacks developed their own criteria for judging one another, which were different from the criteria used by white society. Haskins concluded by saying that the norms of his neighborhood were not only different but in opposition to those of the white society.

The oppositional cultural frame of reference today is not confined to inner-city teenagers or inner-city people. It also has been reported in clinical studies of middle-class blacks, including black executives in white corporations. For example, Bramwell (1972, cited in Fordham, 1984) reported that the black American professionals who "make it" in mainstream culture are people who succeeded in adapting to the basic contradictions arising from the different demands of black and of white norms. According to Taylor (1973), black executives who have "made it" in predominantly white corporations have had to renounce the black cultural frame of reference. That is, they have had to abandon behaving like blacks, to discard symbols used by black peers, and to behave like whites with white symbols or to act in ways that are alien to other blacks.

Distrusting Whites and White Institutions

The last response of blacks that I will discuss is the deep distrust they have developed for white Americans and for the institutions, such as the public schools, controlled by white people. Previous accounts of whites' treatment of blacks show that the two races have been engaged in a perennial conflict with regard to education, jobs, crime and justice, political rights, and residential rights or housing. These conflicts abound with episodes that have left black Americans with the sense that they cannot trust white Americans or the institutions they control.

I will conclude this section by repeating my starting point—namely, that racial stratification includes more than the instrumental dimension. It involves the treatment of racial minorities by the dominant white Americans as well as the minorities' responses to that treatment. Furthermore, racial stratification and its implications for the education of racial minorities cannot be comprehended fully by focusing only on instrumental factors such as minorities' access to education, jobs, housing, and the like. One also must consider the expressive aspects of both the treatment of the minorities and the responses by the minorities. I will now discuss the implications of American racial stratification for the education of black Americans to show how these factors work to influence blacks' school performance and educational attainment.

Educational Consequences

My research has focused on the twin problems of poorer academic performance and lesser educational attainment by black students in comparison with white students. I have concluded that these twin problems are a function of two sets of factors: direct and indirect denial of equal educational opportunity by the dominant white Americans *and* the blacks' responses to their treatment and to schooling. These two sets of factors are represented in Figure 4.

Denial of Equal Educational Opportunity

A historical study of black education in a given community (such as Stockton, California), in a given state or region, or even nationally would reveal that at any given period blacks' access to education and the quality of that education depend on white Americans' perceptions and treatment of blacks in the system of racial stratification described earlier (Ogbu, 1974, 1978, p. 177). Two examples will make this point clear. One concerns the shift in blacks' schooling that occurred in the 1930s. Before that time blacks were said typically to need "industrial education," by which whites usually meant training in low-grade manual skills. Most financial support from the states and from northern philanthropists went into industrial education programs. During the 1930s, however, industrial or vocational education courses became the target of state and federal financial support in order to meet the needs of the mainstream economy for workers with industrial skills. At this point black participation became increasingly restricted (Ogbu, 1978, p. 117). Commenting on this development, Myrdal (1944) noted that southern whites believed that blacks should obtain an industrial education as long as it did not prepare them to compete effectively with whites for jobs.

The other example is the move in the 1960s to redesign black schooling. Title VII of the 1964 civil rights legislation and affirmative action programs gave blacks access to higher level jobs, jobs above the job ceiling, which required more and better education than had been available to them previously. In order to ensure that blacks were "qualified" for their new positions, the mainstream system began to make concerted efforts to "improve" their education, including affirmative action recruitment into predominantly white colleges and universities. Within 10 years, from 1965 to 1975, black college enrollment rose from 349,000 to 948,000 (Wilson, 1979, p. 172).

In general there are four ways in which white Americans have denied blacks equality of educational opportunity and thereby contributed to the problems of poorer academic performance and lower educational attainment. The first and third mechanisms ensure that blacks do not achieve educational qualifications that would enable them to compete effectively with whites for typical jobs above the job ceiling. The second mechanism ensures that those who qualify for such positions do not necessarily get them. This outcome leads to the fourth mechanism, discouragement of blacks from making greater efforts to succeed in school; this will be discussed in connection with blacks' own responses to schooling. I will discuss the first and

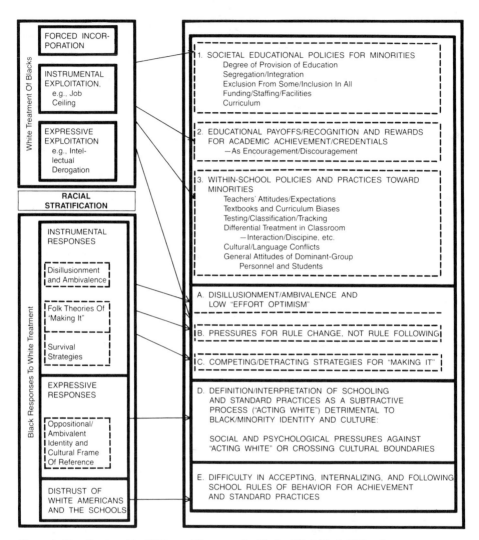

Figure 4 How Treatment by Whites and Responses by Blacks Affect Blacks' Education.

second mechanisms under societal policies and practices and the third under within-school factors.

Societal/community policies and practices. Recent developments and public rhetoric tend to mask the fact that before the 1960s there was no explicit public policy or concerted effort to provide blacks and whites with the same or equal educational preparation for similar jobs and other positions above the job ceiling.

It is true that the education of lower class whites always has been inferior to that of middle-class whites (Hollingshead, 1949; Sexton, 1961; Warner, Havighurst, & Loeb, 1944), but it is equally true that because of racial stratification, the education of black Americans at every class level has been more inferior. Elsewhere I have described in detail the historical pattern of black schooling (Ogbu, 1978); here I will summarize only the salient features. Three points to be emphasized in this summary are that black education was historically different from white education; that it was inferior to white education; and that it was and is determined by white epistemology or by white people's conception of blacks' place in the racial stratification order.

Thus, while slavery lasted, blacks received occasional education in the Bible because their masters believed that it would make them more obedient and more faithful. After the Civil War blacks remained in the peonlike status of sharecroppers or in domestic service and unskilled labor; their education followed suit. The ruling white elite believed that the tenant system would break down if black children, as future laborers, received the same kind of education as whites, because such education would encourage them to question the high interest rates and the exploitative method of account keeping used by the planters in dealing with illiterate tenants. Therefore academic training for blacks was deemphasized and education for blacks was starved of funds (Bond, 1966; Bullock, 1970; Ransom & Sutch, 1977; Vaughn, 1974; Weinberg, 1977).

As the south became urbanized, most blacks initially were provided with some "industrial" education, chiefly for cooking and low-grade building skills. Ironically, however, when many desirable factory jobs began to require special training, the curriculum of black schools began to emphasize classical or academic rather than industrial training, whereas white schools received the necessary funds and began to emphasize industrial education (Bond, 1966; Myrdal, 1944; Weinberg, 1977).

In general, inferior education in the south was institutionalized in legally segregated schools. The processes by which that inferiority was maintained included shorter school terms, inferior curricula and inadequate textbooks, less transportation, fewer library services, fewer supplies, fewer qualified teachers, lower teachers' salaries, and heavier teaching loads (Bond, 1966; Pierce, 1955). Legal segregation was ended officially by the United States Supreme Court in 1954, but actual desegregation did not begin until the late 1960s because of white opposition (Ogbu, 1978).

Black education in the north was not necessarily better. Although in the north blacks had access to more schooling, the quality of that schooling was lower than that of the northern whites; moreover, it deteriorated when more blacks arrived from the south. As black ghettoization in northern cities increased, blacks' education became even more segregated and more inferior. A study conducted in Chicago for the U.S. Commission on Civil Rights shows how northern school systems kept blacks' education inferior. In 1961–1962 the Chicago school system spent almost 25% less per pupil in black schools than in white schools, paid teachers in black schools 18% less than teachers in white schools, and spent 50% less money on nonteaching operating expenses in black schools than in white schools. Black schools had 46.8 pupils per classroom, compared to 30.9 pupils per classroom in white schools (Sexton, 1968). The education committee of the National Association for the Advancement of Colored People (NAACP) in San Francisco found similar differences in the treatment of black and of white schools in the late 1960s; this finding contributed to a later court order for San Francisco to integrate its schools. As recently as 1972 the school district of Washington, DC, spent, on the average, progressively less money per pupil as the number of black children increased in a given school.

Another way in which white Americans and the society at large have contributed to the twin problems is by denying blacks jobs and wages commensurate with their educational attainment. Before the 1960s the American folk theory that more and better education meant better employment opportunities, higher wages, higher social status, and higher self-esteem apparently was not meant to apply to blacks to the same extent as to whites. Blacks who had educational credentials similar to those of whites often were forced to take less desirable jobs, to receive lower wages, and to feel lower self-esteem. Furthermore, the better educated blacks, especially those with a college education, suffered greater discrimination in jobs and wages (Ginzberg, 1956; Kahn, 1968, p. 12; Marshall, 1968; Ogbu, 1978). This treatment in postschool opportunity structure influenced the treatment of blacks within the schools themselves in two ways.

First, as I will show below, the schools might not teach them how to advance within the reward structure of the schools, which is similar to the reward structure of the community. Therefore the way in which black children were made to experience the reward structure of their schools reflected what they would experience as adults in the job market. Until recently black adults in Stockton, California, as elsewhere in the nation, were not hired, paid, or promoted on the basis of their educational qualifications and ability. Thus the schools prepared black children for a predictable future. Second, because school officials were aware of the treatment of blacks in the local opportunity structure, sometimes they channeled black children into educational tracks that merely prepared them for their customary place in the local employment structure—namely, jobs below the job ceiling. These treatments of blacks in the opportunity structure tended directly and indirectly to influence blacks' perceptions of and responses to schooling, a point that will be elaborated in the next section.

Within-school treatment. The gross mechanisms of discrimination described earlier, including deliberate school segregation and differential staffing and funding, probably are no longer widespread; they have been outlawed by legislative statutes or court rulings. Yet many schools continue to use subtle mechanisms to keep blacks' schooling inferior to whites' schooling. Some findings from my own research in Stockton, California, show how minorities and whites may attend the same schools but may not necessarily receive the same education or learn similar rules of behavior for achievement. In the case of 17 black and Chicano students whose records I examined over a 5-year period, I found that all but 1 received the same annual grade of C, regardless of how hard each child had worked and, strikingly, regardless of what the teachers said in their written evaluations. There appeared to be little correspondence between the written assessment and the letter grades. In general, a child who received a C in Grade 1 continued to receive the same mark in subsequent years, although the teacher at each subsequent grade level might write that she was "delighted" at the child's "progress." Because these children received the same average marks whether or not they worked hard, I suggested that obviously they were not being taught to associate effort of hard work with higher achievement (Ogbu, 1974, 1977).

I encountered a typical example of teachers' and administrators' lowered expectations in one family, where I was told that the oldest son ceased to be "smart" because he was bored with courses that were too easy for him. When his parents approached his teacher and the principal to discuss the matter, the latter rejected the parents' explanation and their request for extra work for their son. The boy's work continued to deteriorate, and at the time of my study he was receiving mostly Ds and Fs in 12th-grade courses.

Other researchers (Berkeley & Entwisle, 1979; Entwisle, 1987; Entwisle & Hayduk, 1982, cited in Jackson, 1987) have indicated other school policies and practices that may undermine black children's achievement motivation. Among these is the practice of assigning report card marks on the basis of classroom "conduct expectations" rather than academic effort.

The present situation is complex, but it can be said that in the current educational reform movement there appears to be a growing recognition that black students are at greater "risk" than most other groups of students throughout the country: They lag in school performance at all levels of schooling, and they lag in college admissions and graduation. It also seems to be recognized increasingly that blacks and similar groups need additional help from public and private sources in order to benefit from the current reform movement. No doubt these concerns of the nation's political, civic, and economic leaders are affecting blacks' educational experience in the schools. Blacks' within-school experiences always have been connected intimately with, sometimes determined by, their treatment by whites outside the schools. Yet the educational treatment of blacks by white Americans and by the schools is only one source of the twin problems. The other source is the pattern of response by blacks, which I will discuss next.

Blacks' Responses

The extent to which black children, as a group and as individuals, succeed or fail in school depends not only on how white Americans and the schools they control treat blacks but also on how blacks themselves perceive and respond to schooling. In this section I will consider blacks' own perceptions, interpretations, and other responses as a racial minority group and, to some extent, as individuals.

Instrumental responses and schooling: Disillusionment. Among the responses that impair blacks' school performance and educational attainment is disillusionment, which leads to failure to develop "effort optimism" (Shack, 1970) or incentive motivation in regard to schooling as a culturally sanctioned norm (Ogbu, 1978). Shack suggested how this response might have originated historically. He noted that in the absence of a job ceiling against white Americans, whites have been able to obtain adequate payoffs for their educational efforts, that is, to obtain jobs and wages commensurate with their training and ability. This experience has encouraged whites to develop "effort optimism" toward school and work, as summed up in the maxim, "If at first you don't succeed, try, try again." Effort optimism means being serious and determined and persevering in academic work, test taking, and other such activities. This attitude is less characteristic of blacks, however, because of their different experience.

Faced with the most sustained and most extreme discrimination in American history, particularly a job ceiling, blacks seem to have learned that social and economic rewards are not proportionate to educational efforts; consequently they tended to develop a different maxim: "What's the use of trying?" This disillusionment and its consequences for efforts are not recent in origin. Some of the earliest evidence comes from a speech made by John Rock, the first black American admitted to practice before the U.S. Supreme Court. In that speech, published in *The Liberator* in 1862, Rock spoke of the discouragement caused by limited opportunities in Massachusetts for blacks to achieve a better future through education, employment, or business in spite of the prevailing ideology of equality of opportunity (Gabelko, 1984, p. 265). Sochen (1971) found in her study that although many black writers had accepted the American dream, with its ethic of individual hard work, thrift, and discipline, some writers rejected it simultaneously because racial barriers made it meaningless and irrelevant to black Americans.

I also found disillusionment and ambivalence among black parents and other adults as well as among their children, whom I studied in Stockton, California, in the late 1960s and early 1970s. This situation was paradoxical, however. When questioned, the adults said that a black person who wanted to get ahead and to get a good job should get a good education. Yet (as will be discussed later), they did not seem to match their assertion with effort, even in guiding their children. Part of the reason appears to be that Stockton blacks did not really believe that they had an equal chance with white Stocktonians to be hired for a job or promoted on the job, or that they would do well in examinations designed by white people. They said that if a black person was to be hired or promoted when competing with a white person, the black must be "twice as good" or "twice as qualified" as the white. Because they saw their opportunities as more limited than those of whites, the blacks agreed with the opinion expressed by a Mexican-American parent, who said that although education is important for getting jobs, it is not enough. For a minority applicant to be hired over a white competitor, that parent said,

> You [the minority candidate] have to show that you are better than the white man. And if you are going to take a test or if you are going to interview for a job, your test [score] has to be far better than the superior's—which is supposed to be the white man. Otherwise, they won't even look at you; they won't even hire you.

On the basis of shared knowledge and experience, blacks believed that they would not "make it" or compete successfully with whites simply by adopting the rules of behavior or meeting the criteria for white people (Ogbu, 1974).

Stockton's black youths, like their parents, expressed interest in getting an education, believing that school credentials were important for obtaining mainstream jobs. Yet at the same time they, like their parents, did not match their wishes with effort. They did not put enough time, effort, or perseverance into their schoolwork. Certainly they knew what to do in order to do well in school; during research interviews they explained that one of the reasons why Chinese, Japanese, and some white students did well was that they expended more time and more effort than blacks in doing their schoolwork. This lack of serious academic attitude and effort appears to increase as black students grow older and become more aware that as members of a minority group they have limited future opportunities for obtaining good jobs as a result of their education. They also begin to learn about and to adopt other ways of advancing, influenced by their observations of how older people in their neighborhood succeed and by the prevailing folk theories of success in their community. Accordingly, they divert their time and efforts increasingly away from schoolwork into nonacademic activities. In doing so they contribute further to their low academic adaptation and to their low educational attainment.

To gain further insight into the adverse effect of disillusionment about schooling on contemporary black adolescents, one may read an article sent to *Newsweek's* "My Turn" column by a 15-year-old boy from Wilmington, Delaware (Hunter, 1980). The article describes two types of black teenagers in the inner city: The "rocks," who constitute the majority, have given up hopes of making it in the mainstream economy through the white middle-class strategy of obtaining school credentials. Therefore, they stop trying to do well in school or going to school at all. The "ducks" or "suckers," who are the few, the "minority of the minority," still hope to succeed through schooling. They are derided because they go to school every day and even want to go to college; they don't drink or use drugs. The "ducks" are regarded as "wasting their time waiting for a dream that won't come true" because even their parents cannot find jobs.

Changing the rules or requirements. Blacks do not simply stop trying to succeed because they believe that the rules or requirements do not work for them as they do for whites. Rather, they try to change those rules or requirements for school success and for employment and promotion on the job. The requirements may be related to course placement, tracking, or extracurricular activities in school and to employment and promotion in the public or private sector. Usually these blacks begin with public criticisms of these requirements at public meetings, saying that the requirements are biased; they speak at school board meetings, city council meetings, and other public forums about civil service examinations and other employment-related tests (Ogbu, 1977). Black students, parents, and spokespersons seem to think that the tests or requirements, whether administered by whites or by their black representatives, are designed to keep black people down, not to help them succeed. In many instances nationwide, blacks have taken their case to the courts and have won (Huff, 1974; *Larry P. v. Wilson Riles,* 1979).

Competing and detracting survival strategies. Blacks also have developed several "survival strategies," described previously, to eliminate, lower, or circumvent the barriers they face in trying to obtain desirable jobs and to advance in other ways. The situation is paradoxical, however, with regard to the effects of these strategies on blacks' school performance and educational attainment. For one thing, blacks historically have demanded more and better education; they continue to do so, as was the case in Stockton, California, during my research there. In addition, as I said above, blacks assert that education is the means to improve their social and economic status. Thus they continue to stress the need for education, even though their expectations about the benefits of education historically have not been met by good employment opportunities or in other ways.

I have discussed already some of the likely consequences of these unmet expectations, namely disillusionment, ambivalence, and attempts to change the rules. Here I will stress another likely consequence: Instead of persevering individually for good educations, blacks tend to endorse collective action as offering the best chances for advancement. I suspect that this pooling of efforts may weaken realistic perceptions and may sidetrack the pursuit of schooling as a strategy for self-advancement. Furthermore, collective struggle for employment, better jobs, better education, and better housing, such as occurred during my study in Stockton, may affect the extent to which *blacks as a minority community* sanction school success as a cultural goal (as distinct from merely desiring it), accept the school's criteria for success, and sanction and implement the instrumental attitudes and behaviors that enhance academic success. Other survival strategies, such as patron–client relationships, hustling, and sports, become serious competitors with schooling as a strategy for success. Another likely consequence is that these survival strategies may require and stimulate attitudes, skills, and behaviors that are not necessarily compatible with those required for academic success.

Clientship, or Uncle Tomming, is dysfunctional for young people because it does not create good role models for school success through hard work. Clientship teaches black children the manipulative knowledge, skills, and attitudes used by inner-city adults in dealing with white people and white caretaker institutions. In my research in Stockton, I found that many blacks, both adults and children, believed that most blacks who are successful had played the Uncle Tom game to achieve and maintain their positions (Ogbu, 1977).

Familiarity with other survival strategies, such as hustling and pimping, also has some adverse effects on black children's schoolwork. For one thing, in the norms that support these strategies, the work ethic is reversed by the insistence that one should make it without working, especially without "doing the white man's thing." Also, social interactions such as those between teacher and students and among students in the classroom are seen as opportunities for exploitation, that is, opportunities to gain prestige by putting down another person or other persons. This activity may lead to class disruptions and suspensions. Finally, the skills involved in hustling and in similar activities, as noted before, may conflict with those required for completing schoolwork successfully.

When survival strategies such as collective struggle succeed in increasing the pool of jobs and other resources for the black community, they may encourage black youths to work hard in school. Such success, however, also can lead the youths to blame "the system" and to rationalize their lack of serious efforts at schoolwork.

Identity, Cultural Frame, and Perceptions of Schooling as a Subtractive Process

The instrumental barriers and the black responses described above are important reasons for the twin problems of poorer school performance and lower educational attainment among blacks, but they do not answer three related questions. First, why are some individual black children successful, although they also face a job ceiling and inferior education and share the same folk theories about getting ahead with other blacks? Second, why do some minority groups who also face a job ceiling, other opportunity barriers, and inferior education do better in school than black Americans (Ogbu, 1978)? Third, why are some minority groups doing well in school although they possess cultures and languages different from the culture and language of American public schools (Ogbu & Matute-Bianchi, 1986)? To answer these questions we turn to the influence of black social identity and cultural frame of reference described earlier.

The oppositional process, in terms of blacks' social identity and cultural frame of reference, distinguishes blacks' responses to schooling from those of immigrant minorities. The oppositional process also appears to explain why the elimination of instrumental barriers, such as the job ceiling, does not necessarily lead to the immediate disappearance of the difficulties encountered by blacks and similar minorities with respect to academic performance. The problems created by the oppositional identity and cultural frame of reference may persist after the instrumental barriers in economic and other domains have been removed, for the reasons given earlier in this chapter.

How, exactly, do the oppositional identity and cultural frame of reference affect the process of blacks' education? They do so through the perception and definition or interpretation of school learning as learning white American culture or as "acting white," which leads eventually to identification with white people, loss of black identity, and abandonment of black people and their cause. Consciously or unconsciously, blacks do not distinguish between linear acculturation or assimilation and adopting attitudes and behaviors that lead to academic success. Thus although, like white Americans, blacks and similar minorities say that they want education, they appear simultaneously to assume and to fear that by adopting attitudes and behaviors typical of whites who are successful in school they will give up a part of their own identity, culture, and language.

It is possible that the influence of oppositional identity and cultural frame of reference begins at an earlier age, but thus far research has found evidence of such influence mainly among children approaching adolescence and among adolescents and college students. Studies among black adolescents show that many tend to define academic tasks or behaviors and academic success itself as "white" or as "not black" (i.e., as not appropriate for blacks). In contrast, they define as appropriate for blacks certain extracurricular activities traditionally open to blacks and in which black students excel. Strong peer pressures are applied to black students who try to excel in academic work or who become involved in "white" extracurricular activities to give up such pursuits. These students are called "Uncle Toms" (Petroni, 1970), "crazy," and "brainiacs" (Fordham, 1985).

Petroni's (1970) study provides a good example of the difficulty created by this situation for bright black students who are making the effort to succeed academically. Petroni was told initially by black high school students that they were excluded from certain courses and extracurricular activities by "white racism." Later, however, he found that black students stayed away from these courses and activities partly because of pressures from other black students; furthermore, those who participated in the so-called "white activities," such as student government, madrigals, and the senior play, were called "Uncle Toms" and were rejected by their fellow black students. The following interview excerpt shows the dilemma of one male student who made all As in his courses:

> Well, I participate in speech. I'm the only Negro in the whole group. I find it kind of interesting that I'm the only Negro. I'm always contrasted in pictures of the group. The Negroes accuse me of thinking I'm white. In the bathroom one day, some Negroes wrote in big letters, "B.B. is an Uncle Tom." It's this kind of pressures from other Negro kids which bothers me most. (p. 26)

On the other hand, black students who excelled in nonacademic activities or "black things," such as sports, were praised highly by their black peers. Petroni suggested that the fear of being called "Uncle Toms" or of being accused of "acting white" may prevent black students from working hard to do well in school. Petroni's findings and conclusions are supported by my study in Stockton, California (Ogbu, 1974), and by Fordham and Ogbu's (1986) report on black students in Washington, DC.

Fordham and Ogbu (1986), in an ethnographic study of 33 eleventh graders at an almost all-black high school in Washington, DC, found that black students' peer culture strongly rejected striving for academic success in school because it was perceived as "acting white." These students regarded many behaviors associated with high achievement—speaking standard English, studying long hours, striving to make good grades—as "acting white." Students who were known to engage in such behaviors were labeled "brainiacs," ridiculed, and ostracized as people who had abandoned the group. Interviews with a number of bright students indicated that some had chosen to put brakes on their academic effort in order to avoid being labeled and harassed. Those who continue to try to do well in school were compelled to engage in behaviors that discredited evidence of studying or working hard (e.g., belittling the value of schooling, not speaking up in class, joining athletic teams, taking part in other peer-group-approved extracurricular activities, or behaving like the class clown).

Fordham and Ogbu's interviews with the students indicated a strong awareness of the choice they were making and an explicit concern about what they saw as their own limited economic chances in life. The likely benefit of academic success, however, often was perceived as not worth the burden of peer disapproval. As Fordham and Ogbu stressed, this sort of attachment to peer culture—a peer culture so much at odds with mainstream values and sources of reward—occurs in particular social conditions (see also Ogbu, 1974; Petroni, 1970; Petroni & Hirsch, 1970; Semons, 1987).

One dilemma of a black student, then, is that he or she must choose between "acting white" (adopting attitudes and behaviors that other black students consider inappropriate for blacks but that are conducive to school success) and "acting black" (adopting other attitudes and behaviors that black students approve as appropriate for blacks but that are not necessarily conducive to school success). Thus, unlike immigrant minority students, black students and similar nonimmigrant minority students are unable or unwilling to distinguish attitudes and behaviors that result in academic success and school credentials for future employment from attitudes and behaviors that result in linear acculturation or replacement of their cultural identity with that of white Americans.

The pressure against "acting white" is not limited to lower class black students in the inner city. It is also found among middle-class black students in suburban and private schools (Abdul-Jabbar & Knobles, 1983; Gray, 1985), but it has not been studied systematically among those students. Self-reports indicate that the problem extends to those in college (Mitchell, 1982, 1983; Nemko, 1988). Individual differences exist among lower class as well as middle-class black students: Some students succumb almost totally to peer pressures not to work hard to succeed because that would be acting white; other students, determined to succeed academically, use deliberate strategies to avoid peer pressures; and still others reject the black cultural frame of reference and choose to do their schoolwork in spite of peer pressures.

Distrusting White Americans and the Schools and Acceptance of School Rules

Black Americans' distrust of white Americans and of the public schools also contributes to the twin problems of poorer academic performance and lesser educational attainment by blacks compared to whites. The distrust grew out of past (and to some degree present) treatment of blacks by the public schools and by the white people who control them; this treatment has been documented throughout the history of the public schools in all regions of the country (Bond, 1966, 1969; Bullock, 1970; Kluger, 1977; Ogbu, 1978; Weinberg, 1977). Elsewhere (Ogbu, 1981b, 1985) I have suggested that this phenomenon of distrust might interfere with black childrens' ability to learn in the classroom. The interviews I conducted with black students and their parents in Stockton, California, seemed to indicate that they believed that white children received a better education than black children. Because the children and their parents perceived discrepancies, they said that they did not trust the schools to treat them fairly.

The black students and parents in Stockton also said that they did not trust white people and the schools to teach black people the truth, that the schools taught only white people's knowledge and only what white people wanted blacks to know (see Weis, 1985). In my ethnographic research I encountered several instances in which black students and parents expressed this skepticism. One occasion was at a public meeting following a riot in a predominantly minority high school in 1969. The hero of the occasion was a black youth who had been in and out of jail several times. Holding a high school history textbook, *The Land of the Free*, and strolling from one end of the platform to the other, he repeatedly asked teachers in the audience if they had ever stopped for a moment while teaching their classes to ask themselves whether the title of this textbook had the same meaning for blacks, Indians, and Mexican-Americans as for whites. Each time he asked the question, he was applauded by black parents and students as well as by members of other minorities in the audience.

In an interview I held with a high school student and his mother, they pointed out repeatedly that the public schools are not designed to teach black people the truth or to teach them anything that would "hurt the white man." The following interview excerpt (Ogbu, 1969, #207) illustrates their skepticism:

> **Student:** Now, the white man, like I say, will not teach you something where he will hurt himself. He is not going to do this. And he is not going to fully teach you. I mean—they might bring a book that will tell you something about black history but then he's going to kind of mix it up and make it sound as though the white man was good. Like they said, it was a white man that was there when a black man invented something. See? First, they said the white man invented something but it was the black man that was with him. But now [1969] they sort of change it, saying that the black man invented it but it was the white man that helped him. See? It changed, so that the white man always helped him. See? The white man always won.
> **Mother:** Like the black man never do nothing for himself.
> **Student:** That's it.

To complicate matters, the conflicts between the schools and blacks often force schools to approach black children's education defensively—through control, paternalism, or "contest." These strategies tend to divert attention from the real task of educating black children. Another problem with this type of relationship between blacks and the schools, characterized as it is by distrust and skepticism, is that blacks and whites tend to interpret school rules and requirements differently. Thus white middle-class parents and their children may see completing a given school task or conforming to the school's standard practices as necessary, desirable, and compatible with their educational goals. Inner-city black parents and their children may interpret the same requirements as a deception or as an unnecessary imposition that does not necessarily meet their "real educational needs." In this situation it is probably difficult for black children, especially the older ones, to accept and follow school rules of behavior and to persevere at their academic tasks.

THE FUTURE OF RACIAL STRATIFICATION AND EDUCATION

Racial stratification in the United States has changed significantly since I began to observe it in 1961, but the modification has been uneven. The most noticeable area of change is in the instrumental treatment of blacks by white Americans, especially in certain institutions controlled by whites: in employment above the job ceiling, in elective offices, and in college admissions. The primary reasons for these improvements, as noted earlier, are civil rights pressures, deliberate government policies expressed through legislation, and affirmative action. The effects of these strategies continue to be felt to some degree and will continue at least into the 1990s. Yet the consequences of these changes for the education of black children, particularly the children of the new middle-class blacks, are not clear, because black children continue to lag behind their white peers in school performance and educational attainment. I suggest that if a greater improvement is to occur in the educational achievement of the children of the new (and old) black middle class, greater attention must be paid to the expressive side of racial stratification, including blacks' expressive responses.

The instrumental opportunities of non-middle-class blacks have not changed much, but not because these blacks lack the training and the ability required by the changes in the mainstream economy and institutions. The primary reason is that unlike the case with middle-class blacks, no deliberate, determined official and private employment policies and programs exist to give them jobs and decent wages or to facilitate their upward social mobility. To make matters worse, many middle-class blacks who have benefited from deliberate official and private efforts have moved into the position of caretakers as administrators of "welfare" and remedial programs for non-middle-class minorities, whom they now label disdainfully as "the underclass" and wish to distance themselves from. These factors compound the educational fate of non-middle-class black children as we move into the 1990s. Non-middle-class blacks continue to experience and perceive instrumental and expressive barriers, including expressive barriers such as derogation from middle-class members of their own race. In this situation the instrumental and expressive responses of non-middle-class blacks remain relatively unchanged and continue to contribute to their educational problems.

REFERENCES

Abdul-Jabbar, K., & Knobles, P. (1983). *Giant steps: The autobiography of Kareem Abdul-Jabbar.* New York: Bantam.

Baker, H. A., Jr. (1984). *The journey back: Issues in black literature and criticism.* Chicago: University of Chicago Press.

Berkeley, M. V., & Entwisle, D. R. (1979). *Kindergarten social climate* (Report #284). Baltimore, MD: Johns Hopkins University Center for Social Organization of Schools.

Berreman, G. D. (1960). Caste in India and the United States. *American Journal of Sociology, 66,* 120–127.

Berreman, G. D. (1967). Concomitants of caste organization. In G. DeVos & H. Wagatsuma (Eds.), *Japanese invisible race: Caste in culture and personality* (pp. 308–324). Berkeley: University of California Press.

Blassingame, J. W. (1972). *The slave community: Plantation life in the antebellum south.* New York: Oxford University Press.

Bond, H. M. (1966). *The education of the Negro in the American social order.* New York: Octagon.

Bond, H. M. (1969). *Negro education in Alabama: A study in cotton and steel.* New York: Antheneum.

Boykin, A. W. (1986). The triple quandary and the schooling of Afro-American children. In U. Neisser (Ed.), *The school achievement of minority children: New perspectives* (pp. 57–92). Hillsdale, NJ: Erlbaum.

Bramwell, J. (1972). *Courage in crisis.* New York: Bobbs-Merrill.

Brimmer, A. F. (1974). Economic development in the black community. In E. Ginzberg & R. M. Solow (Eds.), *The great society: Lessons for the future* (pp. 146–173). New York: Basic Books.

Bullock, H. A. (1970). *A history of Negro education in the south: From 1619 to the present.* New York: Praeger.

Burkey, R. M. (1971). *Racial discrimination and public policy in the United States.* Lexington, MA: Heath.

Castile, G. P., & Kushner, G. (1981). *Persistent peoples: Cultural enclaves in perspective.* Tuscon: University of Arizona Press.

CBS Television Network. (1984, August 5). The Rosewood massacre. *60 Minutes, 16*(47), 16–22. (Transcript).

Darity, W. A., Jr. (1983). The human capital approach to black–white earnings inequality: Some unsettled questions. *Journal of Human Resources, 17,* 90–98.

DeVos, G. A. (1967). Essential elements of caste: Psychological determinants in structural theory. In G. A. DeVos & H. Wagatsuma (Eds.), *Japan's invisible race: Caste in culture and personality* (pp. 332–384). Berkeley: University of California Press.

DeVos, G. A. (1984, April 14–16). *Ethnic persistence and role degradation: An illustration from Japan.* Paper presented at the American-Soviet Symposium on Contemporary Ethnic Processes in the USA and the USSR, New Orleans.

DeWare, H. (1978, July 4). Affirmative action plan at AT&T is permitted. *Washington Post,* pp. A1, A7.

DuBois, W. E. B. (1921, December). Editorial. *The Brownies' book.* New York: National Association for the Advancement of Colored People.

DuBois, W. E. B. (1961). *The souls of black folk.* Greenwich, CT: Fawcett. (Original work published 1903).

Elkins, S. M. (1959). *Slavery: A problem in American institutional and intellectual life.* Chicago: University of Chicago Press.

Entwisle, D. R. (1987). *Schooling process and ethnic group membership.* Paper presented at the biennial meeting of the Society for Research in Child Development, Baltimore, MD.

Entwisle, D. R., & Hayduk, L. A. (1982). *Early schooling: Cognitive and affective outcomes.* Baltimore, MD: Johns Hopkins University Press.

Ferman, L. A., Kornbluh, J. L., & Miller, J. A. (Eds.). (1968). *Negroes and jobs: A book of readings.* Ann Arbor: University of Michigan Press.

Folb, E. A. (1980). *Running' down some lines: The language and culture of black teenagers.* Cambridge, MA: Harvard University Press.

Forham, S. (1984). *Ethnography in a black high school: Learning not to be a native.* Paper presented at the 83rd annual meeting of the American Anthropological Association, Denver, CO.

Fordham, S. (1985). *Black student school success as related to fictive kinship.* Unpublished final report to the National Institute of Education, Washington, DC.

Fordham, S., & Ogbu, J. U. (1986). Black students' school success: Coping with the burden of "acting white". *Urban Review, 18*(3), 176–206.

Foster, H. L. (1974). *Ribbin', jivin', and playin' the dozens: The unrecognized dilemma of inner-city schools.* Cambridge, MA: Ballinger.

Frazier, E. F. (1957). *The Negro in the United States.* New York: Macmillan.

Gabelko, N. H. (1984). *Identifying discontinuities through variations in value orientations: Applications to the historiography of American schooling.* Unpublished doctoral dissertation, University of California, Berkeley.

Ginzberg, E. (1956). *The Negro potential.* New York: Columbia University Press.

Gray, J. (1985, March 17). A black American princess: New game, new rules. *Washington Post,* pp. E1, E5.

Greene, L., & Woodson, C. G. (1930). *The Negro wage earner.* Washington, DC: Association for the Study of Negro Life and History.

Gregory, D. (1965). *Nigger: An autobiography.* New York: Pocket Books.

Haley, A. (1976). *Roots: The saga of an American family.* Garden City, NY: Doubleday.

Hall, R. L. (1979). *Black separatism in the United States.* Hanover, NH: University of New England Press.

Hammond, B. E. (1965). *The contest system: A survival technique.* Unpublished manuscript, Department of Sociology and Anthropology, Washington University, St. Louis.

Harrison, B. (1972). *Education, training and the urban ghetto.* Baltimore, MD: Johns Hopkins University Press.

Haskins, K. (1976). You have no right to put a kid out of school. In A. Toblier (Ed.), "Four conversations: The intersection of private and public." *Urban Review, 8*(4), 273–287.

Henderson, V. W. (1967). Region, race and jobs. In A. M. Ross & H. Hill (Eds.), *Employment, race and poverty* (pp. 76–104). New York: Harcourt.

Hollingshead, A. (1949). *Elmtown's youth.* New York: Wiley.

Holt, G. S. (1972). "Inversion" in black communication. In T. Kockman (Ed.), *Rappin' and stylin' out: Communication in urban black America* (pp. 152–159). Urbana: University of Illinois Press.

How whites and blacks feel about racial equality: A new racial poll. (1979, February 26). *Newsweek*, p. 48.

Huff, S. (1974). Credentialing by tests or by degrees: Title VII of the Civil Rights Act and Criggs vs. Duke Power Company. *Harvard Educational Review, 44*, 246–269.

Hunter, D. (1980, August 18). Ducks vs. hard rocks. *Newsweek*, pp. 14–15.

Jackson, J. F. (1987). *Black male underachievement in the elementary school years: A developmental approach*. Unpublished manuscript.

Johnson, C. S. (1938). *The Negro college graduate*. College Park, MD: McGrath.

Johnson, C. S. (1943). *Backgrounds to patterns of Negro segregation*. New York: Crowell.

Kahn, T. (1968). The economics of inequality. In L. A. Ferman, J. L. Kornbluh, & J. A. Miller (Eds.), *Negroes and jobs* (pp. 15–28). Ann Arbor: University of Michigan Press.

Keil, C. (1977). The expressive black male role: The bluesman. In D. Y. Wilkinson & R. L. Taylor (Eds.), *The black male in America today: Perspectives on his status in contemporary society* (pp. 60–84). Chicago: Nelson-Hall.

Kluger, R. (1977). *Simple justice*. New York: Vintage.

Larry P. v. Wilson Riles, (N.D. Calif. 1979). Unp. Document # C-71-2270 RFP. San Francisco.

Lyman, S. M. (1973). *The black American in sociological thought: A failure of a perspective*. New York: Capricorn.

Maquet, J. (1971). *Power and society in Africa*. New York: World University Library.

Marshall, R. (1968). Racial practices of unions. In L. A. Ferman, J. L. Kornbluh, & J. A. Miller (Eds.), *Negroes and jobs* (pp. 277–298). Ann Arbor: University of Michigan Press.

McCord, W., Howard, J., Friedberg, B., & Harwood, E. (1969). *Life styles in the black ghetto*. New York: Norton.

Mickelson, R. A. (1984). *Race, class, and gender differences in adolescent academic achievement attitudes and behaviors*. Unpublished doctoral dissertation, Graduate School of Education, University of California, Los Angeles.

Mitchell, J. (1982). Reflections of a black social scientist: Some struggles, some doubts, some hopes. *Harvard Educational Review, 52*(1), 27–44.

Mitchell, J. (1983). Visible, vulnerable, and viable: Emerging perspectives of a minority professor. In J. H. Cones III, J. F. Noonan, & D. Janha (Eds.), *Teaching minority students* (pp. 17–28). San Francisco: Jossey-Bass.

Myrdal, G. (1944). *An American dilemma: The Negro problem and modern democracy*. New York: Harper.

Nemko, M. (1988). *How to get an ivy league education at a state university: Comprehensive profiles of America's outstanding public colleges*. New York: Avon Books.

Newman, D. K. (1979). Underclass: An appraisal. In C. V. Willie (Ed.), *Caste and class controversy* (pp. 92–97). New York: General Hall.

Newman, D. K., Amidei, B. K., Carter, D. D., Kruvant, W. J., & Russell, J. S. (1978). *Protest, politics, and prosperity: Black Americans and white institutions, 1940–1975*. New York: Pantheon.

Ogbu, J. U. (1974). *The next generation: An ethnography of education in an urban neighborhood*. New York: Academic Press.

Ogbu, J. U. (1977). Racial stratification and education: The case of Stockton, California. *ICRD Bulletin, 12*(3), 1–26.

Ogbu, J. U. (1978). *Minority education and caste: The American system in cross-cultural perspective*. New York: Academic Press.

Ogbu, J. U. (1981a). School ethnography: A multilevel approach. *Anthropology and Education Quarterly, 12*(1), 3–10.

Ogbu, J. U. (1981b). *Schooling in the ghetto: An ecological perspective on community and home influences*. Paper presented at the National Institute of Education Follow-Through Planning Conference, Philadelphia, February 10–11.

Ogbu, J. U. (1982b). *Cultural inversion*. Unpublished manuscript, Department of Anthropology, University of California, Berkeley.

Ogbu, J. U. (1985). Cultural ecological influences on minority education. *Language Arts, 62*(8), 860–869.

Ogbu, J. U. (1986). The consequences of the American caste system. In U. Neisser (Ed.), *The school achievement of minority children: New perspectives* (pp. 19–56). Hillsdale, NJ: Erlbaum.

Ogbu, J. U., & Matute-Bianchi, M. E. (1986). Understanding sociocultural factors: Knowledge, identity, and school adjustment. In *Beyond language: Social and cultural factors in schooling language minority students* (pp. 73–142). Los Angeles: California State University.

Petroni, F. A. (1970). "Uncle Toms": White stereotypes in the black movement. *Human Organization, 29*(4), 260–266.

Petroni, F. A., & Hirsch, E. A. (1970). *Two, four, six, eight, when you gonna integrate?* New York: Behavioral Publications.

Pierce, T. M. (1955). *White and Negro schools in the south: An analysis of biracial education.* Englewood Cliffs, NJ: Prentice-Hall.

Ransom, R. L., & Sutch, R. (1977). *One kind of freedom: The economic consequences of emancipation.* New York: Cambridge University Press.

Rawick, G. P. (1972). *From sundown to sunup: The making of the black community.* Westport, CT: Greenwood.

Rock, J. (1862, June 16). Prospects for colored men. *The Liberator.*

Ross, A. M. (1967). The Negro in the American economy. In A. M. Ross & H. Hill (Eds.), *Employment, race and poverty* (pp. 3–48). New York: Harcourt.

Ross, A. R. (1973). *Negro employment in the south: Vol. 3. State and local governments.* Washington, DC: U.S. Government Printing Office.

Rowan, C. T. (1975). The Negro's place in the American dream. In J. D. Harrison & A. B. Shaw (Eds.), *The American dream: Vision and reality* (pp. 19–21). San Francisco: Canfield.

Scott, J. W. (1976). *The Black revolt: Racial stratification in the USA.* Cambridge, MA: Schenkman.

Sexton, P. C. (1961). *Education and income.* New York: Viking.

Sexton, P. C. (1968). Schools: Broken ladder to success. In L. A. Ferman, J. L. Kornbluh, & J. A. Miller (Eds.), *Negroes and jobs* (pp. 222–236). Ann Arbor: University of Michigan Press.

Semons, M. (1987). *The salience of ethnicity at a multiethnic urban high school.* Unpublished doctoral dissertation, Graduate School of Education, University of California, Berkeley.

Shack, W. A. (1970). *On black American values in white America: Some perspectives on the cultural aspects of learning behavior and compensatory education.* Paper prepared for the Social Science Research Council, Subcommittee on Values and Compensatory Education. New York.

Sochen, J. (Ed.). (1971). *The black man and the American dream: Negro aspirations in America, 1900–1930.* Chicago: Quadrangle.

Spicer, E. H. (1966). The process of cultural enclavement of middle America. *Proceedings of the 36th Congress International de Americanistas* (Seville), 3, 267–279.

Spicer, E. H. (1971). Persistent cultural systems: A comparative study of identity systems that can adapt to contrasting environments. *Science, 174,* 795–800.

Styron, W. (1966). *The confessions of Nat Turner.* New York: Random House.

Taylor, S. A. (1973). Some funny things happened on the way up. *Contact, 5*(1), 12–17.

Vaughn, W. P. (1974). *Schools for all: The blacks and public education in the south, 1865–1877.* Lexington: University of Kentucky Press.

Wallace, M. (1970). The uses of violence in American history. *The American Scholar, 40*(1), 81–102.

Wallace, P. A. (1976). *Equal employment opportunity and the AT&T case.* Cambridge, MA: MIT Press.

Warner, W. L., Havighurst, R. J., & Loeb, M. B. (1944). *Who shall be educated? The challenge of equal opportunity.* New York: Harper.

Weinberg, M. (1977). *A chance to learn: A history of race and education in the United States.* New York: Cambridge University Press.

Weis, L. (1985). *Between two worlds: Black students in an urban community college.* Boston: Routledge & Kegan Paul.

Willie, C. V. (Ed.). (1979). *Caste and class controversy.* Bayside, NY: General Hall.

Wilson, W. J. (1978). *The declining significance of race: Blacks and changing American institutions.* Chicago: University of Chicago Press.

Wilson, W. J. (1979). The declining significance of race: Revisited but not revised. In C. V. Willie (Ed.), *Caste and class controversy* (pp. 159–176). Bayside, NY: General Hall.

2

Current Issues Affecting Blacks and Hispanics in the Educational Pipeline

James E. Blackwell
Department of Sociology
University of Massachusetts—Boston

For more than a century, race as a determinant of life chances has occupied the attention of scholars in the United States. Within the twentieth century some of the more influential treatises, many of which are already classics in the social and behavioral sciences, have addressed patterned social interactions structured on issues of race and color differentiation. W. E. B. DuBois (1906), writing in *The Souls of Black Folk,* was prophetic in his prediction that "the color line" would become the most powerful boundary-maintenance instrument for determining black–white relations throughout the twentieth century. Oliver Cox (1942) was among the first American sociologists to formulate and crystallize exploitation theory as well as to demonstrate fundamental interconnections among colonialism, capitalism, racial dominance, class subjugation, and group exploitation. Similar notions were expanded by Reginald Horsman (1982) when, in *Race and Manifest Destiny,* he traced the spread of the white supremacy doctrine and the power of that belief system as justification for European expansionism, exploitation, and greed as manifested in the institutionalization of slavery, the conquest and decimation of the Native American population, and the expropriation of land from Hispanics and Native Americans in the southwest and west.

Gunnar Myrdal's (1944) *An American Dilemma* served as a major turning point in the study of race relations in the United States. This monumental treatise, richly documented with qualitative data and descriptive statistics, provided a well-organized resource through which a critical assessment of race relations in the United States was made. It also established an institutional framework for understanding features subsequently captured in the term *institutional racism.* It is also important that Myrdal made observations, first expressed almost four decades earlier by DuBois, that identified the existence of parallel institutions among the races in an already racially separated society as a portent of a rapidly rigidifying and crystallizing racial stratification system.

The consequences of a racially stratified social system that perpetuated social, economic, educational, and political inequalities were demonstrated dramatically during the civil rights struggles of the 1950s, 1960s, and early 1970s. They are being realized further in the 1980s as blacks and Hispanics attempt to prevent erosion of crucial gains achieved during the three previous decades. The recent civil rights period (Blackwell, 1982) was not only characterized by racial unrest, interracial turmoil, and civil strife but was a culmination of centuries of alienation, frustration over denial of equal opportunity, and rising expectations that the fundamental precepts and guarantees of a democratic society could not remain the exclusive province of the white population. This period was a time of intense and purposeful mobilization to restructure American society in ways that could transform power relations between the dominant white population and subordinate blacks, Hispanics, Native Americans, and Asian-Americans.

Although the civil rights movement was inescapably concerned about the attitudinal component of prejudice, it focused primarily on observed manifestations of institutional racism as evidenced in systemic patterns of discrimination. Innumerable studies by social and behavioral scientists, such as Williams's (1964) *Strangers Next Door,* described the ravages of prejudice and discrimination in theoretical and affective terms. The National Advisory Commission on Civil Disorders (1968), however, also known as the Kerner Commission, examined the effects of urban riots, civil disturbances, and the socioeconomic conditions of minority groups in the United States. As a result of its assessment, the Commission issued a stark warning, which once again confirmed DuBois's insights of a half-century earlier: Not only did the enormity of racial cleavages and race-based social, political, and economic inequities perpetuate two separate but unequal societies, but policy changes were a sine qua non for that restructuring of the American society that was essential for expanding equality of opportunity.

Minority groups (especially blacks, who assumed primary leadership during the early stages of the civil rights movement, as well as Hispanics, Native Americans, and Asian-Americans) demanded constitutionally guaranteed freedoms, rights, and privileges. Specifically, they demanded equal educational opportunity that would eliminate impoverished schools in their communities and would improve the overall quality of schooling received by minority group students in elementary, secondary, and postsecondary systems. They sought the termination of segregated school systems and of dual systems of higher education. They demanded equity in teachers' salaries and significant improvements in educational facilities and programs. Minority groups demonstrated and litigated for the elimination of barriers to full political participation so that they could play a major role in determining who should be elected as officials from local jurisdictions and should represent their vital interests at the highest level of the federal government. They used pressure and competitive resources (Blalock, 1960) to move toward economic empowerment, political empowerment, and the desegregation of public accommodations.

Blacks, Native Americans, Hispanics, and Asian-Americans mobilized to actualize strategies for change. These changes were initiated by such groups as the National Association for the Advancement of Colored People (NAACP), the Mexican American Political Action Committee (MAPA), the Congress for Racial Equality (CORE), the National Urban League (NUL), the Japanese American Citizens League (JACL), the Student Nonviolent Coordinating Committee (SNCC), the Southern Christian Leadership Conference (SCLC), the United Farm Workers (UFW), the American Indian Movement (AIM), and the National Congress of American Indians (NCAI). Many members of these organizations subsequently would support the aspirations of the "new immigrants" from Southeast Asia (Cambodians, Vietnamese, and Laotians), who experienced indignities against their humanity similar to those suffered by blacks, Hispanics, Native Americans, and other Asian-Americans.

For a short period of time, as long as blacks and Hispanics maintained pressure for continued change and as long as the federal government was supportive (Blackwell, 1985, 1987a), progress was made toward the realization of specific programmatic goals. When concerted pressure slackened, coalitions disintegrated, strategies for change became fragmented and group-specific, and governmental leadership became hostile to the aspirations of minority groups, however, progress was halted and retrogressions slowed the pace of this once all-encompassing social movement.

In this chapter I will use inequities in the educational opportunity structure to illustrate the retrogression and stagnation characteristic of present-day American race relations. My focal concern is the degree to which blacks and Hispanics (a) have been incorporated into the educational mainstream, (b) have been provided with equal educational opportunity, or (c) have achieved progress and either retrogressed or stagnated with respect to educational attainment. Therefore, I will explore the current educational status of blacks and Hispanics and suggest policy issues that must be confronted in order to eliminate identified barriers to educational attainment or to full participation in society by black and Hispanic citizens of the United States.

My theoretical premise in this chapter is that educational attainment is one of several essential strategies that racial and ethnic minority groups may use in their efforts to change power differentials between themselves and the dominant population. In other writings I have described power theory as a means of understanding patterned interaction between dominant and subordinate groups, and power differentials as the basis of racial and ethnic inequality (Blackwell, 1976, 1982, 1987a). The essential argument of this model is that institutional structures exist to serve the needs of individuals and groups who control inordinate power, authority, and resources within a social system and who simultaneously limit the access of others to the advantages of power. This power is used to maintain privilege, to monopolize resources and scarce commodities, and to determine eligibility for sharing privileges and scarce rewards associated with status positions within a racially and ethnically stratified social system. The model also argues that groups in power exercise presumed authority to establish standards, to determine procedural norms, and to make declarations of normative requirements and expectations—all of which serve as gatekeeping methods and boundary-maintenance devices between the powerful dominant group and the relatively powerless minority groups.

Those who control power and the decision-making processes may restructure the rules of the game, alter procedural imperatives, or simply change standards or normative expectations whenever these actions are deemed necessary either to satisfy their needs or to protect their position of power, privilege, and high status. Hence, if minorities are successful on the basis of codified regulatory norms of meritocratic standards (e.g., Asian-Americans on quantitative admissions standards), it is not beyond probability that threatened dominant-group decision makers might alter the rules of the game in order to protect what they define as their own entitlements. Such practices generate enormous conflicts, which may be regarded as a social inevitability in these circumstances because no group that holds a monopoly of power is likely to relinquish significant portions of that power without some form of struggle.

By the same token, groups that either lack power or have limited power and that are convinced of their inalienable rights to a greater share of power and scarce resources may conclude ultimately that struggle is the most efficacious path to changing power relations. Sensing that determination and suspecting that the price for resistance to changes in power relations may be much higher than at least some movement toward placating dissidents, dominant groups sometimes make grudging concessions to some of the more pressing demands of minority and less powerful groups. Such a situation led to a semblance of compliance with selected demands made by minority groups during the civil rights period between 1954 and 1972 (Blackwell, 1982). Improvements were made in the socioeconomic status and educational attainment of these groups. Inroads were achieved in the political process; significant barriers to public accommodations were eliminated.

Change is not self-sustaining, however, especially with respect to alterations or transformations in power relations between dominant and subordinate groups. Enduring change depends on constant mobilization of pressure and competitive resources (Blalock, 1960). Evidence of initial success is often interpreted by dissident minorities as an indicator of the inevitability of progress, without realization of a fundamental fact: Progress in race relations depends, among other things, on sustained pressure.

Cooptation of minorities, the destruction of their leadership structure, and the absence of a central issue around which groups may be mobilized coalesce to create inaction among dissident outsider groups. Complacency follows satisfaction with limited material and social rewards. In the meantime, however, the gatekeepers of power have regrouped and have planned and implemented newer and sometimes less overtly odious strategies to restore their power monopoly. They have devised newer and often substantially more problematic hurdles for minority groups. Hence it was not unexpected that decisions by the U.S. Supreme Court that expanded educational opportunity (e.g., *Brown v. Board of Education of Topeka, Kansas,* 1954), and that approved the race variable as justifiable in meeting compelling state interest (as in *Regents of the University of California at Petitioner v. Allan Bakke,* 1978), as well as lower court decisions (e.g., *Adams v. Richardson,* 1973), would be followed by redefinitions of admissions criteria. The new criteria gives heavier weight to performance on standardized tests when it is evident that the group mean scores of most minority groups are lower than the group mean scores of the white population on such tests, resulting in exclusion of minority groups. Circumvention strategies of this sort, used by the gatekeepers of power, were not anticipated fully by many who sought to change power relations. Consequently a special effort to combat abuses of admissions tests became a major task of groups affected adversely by such strategies. Many institutions now have seized the "quality" criterion as a mechanism for denying equity in higher education.

THE CURRENT STATUS OF BLACKS AND HISPANICS IN EDUCATION

The following analysis is devoted exclusively to the status of blacks and Hispanics in education. By implication, however, the experiences described and the policy implications that follow are highly significant for other minority groups. (The terms *Hispanic* and *Latino* will be used interchangeably throughout this discussion. Both designations encompass the Mexican-American, or Chicano, and the Puerto Rican populations.)

Barriers to Educational Attainment

Educational attainment does not occur in a social vacuum. It is affected in most important ways by conditions that prevail in other dimensions of the opportunity structure. In other words, it is affected by one's position in the economic, occupational, or income structure as well as by conditions and situations inside and outside the family that influence crucial decisions concerning the need and/or desirability for educational attainment.

For the past 30 years, the unemployment rate among blacks has been almost double that among whites. Black teenage unemployment has fluctuated between two and three times that of white teenagers. The unemployment rate among Hispanics is closer to that among blacks than to that among whites. Even in times of economic prosperity for the nation as a whole, blacks and Hispanics do not enjoy economic benefits comparable to those experienced by whites (Blackwell, 1982, 1985, 1987b). This disparity holds for all forms of unemployment: structural, traditional, cyclical, and seasonal, as well as among discouraged workers.

At the same time, blacks and Hispanics are considerably more likely to be relegated to the lower tier of a split labor market characterized by job insecurity, low wages, limitations on upward mobility, and job dissatisfaction. Employment disparities between dominant and subordinate group members, coupled with an occupational distribution that skews blacks and Hispanics toward less remunerative jobs, have undesirable consequences. For example, one third of black families and one fourth of Hispanic families, compared to one tenth of all white families, are in poverty (U.S. Bureau of the Census, 1986). The U.S. Bureau of the Census (1986) reported that the proportion of all black families with children headed by single parents rose from 35.7% in 1970 to 60.1% in 1985. By contrast, the rate for whites rose from 10.1% in 1970 to 20.8% in 1985.

Unemployment, inadequate preparation for newer types of jobs demanding higher educational attainment, inability to leave home without neglecting parental responsibilities, and discrimination in the marketplace are among the factors that conspire to make many black and Hispanic families unable to provide financial support for their children's education. Indeed, data from the U.S. government show that the wealth of this country is concentrated disproportionately in the hands of the white population. White families have a median net wealth of $39,135, compared to $3,397 for black families and $4,913 for Hispanic families. Further, about 30% of all black families have zero or negative net wealth in contrast to 23.9% of Hispanic families and only 8.4% of white families (U.S. Bureau of the Census, 1986).

One consequence of these economic disparities is that many black and Hispanic families find it difficult, if not impossible, to provide the kinds of educational resource materials that foster preschool educational interest and enrichment. They cannot furnish financial assistance for secondary educational needs and postsecondary or college education. Parents cannot inculcate in their children an enduring appreciation for the value of education in a technologically changing society. Neither are some parents available to supervise or monitor their children's college preparation because of time demands. One result of this situation, combined with poor counseling, inadequate guidance, racism among some high school teachers, and some youngsters' penchant to take what they define as the easy way out, is an inordinate concentration of black and Hispanic youngsters in the vocational and general tracks in high school. Aspira (Aspira of New York, Inc., 1987) reported that Hispanic and black youngsters are substantially more likely than whites to be assigned to "special ed" classes.

The slightness of black and Hispanic representation in the academic track in high school, in addition to unsatisfactory schooling and an unstimulating school environment, is reflected in inordinately high dropout rates among black and Hispanic students as well as in their group mean scores on standardized tests. Marcias and Magallan (1987) reported that Hispanic students have a 45% high school dropout rate; 85% of Hispanic 16- and 17-year-olds, compared to 92% of blacks and 91% of whites in the same age cohort, are enrolled in school. At ages 18 and 19, when 50% of all whites and 44% of all blacks are enrolled in school, only 39% of Hispanics are enrolled. Aspira (Aspira of New York, Inc., 1987) reported New York City dropout rates of 80% for Hispanics, 72% for blacks, and 50% for whites. In addition, minority students have difficulty in reading at grade level, in demonstrating verbal skills, and in performing basic mathematical functions. These disabilities are reflected in huge gaps between blacks, Puerto Ricans, Mexican-Americans, and whites on Scholastic Aptitude Test (SAT) scores.

Performance on such determinants of college admission as the Scholastic Aptitude Test generally reflects the quality of the curriculum to which pupils are exposed, their achievement orientation and motivation, their parents' income, and the number of college preparatory courses taken in high school. In general, irrespective of race, youngsters from upper income families who have taken a larger number and wider array of academic subjects perform better on the SAT than do those who have not had such advantages. Pupils in the former group are also much more likely to have opportunities for coaching and test preparation and to be psychologically ready to take standardized tests.

College-Going Rates

The high school completion rate among black and Hispanic students is increasing; however, the college attendance rate among blacks is declining (Arbeiter, 1987). In 1976 the high school completion rates were 79.8% for whites, 64.7% for blacks, and 54.4% for Hispanics. In 1980 the high school completion rates were 78.8% for whites, 66.1% for blacks, and 56.2% for Hispanics. During the same period, the college attendance rate for whites climbed slowly from 29.8% in 1976 to 30.2% in 1980 to 30.5% in 1984. By contrast, the rate for blacks declined precipitously from 26.3% in 1976 to 25.1% in 1980 to 21.2% in 1986. The decline among Hispanics was equally noticeable, dropping from a college attendance rate of 22.5% in 1975 to 20.0% in 1980 to 19.8% in 1984 (U.S. Bureau of the Census, 1976, 1980, 1984).

As mentioned earlier, the college attendance rate is influenced by a number of factors (Thomas, 1981a) including the financial status of one's family, preparation for college, motivation for a college education, attitudes concerning the benefits to be derived from investment of time in a college education, and the quality of counseling and guidance received during elementary and secondary school years.

There is, however, another highly influential determinant of the college attendance rate: the degree to which colleges and universities recruit youngsters from minority groups. Several writers have suggested that predominantly white institutions no longer assign maximum priority to recruiting black and Hispanic students and have concluded that whenever such institutions' recruitment networks are put to work, the target group is the "exceptionally well-prepared" as determined primarily by SAT and American College Testing (ACT) scores (Baratz-Snowden, 1987; Blackwell, 1987a; Clewell, 1987). In addition, financial aid officers that once offered such students adequate aid in the form of grants and scholarships have replaced these more attractive financial incentives with loans. The latter serve to increase the educational and personal indebtedness of minority students. Both factors—the diminution of strong recruitment programs and the reduction in the quality and amount of financial assistance—reflect either declining institutional commitment or insensitivity to the problem of the underrepresentation of minority students in colleges and universities.

Persistence

Among minority students who succeed in meeting college entry requirements, the problem of *persistence* through completion of the baccalaureate degree confronts many individuals. Persistence may be complicated by the type of institution. For example, it is estimated that 54% of Hispanic and 43% of black college students, compared to 36% of white college students, are matriculated in 2-year community or junior colleges (Grant & Eiden, 1985; Reed, 1986). Many of these students are unsuccessful in their efforts to transfer to 4-year institutions. Therefore a tremendous decline occurs among the total number of black and Hispanic students enrolled in undergraduate education programs. Brown (1987) reported on a 1985 study by Hilton and Schrader which showed that fewer than 25% of all Hispanic students who entered 2-year institutions transferred later to 4-year colleges or universities. Specific transfer figures were 24.4% for Mexican-Americans, 36.2% for Puerto Ricans, 27.7% for Cubans, 17.7% for "other Hispanics," 18.3% for blacks, and 30.3% for whites.

Persistence is associated with such variables as financial aid, the quality of the learning environment, academic problems, the magnitude of racism in the classroom and on the campus, the way in which institutions handle racial incidents, home factors, psychological factors, relationships with teachers, and interactions with other students. Regardless of which factor or which combination of these factors predominates in the decision to leave school, minority students have the highest college attrition rates and are less able to remain in college through completion of the baccalaureate degree (Allen, 1987; Brown, 1987; Richardson, de los Santos, & Simmons, 1987; Thomas, 1981b; Valverde, 1986). Brown (1987) showed that blacks suffered a 9.2% decline in the number of baccalaureate degrees earned between 1981 and 1985. The proportion of total bachelor's degrees conferred on blacks fell from 6.6% in 1978 to 6.5% in 1980 to 5.9% in 1984. The proportion of bachelor's degrees conferred on Hispanic students fell from 3.3% of the total in 1978 to 2.3% in 1980, but it rose to 2.9% in 1984. Bachelor's degrees conferred on whites remained at approximately 88% of the total over the same period.

Graduate Education

The slippages noted for blacks and Hispanics at the transition points described above can also be observed in the movement from college to graduate or professional schools. Explanations for the downturn in enrollment of minorities in graduate and professional schools are similar to those proposed for declines in college enrollment. They include (a) inadequate financial aid; (b) limited opportunities to obtain nonrepayable loans, graduate teaching assistantships, and research assistantships; (c) declining institutional commitment and assignment of low priority to recruitment of minority students for graduate or professional schools; (d) a paucity of minority group faculty members; (e) an unfavorable institutional climate; (f) the unwillingness of minority students to incur enormous debts to obtain a graduate or professional degree and then to be confronted with racism in the labor market; (g) inadequate college preparation; (h) faculty indifference to the need for diversity among students; and (i) inappropriate recruitment strategies (Blackwell, 1987a). All of these factors

Table 1   Enrollment in U.S. graduate schools by race and ethnicity: 1976, 1980, and 1984

Categories	1976	1980	1984	Percent change 1976–1984
Total enrollment	1,079,307	1,097,567	1,063,995	−1.4
White	905,371 (83.9%)	899,245 (81.9%)	856,061 (80.5%)	−5.4
Total minority	107,898 (10.0%)	112,172 (10.2%)	104,680 (9.8%)	−3.0
Asian/Pacific Islanders	18,446 (1.7%)	23,534 (2.1%)	27,318 (2.6%)	+8.1
Black	65,338 (6.1%)	59,976 (5.5%)	50,717 (4.8%)	−22.4
Hispanic	20,234 (1.9%)	24,278 (2.2%)	23,144 (2.2%)	+14.4
Native American Indians and Alaskans	3,880 (0.4%)	4,384 (0.4%)	3,501 (0.3%)	−9.8

Note.   Sources: U.S. Department of Education, National Center for Educational Statistics; Carnegie Foundation for the Advancement of Teaching; "Change Trendlines, Minority Access: A Question of Equity," *Change* 19:3 (May/June 1987, pp. 35–39), Tables 3 and 6; James E. Blackwell, *Mainstreaming Outsiders: The Production of Black Professionals* (1987).

reflect the dominant group's power and authority to control access to scarce rewards.

These factors have created a major problem with respect to the future of graduate and professional education among blacks and Hispanics. As depicted in Table 1, whites have a monopoly on graduate school enrollment. The implications of this fact are far-reaching with respect to the access, training, and production of black and Hispanic graduate students and for their availability for future roles as college or university faculty members.

Graduate Enrollment

Total graduate school enrollment in American institutions declined by 1.4% between 1976 and 1984. White students, who constituted 83.9% of the total graduate enrollment in 1976, experienced a 5.4% loss in 1984, when they represented 80.5% of graduate enrollment. By contrast, black students experienced a staggering 22.4% decline in representation among graduate school matriculants, falling from a peak of 65,338 students (6.1%) in 1978 to only 50,717 (4.8%) in 1984. The situation for Hispanic graduate students was considerably more positive; their total enrollment increased by 14.4% between 1978 and 1984. The number of Hispanic graduate students increased from 20,234 (1.9% of total graduate enrollment) in 1978 to 25,144 (2.2%) in 1984. The only other group to increase its proportion of the graduate school enrollment during that period was Asian/Pacific Islanders, who experienced an 18.1% increase in absolute terms (see Table 1).

Financial Support

As noted previously, the inadequacy of financial assistance is one explanation for the loss of such a large number of black students from graduate schools. One third of all black families are in poverty, and blacks' median family income is only about 56% of that of white families. In view of the escalating costs of graduate and professional education, the need for significant financial assistance is apparent and real. As shown in Table 2, racial inequities in financial support for graduate students work to the detriment of black, Puerto Rican, and Mexican-American students. An examination of the data presented in Table 2 reveals that blacks and Puerto Ricans consistently fare worse than other graduate students in the allocation of research and teaching assistant-ships. On the other hand, they are substantially more likely than all other students to receive educational institutional funds. In 1985, the last year for which systematized data are available, almost half (46.6%) of all graduate students depended on teaching assistantships as a source of financial support for graduate education, but only 26.1% of black and 39.3% of Puerto Rican students were awarded teaching assistantships. By contrast, almost half (48.1%) of Mexican-American students and 48.1% of white students supported their graduate education in total or in part through teaching assist-antships. Mexican-American students (37.2%) approximated the national average of research assistantships awarded. By contrast, Puerto Rican graduate students (16.8%) fared worse than other graduate students in being selected as research assistants (see Table 2).

Without teaching or research assistantships, students are denied participation in an integral element of graduate training and in an experience that is extraordinarily important for their postgraduate school careers. It is primarily through the interaction between faculty supervisors and their graduate students during such apprenticeships that mentoring is developed, nurtured, and facilitated. From the graduate student's perspective, the teaching assistant develops a much broader understanding of the subject matter, becomes confident, poised, and self-assured in the classroom, and learns to sharpen communication skills, to articulate ideas with clarity and persua-sion, and to engage students in the learning process—all skills that will be needed as an independent member of a college or university faculty.

As a research assistant, the graduate student tends to have an even closer and more intense relationship with his or her faculty mentor. On-the-job training is received not only in the actual conduct of a research program but also in developing the student's own research interest, research agenda, and program direction and in writing papers for presentation at professional meetings or for publication. Mentors in both situa-tions use their knowledge of their protégés in writing assessments and recommenda-tions for job placement and for other forms of sponsorship, such as postdoctoral fellowships. Students not selected for these forms of assistance are not only deprived of a rich experience but are also locked out of the social network among graduates and out of the mentor's professional network.

Doctorate Production

Enrollment fluctuations of blacks and Hispanics in graduate education are re-flected, not unexpectedly, in degree production. Between 1977 and 1986 (see Table 3) the number of black U.S. citizens who received doctoral degrees fell sharply from 1,116 to 820, a loss of 296 graduates and a decline from 4.5% to 3.5% of the total. By contrast, the number of Hispanic Americans who received doctorates rose from 423 in 1977 to 554 in 1986, an increase from 1.7% of total doctorates conferred to 2.4%. It may be observed that as Hispanic doctoral degree production climbed, production of blacks with doctorates declined. It is also evident, however, that despite improvements among Hispanics in the absolute number and percentage of doctorates earned, they still received fewer than 3% of all doctorates conferred on U.S. citizens. Not only has the downturn in the production of doctorates among black Americans

Table 2 Graduate school support by race and ethnicity: 1981 and 1985

Sources of support	Total U.S. citizens		American Indian		Asian		Black		White		Puerto Rican		Mexican-American	
	1981	1985	1981	1985	1981	1985	1981	1985	1981	1985	1981	1985	1981	1985
Federal fellow trainee	20.7	16.0	25.8	21.5	24.3	21.2	17.8	18.9	21.0	15.6	19.1	26.9	29.9	29.4
G.I. Bill	6.9	4.2	7.9	5.4	2.6	1.4	7.9	3.0	7.0	4.3	5.2	4.1	11.0	3.9
Other fellowship	20.4	3.8	15.7	7.5	19.1	4.5	22.3	8.3	20.4	3.4	37.4	7.6	27.9	15.6
Teaching assistantships	45.6	46.6	31.5	35.5	42.0	47.4	25.7	26.0	47.4	48.1	27.8	39.3	36.4	48.1
Research assistantships	33.8	37.8	13.5	31.2	43.3	51.1	15.4	16.0	35.1	29.6	23.5	29.4	22.1	37.2
Educational institutions' funds	10.7	29.5	5.6	21.5	14.1	29.5	11.7	32.0	10.7	5.6	21.7	12.4	15.6	4.4
Own/spouse's earnings[a]	69.1	81.8	77.5	81.7	53.7	71.8	73.3	82.0	70.4	82.9	57.4	73.6	71.4	82.8
Family contributions[a]	15.9	—	6.7	—	16.5	—	10.8	—	16.6	—	10.4	—	7.8	—
National Direct Student Loan	12.8	28.1	14.6	33.3	10.9	24.7	17.6	27.0	12.8	28.2	27.8	49.7	14.9	34.4
Other loans	12.1	11.1	14.6	11.8	9.1	11.5	17.7	15.8	12.0	10.7	21.7	22.1	10.4	14.4
Other	4.3	3.3	3.4	0.0	3.5	2.3	5.3	3.4	4.3	3.3	7.8	5.5	4.5	2.8
Unknown	—	1.6	0.0	0.0	1.7	1.2	1.6	1.7	1.0	0.7	4.3	0.0	1.3	1.1

Note. Figures denote percentages using source of support. Source: National Research Council (1981, 1985).
[a]In 1985 these items were combined in doctoral survey reports.

Table 3 Total doctorates earned by U.S. citizens by race and ethnicity: 1977–1986

Race/ethnicity	1977	1978	1979	1980	1981	1982	1983	1984	1985	1986
Total U.S. citizens	25,008	23,767	23,947	23,970	24,006	23,785	23,704	23,394	22,717	22,984
American Indian										
n	65	60	81	75	85	77	80	73	93	100
%	0.3	0.3	0.3	0.3	0.4	0.3	0.3	0.3	0.4	0.4
Asian										
n	339	390	428	458	465	452	492	512	515	527
%	1.4	1.6	1.8	1.9	1.9	1.9	2.1	2.2	2.3	2.3
Black										
n	1,116	1,033	1,056	1,032	1,013	1,047	921	953	909	820
%	4.5	4.3	4.4	4.3	4.2	4.4	3.9	4.1	4.0	3.5
Hispanic										
n	423	473	462	412	464	535	538	535	559	554
%	1.7	2.0	1.9	1.7	1.9	2.2	2.3	2.3	2.5	2.4
White										
n	23,065	21,811	21,920	21,920	21,993	21,979	21,674	21,321	20,641	22,538
%	92.2	91.8	91.5	91.8	91.6	91.1	91.4	91.1	90.9	89.3

Note. Source: National Research Council, 1985, p. 13; Susan Coyle, National Research Council, unpublished 1986 data.

reached an alarming state but it presents graphic evidence of failed institutional policies, inadequate practices, and weakened outreach.

In addition to the general problem of black and Hispanic underrepresentation among recipients of the doctoral degree, a serious problem also exists with respect to the field distribution of those degrees. Table 4 shows that in 1986, for example, black, Puerto Rican, and Mexican-American recipients of the doctorate were concentrated in education and in the social and behavioral sciences. More than half of all doctorates conferred on blacks were degrees in education. This observation reflects a pattern that has persisted among blacks for at least two decades (Blackwell, 1987a).

Maldistribution of earned doctorates among blacks, Puerto Ricans, and Mexican-Americans is equality evident in the absence or the abysmally low proportion of doctorates earned in the natural and physical sciences. A few examples from Table 4 illustrate the seriousness of this underrepresentation. Only 15 physical sciences doctorates each were conferred on Puerto Ricans and Mexican-Americans in 1986. This number accounted for about 11% of the total number of doctorates earned by Puerto Ricans and fewer than 10% of those obtained by Mexican-Americans. The 25 doctorates earned in this field by blacks constituted approximately one fifth of the total earned by blacks. A similar pattern of underrepresentation is observed for these three groups in such fields as engineering, health, and medical sciences. It is quite evident that no discipline, field, or specialization can be characterized as oversaturated with blacks, Puerto Ricans, Mexican-Americans, and "other Hispanics." The need to increase the production of minority students with doctoral degrees remains a crisis. The demand for a well-defined educational policy designed to address the problems of recruitment, enrollment, and degree production among black and Hispanic students in our nation's graduate schools is not only urgent but in the national interest.

POLICY IMPLICATIONS

This description of the situation for blacks and Hispanics in the educational pipeline attests to the urgent need for change in a broad range of educational policies and practices. Such changes, like educational reform in general and like specific efforts to alter power relations between minorities and majorities, will not occur without a clearly and forcefully articulated institutional commitment. "Institutional commitment" means that the leadership structure has a responsibility to create a framework through which to implement well-defined guidelines and policies that lead to accelerated educational opportunity.

Leadership for the kind of change envisioned should be system-wide in publicly supported sectors of higher education. That mandate in itself, however, does not preclude positive, aggressive action by single institutions or by units within a system. Nor does it mean that a single department is exempt from assuming direct, aggressive leadership in moving to implement policies and practices that expand equal educational opportunity for the underrepresented groups that it wishes to target. Such departments could become models for other departments when they succeed in developing outreach programs that result in substantially higher admission, retention, and graduation of minority students in colleges and graduate schools.

Examples of specific courses of action include the following:

Table 4 Doctoral degrees awarded to U.S. citizens by field and race ethnicity: 1986

Field	Total U.S. citizens	American Indian	Asian	Black	White	Puerto Rican	Mexican-American	Other Hispanic
All fields	22,894	100	527	820	20,538	137	182	248
Physical science	3,003	8	107	25	2,714	15	15	23
Mathematics	367	1	14	5	327	3	3	3
Computer science	203	0	12	1	176	2	0	2
Physics	692	0	19	7	633	4	2	5
Chemistry	1,319	5	56	13	1,180	5	10	9
Earth/environment science	422	2	6	0	398	1	0	4
Engineering	1,379	6	80	14	1,224	11	5	9
Life sciences	4,342	24	152	64	3,958	20	14	38
Biological science	3,119	18	124	40	2,835	13	9	31
Agricultural science	657	0	14	7	616	4	2	2
Health/medical sciences	566	6	14	17	507	4	3	5
Social science and psychology	4,548	20	69	163	4,080	27	23	60
Humanities	2,728	7	30	70	2,496	14	20	42
Languages and literature	896	2	11	16	805	9	11	24
Professional fields	1,373	9	31	53	1,230	5	6	12
Education	5,595	26	58	421	4,820	45	79	64
Teaching fields	943	2	6	58	835	8	3	9
Other, unspecified	16	0	0	1	15	0	0	0

Note. Source: Susan Coyle and Yupin Bea, National Research Council, unpublished data.

1. Stronger coalitions and areas of cooperation between collegiate departments and teachers of corresponding subjects in "feeder" high schools or nearby high school departments are needed.

2. Such cooperative arrangements should be used to facilitate *early identification* of potential majors in a specific field. These students may be selected for college admission, mentored, and guided through the baccalaureate degree and may be selected for graduate education.

3. Admission and selection policies, procedures, and practices must be reexamined so that a good mix of quantitative and qualitative measures for selection and admission is fostered.

4. Aggressive, well-organized, well-funded recruitment programs must be instituted at the undergraduate and graduate school levels. Such programs need to use a broad range of individuals for outreach strategies; those persons must communicate to the potential student that the institution or a specific college or department is seriously interested in the educational development of that particular student.

5. The institutional climate into which the minority student is recruited must be made favorable for that student's growth and development.

6. Financial assistance must be provided for persons in need and for students who compete successfully for scholarships based on academic merit or on the basis of special talent. In this regard, it is imperative for graduate departments to award larger numbers of teaching and research assistantships and nonrepayable funds to minority students (Nettles, 1987).

7. Mentoring opportunities for minority students are essential for their retention in schools until they complete their baccalaureate and graduate degrees (Blackwell, 1983). Through the mentoring process many students not only are retained but also achieve their maximum intellectual potential, expand their interest in and commitment to a general field, are inspired to continue their professional growth, and are socialized into their chosen profession.

8. Institutional and departmental policy changes and practices that promote the recruitment, hiring, and retention of minority faculty are needed. Blacks represent only about 4% of all college and university faculty members and a dismal 1% of the total faculty in predominantlly white institutions. The situation is worse for faculty members of Hispanic descent. A close association has been demonstrated between the presence of black faculty and the recruitment, matriculation, retention, and graduation of blacks from graduate and professional schools (Blackwell, 1982, 1987a). Institutions seriously committed to the democratization of higher education will recruit and retain both students and faculty from underrepresented minority groups. Such institutions will devise and implement coordinated programs that will lead ultimately to cultural and racial diversity and will enrich the learning milieu in colleges and universities.

IMPLICATIONS FOR RACE RELATIONS

Education is a social institution that reflects patterns of race relations throughout American society. It mirrors conditions that prevail in other components of the social system. Not unexpectedly, power in education is vested disproportionately among dominant-group members, who control administrative and supervisory functions, decision-making authority, and financial resources that support the structure and operation of the institution. As demonstrated in this chapter, control over power, decision making, and resources determines access, progression, retention, and expulsion at all levels of the institutional structure.

As in other institutions, progress and retrogression in patterns of race relations also have been observed in education. For example, American society has moved from de jure segregation toward de jure desegregation; however, integration has never been fully achieved. As in all relationships characterized by unequal distribution of power, systemic transformations and enduring change depend in part not only on the willingness of dominant groups to share power and to make concessions but also on the minority groups' ability to mobilize resources and to sustain unremitting pressure on powerful dominant groups in order to force the sharing of social, economic, educational, and political rewards.

In 1990 there is still increasing concern over retrogression in race relations and over the slippages observed during the previous 7 years. The term *racial slippages* refers to patterns and conditions that indicate (a) a retreat from the ideal of equal opportunity across racial lines, (b) efforts suggesting white supremacy as both a modus vivendi and a modus operandi among all age cohorts, and (c) a pernicious disintegration of even the level of interrracial harmony that followed the events of the 1960s. Racial slippages are evident in the following:

1. The apparent contempt of the federal government for the support of minorities in education, especially with respect to enforcing the mandates ordered by the decision in *Adams v. Richardson* (1973). The one major exception is the occasional financial relief granted to seriously troubled, historically black colleges and universities (HBCUs), such as Meharry Medical College (which was not mandated in the *Adams* case), the medical college of Morehouse College, and/or HBCUs outside the *Adams* mandate.

2. The declining numbers of blacks in graduate schools.

3. The declining production of blacks with doctoral degrees, as evidenced in the fact that the 820 doctorates received by black Americans in 1986 were equal to the number received in 1976.

4. The decline in the number of blacks in college and university faculty positions in predominantly white institutions and the continuing underrepresentation of Hispanics in such positions, despite slight increases in their numbers. This situation is already a catalyst for student protest at several institutions and is potentially much more explosive than were the campus demonstrations during the late 1960s.

5. The persistence of academic tokenism and the ghettoization of minority faculty and administrators in predominantly white institutions.

6. The resurgence of campus racism, as manifested in outbreaks of racial assaults against blacks, Hispanics, Asians, and Native Americans: physical assaults, beatings, attempted rapes, racial epithets, slurs, ethnophaulisms, cross burnings, racial graffiti, and the wearing of Ku Klux Klan garb on campus. The resurgence of racism is also manifested in the articulation of a belief among some white students that "institutions are doing too much for minorities" or that "most minorities do not belong" in white colleges. Racism is often evident in the manner in which some white professors treat minority students. Often conveyed either verbally or nonverbally are such sentiments as "minority students do not belong here" (in the predominantly white institution) or the notion that standards, by definition, have been lowered in order to admit minority students. Occasionally, similar ideas are expressed by a few professors who are themselves members of a minority group.

7. The perpetuation of stereotypes about dominant and minority groups. These stereotypes impede interracial and intercultural understanding and cooperation within an institution that should provide leadership in this area for the majority of Americans.

8. The virtual absence, as in the external labor marketplace, of informal social interaction among colleagues and students once they have left their own workplaces or the classroom environment.

9. The failure of black and Hispanic students to achieve parity with white students in moving through the educational pipeline.

10. The declining number and proportion of public school teachers from minority group populations. Some researchers (Larke & Thomas, 1989) project that at the present rate of entry of blacks and Hispanics into teacher training programs, and at the present rate of failure of these groups to meet certification requirements, the number of minority group members in public school teaching positions will have been reduced by 50% over the next 12 years.

National concern over these organizational, structural, and interpersonal dimensions of education has recently attracted much-needed attention from influential bodies and institutions. As a result, serious efforts are being undertaken to construct strategies that will help alleviate these situations. Examples include the following:

1. A recent conference held at the American Council on Education, which was devoted to several of the racial slippages identified in this chapter.

2. The November 1987 conference "From Access to Achievement: Strategies for Urban Institution," sponsored by the National Center for Postsecondary Governance and Finance.

3. The November 1987 conference on "The Role of Faculty in Meeting the National Need for African American, American Indian and Latino Scholars," sponsored by the State University of New York at Stony Brook and coordinated by Myrna Adams.

4. The May/June issue of *Change* magazine (1987), which was devoted entirely to blacks in higher education.

5. The beginning of a response by many state systems of higher education to Harold Hodgkinson's (1985) notion of "demographic imperatives" and to what I view as "the vested interest thesis." Because of an aging white population and a younger minority population, demographics alone dictate that the national interest will be served best by educating as many members of minorities as possible in order to sustain our nation's economy and competitiveness and to assure the preservation of social security and other human services and benefits that will continue to be needed by the society as a whole.

The future of race relations in the coming decade depends in large measure on how well these issues are addressed and how well solutions to the problems are found and implemented.

REFERENCES

Adams v. Richardson, 480 F.2d.1159 (D.C. Cir. 1973).

Allen, W. (1987). Black colleges vs. white colleges: The fork in the road for black students. *Change, 19,* 28–39.

Arbeiter, S. (1987). Black enrollment: The case of the missing students. *Change, 19,* 14–19.

Aspira of New York, Inc. (1987). *Demographics of Puerto Rican/Latino Students in New York and the United States* (Compiled by Luis O. Reyes). New York: Author.

Baratz-Snowden, J. (1987). Good news, bad news: Black performance on standardized tests. *Change, 19,* 50–54.

Blacks in higher education: The climb toward equity. *Change* (Special issue). *19*:3 (May/June 1987).

Blackwell, J. E. (1976). The power basis of ethnic conflict in American society. In L. Coser & O. Larsen (Eds.), *The uses of controversy in sociology* (pp. 179–196). New York: Free Press.

Blackwell, J. E. (1982). *Mainstreaming outsiders: The production of black professionals* (1st ed.). Bayside, NY: General Hall.

Blackwell, J. E. (1983). *Networking and mentoring: A study of cross-generational experiences of blacks in graduate and professional schools.* Atlanta, GA: Southern Education Foundation.

Blackwell, J. E. (1985). *The black community: Diversity and unity.* New York: Harper & Row.

Blackwell, J. E. (1987a). *Mainstreaming outsiders: The production of black professionals.* Dix Hills, NY: General Hall.

Blackwell, J. E. (1987b). *Youth employment and unemployment: Outreach initiatives in Massachusetts and the city of Boston.* Boston: William Monroe Trotter Institute.

Blalock, H. M. (1960). A power analysis of racial discrimination. *Social Forces, 39,* 53–69.

Brown v. Board of Education of Topeka, Kansas, 347 U.S. 483 (1954).

Brown, S. V. (1987). *Minorities in the graduate education pipeline.* Princeton, NJ: Educational Testing Service.

Clewell, B. (1987). Effective institutional practices for improving minority retention in higher education. *Journal of College Admissions, 116,* 7–13.

Cox, O. C. (1942). The modern caste school of race relations. *Social Forces, 21,* 218–226.

DuBois, W. E. B. (1906). *The souls of black folk.* New York: Fawcett.

Grant, E. V., & Eiden, L. (1985). *Digest of education statistics 1983–84.* Washington, DC: Department of Education, National Center for Educational Statistics.

Hodgkinson, H. L. (1985). *All one system: Demographics of education, kindergarten through graduate school.* Washington, DC: The Institute for Educational Leadership.

Horsman, R. (1982). *Race and manifest destiny.* Cambridge, MA: Harvard University Press.

Larke, P., & Thomas, G. E. (1989). Gender differences among blacks in education career orientation. *Education and Urban Society, 21,* 283–298.

Marcias, R. F., & Magallan, R. (1987). *Hispanics and education.* Pomona, CA: Tomas Rivera Center.

Myrdal, G. (1944). *An American dilemma.* New York: Harper & Row.

National Advisory Commission on Civil Disorders. (1968). *Report 1968.* New York: Bantam.

National Research Council. (1981). *Summary report, 1981: Doctorate recipients from United States universities.* Washington, DC: Author.

National Research Council. (1985). *Summary report, 1985: Doctorate recipients from United States universities.* Washington, DC: Author.

Nettles, M. (1987). *Financial aid and minority participation in graduate education.* Princeton, NJ: Educational Testing Service.

Reed, R. J. (1986). Faculty diversity: An educational and moral imperative in search of institutional commitment. *Journal of Educational Equity and Leadership, 8,* 274–294.

Regents of the University of California at Petitioner v. Allan Bakke (No. 76-811), 97 S.C. 1098 (1978).

Richardson, R. C., de los Santos, A., & Simmons, H. (1987). Graduating minority students: Lessons from ten success stories. *Change, 19,* 20–27.

Thomas, G. E. (1981a). *Black students in higher education: The conditions of blacks in the 1970s.* Westport, CT: Greenwood.

Thomas, G. E. (1981b). College characteristics and black students' four year college graduation. *Journal of Negro Education, 50,* 328–345.

U.S. Bureau of the Census. (1976). *Educational attainment in the U.S.* Washington, DC: U.S. Department of Commerce.

U.S. Bureau of the Census. (1980). *Educational attainment in the U.S.* Washington, DC: U.S. Department of Commerce.

U.S. Bureau of the Census. (1984). *Educational attainment in the U.S.* Washington, DC: U.S. Department of Commerce.

U.S. Bureau of the Census. (1986). *Household wealth and asset ownership: 1984.* Washington, DC: U.S. Government Printing Office.

Valverde, L. (1986). Low income students. In N. Lee (Ed.), *Increasing student retention* (pp. 79–84). San Francisco: Jossey-Bass.

Williams, R. (1964). *Strangers next door.* Englewood Cliffs, NJ: Prentice-Hall.

3

Issues of Race and Education Affecting Blacks and Hispanics: Commentary on Ogbu and Blackwell

Grace L. Butler
University of Houston

Indicators of the status of race relations suggest that there is a need to reassess systemic policies and practices in education that stratify learners by race, ethnicity, and class. America's children risk the prospect of ever-widening cleavages between the educated and the undereducated and between the educational experiences provided to upper class children and those given to lower class children (Wilson, 1987). Education is viewed as the great equalizer. It is said to be available to everyone; therefore it is assumed to provide advantages for all, regardless of race, ethnicity, or class. Ethnic minority students arrive on the educational scene with the same excitement and enthusiasm for learning as nonminority students (Katz, 1967; Mingione, 1965; Rosen, 1959). For too many of those students, however, the great equalizer is known to diminish in its effectiveness (usually in the upper elementary grades and beyond); as a result, many students are ensnared by stratification because of race and economic status. Thus the question emerges: Is education the great equalizer? If so, why is society still highly stratified by race and by social class?

Ogbu, in "Racial Stratification and Education," and Blackwell, in "Current Issues Affecting Blacks and Hispanics in the Educational Pipeline," provide insightful and critical analyses of the role and status of blacks and Hispanics in education. Each provides a unique interpretation and direction for solutions to the problem of race, education, and social class stratification. First let us consider Ogbu's chapter.

Ogbu opens and closes with two unnerving and perturbing questions: "Why [do] black Americans continue to lag in school performance and educational attainment?" and "Why [is it that] inequality persists after all the improvements in race relations in the last two or three decades?" (p. 3). His conceptual and analytical focus embraces the twin problems of poorer school performance and lesser educational attainment among black Americans, and he analyzes these problems and those of other ethnic minorities in the context of "racial stratification" rather than of race relations.

Ogbu acknowledges the persistence of stratification by race and effectively challenges those social scientists who contend that "the significance of race in determining black Americans' life chances has declined" (p. 4) and that "the emergence of an 'underclass'" (p. 4; i.e., class rather than race) is the major factor that explains blacks' current problems in education, employment, and housing. Given the importance Ogbu attributes to race and racial stratification in explaining black achievement, he elaborates to ensure that the reader has a correct conception of the term *racial stratification.*

Ogbu contends that racial stratification is a construct consisting of instrumental and expressive barriers erected by the dominant culture and of expressive responses to those barriers manifested by those being dominated, namely racial minorities. His model of racial stratification includes four dimensions or integral components: (a) instrumental exploitation of black Americans by white Americans, (b) responses by blacks to that exploitation, (c) expressive exploitation, and (d) responses to expressive exploitation. Ogbu explains that "expressive exploitation refer[s] to conscious or unconscious treatment of racial minorities that satisfies the psychological needs of the members of the dominant group—namely, white Americans. . . . Expressive responses refer to the conscious or unconscious responses by minorities to this treatment; these responses satisfy their own psychological needs, such as the need to maintain their sense of self-worth and integrity" (p. 4). Instrumental factors, on the other hand, emerge within those institutions of society—church, school, family—that perform important roles in socializing children and developing their attitudes. Regarding instrumental exploitation, Ogbu notes that job ceilings—formal statutes and informal practices by which blacks are denied equal access—continue to be pervasive in limiting blacks' employment and aiding whites' advancement. There has been an improvement in work force conditions for some blacks, but Ogbu's analysis suggests that although job ceilings may have risen, stratification by race remains.

Ogbu makes another important observation regarding the relationship between educational attainment and job ceilings among black Americans. Substantial progress in raising the job ceiling for blacks usually occurred during times of national crisis and turbulence. Surely there must be alternatives to this "employment with turbulence" relationship, which has been the primary driving force behind progress in the past. The interplay between employment opportunity and job ceilings for blacks should serve as the locus of change, for it is the prospect of employment that motivates one to pursue educational goals.

Ogbu makes another important contribution with his notable distinction between voluntary and nonvoluntary entry into this country and between immigrant and nonimmigrant minority status; he believes that each of these factors strongly influences the educational consequences for persons in those groups. It is interesting to note Ogbu's application of the term *immigrant* in referring to black Americans. Indeed, blacks came to this nation not as immigrants but as "soon-to-be-slaves." Because they did not arrive in this country voluntarily, it is understandable that their social identity and acculturation have been quite different from those of voluntary immigrants. Although often overlooked and not understood, the expressive exploitation of nonvoluntary immigrants and their subsequent responses are particularly important in comparing the status of black Americans to that of other racial and ethnic minorities. Thus Ogbu's distinction between voluntary and nonvoluntary immigrants is valuable because attitudes and perceptions are shaped by membership in these groups.

Ogbu offers an instructive explanation that expressive dimensions of racial stratification may persist even after formal instrumental barriers have been eliminated or after more opportunities have been made available to minorities. Blacks who are considered to be among the economically advantaged, who live in upper income neighborhoods, who have taken on the life-styles and accoutrements of the upper class, assert that there are still areas of limited access even for them. This observation can be verified in the educational sector alone when one considers the disproportionately low percentages of blacks and Hispanics among school superintendents, principals, and assistant principals (Jones & Montenegro, 1983, 1988; Revere, 1987).

Instrumental changes have resulted in structural modification of societal institutions. For example, there are no laws prohibiting blacks and Hispanics from holding positions above their ascribed job ceilings; yet because of attitudes (expressive factors), blacks and members of similar minorities continue to gain only limited opportunities for employment in the upper strata. Ogbu makes a valuable point in attributing the persistence of expressive oppression primarily to a lack of awareness and understanding of this dimension by both whites and blacks.

In his discussion of the treatment of blacks by whites, Ogbu elaborates on the two modalities mentioned earlier—instrumental and expressive—and notes that education falls within the instrumental domain. We should expand this conceptualization to consider education as expressive as well as instrumental. Expressive (psychological) exploitation of blacks has been just as destructive as instrumental (structural) exploitation, if not more so, in restricting access to opportunities. When one is denied opportunity to develop a sense of well-being, a self-concept, and self-assurance, one puts forth minimal effort to negotiate the system successfully—in this case, the educational system. The ultimate outcome is a reduction of effort in the pursuit of educational goals (Alderfer, 1972; Locke, 1968; Vroom, 1964).

Expressive exploitation denies the self-affirmation so vital to achievement in the educational process. As a matter of fact, self-disapprobation is often observed among black learners who do not do well in school. Negative projections that stem from societal influences are often internalized; thus the cycle of expressive exploitation and consequent expressive responses is perpetuated. The point is that as long as expressive exploitation persists, effective relations and interactions between teacher and learner will not occur.

Educational processes and educational consequences are associated directly with the twin problems identified by Ogbu: poorer academic performance and lesser educational attainment among black Americans. He traces briefly the pattern of schooling for blacks, noting that the earlier emphasis had been on "industrial education." But as Myrdal (1944) in his treatise confirmed the belief of Southern whites that industrial education was the desired end, thereby assuring that blacks would not compete effectively against whites in the labor market. In their expressive responses, black educators promoted a sense of belonging and esteem among black students; they had high expectations for students' performance in school. Comer (1988), recalling his schooling, stated,

> When I was in elementary school in the 1940s, I went on a shopping expedition to the A&P store every Friday with my parents and siblings. I can't remember a week that we did not encounter someone from the school—the custodian, principal, teacher, school clerk. There was always an exchange of information about how we were doing in school, what was expected of us, and what to do if we didn't meet those expectations. The positive relationship between my parents and school people—and the probability of a weekly report—made it difficult for me to do anything short of live up to the expressed expectations. (p. 35)

In one sense, expressive responses provided a dimension to the education of blacks that served to offset the debilitating effects of inferior education mentioned by Ogbu. Vestiges of the former treatment of blacks by white Americans in educational settings and in society today are painful reminders of difficulties encountered, responses made, and the impact of membership in those groups on academic performance.

Ogbu notes that within-school segregation has resulted in different educational experiences for blacks and whites and has perpetuated inequities in grading and placement of students on the basis of conduct rather than academic performance. He offers this situation as one explanation of blacks' lower educational attainment. Researchers have substantiated the assertion that black children learn in distinctly different ways from white children and that teaching styles should be adapted to accommodate those differences in learning styles (Claxton & Murrell, 1987; Cohen, 1976; Gilbert & Gay, 1985; Hale, 1982). Although convincing research findings are readily available, teachers have been slow to adapt their instructional methodology to accommodate those differences. In many schools where racial minorities' academic records continue to reflect poor performance, overt, covert, and subtle educational practices have truncated achievement and have obviated recognition of progress made by racial minorities. Such practices include inappropriate tracking, mislabeling, and failure to provide a supportive environment that communicates to learners that the lack of knowledge is acceptable, providing there is a desire to attain that knowledge (Oakes, 1985, 1988).

Ogbu cites several responses by blacks to these conditions, including disillusionment, attempts to change the rules and requirements for success, competition, and demands for better education. Yet in view of the continuing, distinct, and disparate stratification of the races and its consequences for their educational attainment, new modalities of response must be sought. This point certainly seems to be true as one ponders three critical questions Ogbu sets forth (p. 27):

> *First, why are some individual black children successful, although they also face a job ceiling and inferior education and share the same folk theories about getting ahead with other blacks? Second, why do some minority groups who also face a job ceiling, other opportunity barriers, and inferior education do better in school than black Americans? Third, why are some minority groups doing well in school although they possess cultures and languages different from the culture and language of American public schools?*

Ogbu asserts that the influence of black social identity and cultural frame of reference are plausible explanations. Moreover, it has been observed that black children regard successful outcomes in school as "acting white" and reject the pursuit of those outcomes as an acceptable endeavor. Positive self-imaging therefore should be reinforced because it is an essential ingredient that must be incorporated into the educational process.

Ogbu concludes his chapter most appropriately with the poignant assessment "that if a greater improvement is to occur in the educational achievement of the children of the new (and old) black middle class, greater attention must be paid to the expressive side of racial stratification, including blacks' expressive responses" (p. 31). Thus in responding to the opening questions, I would conclude that there is also a dire need to build trust between black students (and parents) and white educators. To the extent that distrust exists, the system will be questioned constantly by blacks, the curricula content often will be suspect, and white teachers and administrators will be challenged by black students and their parents to accede to their demands. Among the many factors that influence trust building is the primacy of open and honest communication among students, educators, and parents. A climate that fosters understanding, collaboration, partnership, and support among each of these constituencies is an absolute necessity for improving educational conditions for low-achieving ethnic minority children.

What then, does the evidence reveal regarding the educational attainment of blacks and Hispanics? Has there been any improvement in their educational achievement? These questions are explored in James Blackwell's chapter, "Current Issues Affecting Blacks and Hispanics in the Educational Pipeline." Blackwell sets the stage for his analysis by highlighting social scientists' findings that dominance, exploitation, and subjugation have characterized race relations and been powerful tools in determining the life chances of blacks and other ethnic minorities. Throughout his chapter Blackwell provides evidence that inequities in education have not been ameliorated; rather they have been sustained and have resulted in the stagnation of relations among the races.

Blackwell's discussion of minorities college attendance rates and persistence through completion of the degree presents a rather bleak picture. Blackwell notes that predominantly white universities are returning to the practice of focusing recruitment primarily on the "exceptionally prepared" students. Such practices lead to a "bidding war" among competing institutions to offer attractive inducements to the limited number of students who meet highly selective criteria. Many ethnic minority students consider this practice an affront because it gives them the impression that they are pawns in a lottery. Institutions of higher education must become more deeply involved in developing and expanding the potential talent pool and in working more closely with elementary and secondary educators in order to reduce the need for such bidding. In addition, predominantly white institutions should reevaluate their motivations and strategies for recruiting only "outstanding" ethnic minority students. They should acknowledge that just as white students who are admitted have a wide range of abilities and background experiences (many are well prepared but others are not as well prepared), so should blacks and Hispanics with a range of abilities and experiences be admitted.

Blackwell contends that educational attainment is a primary requisite if change in power differentials is to occur. Etzioni (1961) used a compliance typology to suggest that a relationship exists between the types of power used by those in dominant positions and the characteristic responses (involvement) used by those in subordinate positions. He defined power as "an actor's ability to induce or influence another actor to carry out his [or her] directives or any other norms he [or she] supports" (p. 4). Etzioni identified three types of power: (a) coercive—the use of physical force to control others; (b) remunerative—material resources that are granted or withheld as a means of control; and (c) normative—symbolic means such as praise, reprimand, or granting of privileges, which are used to influence others. For each type of power there is a characteristic type of involvement (response). Individuals comply with the use of coercive power by becoming alienated. Response to remunerative power tends to yield calculative involvement. The use of normative power usually evokes commitment to the cause or the institution. Therefore, persons in dominant and subordinate positions, either in order to control or to respond to control, would be expected to behave in the manner predicted by Etzioni.

In connection with this discussion, it should be understood that power resides most often within the dominant population—namely, white Americans: those who possess the highest proportion of educational attainment. The dominant group has used coercive power to sustain segregated educational systems. It has used remunerative power in granting inferior or substandard material resources. It has used normative power in its failure to acknowledge blacks' educational achievements. Therefore, the difficulty for blacks and other underrepresented minorities becomes apparent: If the lack of educational attainment limits life chances and if educational attainment is an essential ingredient to the elimination of power differentials, how can blacks who are virtually devoid of power expand their limited access to opportunity and thus make their life chances equal to those of whites? The impact of this anomaly becomes clear as we sharpen our understanding of power and compliance.

The concepts inherent in Etzioni's notions of power can be used to describe the strategies that persons in power use to maintain that power. Those strategies include changing the rules of the game, altering procedural imperatives, and changing standards to suit the desires of the privileged. Blackwell contends that those who possess power are not likely to relinquish it merely for the asking. Dominated groups therefore are likely to respond with confusion, disagreements, despair, alienation, and consequently the acquisition and actualization of very little power. Blackwell contends justifiably that the gatekeepers of power have devised new and more complex strategies for circumventing the attainment of equity. He asserts that "institutions now have seized the 'quality' criterion as a mechanism for denying equity in higher education" (p. 38). To his contention I would add that "quality" has been seized as the counterpart criterion for controlling the access and progress of faculty and administrators. In referring to ethnic minority candidates, the question of qualification immediately becomes part of the decision-making agenda; when white candidates are considered, their qualifications are taken for granted.

Regarding the current state of educational and occupational attainment among blacks and Hispanics, Blackwell cites persistent unemployment rates, widespread labor-force participation in the lower stratum of the job market, inadequate training to meet requirements for new job markets, and disproportionality in the distribution of wealth. Blackwell's findings regarding the persistence of minorities in higher education are troubling, especially because "minority students have the highest college attrition rates and are less able to remain in college through completion of the baccalaureate degree" (p. 41). This fact, coupled with the continuing decline in graduate enrollment of minorities, portrays vividly the fragile status of blacks and, to a lesser extent, Hispanics in the educational pipeline. All of these elements portend a continuation of constraints consistent with minorities' past experiences. Howe (1988) further underscored the potential outcomes of these conditions in his conclusion that "the plight of the young person without advanced education, never easy, has become alarming in recent years. In a fast-changing economy that demands increasingly specialized skills, these young people are in danger of being left at the starting gate."

These factors, coupled with blacks' declining rate of participation in postsecondary education (American Council on Education, 1987; U.S. Bureau of the Census, 1985), suggest that serious problems exist for the future. Without college degrees, minorities will have fewer and fewer places to turn for meaningful employment. For example, the expected median income for a male with a high school diploma in 1985 showed a decrease of 24% from 1972 (after adjusting for inflation). For a male college graduate, the figure dropped only 7% (Gamarekian, 1988). In a technological world, an uneducated populace is an unproductive populace. If these conditions persist, they could become catastrophic to the nation's economy.

Blackwell presents a dismal account of the number of doctoral degree recipients who are black and Hispanic. He speaks not only of the declining numbers but also of the "maldistribution of earned doctorates among blacks, Puerto Ricans, and

Mexican-Americans'' (p. 46). I agree that there is a dire need for more blacks and Hispanics to pursue doctoral degrees in the physical and biological sciences. Reports show that in 1985, of the doctoral degrees earned in the physical and biological sciences, only 8.2% and 19.5% were awarded to blacks and Hispanics, respectively (U.S. Department of Education, 1980, 1988).

Other concerns also persist. Although 45% of all doctoral degrees earned by blacks were in the field of education, that number is not sufficient to offset the growing trend among blacks and other minorities to pursue degrees in fields other than education. This trend will intensify the critical shortage of ethnic minority teachers. One thing is certain, as Blackwell states clearly: "No discipline, field, or specialization can be characterized as oversaturated with blacks, Puerto Ricans, Mexican-Americans, and 'other Hispanics'" (p. 46).

Blackwell's call for policy development and systemic change is well taken. His directions for change and suggested courses of action constitute basic beginnings that can guide our actions. More is needed, however; although Blackwell's suggestions are appropriate and necessary, they do not include changes in the affective (as opposed to structural) or expressive dimensions described by Ogbu. Affective changes—psychological dimensions of attitudes, motivations, and values—are less easy to quantify and to rectify; yet they are as important as instrumental factors, if not more so. Students are affected by the affective orientations of teachers, administrators, and peers. In turn, they influence the affective orientations of siblings, peers, and offspring. Insights regarding these factors are vitally important to our understanding and consequently to our capacity to reconcile and/or resolve the twin problems articulated by Ogbu.

Although Ogbu and Blackwell agree about the fundamental issues that must be addressed, they differ in their conceptualization of the problems. Ogbu's reasoning suggests that differences in school adjustment and educational attainment among minorities can be attributed in part of voluntary immigrant status or to nonimmigrant or involuntary immigrant status (Ogbu, 1978). Minority students' educational performance is shaped by their perceptions of their status. Accordingly, minorities whose immigrant status is voluntary tend also to perceive that status as temporary. Therefore they believe that with sufficient time, their educational success can be assured by hard work. Ethnic minorities who perceive their status as involuntary see themselves and their culture as different from voluntary immigrants and their culture; therefore their psychological orientations and their perceptions of academic achievement are influenced by the belief that they will not be rewarded and that discriminatory job ceilings will limit their occupational attainment.

Blackwell, in contrast, focuses on extrinsic or systemic factors. He believes that societal barriers impose limitations and subordinate status on ethnic minorities. Blackwell reminds us that within society, it is still difficult to make progress toward eliminating access barriers and closing equity gaps between blacks and whites or Hispanics and whites. Slippages in the educational pipeline continue, but Blackwell expresses hope that the strategies that have been implemented will deal with the problems that continue to limit and stratify blacks and Hispanics by class and educational attainment.

Ogbu and Blackwell offer views that are essential to our understanding and, more important, to the resolution of the twin problems. Even so, a universe of additional issues surrounds race and education. Consider the following:

What will the effect of educational reforms be on the status and the persistence of blacks and Hispanic Americans in education in the 1990s? Proponents of educational reform, in their efforts to ensure higher standards and higher academic performance among students, have not adequately addressed the potential negative effects of reform proposals on ethnic minority students. For those students who need or want to work, such changes as lengthening the school day or school year may impose an additional burden by forcing them to choose between earning an income and staying longer in school. In making that choice, students may find that money to provide or supplement their income has greater appeal than staying in school. In addition, although it is vital that high standards be set and met, the student whose academic skills are marginal may perceive the higher standards as an added barrier unless appropriate support and/or remediation are provided. Thus such students will be less likely to view success in school as a realistic outcome. We must monitor carefully and must be willing to make immediate adjustments to the reform measures that negatively affect the educational attainment of racial minorities and of academically marginal students.

How will increased entry and certification standards affect the growing shortage of ethnic minority elementary and secondary school teachers? A corollary to reform efforts and their effects on students is the potential effect on the minority teaching force. In an attempt to improve teaching and learning, standards of entry and certification are being raised. Minorities are being screened out of teaching through the use of competency testing at an alarmingly high rate at every level. Additional testing should be studied thoroughly for its possible effect on the supply of minority teachers (Wilson, 1987).

> While enrollment in teacher education programs is rising, the vast majority of those students have no intention of working in urban school districts, where the need for new teachers is most critical . . . Eighty-nine percent of the students now enrolled in teacher training programs are white. Only 5 percent are black and 3 percent are Hispanic. The numbers for minority groups are down from those in 1980, when 17 percent of all undergraduates majoring in education were black or Hispanic. (Wells, 1988, p. A28. Copyright © 1988 by The New York Times Company. Reprinted by permission.)

Not only will ethnic minority students be left with insufficient numbers of ethnic minority role models, mentors, and sponsors, but nonminority students will also be denied opportunities to develop wholesome attitudes and respect for the knowledge, skills, and abilities of minority educators. Further, nonminority students will be denied the benefits of meaningful interaction with and role modeling of ethnic minority teachers and administrators.

How will the declining postsecondary participation rates among ethnic minority students affect the dearth of minority faculty, particularly in the areas of severest underrepresentation? Doctorates earned by blacks declined by 27% from 1976 to 1986. In 1986 blacks earned 820 doctorates, or 3.6% of all doctoral degrees; Hispanics earned 2.5%. In all fields (with the exception of education and the social sciences) the numbers of degrees earned by blacks and Hispanics in 1986 were less than 100 in each field. In engineering, for example, only 14 doctoral degrees were earned by blacks and 25 by Hispanics. In the physical sciences, the total number of doctoral degrees earned by blacks was 23; Hispanics earned 53. If ethnic minorities are underrepresented among doctoral degree recipients, it stands to reason that they will continue to be underrepresented on university faculties. University officials must participate in the struggle to increase the academic participation and achievement rates of racial minorities. Their involvement must begin with the establishment of partnerships with elementary and secondary school systems. Programs and policies that promote outreach to parents and community are essential to the resolution of the twin problems confronting minorities in education.

Assessments and projections of educational attainment indicate ethnic minority students are less likely than white students to earn college degrees. In 1986, 20.1% of white persons over age 25 had completed 4 years of college or more. For blacks the figure was 10.9%; for Hispanics, 8.4% (U.S. Bureau of the Census, 1986). It is predicted that by the year 2000, almost 42% of all public school students will be members of ethnic minority groups (U.S. Bureau of the Census, 1986). Further, according to Hodgkinson (1987, 1988), by the year 2020 the population of school-age children (ages 5–17) will be 48% ethnic minority. Recent decreases in the participation rates of ethnic minorities in the educational pipeline and the inadequate quality of educational experiences for those who continue in the system are problems that cannot be ignored or left to happenstance. Allowing stratification by race and economic class to persist works to the detriment of us all; ultimately it jeopardizes the competitive advantage of this nation in the world. The reason is clear: Not only are race and social class stratification counterproductive and contradictory to American values, they are restrictive and debilitating. They impose ceilings on the growth and development of all who are subjected to these conditions.

What will be the status of race relations in the coming decade? First, if present trends persist, it is likely that class differences will continue to be the determining factor for conditions among blacks and Hispanics. It is projected that the minority school-age population will increase from 20% in 1985 to 33% in 2000 (U.S. Bureau of the Census, 1988) and that 43.1% of black children and 39.6% of Hispanic children under age 18 will live in poverty; for children living in female-headed families the figure is 54%. In addition, disparities persist in median family income levels: Blacks earn 57% and Hispanics earn 65% of the income earned by whites (U.S. Bureau of the Census, 1987). Accordingly it is clear that class differences are unlikely to be eliminated in the coming decades, even with our best efforts and intentions. I do not wish to suggest that despair is in order; rather, our efforts must be clear in focus and purpose, and we must be determined to improve the educational and economic conditions of racial minorities. Members of minorities (particularly those who have achieved middle-class status or above) and nonminority persons must make stronger commitments to provide better education for all children. Education is an important contributor to this nation's well-being; thus it is imperative that we do a better job of educating all children in the future.

Second, the declining numbers of minority teachers and administrators may result in less understanding and less tolerance of cultural differences. Even among the few members of ethnic minorities who hold positions in education, there are some who do not wish to have duties and responsibilities assigned to them solely on the basis of their race or ethnicity. They contend that they have trained and prepared themselves as scholars in the disciplines of their choice; they do not wish to have an interest in cultural or ethnic concerns assumed, taken for granted, or imposed. As a consequence, the numbers of ethnic minority members who wish to establish strong cultural identities is reduced further. Thus the enculturation of minorities and nonminorities within different cultural contexts may become an even greater challenge than in the past.

Third, stronger emphasis must be placed on the development of intellectual resources that will empower blacks and Hispanics with the skills, knowledge, and behaviors needed to eradicate racial stratification. Professional preparation programs (teacher education and educational administration) have a crucial responsibility in providing learning experiences for potential teachers and administrators; these experiences must foster awareness and understanding of expressive and instrumental factors, cultural differences, and differences in learning styles and must help to develop an appreciation for those differences and their effect on the teaching/learning process.

Fourth, the widening gap in the postsecondary participation rates of minority men and women, as indicated by serious declines in the percentage of black males who enter and complete baccalaureate, graduate, and professional studies, must not be allowed to continue. Closing this gap will require intensification of efforts toward change in the early childhood, elementary, and secondary school years to offset and/ or prevent disparities in literacy among racial and ethnic groups.

In sum, the projections and assessments provided by Ogbu and Blackwell compel us to ask whether people are truly concerned about the education of all children in this nation. Surely in the United States we can find the knowledge and resources needed to improve present conditions. I am convinced that we have the know-how, the skills, and the resources. Yet I question whether there exist the commitment and the determination to do what we know is right, just, and necessary. New focuses are needed: those that shift away from power and involvement, away from exploitation and stratification, and toward empowerment. Empowerment means simply that blacks and Hispanics must assume greater control over the economic and social conditions of their lives. They must seize control over instrumental and expressive factors that limit or facilitate their educational and occupational access and attainment. They must garner resources and use them to their collective advantage in eliminating the stratification and exploitation that have limited their life chances in the past. Blacks and Hispanics have within their control the most powerful mechanisms imaginable for change: commitment, motivation, and determination.

REFERENCES

Alderfer, C. P. (1972). *Existence, relatedness and growth: Human needs in organizational settings.* New York: Free Press.

American Council on Education. (1987). *Minorities in higher education: Sixth annual status report.* Washington, DC: American Council on Education.

Claxton, C. S., & Murrell, P. H. (1987). *Learning styles: Implications for improving educational practices.* (ASHE-ERIC Higher Education Report #4. Clearinghouse on Higher Education). Washington, DC: George Washington University.

Cohen, R. A. (1976). Conceptual styles, cultural conflicts, and non-verbal tests of intelligence. In J. I. Roberts & S. K. Akinsanya (Eds.), *Schooling in the cultural context* (pp. 290–322). New York: David McKay.

Comer, J. P. (1988). Is "parenting" essential to good teaching? *NEA Today, 6,* 34–40.

Etzioni, A. (1961). *A comparative analysis of complex organizations.* New York: Free Press.

Gamarekian, B. (1988, May 18). Women are liberating a citadel of male power. *New York Times,* p. A24.

Gilbert, S. E., II, & Gay, G. (1985). Improving the success in school of poor black children. *Phi Delta Kappan, 67,* 133–137.

Hale, J. E. (1982). *Black children, their roots, culture and learning styles.* Provo, UT: Brigham Young University Press.

Hodgkinson, H. (1987). Courage to change: Facing our demographic destiny. *Currents, 13,* 8–12.

Hodgkinson, H. (1988). The right schools for the right kids. *Educational Leadership, 45,* 10–14.

Howe, H. (1988, January 20). Commentary on: *The forgotten half: Non-college youth in America.* Washington, DC: The William T. Grant Foundation, Commission on Work, Family and Citizenship.

Jones, E. H., & Montenegro, X. P. (1983). *Perspectives on racial minority and women school administrators.* Arlington, VA: American Association of School Administrators, Office of Minority Affairs.

Jones, E. H., & Montenegro, X. P. (1988). *Women and minorities in school administration*. Arlington, VA: American Association of School Administrators, Office of Minority Affairs.

Katz, I. (1967). Socialization of academic achievement in minority group children. In D. Levine (Ed.), *Nebraska Symposium on Motivation* (pp. 133–191). Lincoln: University of Nebraska.

Locke, E. A. (1968). Toward a theory of task motivation and incentives. *Organizational Behavior and Human Performance, 3*, 157–189.

Mingione, A. (1965). Need for achievement in Negro and white children. *Journal of Consulting Psychology, 29*, 108–111.

Oakes, J. (1985). *Keeping track: How schools structure inequality*. New Haven, CT: Yale University Press.

Oakes, J. (1988). Tracking: Can schools take a different route? *NEA Today, 6*, 41–47.

Ogbu, J. (1978). *Minority education and caste: The American system in cross-cultural perspective*. New York: Academic Press.

Revere, A. B. (1987). Black women superintendents in the United States: 1984–1985. *Journal of Negro Education, 56*, 510–520.

Rosen, B. C. (1959). Race, ethnicity, and the achievement syndrome. *American Sociological Review, 24*, 47–60.

U.S. Bureau of the Census. (1985). *School enrollment—Social and economic characteristics of students*. Washington, DC: U.S. Government Printing Office.

U.S. Bureau of the Census. (1986). *Money income and poverty status of families and persons in the U.S.: 1986*. Washington, DC: U.S. Government Printing Office.

U.S. Bureau of the Census. (1987). *What's it worth? Educational background and economic status: Spring 1984*. Washington, DC: U.S. Government Printing Office.

U.S. Bureau of the Census. (1988). *Statistical abstract of the United States*. Washington, DC: U.S. Government Printing Office.

U.S. Department of Education, National Center for Education Statistics. (1980). *Digest of education statistics*. Washington, DC: U.S. Government Printing Office.

U.S. Department of Education, National Center for Education Statistics. (1988). *Digest of education statistics*. Washington, DC: U.S. Government Printing Office.

Vroom, V. H. (1964). *Work and motivation*. New York: Wiley.

Wells, A. S. (1988, May 10). Teacher shortage termed most critical in inner-city schools. *New York Times*, p. A28.

Wilson, R. (1987). Recruitment and retention of minority faculty and staff. *American Association for Higher Education Bulletin, 39*, 3–6.

4

Inner-City Schools–Poverty and Segregation: Has the Picture Changed Since 1967?

James L. Parsons
College of Education
Texas A&M University

In the summer of 1967, cities throughout the nation erupted in violence and destruction. Urban civil disorder was concentrated in the heavily black ghettos of Newark and Detroit, but violence spread throughout the country and occurred in Atlanta, Cleveland, Dayton, Houston, and other cities. The problems were limited by neither time nor place. Watts, a Los Angeles ghetto, had been devastated by rioting just two summers before; in the intervening period, flare-ups demonstrating the volatile tension between blacks and the police had occurred in both the North and the South. Nationally it was feared that the worst was just beginning.

President Lyndon Johnson responded to this crisis by appointing a special commission. The National Advisory Commission on Civil Disorders (the Kerner Commission, or NACCD) was established by presidential order on July 28, 1967. Headed by former Illinois governor Otto Kerner, the Commission began the task of learning what had happened in the cities, what had caused the riots, and what could be done to prevent similar occurrences in the future.

The Commission met through the fall and winter of 1967. They heard hundreds of witnesses, visited the sites of the riots, and issued a final report in February 1968. The report listed causes of the riots and suggested many changes in local, state, and federal responses to civil disorder. In addition, the Commission made a number of policy recommendations to improve conditions in the ghettos. These included recommendations about public welfare, increasing employment, and improving education.

Many people saw educational reform as the key to long-term improvement of life in the inner city, movement out of the ghetto, and a starting point for economic growth away from poverty and inequality for blacks and Hispanics. The Commission's report described inner-city schools as dilapidated, marginally maintained, and poorly equipped. It documented the continuing segregation of city school districts. Most teachers in inner-city schools were commuters, neither living in the neighborhoods served by the school nor involved in school or community activities after the dismissal bell. Community–school relations were characterized by parents' and students' hostility toward teachers and schools. The Commission suggested use of federal money and power to improve both the physical and the social conditions of ghetto schools. De facto segregation was to end, teaching improvements were to be made, and schools were to become integral parts and participants in the inner-city community.

It is now 20 years since these recommendations were made. Has the situation described by the Kerner Commission changed? To what extent are inner-city schools still segregated? Are teachers and schools part of the communities that they serve? If not, to what extent are poverty-stricken schools moving toward the Commission's goals, and at what rate?

In a study of the sociology of education, few issues are more vital than those raised by an examination of change in inner-city schools. Today the numbers of minority students are larger in both absolute and relative terms than in 1967. The rate of growth for the minority population also has outstripped the growth of the population as a whole. In 1987 the rate of U.S. population growth from 1984 to 1990 was projected to be 5.5%, but black population growth was projected to be nearly double that rate (9.8%); Hispanics were expected to increase at an even higher rate, 18.5% (Sternlieb & Hughes, 1987). Continuing demographic changes mean that in many of the cities studied, white populations will be in the minority by the year 2000.

Many large American cities already have majority populations that are nonwhite. Of the 100 largest cities, 8 are more than 50% black and 3 are more than 50% Hispanic. Six cities have between 40% and 49% black populations; an additional 12 are at least 30% black. Thus 26 of the 100 largest U.S. cities are 30% or more black (Robey, 1985). Even more important for education, the proportion of blacks in the population is increasing at a greater rate at the younger end of the age distribution, resulting in national proportions of blacks by age group ranging from 15.3% for ages 14 to 17 to 17.0% for children under 5. By contrast, the total national proportion for 1995 is projected to be 13.0% (U.S. Bureau of the Census, 1984). Some of the larger school districts of the riot-stricken cities are approaching or have surpassed majority black and Hispanic student enrollment.

Given that education is a good predictor of employment and that employment is a means for economic security, the potential impact of more generations of unemployed and unemployable inner-city residents becomes obvious. The economic and social disruptions described by the Kerner Commission in 1967 will be insignificant compared to those described by some future presidential commission examining the causes and cures of the next round of urban unrest.

It is important to examine the inner-city school of 1987 and to compare it with the conditions described in 1967. In this chapter I use statistics from both government and private sources to describe and highlight the racial and ethnic composition of urban school districts. Statistics merely describe, but from that description the impact of governmental policy decisions may be inferred. Federal policy toward education, civil rights, poverty, and urban growth has changed since the Johnson administration. Thus the second step of an analysis of urban schools is to chart and consider these policy changes. In essence, this chapter provides a historical summary of 20 years of educational change in schools that received international attention as the most disadvantaged in the United States.

THE SITUATION IN 1967

The Cities

What white Americans have never fully understood—but what the Negro can never forget—is that the white society is deeply implicated in the ghetto. White institutions created it, white institutions maintain it, and white society condones it. (National Advisory Commission on Civil Disorders [NACCD], 1968, p. 2)

The Commission's report describes the inner city in stark terms, outlining fundamental problems in housing, education, and basic family security and welfare. The ghetto grew in the twentieth century, with the most rapid expansion in the period after the Great Depression, as the black population moved from farms to the cities. The movement generally led black families from the South to the North or to the West. Hart (1976) asserted that the movement of the black population was "one of the most dramatic aspects of population geography of the United States over the last half century" (p. 49). By 1950 more than two thirds of the American black population lived in cities, accounting for nearly 10% of the urban population. By 1966, 70% of all blacks lived in large cities, compared to 64% of all whites. The growth of black population in the United States from 1950 to 1960 was primarily within central cities. The overall black population grew by more than 6.5 million; 98% of that growth occurred in metropolitan areas, with 86% of the growth in the most crowded central cities themselves (U.S. Bureau of the Census, 1985). By contrast, most (77.8%) of the white population growth in the same period took place in the suburbs; only 2.5% of the white increase occurred in the central city. Absolute white population in the central cities declined by 1.3 million in the same period (NACCD, 1968). The result is that by 1966 the central city had become primarily black, surrounded by a suburban fringe that was primarily white. Put another way, from 1950 to 1960 the suburban fringe remained about 95% white; by 1966 it had increased its homogeneity by another percentage point to 96%.

The inner city became more and more black as birth rates for blacks increased faster than those for whites and as migration from rural to urban areas continued during the period. Yet one of the traditional roles of the inner city was as a way station for immigrants and a meeting place for those of similar racial or ethnic origins. For European immigrants as well as for white newcomers from the rural areas, low-cost housing, available public transportation, and friends and relatives in a similar situation made the inner city attractive. As the white immigrants, whether foreigners or farmers, found jobs and became assimilated into mainstream society, they moved from the inner city and settled into developing suburban areas with newer houses and better schools (Hummel & Nagle, 1973).

Similarly, blacks moved into the inner city for its advantages of housing, transportation, and society, but there the similarity ends. According to Ornstein (1974, 1982), even as blacks joined the work force, and even when they achieved incomes and living standards equaling or surpassing those of whites, they did not move from the inner city. Brown (1976) described the history of discrimination in housing. As blacks attempted to leave the inner city, following the path of other immigrants, they found their way effectively blocked by both overt and covert attitudes and practices. The suburbs were essentially white and were intended by their residents to remain that way. Even economically successful blacks were prevented from buying houses in predominantly white neighborhoods. Residential patterns were defined first by law, as in the South, where many cities had zoning restrictions barring the sale of houses to blacks. After such statutes were declared unlawful, residential neighborhood covenants or private agreements between homeowners restricted the sale of houses to those who were not of the same race as the general community (Brown, 1976). Real estate agents refused to show property in white neighborhoods to blacks; banks refused to lend to blacks in certain areas. Blacks, then, were forced to remain where they were. Well-to-do blacks who attempted to distance themselves from poverty-stricken neighborhoods were forced to develop all-black neighborhoods with better housing, usually on the boundary between the increasingly black inner city and the increasingly white suburb.

In 1966, the inner-city ghetto became the place where blacks moved, stayed, and reproduced. Economically able blacks were able to move out of the poorer areas of the city, but they did so only with difficulty. Whites who had migrated for traditional reasons moved out as quickly as they could afford housing in the suburbs. Other ethnic groups who migrated to the inner city, primarily Hispanics, similarly found their exit blocked, but not to the same degree as blacks. Those left behind in the inner city in 1966 were the least economically successful of the nonblacks, as well as the blacks themselves.

The Schools

At the request of President Johnson, the U.S. Commission on Civil Rights prepared a report that described the continuing racial isolation of black students in the public schools (U.S. Commission on Civil Rights, 1967). Though school segregation had been illegal since the 1954 *Brown v. Board of Education* decision, racial segregation persisted "from circumstances other than legal compulsion" (U. S. Commission on Civil Rights, 1967, p. v.). As noted previously, some of the circumstances that contributed to continuing de facto segregation are those related to the growth of the inner city. Other reasons included attitudes of both blacks and whites and certain educational policies and practices of school districts and individual schools.

The extent of racial isolation—the separation of blacks into predominantly black schools and whites into predominantly white schools—is clear from the report, which made extensive use of data gathered by James Coleman (1966) in preparing *Equality of Educational Opportunity.* Nationally, school segregation in 1966 was severe and pervasive, as shown by these figures:

- 65% of black first graders attended schools with 90% or more black enrollment;
- 80% of white first graders attended schools with 90% or more white enrollment;
- 87% of all blacks attended schools that were more than 50% black; 72% of these schools were in urban areas in the North; 97% of these schools were in urban areas in the South.

The situation was even more extreme in the metropolitan areas:

- 79% of nonwhite enrollment was in central city schools;
- 68% of white enrollment was suburban;
- 75% of black elementary students attended schools 90% or more black;
- 83% of white elementary students attended schools 90% or more white.

In sum, about 90% of black elementary children attended schools that were more than 50% black: In selected cities, the percentages were even higher. In 1966, for example, 97% of black elementary children attended schools that were predominantly black. This was not merely a regional problem; black students, whether in Houston or in Newark, were likely to find themselves in predominantly black schools (U.S. Commission on Civil Rights, 1967).

Teachers

In the mid-1960s, black children in the central city lived in black neighborhoods and attended black schools. It could be speculated that because the dual school systems were abolished by court action in 1954, faculties would be integrated; though children might not sit beside other children of a different race, at the very least a teacher of a different race would stand in the front of the classroom. This proved not to be the case, however. As Witty (1982) showed in her study of black teachers, the period from the *Brown* decision through 1970 was a time of difficulty for black teachers. As school districts were combined after the 1954 Supreme Court decision, many black teachers were dismissed. Some were fired outright, but most simply found that their contracts were not renewed for the next school year. Newly graduated black teachers were not hired. According to school administrators, there were not enough teaching positions for all available teachers. Some of those black teachers who retained employment were given nonteaching duties. Some were assigned to low-level supervisory positions that some critics discounted as "window-dressing" (Witty, 1982).

A few black teachers were transferred to white schools, but most remained in the classrooms in predominantly black schools. White teachers with experience and seniority exercised horizontal mobility; they moved to teaching positions in the predominantly white suburban districts as the big city districts became more and more black (Morgan & McPartland, 1981). According to Morgan and McPartland (1981), in 1967 only about 20% of the black students in their survey of public schools had white teachers; only about 5% of white students had black teachers. This discrepancy was greatest in the largest school districts, but the ratios generally held throughout the sample.

Race was not the only factor in staffing inner-city schools. According to Hummel and Nagle (1973), "Teacher placement in the big-city school districts typically results in a high concentration of the youngest, least experienced, and least well qualified teachers in the most disadvantaged schools" (p. 123). They cited figures from a 1968 report of the U.S. Department of Health, Education, and Welfare that showed a disproportionate number of public school teachers *without bachelor's degrees* in four of the largest urban districts with high minority enrollments: Boston, Detroit, Cleveland, and Baltimore. In those cities 10.3%, 11.4%, 12.1%, and 15.9% respectively, of public school teachers were employed without college degrees. Noncertified teachers in Baltimore, a predominantly black district, accounted for more than 20% of full-time teaching employees. In contrast, cities such as Chicago, Denver, Los Angeles, Atlanta, and Dallas had virtually no teachers without minimum teaching credentials.

Hummel and Nagle (1973) noted that as teachers gained experience and acquired advanced credentials they tended "to transfer *from* schools with high percentages of economically and socially disadvantaged students *to* schools where those from middle- and upper-income families are more numerous" (p. 123). If we apply this trend to inner-city black schools, it is reasonable to infer that teachers moved from black schools to white schools. It is important to remember as well that teaching is a profession with a high turnover. Many teachers leave after only 2 years in the classroom. Thus inner-city schools are continual training grounds for new teachers who are least able to cope with the demands of the environment. As James Irwin (1973) said in his account of life in the Detroit schools, "Given the proposition that teaching in the inner-city school, with its legions of problems, is somewhat less than the most desirable position in the educational firmament, one might well ask why anyone would take such a job" (p. 60).

Poverty

In the words of the Kerner Commission's report (NACCD, 1968), "The conditions of life in the racial ghetto are strikingly different from those to which most Americans are accustomed" (p. 266). Crime was a way of life; the rate of crimes against persons in the lowest-income black area was 35 times the rate in the highest-income white area (NACCD, 1968). The study reported a strong correlation between both income and race and the crime rate: The lower the income, the higher the crime rate, but low-income white areas had a lower crime rate than low-income black areas. The report noted that "most of these crimes are committed by a small minority of the residents, and the principal victims are the residents themselves" (p. 268).

More so than crime, poverty constitutes the greatest disparity between the inner city and mainstream society. Michael Harrington's (1963) *The Other America* sounded the alarm that poverty was rampant amid the prosperity of the United States. Harrington estimated that 40 to 50 million people—about one fourth of all Americans—lived in poverty. In *Dark Ghetto,* Clark (1965) described the American inner city as "urban ghettos [having] overcrowded and deteriorated housing, high infant mortality, crime and disease" (p. 11). Harrington, Clark, and others (Conant, 1961; Riessman, 1962) "helped to spark the War on Poverty" (Ornstein, 1982, p. 197).

Jencks (1972) criticized the war on poverty as being misdirected in its emphasis on educational attainment as the escape hatch from the poverty cycle. He argued for an approach that would "change the rules of the game so as to reduce the rewards of competitive success and the costs of failure" (p. 8). Despite his controversial emphasis on a needs-based economic equality, his study emphasized the economic disparity between the top and the bottom groups in America and the relationship of that disparity to educational and occupational attainment.

Regardless of discussions about the tactics of waging the war on poverty, the facts about the inner city in 1966 were brutal:

- 54% of all poor children in the inner city were nonwhite;
- 15.3% of the U.S. population (29.7 million people) were living below the poverty level;
- 40.6% of all nonwhites in the United States were living below the poverty level (U.S. Bureau of the Census, 1986).

Poverty was part of the lives of 30 to 40 million Americans in the 1960s, with a disproportionate number of these individuals belonging to racial minorities. Malnutrition, substandard housing, and inadequate health care marked the existence of those living in the inner city. For whatever causes, the impact on school children was immense. A solution to the problem of poverty was regarded by the Commission as critical to improving the schools, the neighborhoods, and the people themselves.

THE SITUATION IN THE 1980s

Conditions in the inner city two decades ago were tragic. A child who was born, or whose family moved, into the inner city of one of America's metropolitan areas faced a future of poverty and deprivation, with little chance of exposure or access to the majority white culture or society. Moreover, the child's future seemed bleak if that child survived to maturity. That possibility was problematic because infant mortality rates for nonwhites were 58% higher than for whites in 1968, and life expectancies for 25-year-old nonwhites were 11% less than for whites of the same age (NACCD, 1968; U.S. Bureau of the Census, 1986).

In 1987 the hypothetical child born in 1968 would turn 20 within the year. Perhaps this child, or one of his or her younger brothers, sisters, cousins, or friends, is described in *Growing Up Poor,* a study of disadvantaged youth in four American cities by Terry Williams and William Kornblum (1985). These authors found that youth who grow up in poverty follow one or more of several paths to maturity: "Achieving in school and participating in street hustles are just two" (p. 12). Work, prostitution, crime, military service, and prison are other paths taken by these youth. Yet Williams and Kornblum asserted that their greatest concern for

> poor teenagers, especially those from minority backgrounds, [is that they] are in danger of becoming superfluous people. Their disadvantages make them the least competitive members of the labor force. Without special efforts to improve their basic educational level, foster their interpersonal skills, and provide them with successful work experiences, it is unlikely they will be able to find roles in a society whose economic institutions are undergoing rapid change. (p. 13)

William Wilson (1987) more recently documented these trends for minorities in *The Truly Disadvantaged.*

The picture for minority youth in poverty, born after the Kerner Commission report, does not look optimistic. Among its recommendations for change in the schools concerning segregation, teachers, and instructional quality, the Commission held out the hope that such changes, if made, would improve the lot of the next generation of urban poor. *Racial Isolation in the Public Schools* (U.S. Commission on Civil Rights, 1967), directed solely at segregation in public schools, contained a similar idea. In the words of Commissioner Freeman, on schools as the beginning of a general betterment of society, "If in the future the adults in our society who make decisions about who gets a job, who lives down the block, or the essential worth of another person, are to be less likely to make these decisions on the basis of race or class, the present cycle [of segregation] must be broken in classrooms" (p. 214).

Thus the end of school segregation, the increase in classroom diversity, and the alleviation of poverty and deprivation in the inner city have consequences reaching beyond persons born in the ghetto. The coming together of those from diverse backgrounds was regarded as enriching to all. However, for the youth described by Williams and Kornblum (1985) and Wilson (1987), their younger siblings, and their children, the question remains: Have the conditions changed? Has there been an end to circumstances that were seen to cause and perpetuate poverty and racial division in 1968?

The Cities

The population shift of Americans from rural to urban areas, which paralleled the movement of blacks from the farms to the inner city, has continued at an increasing rate in the past 20 years. The population of the central cities throughout the United States increased at a rate of 57.6% from 1970 to 1980 and at 61.8% from 1980 to 1984 (U.S. Bureau of the Census, 1985). City growth has been greatest in the South and the West. Although cities in the Northeast and the Midwest experienced a decreasing rate of growth during the 1970s, the overall growth of the cities outpaced the growth of the suburbs (U.S. Bureau of the Census, 1985). Thus in 1987, the inner city is even more crowded than in 1967. One significant change, however, is the increasing urbanization of the South and the West. This finding suggests that the masses of people living in inner-city slums—ghettos—which had been viewed commonly as a northeastern phenomenon, are no longer limited to a single region.

The growth of the inner cities in the past two decades can be traced less to migration than to the high birth rates of the inhabitants. In the 1960s, the proportion of blacks in the population was placed at less than 11%. According to estimates made by the U.S. Bureau of the Census, as reported in the Kerner Commission report, the percentage of blacks in the United States would surpass 12% by 1985. Current data confirm that projection (U.S. Bureau of the Census, 1987b). The proportion of blacks living in the inner city is approaching one third of the current black population; this figure is in contrast to the 12.1% of blacks who lived in the central city in 1965 (NACCD, 1968; U.S. Bureau of the Census, 1985, 1987b). The 1968 estimates did not consider the growth of the nonblack minority population; in 1965, less than 5% of the U.S. population was of Spanish origin or descent. Census Bureau (1987b) figures report a 1985 percentage exceeding 7% of the population. As in the case of blacks, much of this growth occurred in the inner cities.

Today as in 1968, the inner cities are inhabited primarily by members of minority groups. The difference between then and now lies in the extent of the concentration of minorities. Inner cities today are even more exclusively minority enclaves than in the past. Although discrimination in housing currently restricts exit to the suburbs to some extent relative to 1968, there appear to be more than enough people to replace those who escape the inner city. Moreover, if the classic pattern of inner-city habitation is still operative today, the inner city is left to the new arrivals, those most economically deprived, and those with the least ability to leave.

The Schools

The segregation of the public schools has decreased since 1968. Nationally, the percentage of black students attending public schools with 90% to 100% minority enrollment has declined steadily since the time of the Kerner Commission report. Estimates for the 1984 school year showed an average state proportion of about 17%, but percentages for the most populous states were 69.0% for Illinois; 50% to 60% for New York and Michigan; 40% to 50% for New Jersey, Missouri, and Pennsylvania; and 30% to 40% for Maryland, California, Connecticut, and Texas. Moreover, the low percentage nationally was primarily the result of figures for 14 New England, northern-tier, and far-western states with negligible black populations. The District of Columbia school district reported that 95.2 percent of its black students attended schools with more than 90% minority enrollment (Orfield, 1987).

Though the figures above show a trend toward improvement from 1968 to the present, a cautionary note must be added. The change in desegregation of blacks, as estimated by Orfield (1987), is practically nil for the period from 1980 to 1984. The average change for any state in that period is a decline of 0.05%. In 21 states the percentage of blacks who attend 90% to 100% minority schools increased; 11 states showed no change; and only 18 states (including the District of Columbia) showed a decline. Hentschke, Lowe, and Royster (1985), who interpreted Orfield's studies of segregation for the period, noted that most of the improvement occurred in states that were segregated by law before 1954 and that segregation in the schools shifted from the South to the North and the Northeast. As can be seen from percentages previously cited, no states of the "Old South" are listed above the 40% level. Most of the states in the over-30% range are northern or northeastern.

In addition, since 1964 the increase in the Hispanic population has caused new racial isolation for that group. Nearly three of five (59.1%) Hispanics in New York and two of five in Illinois (41.2%) and Texas (40.0%) attend schools with more than 90% minority enrollment. Between 1980 and 1984 the states showed an average of 1.8% of Hispanic students attending 90% to 100% minority schools. In 29 states the percentage of Hispanics in largely minority schools increased.

To consider the matter of school segregation from a different perspective, the percentage of white students in the school of a typical minority student serves as an index of isolation. Racial isolation, however, is a two-way process; in racially isolated schools, both whites and minorities are denied the benefits of association. According to Orfield's (1987) estimates, in 1984 only 14 states contained schools in which the typical black student had 40% to 60% white classmates. In only eight states did a typical Hispanic student attend classes with 40% to 60% whites. The percentage of whites in the school of a typical Hispanic student is 18.9% in New York, 27.6% in Texas, and 28.0% in Illinois. Racial isolation is most severe in Illinois when we consider that only 8.0% of the state's public school students are Hispanic (Orfield, 1987).

Thus segregation in the schools continues. This trend is confirmed by Morgan and McPartland (1981), who report that in their survey of school districts of 29 large cities (with populations of 400,000 or more), the percentage of blacks in the school of a typical white child increased from 11.2% in 1967 to 27.3% in 1978. The percentage of whites in a school attended by a typical black child increased from 18.9% to

23.5% during the same period. Again, according to Morgan and McPartland (1981), the greatest positive change occurred in cities in the South with large black populations. They also found resegregation increasing by grade: Elementary schools were the least segregated, junior high schools were next, and high schools were the most segregated. Much of the secondary-level resegregation was found in the South, especially in the newly growing urban areas.

The U.S. Commission on Civil Rights (1977a, 1977b) reported improvement in school segregation patterns in the period from 1966 to 1975. According to the report, 38% of districts with at least a 5% minority enrollment had a high degree of segregation, but high levels of segregation were found in only 7% of those districts in 1972. Most of the districts experiencing the largest change were those under court order or other pressure to desegregate.

Overall population trends for minority students tend to reflect the patterns of minority population growth for the nation. The U.S. Bureau of the Census (1987c) and the U.S. Department of Education (1987) reported that the proportion of minority students in American schools rose from 24% to almost 27% between 1976 and 1980. For blacks, the proportion in 1976 was 15.5%; this figure increased to 16.1% in 1980. This change in itself does not seem large, but when combined with a decrease in white student population from 76.0% in 1976 to 73.3% in 1980, it shows a clear trend. In fact, in Texas and California, minority enrollments grew, respectively, from 41.8% and 34.9% in 1976 to 45.9% and 42.9% in 1980. Again, as in the general population, the trend is toward an increasing minority population in the public schools.

Poverty

The U.S. poverty rate was 13.6% in 1986, compared with 14.0% in 1985 (U.S. Bureau of the Census, 1987a, p. 3). So begins the federal government's official account of an improvement in poverty rates in the United States. According to the Kerner Commission, the 1966 percentage of persons below the poverty level was 15.3%. A cursory examination of the statistics suggests that poverty has declined, though not drastically, over the past two decades. Blacks represented 31.1% of those below the poverty level in 1986, compared with the total nonwhite figure of 31.7%. The poverty rate for blacks in 1986 was 36% nationwide, compared to 11% for whites. More than 29% of the blacks below the poverty level lived in the central city; 38.8% lived in federally designated "poverty areas," which included the central city (or inner city, as it is referred to here) and a fringe area immediately adjacent to the central city, or specific regions, such as the Appalachians. For public school students, the Center for Education Statistics reported that approximately 47% of black children were living in poverty in 1983 (U.S. Department of Education, 1987).

Poverty remains a major fact of life for children of the inner city. The impact of poverty on a child has been documented by Jencks (1972), Coleman (1966), and others. The Kerner Commission promised a reduction in poverty, or in the effects of poverty, for those in the inner city, but in 1986, 3.7 million black children under the age of 16 lived below the poverty level (U.S. Bureau of the Census, 1987a). More than one of every five American children is poor, but the rate for black children is about one in two. This figure stands in contrast to the 1.0 million nonwhite children in the same age range reported by the Kerner Commission in 1968. Because close to one third of these children live in the inner city, poverty remains a major problem for inner-city public schools in the 1980s.

CONCLUSION AND RECOMMENDATIONS

The Kerner Commission report described schools that were attended by students who were poor, staffed by teachers who were minimally competent, and housed in communities that were crowded and poverty-stricken. Superintendent Briggs of the Cleveland public schools was quoted in his testimony before the Commission: "Many of those whose recent acts threaten the domestic safety and tear at the roots of the American democracy are the products of yesterday's inadequate and neglected inner-city schools. The greatest unused and underdeveloped human resources in America are to be found in the deteriorating cores of America's urban centers" (NACCD, 1968, p. 425). Analysis of available statistics on urban population, student attendance, faculty composition, and poverty presented in this chapter shows little change from the corresponding statistics reported by the Kerner Commission.

The inner cities of our large metropolitan areas are filled with the poor and with members of minorities. The schools, as surveyed on the basis of the limited available information, are staffed by a decreasing cadre of black teachers. Though segregation in total has decreased in the past 20 years, specific pockets of resegregation are emerging in urban areas. The classrooms, though improving in the aggregate, are experiencing a similar resegregation. Also, white students are increasingly unlikely to have a black teacher during their school careers.

This chapter was hampered to some extent by the dearth of recent material on inner-city schools. Even the federal government's Office of Civil Rights seems to have decreased and in some instances eliminated its coverage of racial and ethnic composition of students and faculties in the nation's schools. Bowser (1985) confirmed this by stating that "our present dilemma of perspectives is not the result of trying to assimilate endless amounts of direct information. The research that is most needed is not being done" (p. 319). Private researchers seem to have abandoned conditions in schools as a research topic. From 1965 through 1975 there appeared dozens of books and many journal articles documenting the progress of school desegregation and poverty initiatives. But as evidenced by the great gaps on library shelves and in journal indexes, follow-up studies or reexaminations have not taken place from 1975 to the present.

Most of the statistical information about racial composition presented here had to be obtained from primary sources, such as census bureau documents. Most researchers have not recently attempted a direct investigation of schools in the poverty-stricken inner cities. Therefore more research is needed. Perhaps we have made more progress in race relations and in improving inner-city schools than the present limited data suggest. Or, alternatively, the data may be definitive and correctly suggest that our policies have failed and that conditions are ripe for a repetition of the summers of 1965 and 1966. However, we do not really know. Thus a better understanding of the state of inner-city schools is needed. Such an understanding might serve two purposes: First, it would facilitate a better evaluation of the past; second, and more important, it would provide the starting point and a guide for more effective planning and policy implementation in the future.

Most literature on inner-city schools also reflects a continuing confusion or lack of clear specification regarding the significance of race versus socioeconomic status.

Thus future studies that successfully differentiate the two should be valuable. My own hypothesis is that family socioeconomic status is an overriding determinant of educational and occupational attainment; but I hope we have passed the point of not even asking the question for fear that the answer might point to race alone as a factor. Sandra Scarr (1988) cautioned social scientists who investigate racial differences about the dangers that may be present when research results reflect "unfavorable possibilities for the underdog" (p. 56). She also asserted that "investigators cannot be held responsible for politically unfavorable outcomes of their research" (p. 58). Again, a thorough and honest evaluation is the first step to developing a broader focus and possible solutions.

In summary, from the various indicators and descriptive data presented, it appears that the promises of the Kerner Commission regarding education are yet to be fulfilled in the 1980s, although progress has been made in some areas. It is up to major future research and governmental and social policies to determine the success of the Commission in preventing a recurrence of urban rioting stemming from the present lack of progress and declining status of America's poor racial minorities.

REFERENCES

Bowser, B. P. (1985). Race relations in the 1980s: The case of the United States. *Journal of Black Studies, 15,* 307–324.

Brown, W. H., Jr. (1976). Access to housing: The role of the real estate industry. In R. T. Ernst & L. Hugg (Eds.), *Black America: Geographic perspectives* (pp. 157–174). Garden City, NY: Anchor/Doubleday.

Brown v. Board of Education of Topeka, Kansas, 347 U.S. 483 (1954).

Clark, K. B. (1965). *Dark ghetto.* New York: Harper & Row.

Coleman, J. (1966). *Equality of educational opportunity.* Washington, DC: U.S. Government Printing Office.

Conant, J. B. (1961). *Slums and suburbs.* New York: McGraw-Hill.

Harrington, M. (1963). *The other America.* Baltimore, MD: Penguin.

Hart, J. F. (1976). The changing distribution of the American Negro. In R. T. Ernst & L. Hugg (Eds.), *Black America: Geographic perspectives* (pp. 49–70). Garden City, NY: Anchor/Doubleday.

Hentschke, G. C., Lowe, W. T., & Royster, E. C. (1985). School desegregation policy for the next thirty years. *Urban Education, 20,* 149–175.

Hummel, R. C., & Nagle, J. M. (1973). *Urban education in America: Problems and prospects.* New York: Oxford University Press.

Irwin, J. R. (1973). *A ghetto principal speaks out: A decade of crisis in urban public schools.* Detroit: Wayne State University Press.

Jencks, C. (1972). *Inequality.* New York: Basic Books.

Morgan, P. R., & McPartland, J. M. (1981). *The extent of classroom segregation within desegregated schools.* Baltimore, MD: Center for Social Organization of Schools, Johns Hopkins University.

National Advisory Commission on Civil Disorders. (1968). *Report of the National Advisory Commission on Civil Disorders.* New York: Dutton.

Orfield, G. (1987). *School desegregation in the 1980s: Trends in the states and metropolitan areas.* Chicago: University of Chicago Press.

Ornstein, A. C. (1974). *Metropolitan schools: Administrative decentralization vs. community control.* Metuchen, NJ: Scarecrow.

Ornstein, A. C. (1982). The education of the disadvantaged: A 20-year review. *Educational Research, 24,* 197–211.

Riessman, F. (1962). *The culturally deprived child.* New York: Harper & Row.

Robey, B. (1985). *The American people: A timely exploration of a changing America and the important new demographic trends around us.* New York: Dutton.

Scarr, S. (1988). Race and gender as psychological variables. *American Psychologist, 43,* 56–59.

Sternlieb, G., & Hughes, J. W. (1987). *The dynamics of America's housing.* New Brunswick, NJ: Center for Urban Policy Research.

U.S. Bureau of the Census. (1984). *Projections of the population of the United States: 1983 to 2050.* Washington, DC: U.S. Government Printing Office.

U.S. Bureau of the Census. (1985). *Patterns of metropolitan areas and county population growth: 1980-1984.* Washington, DC: U.S. Government Printing Office.

U.S. Bureau of the Census. (1986). *Characteristics of the population below poverty level: 1984.* Washington, DC: U.S. Government Printing Office.

U.S. Bureau of the Census. (1987a). *Money income and poverty status of families and persons in the United States: 1986.* Washington, DC: U.S. Government Printing Office.

U.S. Bureau of the Census. (1987b). *Population profile of the United States: 1984-85.* Washington, DC: U.S. Government Printing Office.

U.S. Bureau of the Census. (1987c). *Social and economic characteristics of students: October 1983.* Washington, DC: U.S. Government Printing Office.

U.S. Commission on Civil Rights. (1967). *Racial isolation in the public schools.* Washington, DC: U.S. Government Printing Office.

U.S. Commission on Civil Rights. (1977a). *Reviewing a decade of school desegregation, 1966-1975.* Washington, DC: U.S. Government Printing Office.

U.S. Commission on Civil Rights. (1977b). *Statement of metropolitan school desegregation.* Washington, DC: U.S. Government Printing Office.

U.S. Department of Education, Center for Education Statistics. (1987). *The condition of education, 1986 edition.* Washington, DC: U.S. Government Printing Office.

U.S. Department of Health, Education, and Welfare. (1968). *Equality in educational opportunity.* Washington, DC: U.S. Government Printing Office.

Williams, T. M., & Kornblum, W. (1985). *Growing up poor.* Lexington, MA: Heath.

Wilson, W. J. (1987). *The truly disadvantaged.* Chicago: University of Chicago Press.

Witty, E. P. (1982). *Prospects for black teachers: Preparation, certification, employment.* Washington, DC: National Institute of Education.

5

Black Teachers: An Endangered Species in the 1990s

Patricia J. Larke
Department of Educational Curriculum and Instruction
Texas A&M University

The decreasing number of black elementary and secondary teachers[1] in the United States has captured national, state, and local attention. The entire minority teacher population in the United States constitutes only 10.3% of the total and includes 6.9% blacks, 1.9% Hispanics, 0.9% Asian-Americans, and 0.6% Native Americans (National Education Association [NEA], 1987; Office of Educational Research and Improvement, 1987). To compound that problem, demographic projections suggest that by 1990, minority teachers will make up much less than 10% of the total precollege teaching population. Black teachers are expected to account for only 5% (NEA, 1987). Moreover, the overall number of blacks entering institutions of higher education is decreasing, especially the number pursuing degrees in education (Arbeiter, 1987; Frankel & Gerald, 1980; Thomas, 1987). National and regional demographics, however, show that blacks, Hispanics, Asian-Americans, and Native Americans make up more than 30% of the student population in this country (Hodgkinson, 1985; Office of Educational Research and Improvement, 1987). Therefore in the 1990s, when more black students are expected to be in elementary and secondary schools, fewer black teachers will be at work than ever before.

The 26 largest school districts in the country, as well as the state of Texas, reflect the growing minority student population (Hodgkinson, 1985, 1986). Twenty-three of these 26 districts have more than 50% minority student populations. For the first time in Texas at the kindergarten and first-grade levels, minority students (Hispanics, blacks, Asian-Americans, and Native Americans) are the majority; thus the minority/majority reversal will be total by the year 2000 (Hodgkinson, 1986). If this demographic imbalance between minority teachers and minority students continues—and all evidence indicates that it will—the American educational system will become much more unbalanced and more educationally unsound for minority groups. Such a system is seriously detrimental to educational development and may have an adverse affect on racial and ethnic relations in the 1990s.

The severe shortage of black teachers in the 1990s will have the following negative effects: Few, if any, black teachers will be available to serve as role models for black

---

[1]"Black teachers" in this chapter refers to elementary and secondary teachers; "black students" refers to elementary and secondary students.

students, other minority students, and nonminority students, and little gain, if any, will be evident in black students' academic achievement levels. In addition, black students and students in general may think that a career in education is not valuable or feasible. Most important, the absence of black teachers' contributions to the richness of this country's educational system and to their communities will be a noticeable and irreplaceable loss for the nation. Accordingly, in this chapter I will attempt to address four important questions: (a) How and why did the shortage of black teachers occur? (b) What are the effects of the shortage? (c) What type of intervention can be used to affect the shortage for the 1990s? and (d) What are the implications of the present and projected future shortage of black teachers for race relations in the United States?

CONTRIBUTIONS TO THE SHORTAGE

The shortage of black teachers did not occur overnight; it came about through a gradual process that involved a number of elements. In general, the declining number of black teachers can be attributed to several related factors: (a) the *Brown v. Board of Education of Topeka, Kansas* (1954) decision, (b) competency testing, (c) educational reform movements, and (d) improved employment opportunities for blacks.

The *Brown* Decision

Historically, black teachers were plentiful, especially during the era of segregated schools from *Plessy v. Ferguson* (1896) to *Brown v. Board of Education* (1954). Yet a severe shortage of black teachers developed during the 34-year period since the *Brown* decision. The intent of the *Brown* decision was to provide all students with an equal education, regardless of race, by overruling the *Plessy* decision of "separate but equal facilities." During the last 30 years, many physical facilities have been improved through major renovation and construction of public school buildings. Some suggest that it would have been more beneficial if that growth could have been reflected in minority students' academic achievements (Hooks, 1984; Reid & Foster-Davis, 1984; Webb, 1986). Clark (1988) pointed out that the human aspect of the *Brown* decision has not materialized for blacks.

As a result of the "unforeseen circumstances" (Webb, 1986, p. 1) of the *Brown* decision, many black teachers and administrators lost their jobs, many black schools were closed because of inadequate facilities, and a disproportionate number of black students were bused to white schools, where supposedly better facilities and academic programs existed (Ethridge, 1979; George, 1985; Hooks, 1984; Reid & Foster-Davis, 1984; V. B. Smith, 1988; Webb, 1986). As black students were bused to "white" schools, black teachers were assigned to those schools. Many black teachers were given teaching assignments in noncertified areas and were demoted from their previous positions, as from department head to teacher, from administrator to teacher, and even from teacher to teacher's aide. It was not uncommon for black teachers to be placed in teaching assignments for which they were not certified and to be asked to seek certification in a new area, often according to new standards. Many were unable to obtain certification in the new areas; therefore, frequently they were dismissed, were given teacher's aide positions or office aide assignments, or sought early retirement (Ethridge, 1979; Witty, 1982).

One indirect result of the *Brown* decision concerns disparities between the rates of employment for black teachers and for white teachers (Ethridge, 1979; George,

1985; Witty, 1982). In Kentucky from 1954 to 1984, for example, the number of employed black teachers increased by only 14%, compared to a 78% increase in the number of employed white teachers. For every 76 white teachers employed, only *1* black teacher was employed (George, 1985, pp. 2–4). Unfortunately, similar statistics are reported for many other states: South Carolina, North Carolina, Georgia, Missouri, West Virginia, Mississippi, Texas, Alabama, and Arkansas (Ethridge, 1979, pp. 217–232). Clearly, the 30-year period following the *Brown* decision has had a devastating effect on black teachers and administrators. Their numbers were reduced drastically to support the consolidation of facilities and services, a move designed to provide equal facilities that were no longer separate (Ethridge, 1979; George, 1985; Webb, 1986; Witty, 1982, 1986).

Competency Testing

Numerous researchers and educators have noted that the impact of competency testing (such as that achieved through the National Teacher Exam, the California Basic Educational Skills Test, and the Preprofessional Skills Test) has reduced dramatically the number of black teachers (Davis, 1984; Dilworth, 1986; Dupré, 1986; Gifford, 1985, 1986; Hilliard, 1986; Oliver, 1988; Popham, 1986; G. P. Smith, 1984a, 1984b, 1984c, 1988; Witty, 1982, 1986). This reduction occurred in part because many black education majors and black teachers were unable to meet the new score requirements for certification. As of 1987, 48 states had adopted or were considering some form of competency-based testing for teachers, such as an admissions test, a certification test, a recertification test, and/or a performance assessment test (Burks, 1987; Rudner et al., 1987). Burkes and Rudner et al. noted further that 24 states use admissions tests for teacher applicants, 26 states use certification tests as a requirement for teacher certification, 3 states (Texas, Georgia, and Arkansas) have tested in-service teachers, and 7 states have used performance assessments to evaluate first-year teachers. According to Jones (1986), black teachers in Virginia score significantly higher on performance tests than their white counterparts. One implication of this research is that an alternative process for selecting minority teachers is to rely on more applied knowledge (Jones, 1986).

The most popular certification test for teachers is the National Teacher Examination (NTE). Twenty-two states now use the NTE as one of their criteria for teacher certification (Burks, 1987). Many studies have revealed that substantial decreases in the number of black teachers are correlated with the states' adoption of the NTE as a requirement for certification (Ethridge, 1979; Gifford, 1986; Pressman & Gartner, 1986; G. P. Smith, 1984a, 1984b, 1984c, 1988; Witty, 1982). Garibaldi (1986) reported that in Louisiana between 1978 and 1982, only 211 of 1,400 blacks, or 15%, passed the NTE. During the same period, the rate of passing among whites was 4,000 of 5,200, or 77%. Similar trends have been identified in studies by G. P. Smith (1984a, 1984b, 1984c) and Gifford (1986). According to G. P. Smith (1984a, p. 125), the legal decision in *United States v. State of South Carolina* (1977) provided the impetus to many states' acceptance and adoption of a competency test such as the NTE as a means of certifying teachers. In this decision it was held that states legally could use minimum score requirements on the National Teacher Examination both to certify teachers and to determine their pay levels. It was held that this procedure should not violate a person's rights as guaranteed by the Fourteenth Amendment or by Title VII of the Civil Rights Act of 1964.

Historically, some states—South Carolina, North Carolina, and Louisiana—awarded differentiated certificates with various cutoff scores. Today the score is an integral part of the certification process; it determines entry into the profession regardless of the academic performance of education majors in undergraduate classes or their performance as student teachers. This change in the certification process also seems to be correlated with the loss of black teachers (Ethridge, 1979; Witty, 1982).

Because it regulates the number and the race or ethnicity of participants, competency testing has been regarded as the gatekeeper of the teaching profession (Porter & Freeman, 1986). Unfortunately, as Porter and Freeman pointed out, the gate is closed more often to black and Hispanic teacher candidates than to white candidates. In California, Georgia, Oklahoma, and Florida, for example, the failure rate on competency-based exams is 50% higher for black and Hispanic candidates than for white candidates (Pressman & Gartner, 1986).

As states mandate and approve legislation to implement competency testing for teachers, evidence from educational research continues to accumulate showing that these tests do not conclusively improve education or evaluate a teacher's performance fairly. Many educators and researchers maintain that the most valid assessment of a teacher's instructional skills and quality is student outcomes (Garcia, 1986; Gifford, 1986; Pressman & Gartner, 1986).

Educational Reform

The current educational reform movement started years before the National Commission on Excellence in Education (1983) released *A Nation at Risk*. Historically, the purpose of educational reform movements was to devise or develop programs and policies to improve students' academic achievement, teacher education, and teacher certification. For example, the "Sputnik revolution" of the 1950s was implemented in order to strengthen the mathematics, science, and foreign language curricula and to improve students' performance in those areas.

In the early 1980s, however, *A Nation at Risk* drew national attention and galvanized the current reform movement in education. Presently, all states except Alaska and Iowa have implemented or will implement some type of educational reform policy and/or program (Rudner et al., 1987). States initially began to adopt reform legislation for elementary and secondary students, such as competency-based testing. Later they adopted or considered legislation to reform teacher education, especially teacher certification requirements such as entrance and exit examinations. The actions of these states also may be related to the diminishing number of black teachers in many states. Texas, Florida, Georgia, Louisiana, and Virginia readily embraced the new certification initiatives (Gifford, 1985; G. P. Smith, 1984a, 1984b, 1984c).

As reforms are implemented, one study reveals, many states are unable to supply the required number of certified teachers because teacher education institutions are not producing the necessary number of new teachers (Corrigan, 1986). Corrigan pointed out that in Texas during the 1982–1983 academic year, the Texas Education Agency issued more emergency permits (1-year certificates issued when certified teachers are unavailable) than the number of qualified graduates. This trend is evident in many other states (such as Florida, North Carolina, and California), particularly those in which the minority school-age population is increasing (G. P. Smith, 1984a, 1984b, 1984c). Research confirms that as states promote mandates intended to improve education, many state offices of education issue emergency permits to individuals who by definition are unqualified to teach (Corrigan, 1986; Graham, 1987).

Largely as a result of national reports such as *Tomorrow's Teachers* (The Holmes Group, 1986) and *A Nation Prepared* (Carnegie Forum on Education and the Economy, 1985), institutions of higher education are implementing curriculum changes in their teacher education programs, some as a direct response to these reports and others in response to state mandates. These reports have had and are continuing to have a major impact on teacher preparation throughout this country. Many educators, however, are concerned that the issue of increasing minority (especially black) representation in the teaching profession is not addressed adequately in these reports. Dilworth (1988), B. Gordon (1988), and G. P. Smith (1988) are among the many who have pointed out that the Holmes and Carnegie reports did not adequately discuss the increasing shortage of minority teachers and its impact on education. Specifically, the Holmes report, which is 97 pages long, discusses minority issues in only two paragraphs; the Carnegie report discusses minority issues in only 8 of 135 pages (B. Gordon, 1988, p. 149).

In addition to giving minimal coverage to minorities in its report, The Holmes Group committee included only one committee member (Howard University) from the 116 historically black colleges and universities (HBCUs), even though the HBCUs have produced a significant percentage of the black teachers to date (Dilworth, 1988; B. Gordon, 1988; G. P. Smith, 1988). Thus the educational reform initiatives have shown little visible concern about the shortage of black teachers. It is evident, however, that even as reforms are implemented and discussed at length, the number of black teachers is decreasing steadily (B. Gordon, 1988).

Improved Employment Opportunities

The civil rights movement of the 1960s, coupled with federal decisions (Title VII of the Civil Rights Act, Title IX of the 1972 Education Amendments, and affirmative action policies), made many employment opportunities other than teaching available to blacks (Graham, 1987). Historically, teaching was a career for many blacks because of its link to upward mobility and improved socioeconomic status. Today, however, teaching is only one of many career options available to blacks and other minorities (Graham, 1987).

Over the last two decades, recruitment efforts and affirmative action policies in other careers such as engineering and business began to attract blacks who previously might have considered teaching careers. Between 1976 and 1985, the number of black students in engineering increased from 10% to 11.6%; blacks in business increased from 7.3% to 11.2%. During the same period, the number of education students decreased from 12% to 10.5% (American Council on Education [ACE], 1987). Research data show increases in the percentage of black students in fields other than education (ACE, 1987), but recent studies indicate a decline in the overall number of black graduate and undergraduate students (Arbeiter, 1987; Darling-Hammond, 1985; Thomas, 1987). This development means not only that fewer blacks are going to college, but that within that reduced pool of eligibles, fewer blacks are seeking teaching careers.

Throughout their elementary and secondary school years, black students (potential teacher candidates) will encounter many black teachers and administrators who have been displaced, demoted, or even dismissed because of desegregation plans, racism, and discrimination (Ethridge, 1979; Witty, 1982). This situation creates a sense of hopelessness for many potential black teachers. Therefore black students seek careers in industry and government, which seem to provide greater job security and financial rewards. In addition, many minority and nonminority teachers are encouraging high-achieving black students to seek careers in fields other than education in order to combat or overcome previous denial of access to nontraditional careers and working conditions that perpetuate overt as well as subtle racism, sexism, prejudice, and individual and institutional discrimination (S. Johnson & Prom-Johnson, 1986). Therefore the shortage of black teachers also may be attributed to black students' decisions to seek employment opportunities in noneducation careers.

EFFECTS OF THE SHORTAGE

The effects of the shortage of black teachers are devastating to the teaching profession and, more important, to the lives of black children. Black teachers are seen as visible and contributing professionals in their respective communities. It is important that black children observe and associate with teachers of their own racial group; such association reinforces for black students and others the fact that blacks are and can be productive and contributing members of society (Graham, 1987; Holmes, 1988). Because of today's shortage, many children have only a 1 in 20 probability of being taught by a black teacher (NEA, 1987). Many students will pass through school without ever having a black teacher, especially in regions where a large black student population exists. The most catastrophic result of such a shortage is the loss of role models for black students (Cooper, 1988; Graham, 1987; Holmes, 1988; Mercer, 1983) as well as for other minority and nonminority students. In addition, the increase in black high school dropouts and the decrease in black college enrollments mean an irreclaimable loss in the number of black students who might have become teachers (Arbeiter, 1987; Graham, 1987; Intercultural Development Research Association, 1986).

Role Models

Role models, particularly teachers, are highly instrumental in shaping children's attitudes, beliefs, and values (Biddle, 1979). Overtly and covertly, children emulate their teachers' values and behaviors. Studies reveal that black students' lack of access to black role models in education is perpetuating a system of white middle-class values, beliefs, and attitudes that are counterproductive to the self-concept and the cultural and educational development of black students (Cooper, 1988; Graham, 1987; Holmes, 1988; Mercer, 1983). The visibility of black teachers provides some stability for black students. This visibility also assures others, especially parents, that black students' educational needs will be addressed adequately by someone who shares their racial/ethnic identity (Franklin, 1987). The dominant group in American society and schools has not addressed blacks' educational concerns or needs (Gilbert & Gay, 1985; Gollnick & Chinn, 1986; Sleeter & Grant, 1988). Hayes (1987) suggested that the loss of black teachers will greatly reduce the ambitions of black students. Therefore one of the most direct ways to address black students' concerns is through increased black representation within the teaching profession.

DECREASING THE SHORTAGE

To increase the number of black teachers, more effective programs and policies must be implemented on all educational levels. A prerequisite is to increase the pool of black students enrolling in college and entering the teaching profession. Programs and policies designed to achieve this goal and the broader objective of increasing the number of black teachers must be developed and directed toward the following: (a) black elementary and secondary students, (b) in-service teachers and administrators, (c) black parents, (d) institutions of higher education, (e) teacher education programs, (f) predominantly black colleges and universities, and (g) educational decision makers.

Black Elementary and Secondary Students

The quality of education for black students determines strongly the size of the pool of potential black teachers. Specific career awareness and recruitment programs must be initiated in the early stages of black students' educational development. Educational research supports overwhelmingly the idea that black students need black role models (Cooper, 1988; Graham, 1987; Holmes, 1988; Mercer, 1983). According to the National Education Association (1987), blacks constitute 16.2% of the student population in this country but only 6.9% of the teachers. Because blacks constitute such a small percentage of teachers, it is obvious that many schools have few, if any, black teachers. Yet through the use of school adoption programs, black fraternities and sororities (both graduate and undergraduate chapters) could adopt these schools. A school adoption program would allow fraternity and sorority members to serve as role models for black students. In addition, they could provide academic support for black elementary and secondary students and community involvement for many black undergraduates.

Such involvement would provide black undergraduates at predominantly white institutions with more involvement and ties to the community. Retired black educators, an important resource group, also could provide effective role models. School districts could use this group as substitute teachers. Wherever possible, school districts should collaborate with institutions of higher education to develop innovative educational programs that would encourage equity and excellence for black students. In addition to developing programs, educators from higher education, graduate students, public school teachers, and teachers' associations could initiate a "Teaching As a Profession" organization. The purposes of this organization would be to campaign for teaching careers (using the media, clubs, organizations, and churches) and to visit and speak with black students on aspects of teaching as a career (e.g., preparation, career options, and intrinsic rewards).

As early as possible, black students must be exposed to college campuses in order to implant the idea that higher education is a viable option for them. Texas A&M University's Minority Mentorship Project (Larke & Wiseman, 1987) is an example of a program designed for this purpose. This program provides opportunities for sixth-grade black and Hispanic students to be paired with a preservice teacher for 3 years. The Minority Mentorship Project provides 25 minority students (blacks and Hispanics) with academic, educational, and social support, tutoring, and mentoring that encourage and promote success and achievement in school. Many of these activities take place on the university campus. In addition, the Minority Mentorship Project is designed to sensitize preservice teachers to the needs of minority students while simultaneously sharpening their pedagogical knowledge and expanding their teaching and instructional skills. Most important, this project serves as an early recruitment effort to attract more black and Hispanic students into teaching careers.

In-Service Teachers and Administrators

Effective research on schools, teachers, and principals suggests that high levels of commitment and sensitivity, coupled with acceptance, respect, and high expectations, are instrumental in producing high-achieving black students (Brookover, 1985). High commitment is demonstrated by staffing patterns, curricula, instructional practices, and school–community relations. High sensitivity is demonstrated by knowledge of the students' culture, values, beliefs, and home environment (Brookover, 1985; Mills, 1983). Therefore, through the use of their in-service training programs, school districts could develop and disseminate relevant research findings to their teachers and administrators.

In addition, training in multicultural education could be required and reinforced strongly. This training should be thorough and extensive and should be conducted by personnel trained in this area. Many teacher education institutions have staff members who are trained as multicultural education specialists. Multicultural in-service programs often require 1-hour training sessions that are expected to provide quick fixes for complicated problems; administrators must set the tone for the success of such training. In addition, teachers must be trained to match their teaching styles with their students' learning styles. The fact that students possess different learning styles implies that all students can learn.

At every opportunity, teachers and administrators should encourage black students to seek careers in education. These educators must influence and recruit black students to participate in various student–teacher organizations (such as Future Teachers of America) and activities (such as working with younger children or taking part in a student-as-teacher day).

Black Parents

Research by Slaughter and Epps (1987) summarized several studies which found that black parents are instrumental in setting the educational goals for their children. Far too often, poor black parents have been labeled as uncaring in regard to their children's education (Webster, 1974). Most poor black parents, however, do care and want the best for their children. Many educators may not be aware of the various problems that diminish some black parents' ability to give full support to the educational process. These problems include parents' perceptions of negative attitudes exhibited toward them by office staff members, teachers, counselors, and administrators in school settings (Webster, 1974, p. 146). According to Webster, many black parents of lower socioeconomic status believe that by avoiding the school, they will not be embarrassed because of their incorrect speech, inexpensive dress, and/or limited academic knowledge. Because of these perceptions, when parents see their children failing or being suspending, retained, or placed in special classes, they feel a sense of hopelessness in attempting to interact with school personnel (Webster, 1974, pp. 147–151).

As former students, many black parents remember negative experiences such as low expectations by teachers, low achievement, academic failure, and even mistreatment by teachers and administrators (Webster, 1974). Therefore they view the school as an external institution rather than as a vital part of their community. Within many schools, activities designed for parental involvement do little to encourage the participation of black parents; most executive offices of parent–teacher groups are held by white middle-class parents. Therefore sustained and concerted efforts must be made to include and encourage black parents' participation. Programs should be developed that solicit and consider black parents' opinions on school matters. Such programs also must encourage black parents to feel a sense of ownership in their children's school, thus increasing their involvement.

Predominantly White Institutions of Higher Education

As shown by national reports (Carnegie Forum on Education and the Economy, 1985; The Holmes Group, 1986), institutions of higher education—particularly colleges and departments of education (CDEs)—need to think seriously about enhancing educational opportunities for black students who seek careers in education. Recruitment and retention of black students should be a top priority of CDEs, as expressed through the development and implementation of the necessary supportive policies and programs. These programs should provide financial, academic, and interpersonal or social mechanisms to enhance and support recruitment and retention efforts.

As CDEs set goals to increase the numbers of black students, staff development programs also must be developed to raise levels of awareness about black students' concerns and needs. To recruit black students from junior colleges (many black students attend junior college before becoming eligible for admission to major 4-year institutions), CDEs should organize a mentor network between junior college students and professors in the CDEs. This mentoring network could (a) help black students to build appropriate academic records for pursuing a degree in education; (b) help ease the black student's transition between junior college and the 4-year college; and (c) provide academic and moral support for black students transferring to the CDEs.

CDEs should establish a network of teachers to assist counselors in their efforts to prepare and recruit black students. Historically, institutions of higher education have relied on counselors to recruit black students, but this method has proven ineffective. Use of additional personnel such as teachers and administrators should enhance success in recruiting black students.

Finally, CDEs should encourage and reward faculty members for conducting research on the concerns and needs of black students, for developing programs that foster equity in academic success, and for implementing programs to improve the recruitment and retention of black students. This recognition should be incorporated into the tenure and promotion process and into the merit system. Faculty members should receive release time in which to conduct much-needed research on minority concerns such as learning styles, instructional strategies, and socioeconomic factors related to education.

Teacher Education Programs

Teacher education programs should prepare all teachers to teach in a culturally diverse society. Current demographics show a steady increase in the minority student population (Hodgkinson, 1985, 1986). This finding suggests that teacher education programs need to reflect an integrated, multicultural approach in general methods and education courses, in addition to offering specific multicultural education courses. Teacher education programs must broaden pedagogical knowledge and sharpen teachers' instructional skills so that teachers can work more effectively with the growing number of black and other minority students in elementary and secondary schools. In addition, these programs must modify attitudes, values, and beliefs of preservice and in-service teachers to eradicate stereotypical misconceptions about black students.

The field component of teacher education should provide students with experiences in working with black and other minority children in urban, suburban, or rural settings. Too often, the academic view of school is incompatible with the reality in classrooms; thus preservice and in-service minority teachers often become disillusioned and confused, and students may suffer. It is imperative that preservice teachers receive accurate and current information about blacks' and other minority students' racial and ethnic heritage, cultural characteristics and values, home environments, learning styles, language diversity, and behavioral interactions, and be given appropriate, effective, and relevant teaching strategies. These are necessary components that teacher education programs should implement in preparing teachers to work more effectively with the changing student population.

Historically Black Colleges and Universities

The contributions of HBCUs to the teaching profession are numerous (Hatton, 1988; Witty, 1982). A significant percentage of black teachers were trained in HCBUs, and most black professionals received their undergraduate degrees from black institutions of higher education (Hatton, 1988). Yet today, colleges of education at HCBUs are experiencing declines in the number of black students (some of whom are potential teachers), and their graduates are suffering high failure rates in both entrance and exit competency examinations (Spencer, 1986).

As depressing as this condition may seem, however, some HBCUs (such as Xavier University and Grambling State University, both located in Louisiana) are experiencing successes. Data from Xavier University show that an average of 90% of its education students pass the National Teacher Examination for certification (Garibaldi, 1986). In 1978–1979 only 20% of the education students at Grambling State University passed the National Teacher Examination; in 1983–1984 the rate had risen to 86% (Spencer, 1986). HBCU faculty members who are experiencing low success rates could collaborate with those at sister institutions which are enjoying high success rates. These faculty members could work together to develop and design strategies for improvement. Foundations, such as The Woodrow Wilson Foundation, also might support faculty exchange programs to bring faculty from predominantly black institutions to predominantly white institutions, and vice versa, in order to develop innovative programs to increase black students' success rates on competency-based tests.

Educational Decision Makers

Most decisions regarding educational policies and practices are made not by educators (Callahan & Clark, 1983; Provenzo, 1986) but by politicians, business people, school board members, and members of other concerned interest groups (Provenzo, 1986). Most of these individuals are white males of middle to high socioeconomic status. Advisory groups could provide these decision makers with accurate, factual information so that policies and laws would not reflect subtle discriminatory practices. As state legislatures designate funding for public education, they might be encouraged to set salaries for teachers that are competitive with those in other careers. In many instances, public school funding is the first item to be cut when states face budget deficits. The average teacher's salary in 1987 was $26,551 (Johnson, 1988); compared to salaries in other professional careers, this figure is quite low. Increased salaries will help make teaching a more attractive career and conceivably will increase blacks' participation (NEA, 1987). Educational decision makers must develop and propose policies that incorporate strategies to increase the number of black teachers. These decision makers, whether they are local, state, or national, must become aware that the absence of black teachers reduces the quality of the educational programs within their jurisdictions.

Black Teachers and Race Relations in the United States

In the 1990s American society will be depleted of an important human resource: the black teacher. Historically, black teachers have been a formidable force, contributing greatly to the educational and developmental needs of black students (Ethridge, 1979; Hatton, 1988; Holmes, 1986; Witty, 1982). They have molded and educated a vast number of black students (Holmes, 1988). Without these individuals, in the next decade this nation will be robbed of a human element hat provides immeasurable warmth, encouragement, and support to many black Americans.

The impact of the shortage of black teachers suggests three specific implications for race relations in the 1990s. First, the absence of black teachers means that a group of black professionals no longer will contribute as abundantly to economic, political, and social agendas at all levels of government. In addition to providing educational leadership, many black teachers are the spokespersons for their communities on political and social concerns.

Second, the absence of black teachers will mean an absence of black representation in civic affairs. School board members and other elected officials educate nonblacks about the concerns and needs of the black community. These social concerns may include acts of racial injustice, discriminatory practices, or prejudicial attitudes faced by members of local communities. In some areas, black teachers and preachers are the only educated persons in their communities and have the authority to speak on behalf of the community about race-related issues. Thus when these individuals are not adequately represented, the stability and the well-being of the black community are affected directly and indirectly.

Finally, if black teachers are absent, their views will not be voiced in the colloquy that strengthens black and white race relations. Black teachers serve to facilitate race relations because of the trust and respect accorded to them by their community. In addition, black teachers have the responsibility to articulate the needs and concerns of the black community. They bring stability to black communities, whereas black professionals in management or in business are more mobile. Blacks teachers are the largest group of successful black professionals contributing to American society. As the number of black teachers decreases in the 1990s, the number of resource persons for improving race relations will decrease just when they are needed more than ever. This need is evident for two reasons: (a) the increase in racial incidents in the United

States within the last few years (notably those on college campuses), and (b) the resegregation within schools, as evidenced by desegregated school buildings and segregated
classrooms (P. Gordon, 1988; V. B. Smith, 1988).

It has been noted that the more educated a person is about other cultures and races,
the less threatening persons of a different culture or race become (Banks, 1988;
Simpson & Yinger, 1985). Thus one of the black teacher's many roles has been to
educate others about the black culture in order to improve race relations. From all
indications, in the 1990s the intercultural education provided by black teachers will
still be needed greatly.

CONCLUSION

There is no doubt that the substantial loss of black teachers jeopardizes the educational system in this country. The seriousness of this concern has warranted much
attention from persons both inside and outside education. The professional literature
has been inundated with articles, studies, and research reports on the catastrophes
attending the decline in the number of black teachers. Many professional meetings
have included the topic on their agendas. Thus it is not surprisingly that this issue will
be a major concern for the 1990s. At that time it is projected that the percentage of
black teachers will reach a record low of about 5%. This downward trend is occurring at the same time as the student population of blacks and other minorities is
increasing.

As this chapter suggests, several factors contributed indirectly or directly to the
shortage. The decision in *Brown v. Board of Education* is an indirect factor in that it
was intended to correct the injustices in education in this country; yet those injustices
still exist. Many school districts are being released from desegregation rulings that
were mandated in the 1970s, and schools are becoming more segregated. Therefore
the *Brown* decision has not been implemented fully for black teachers or black students.

Competency-based testing is a more direct concern in that states have agreed to
adopt competency-based testing to improve educational standards. Yet no conclusive
evidence exists that such testing improves the quality of education. The quality of
teaching is measured more appropriately by the quality of student outcomes. It is
evident that more black teachers have lost their jobs and that black education majors
are not passing the competency-based tests for certification. At the same time, however, white students are passing at high rates. Although some black institutions are
showing increased rates of success, these increases constitute a rather small number
of black candidates in teacher education programs. In one black institution, 6 of 156
students passed the NTE in 1976; in 1983, 39 of 43 passed this test. Although the
latter percentage is much higher, the number of candidates seeking and attaining
degrees in education is considerably lower.

As more teacher education reform mandates are implemented, the number of black
teachers who lose their jobs becomes disproportionately high. In addition, black
education students frequently are unsuccessful in meeting the new program requirements instituted by reform legislation. Therefore the educational agenda for the 1990s
must include alternative and valid certification methods that do not inhibit racial or
ethnic groups' representation in the teaching profession. According to Cooper (1988),
the teacher not only imparts knowledge to students but also contributes to students'
cultural development. Therefore the shortage of black teachers will ensure that many

students are denied such experiences. This denial will hinder students from participating actively in the pluralistic society of America.

To change the conditions producing underrepresentation of black teachers, all educational institutions (from elementary schools to colleges and universities), parents, communities, and educational decision makers must be involved. This involvement must be exhibited equally in schools by students, teachers, administrators, parents, and school board members. If programs and policies are not developed and implemented to increase the number of black teachers, the possibility of black teachers and other minority teachers becoming an endangered species in the 1990s will be a depressing reality throughout the educational system. Such a situation would have a negative effect on the political, economic, and social systems in this country. S. Johnson and Prom-Johnson (1986) captured the seriousness of the situation when they stated, "To lose [black] teachers who would teach well is a tragedy; to replace [black] teachers with those who may teach punitively and carelessly is criminal" (p. 283).

It is unsound educationally to justify, however subtly, an educational system that does not reflect the prevailing racial and ethnic makeup of the United States within its professional ranks. The evidence indicates clearly that black teachers make a significant difference in the education of black children and such valuable lives are not worth the excuse "I can't find any"; more school-age black children exist than ever before who need the exposure to black teachers. Because of changes during the 1990s and into the twenty-first century, one of every three members of the work force ultimately will belong to a minority group. Statistically, that minority person has a 40% probability of being black.

Thus increasing the number of black teachers must be included among the priorities for educational agendas in the next decade. As programs and policies are developed to improve education, procedures must reflect a means to increase the number of black teachers. Suggestions include external monetary rewards (fellowships and scholarships) and intrinsic incentives (the need for black professional role models) to encourage black students to seek careers in education. Most important, black students must be provided with the assistance necessary to pass the entrance and exit examinations.

If steps are not taken to increase the number of black teachers, it is highly probable that race relations in the United States will be threatened. As Walter Mercer (1983) pointed out, the absence of black teachers in public schools teaches "white supremacy" in its most subtle form. This ideology is antithetical to cultural pluralism and can only foster negative interactions. Without question, the shortage of black teachers will continue to be detrimental to healthy school environments if the problem goes unaddressed in the 1990s.

REFERENCES

American Association of Colleges for Teacher Education. (1987). *Minority teacher recruitment and retention: A call for action.* Unpublished manuscript.

American Council on Education. (1987). *Minorities in higher education: Sixth annual status report.* Washington, DC: Author.

Arbeiter, S. (1987). Black enrollments: The case of the missing students. *Change, 19*, 14–19.

Banks, J. (1988). *Multiethnic education.* Boston: Allyn & Bacon.

Biddle, B. (1979). *Role theory expectations, identities and behaviors.* New York: Academic Press.

Brookover, W. (1985). Can we make school effective for minority students? *Journal of Negro Education, 54,* 257–268.

Brown v. Board of Education of Topeka, Kansas, 347 U.S. 483 (1954).

Burks, M. P. (1987). *Requirements for certification* (57th ed.). Chicago: University of Chicago Press.

Callahan, J. F., & Clark, L. (1983). *Foundations of education* (2nd ed.). New York: Macmillan.

Carnegie Forum on Education and the Economy. (1985). *A nation prepared: Teachers for the 21st century.* New York: Carnegie Corporation.

Clark, K. B. (1988). The Brown decision: Racism, education, and human values. *Journal of Negro Education, 57,* 125–127.

Cooper, C. C. (1988). Implications of the absence of black teachers/administrators on black youth. *Journal of Negro Education, 57,* 123–124.

Corrigan, D. (1986). Politics and teacher education reform. *Journal of Teacher Education, 36,* 8–11.

Darling-Hammond, L. (1985). *Equality and excellence: The educational status of black Americans.* New York: College Entrance Examination Board.

Davis, M. (1984). *Prospective black teachers and the closing door: Strategies for entry.* Birmingham: Alabama Center for Higher Education.

Dilworth, M. (1986). Teacher testing: Adjustments for schools, colleges and departments of education. *Journal of Negro Education, 55,* 368–378.

Dilworth, M. (1988). A continuing critique of the Holmes group. *Journal of Negro Education, 57,* 199–201.

Dupré, B. (1986). Problems regarding the survival of future black teachers in education. *Journal of Negro Education, 55,* 56–66.

Ethridge, S. B. (1979). Impact of the 1954 *Brown v. Topeka Board of Education* decision on black educators. *Negro Educational Review, 30,* 217–232.

Frankel, M., & Gerald, D. E. (1980). *Projections of education statistics to 1988–89.* Washington, DC: National Center for Education Statistics.

Franklin, J. H. (1987). The desperate need for black teachers. *Change, 19,* 44–45.

Garcia, P. A. (1986). The impact of national testing on ethnic minorities: With proposed solutions. *Journal of Negro Education, 55,* 347–357.

Garibaldi, A. (1986). Sustaining black educational progress: Challenges for the 1990's. *Journal of Negro Education, 55,* 386–396.

George, E. (1985). *Black teachers lose employment ground, 1954–84.* Louisville: Kentucky Commission on Human Rights.

Gifford, B. R. (1985). Minority representation in the teaching profession: An affirmative program. *American Educator, 9,* 16, 18–19, 43.

Gifford, B. R. (1986). Excellence and equity in teacher competency testing: A policy perspective. *Journal of Negro Education, 55,* 251–271.

Gilbert, S. E., II, & Gay, G. (1985). Improving the success of poor black children. *Phi Delta Kappan, 67,* 133–137.

Gollnick, D. M., & Chinn, P. (1986). *Multicultural education in a pluralistic society* (2nd ed.). Columbus, OH: Merrill.

Gordon, B. M. (1988). Implicit assumptions of the Holmes and Carnegie reports: View from an African-American perspective. *Journal of Negro Education, 55,* 141–158.

Gordon, P. (1988, February 20). School busing for desegregation ordered halted in Fort Worth. *Dallas Morning News,* Section B, pp. 13–14.

Graham, P. A. (1987). Black teachers: A drastically scarce resource. *Phi Delta Kappan, 68,* 598–605.

Hatton, B. R. (1988). A game plan for ending the minority teacher shortage. *NEA Today, 6,* 66–69.

Hayes, D. W. (1987). The children of the baby boomers need teachers. *Black Collegian, 17,* 120–125.

Hilliard, A. G., III. (1986). Hurdles to standards of quality in teacher testing. *Journal of Negro Education, 55,* 304–315.

Hodgkinson, H. L. (1985). *All one system: Demographics of education—kindergarten through graduate school.* Washington, DC: Institute for Educational Leadership.

Hodgkinson, H. L. (1986). *Texas: The state and its educational system.* Washington, DC: Institute for Educational Leadership.

Holmes, B. (1986). Do not buy the conventional wisdom: Minority teachers can pass the tests. *Journal of Negro Education, 55,* 293–303.

Holmes, B. (1988, August 19). Why black teachers are essential. *Black Issues in Higher Education,* pp. 17, 19.

The Holmes Group. (1986). *Tomorrow's teachers.* East Lansing: Michigan State University.

Hooks, B. (1984). Thirty years after *Brown v. Board of Education. Crisis, 91,* 24.

Intercultural Development Research Association. (1986). *Texas school dropout survey project: A summary of findings.* San Antonio: Author.

Johnson, S., & Prom-Johnson, S. (1986). The memorable teacher: Implications for teacher selection. *Journal of Negro Education, 55,* 272–283.

Jones, C. (1986, April 1). Evaluation shows black and white teachers equal: Virginia results diminish validity of test use. *Black Issues in Higher Education,* p. 1.

Larke, P. J., & Wiseman, D. (1987). *Minority Mentorship Project, Texas A&M University.* Unpublished manuscript, Texas A&M University.

Mercer, W. (1983). The gathering storm: Teacher testing and black teachers. *Educational Leadership, 41,* 70–71.

Mills, J. (1983). Multicultural education: Where do we go from here? *Journal of Social and Behavioral Sciences, 2,* 43–51.

National Commission on Excellence in Education. (1983). *A nation at risk: The imperative for educational reform.* Washington, DC: U.S. Government Printing Office.

National Education Association. (1987). *Status of the American public school teachers, 1985-1986.* Washington, DC: Author.

Office of Educational Research and Improvement. (1987). *U.S. Department of Education digest of educational statistics, 1987.* Washington, DC: U.S. Government Printing Office.

Oliver, B. (1988). Structuring the teaching force: Will minority teachers suffer? *Journal of Negro Education, 57,* 159–165.

Plessy v. Ferguson, 163 U.S. 537 (1896).

Popham, W. J. (1986). Teacher competency testing: The devil's dilemma. *Journal of Negro Education, 55,* 379–385.

Porter, A. C., & Freeman, D. J. (1986). Professional orientations: An essential domain for teacher testing. *Journal of Negro Education, 55,* 284–292.

Pressman, H., & Gartner, A. (1986). The new racism in education. *Social Policy, 17,* 11–15.

Provenzo, E. F. (1986). *An introduction to American society.* Columbus, OH: Merrill.

Reid, H. O., & Foster-Davis, F. M. (1984). Three decades of "All deliberate speed". *Crisis, 91,* 12–15.

Rudner, L., Adelman, N., Algina, J., Galluzzo, G. R., Gifford, B. R., McCarthy, M. M., McKinney, K. C., & Sandefur, J. T. (1987). *What's happening in teacher practices.* Washington, DC: Office of Educational Research and Improvement.

Simpson, G., & Yinger, M. (1985). *Racial and cultural minorities.* New York: Plenum.

Slaughter, D. T., & Epps, E. G. (1987). The home environment and academic achievement of black American children and youth: An overview. *Journal of Negro Education, 56,* 3–20.

Sleeter, C., & Grant, C. (1988). *Making choices for multicultural education.* Columbus, OH: Merrill.

Smith, G. P. (1984a). Competency testing: Excellence without equity. *Journal of Teacher Education, 35,* 6–9.

Smith, G. P. (1984b). Critical issues of excellence and equity in competency testing. *Texas Tech Journal of Education, 12,* 125–129.

Smith, G. P. (1984c). *Impact of competency tests on teacher education: Ethical and legal issues in selecting and certifying teachers.* Unpublished manuscript.

Smith, G. P. (1988). Tomorrow's white teachers: A response to the Holmes group. *Journal of Negro Education, 57,* 178–194.

Smith, V. B. (1988, March 7). Busing: How to get everyone mad. *Newsweek,* pp. 39–40.

Spencer, T. L. (1986). Teacher education at Grambling State University: A move toward excellence. *Journal of Negro Education, 57,* 178–194.

Thomas, G. E. (1987). Black students in U.S. graduate and professional schools in the 1980s: A national and institutional assessment. *Harvard Educational Review, 57,* 261–282.

United States v. State of South Carolina, 445 F. Supp. 1904 (1977).

Webb, M. B. (1986). *Increasing minority participation in the teaching profession.* New York: ERIC Clearinghouse on Urban Education.

Webster, S. (1974). *The education of black Americans.* New York: John Day.

Witty, E. P. (1982). *Prospects for black teachers: Preparation, certification, employment.* Washington, DC: ERIC Clearinghouse on Teacher Education.

Witty, E. P. (1986). Testing teaching performance. *Journal of Negro Education, 55,* 358–367.

6

The Current Status of America's Inner-City Schools and Black Teachers: Commentary on Parsons and Larke

Wanda E. Ward
Center for Research on Minority Education
University of Oklahoma

The familiar saying that "the more things change, the more they stay the same" seems, unfortunately, to be a major conclusion drawn by scholars examining the status of desegregation efforts over the last few decades. In fact, some point out that ethnic and racial minority groups are relatively worse off today educationally (e.g., blacks; Wilson & Melendez, 1985), economically (Jones, 1986), and socially in America than two decades ago. While many correctly point to the devastating effects of the callous insensitivity of the Reagan administration to civil rights issues, fewer consciously reflect on the fact that, since the establishment of the Kerner Commission in 1967, Republicans won five of the six Presidential elections and that the slowing down of significant strides in civil rights really did not happen overnight or even over only the last 8 years.

Most ironically, at a time when demographic projections suggest that it is in the nation's interest to ensure significant and effective minority participation in all sectors of society, we see instead a steady, if sometimes subtle, degeneration of race relations in America. From the primary to the postsecondary levels of education, problems associated with race, class, and gender persist. Social disorganization looms larger, as reflected by homelessness, increasingly deviant crime, and escalating racial tensions in urban communities (e.g., Miami; Forsyth County, Georgia; Howard Beach, New York) and even on college campuses, the presumed bastions of intellectual exchange and enlightenment.

In addressing the problems of poverty and segregation in inner-city schools over the past two decades, James Parsons recalls the violence, destruction, and general urban social disorder in the summer of 1967 that prompted the establishment of the National Advisory Commission on Civil Disorders (or the Kerner Commission) by President Lyndon Johnson that same summer. Parsons notes that one of the Commission's major recommendations to improve the plight of those living in the urban ghetto was educational reform, which was viewed by many as the key to significant long-term improvement in the inner city. With federal money and power to improve the quality of life in the ghetto, segregation was to be halted, improvements in teaching were to be made, and schools were to become a core of the urban community.

The crux of Parson's chapter is the examination of change in the inner-city schools since 1967. He asks whether the picture has changed since the Kerner Commission's report in terms of segregation, teaching conditions, and the involvement of schools in the general community, and he presents a historical summary of two decades of educational change in such schools. Parsons outlines a two-stage treatment of the issue: The first stage is a descriptive analysis in which he traces the racial and ethnic composition of urban school districts using governmental and private statistical sources. Next, pointing out that federal policy toward education, civil rights, poverty, and urban growth has changed since 1967, he states that, by using such data to infer the impact of governmental policy decisions, the second stage of his analysis will "chart and consider these policy changes" (p. 66). Parsons then sets out to compare the cities, the schools, the teachers, and the poverty of 1987 to those of 1967.

His examination of the cities reveals that as black birth rates exceeded those of whites and as migration from rural to urban areas increased, the inner city of 1966 became primarily black and encircled by a primarily white suburb. Whereas the city traditionally served as a transition point for white foreigners or farmers who later moved into the suburb with its newer and better houses and schools, discriminatory housing practices (i.e., residential patterns, neighborhood covenants, or private agreements among homeowners) effectively served to block blacks from such moves and to lock them in the inner city. Parsons also describes the route taken by middle-class blacks seeking better housing: all-black neighborhood developments within the city limits sandwiched between an increasingly poorer black inner city and an increasingly white suburb. Similar patterns emerged for other ethnic groups such as Hispanics, but to a lesser degree than for blacks.

Parsons describes the inner city in 1987 as "even more crowded than in 1967" (p. 72). A major difference, he states, is the growing rate of urbanization in the South and West, resulting in the expansion of inner-city ghettos beyond the conventional regional boundaries of the Northeast. He points out that this growth is due less, however, to migration than to birth rates. Whereas 12.1% of blacks lived in the inner city in 1965, currently nearly one third do. An additional difference between the cities of 1967 and those of the late 1980s is the current increase in the nonblack minority population as well as an even more exclusively minority overrepresentation.

Parsons contributes to our understanding of the plight of urban America by examining the impact of birth rates, migration patterns, and discriminatory practices. Discussion of this topic might have been strengthened by considering major federal policy changes that affected the inner city. For instance, what have been the nature and impact of policy changes on public housing? To what extent is the increase in urban homelessness—an embarrassing and distressing commentary on the U.S. city— due to federal, state, or local policy? Given reported increases in housing discrimination (e.g., redlining in Atlanta; residential steering in the Belview area of Chicago), what do such occurrences portend for the advancement of desegregation? Beyond the historical account, what improvement for inner-city minorities is likely to result from urban revitalization efforts (e.g., housing restoration, downtown business redevelopment)? How likely are such efforts to reverse the impact of suburban shopping malls and the economic drain on the city caused by suburbanites taking resources earned in the city to the suburb?

After addressing changes in the inner cities, Parsons focuses on the schools. The status of schools in 1967, according to Parsons, was one of continuing segregation despite the fact that such schooling had been illegal since the landmark 1954 decision in *Brown v. Board of Education*. Citing the nature of the growth of the inner city as one contributor to the persisting racial isolation of blacks, he also cites the attitudes of blacks and whites and various educational policies and school practices (at the individual school and district levels) as additional contributors. He does not, however, specify what some of those attitudes and practices were. He does state that such isolation is not restricted to geographic region.

In terms of the national percentage of black students attending schools with 90% to 100% minority enrollment, Parsons describes a steady decline of school segregation since 1968. This natural picture of decline is due largely, he states, to the fact that 14 states have negligible black populations. He cautions, however, that the change in desegregation of blacks was practically nil between 1980 and 1984 and that the states that showed the greatest improvement were those that were segregated by law prior to 1954. In addition, school segregation shifted from the South to the North and Northeast. Parsons also discusses the school segregation of nonblack minorities. That is, the increase in Hispanic representation in the inner city has brought about an accompanying increase in the percentage of Hispanics attending predominantly minority schools.

Approaching the issue of school segregation from a different perspective, Parsons notes that the percentage of white students attending the school of a typical minority student is an additional measure of racial isolation. The reported findings indicate continued racial isolation. Moreover, other reported findings reveal increasing resegregation by grade, elementary schools being the least segregated and high schools being the most segregated. Finally, Parsons traces overall population growth and points out that increases in the proportion of minority students in school correspond to increases in minority population growth nationally.

Parsons provides an informative and important description of school segregation, or racial isolation in the schools, in the 1960s and in the 1980s. Noticeably absent from his examination of this issue, however, is any treatment of the integral role schools are to play in the inner-city community at either point in time. Institutions such as the family, school, and church have traditionally been regarded as playing foundational roles in the establishment and maintenance of a sense of community. Discussion of changes in the role of the school in the community in the 1980s as compared to the 1960s, as well as suggestions about what the current role of the school can reasonably be expected to be, would have made a major contribution to our understanding of the inner-city school.

Also absent from Parson's chapter is any discussion of changes in allocation of financial resources among school districts, changes in the conditions of school facilities, or changes in minority representation in school governance. Finally, while the issue of school segregation is addressed, the emerging problem of classroom segregation even in desegregated schools is not.

The final topic Parsons addresses is poverty. He describes reports of correlations between income and race and between crime and race, structural problems in the American economy and society that contribute to inner-city poverty, and problems such as malnutrition, substandard housing, and insufficient health care that were associated with living in the inner city in the 1960s. In the 1980s poverty is still a major problem in urban America, including its public schools. The poverty rate for blacks is more than three times that of whites, with nearly a third of poor blacks living in the inner city and nearly 40% living in federally designated poverty areas. In addition, the rate of poverty among black children is alarming.

Other dynamics related to poverty are unfolding in the urban America of the 1980s that Parsons has not addressed in his chapter but that warrant serious attention. For example, the feminization of poverty is an issue that has a major impact on the learning opportunities and capabilities of inner-city youth as well as on parental involvement in the schools. In addition, the identification by the minority community of the need for economic self-empowerment (partly as a result of the lack of concern and accompanying lack of effective policy on the part of the Reagan administration) is a major priority on the national agenda to improve the status of minorities in America. For example, minorities need to identify effective means to maximize the buying power of their dollars within their own communities before releasing such funds to the broader community. Finally, some comment on the ominous problem of the growing underclass in the inner city would have been helpful, especially as it concerns class problems within various ethnic and racial groups. How, for example, will the sense of community and traditional cooperativeness within the minority community be affected by the growing economic and sociocultural distance between the minority middle class and underclass, between the "haves" and the "have nots"?

Parsons basically concludes that there has been little change in the picture of inner-city schools since 1967. Noting that the promises of the Kerner Commission regarding education have yet to be fulfilled, his recommendations call for (a) more research because of the paucity of recent data on inner-city schools, and (b) research focusing specifically on distinctions between race and economics, especially as they impact classroom performance.

A major strength of Parsons's chapter is that he crystallizes how little cumulative progress has actually been made in this area. Thus he completes the first step of the two-step analysis he outlined for the chapter. The overall goal of the chapter goes only partially accomplished, however, because little or no serious attention is devoted to the stated (and extremely important) second step of the analysis: to use the data described to "chart and consider" the impact of changes in governmental policy decisions on education, civil rights, poverty, and urban growth. A serious treatment of such changes could have yielded valuable information on the systematic, structural factors that have resulted in little net gain in this area. The benefit of such a discussion might have been identification of needed policy research aimed at reversing the problems of the inner city.

In addition, such treatment may have better equipped social scientists to engage in what Parsons refers to as "a thorough and honest evaluation" of the role race plays in the dilemma of the inner-city school. He cites assertions by Scarr (1988) that social scientists examining the role of racial differences must be objective and report research findings even if they suggest "unfavorable possibilities for the underdog" (p. 56) and that "investigators cannot be held responsible for politically unfavorable outcomes of their research" (p. 58).

An actual reading of Scarr's work reveals her view that social scientists have shied away from conducting (psychological) research involving race and gender for fear of being seen as malevolent toward socially disadvantaged groups but that good science behooves them to conduct the studies and report the findings even if they shed unfavorable light on those groups. A full response to the issues and perspectives presented in Scarr's paper is beyond the scope of this commentary, but I find reference to Scarr's position in Parson's chapter somewhat puzzling. It is puzzling because of the general context of the dire picture he paints about inner-city schools and segregation throughout his chapter.

A number of the issues Parsons addresses reflect structural flaws in the American system that have resulted in the disadvantaged status of racial and ethnic minority groups. It is not so much that many of the scholars committed to the balanced and objective investigation of issues involving race, gender, or class fear being labeled reactionary or biased. Rather, the longstanding scientific battle for many has entailed the needed inclusion of scientific inquiry reflecting perspectives and methodologies that more accurately and objectively account for the status of racial minority groups in America. Indeed, thorough and honest evaluations are essential to solving the multifaceted problems involved in the study of inner-city schoools and segregation in particular and of race relations in general, but unfortunately, truth, honesty, and objective science are often in the eye of the beholder.

Whereas Parsons presents a historical summary of the broader issue of the inner-city school (including some discussion of the status of minority teachers), Patricia Larke's chapter focuses exclusively on the present and future status of black elementary and secondary school teachers. Larke provides a thorough discussion of the projected shortage of black teachers in the 1990s by addressing four aspects of the problem: its causes, its effects, viable intervention strategies, and the implications of the shortage of black teachers for U.S. race relations.

Examining causes of the shortage, Larke cites four contributors to the problem: the *Brown* decision, the competency testing movement, the educational reform movement, and an increase in alternative career opportunities for blacks. Regarding the first factor, she points out that although the *Brown* decision was designed to counteract the "separate but equal facilities" intent of the *Plessy v. Ferguson* (1896) decision, it actually contribued to the unpredicted shortage of black teachers. She states, for example, that the consolidation of facilities and services (presumably to provide equal facilities that were not separate) actually resulted in the reduction and displacement of black teachers and administrators. These consolidations often took the form of black schools' being closed because of inadequate facilities, a disproportionate number of black students being bused to white schools (with presumably better facilities and academic programs), and, concurrently, black teachers being assigned to white schools.

Larke also points out that an indirect result of the *Brown* decision has been fewer new hirings of black teachers relative to white teachers over the past three decades in many states. Importantly, she also notes the failure of the *Brown* decision to lead to a degree of human development (i.e., academic achievement of minority students) equal to that of the development of physical facilities (i.e., new or renovated public school buildings).

Competency testing and educational reform have also led to the shortage of blacks in the teaching profession. Noting that some regard competency-based testing as the gatekeeper of the teaching profession, Larke describes the large number of states that have adopted or have considered adopting this kind of testing whether in the form of admission, certification, recertification, and/or performance tests. She reports that the reduction in the number of black teachers is due partly to the fact that more blacks (i.e., teacher education students as well as actually employed teachers) fail to pass the tests than do whites. She does cite reports that black teachers in Virginia score significantly higher on performance tests that their white counterparts and suggests the use of knowledge applicability as an alternative process in the selection of minority teachers. She makes the important point that the accumulated research continues to yield inconclusive evidence that competency-based tests actually improve education (in the sense of improving student outcomes) or evaluate teachers' performance fairly.

Larke states that the purpose of educational reform movements traditionally has been to develop programs and policies to improve students' academic achievement, teacher education, and teacher certification and that these movements date back to the Sputnik revolution of the 1950s. The more recent reform movement, prompted by publication of A Nation at Risk (National Commission on Excellence in Education, 1983), was directed initially at reform legislation for elementary and secondary students but later included reform legislation for teacher education (e.g., competency-based testing). Larke points out the irony involved in the national reform movement, however, by noting that as state mandates for competency testing are enacted, many state offices of education are increasingly having to issue emergency teaching permits to "individuals who by definition are unqualified to teach" (p. 82). She explains that this is due partly to the fact that many states cannot provide the required number of certified teachers because teacher education institutions are not producing the needed number of new teachers.

Larke states that higher education institutions are now implementing curriculum changes in their teacher education programs partly as a result of state mandates and partly as a result of national reports such as The Holmes Group's (1986) *Tomorrow's Teacher* and the Carnegie Forum on Education and the Economy's (1985) *A Nation Prepared*. A major criticism she levels against these two reports is their apparent lack of concern about the shortage of black teachers, reflected both by the report's scant attention to the issue of increasing minority representation in the teaching profession and by the lack of minority representation (i.e., from historically black colleges and universities) on the Holmes Group committee.

Alternative career options for blacks have also contributed to the black teacher shortage, according to Larke. In an overall reduced pool of black college applicants, fewer blacks pursue teaching careers. This is due partly to disillusionment with the profession caused by observing the displacement, demotion, or dismissal of black teachers and administrators and partly to both minority and nonminority teachers' encouraging of talented black students to seek careers in nontraditional fields as a means of combatting previous denial of access to such fields.

After addressing the causes of the black teacher shortage, Larke focuses on its effects. An issue of paramount concern is the loss of needed role models for black students in particular and for other minority and nonminority students in general. Such a loss reduces minority students' chances of interacting with instructors who share their cultural values, beliefs, and racial/ethnic identity.

While it is important to understand the causes and effects of the shortage of blacks in the teaching profession, identification of intervention strategies is essential to the reversal of this problem. Larke states that the primary task is to enlarge the pool of those who pursue teaching careers. Pointing out that programs and policies must be developed and implemented in order to achieve this goal, she targets seven groups at which such initiatives must be directed: black elementary and secondary students; in-service teachers and administrators; black parents; higher education institutions; teacher education programs; historically black colleges and universities (HBCUs); and education decision makers.

Regarding black elementary and secondary students, she notes that initiation of career awareness and recruitment programs early in the educational pipeline are critical to students' educational development. School adoption programs are mutually beneficial for all students involved: Elementary and secondary students receive academic support from black undergraduates, who themselves benefit from the community involvement. Collaborations between school districts and colleges/universities are also important. In addition, college campus programs such as Texas A&M's Minority Mentorship Project provide social and academic functions that foster an appreciation of academic achievement and higher learning as well as serve an early recruitment function.

In-service training should involve multicultural education training, and in-service teachers and administrators should maximize every opportunity to encourage black students to pursue education careers, Larke asserts. She also raises an important point about the invaluable role of black parents in the education of their children. She states that many parents perceive negative attitudes held about them by school staff (e.g., teachers, counselors, administrators) and that such perceptions distance the parents from the staff. When their children have problems, parents may be reluctant to interact with the staff on their children's behalf. They view the school as alien to the community rather than as a vital part of it. Parents must be actively involved in their children's education, Larke suggests, and a sense of ownership in this process must be instilled in them.

More efforts have to be made by predominantly white colleges and universities to enlarge the pool of black students, according to Larke. In addition to the development and implementation of supportive policies and programs, these institutions need to provide adequate financial, academic, and social systems to facilitate these efforts. Moreover, academic units should reward faculty for developing and/or implementing recruitment and retention programs as well as acknowledge their research on such issues (e.g., explicitly incorporate consideration of such efforts in tenure and promotion decisions; provide release time).

In examining the contribution of HBCUs to the teaching profession, Larke notes the significant proportion of black teachers trained at these schools. Although noting the high failure rates of graduates of these schools on competency tests, Larke identifies some HBCUs that are experiencing success in this area and suggests that sister schools might collaborate with the more successful institutions to improve their records on competency testing.

Larke asserts that education decision makers must develop and adopt policies that include strategies designed to increase the number of black teachers. Also, she notes, these decision makers should call upon advisory groups that provide accurate information in order to prevent adoption of discriminatory practices.

Larke cites three implications of the shortage of black teachers for race relations in the 1990s: a reduction in the contribution of this group of professionals to America's educational, political, economic, and social agendas; a threat to black leadership in civic affairs; and a conspicuous void in the promotion of black and white race relations. Larke concludes by noting that the substantial loss of black teachers threatens the survival of the American educational system. A casualty of teacher education reform mandates is the loss of jobs by a disproportionately high number of black teachers and a failure of a high number of teacher education students to meet the new requirements, thus reducing the pool further. She suggests, therefore, the necessity for educational agendas to include valid and alternative certification methods that do not disproportionately restrict ethnic and racial representation in the teaching profession.

Larke provides a thorough and informative discussion of the problem of a black teacher shortage, citing a large amount of the extant literature on the issue. Her discussion of the need to increase the proportion of blacks in teaching careers would have been strengthened by articulating in what areas the greatest needs exist. For example, it is clear that the pool of students in education needs to be enlarged; however, it is not clear in which areas of education the greatest needs for more ethnic and racial representation exist. At the graduate level, for example, Pruitt (1989) points out that by examining the representation of minorities at the level of subfield as well as field of specialization, one can see even more clearly the existing disparities in minority representation. She notes that in 1985, 52.3% of the doctorates awarded to blacks were in the field of education versus 2.1% in engineering and 3.3% in physical sciences. Disaggregating data by subfield, however, Pruitt found that most of the doctorates awarded in education in 1984 were in educational administration and supervision. In the subfields of educational statistics and research, educational testing, school psychology, preschool education, and educational media, fewer than 10 doctorates each were awarded. The point here is that such an approach allows for more strategic planning to better balance the representation of blacks and other ethnic/racial groups in teacher education.

One of the most strongly debated issues in education today is educational reform, a debate that often focuses on the issue of competency-based testing. Larke makes the point that there is a lack of conclusive evidence that competency-based testing (in its current forms) actually improves the quality of education for students. She also briefly refers to the need for alternative and valid assessment methods but provides little insight into what she sees critical components of such clearly needed alternatives to be. Admittedly, many in the field are grappling with this critical issue and have yet to resolve it fully. Such a discussion, however, would facilitate advancement on this issue and bring us closer to satisfactory solutions to the problem.

REFERENCES

Brown v. Board of Education of Topeka, Kansas, 347 U.S. 483 (1954).
Carnegie Forum on Education and the Economy. (1985). *A nation prepared: Teachers for the 21st century*. New York: Carnegie Corporation.
The Holmes Group. (1986). *Tomorrow's teachers*. East Lansing: Michigan State University.
Jones, J. (1986). Racism: A cultural analysis of the problem. In L. Gaertner & J. F. Dovidio (Eds.), *Prejudice, discrimination and racism* (pp. 279–314). New York: Academic Press.
National Commission on Excellence in Education. (1983). *A nation at risk: The imperative for educational reform*. Washington, DC: U.S. Government Printing Office.
Plessy v. Ferguson, 163 U.S. 537 (1896).
Pruitt, A. S. (1989). Access and retention of minority graduate students. In W. E. Ward & M. M. Cross (Eds.), *Key issues in minority education: Research directions and practical implications* (pp. 73–96). Norman: University of Oklahoma Center for Research on Minority Education.
Scarr, S. (1988). Race and gender as psychological variables. *American Psychologist, 43*, 56–59.
Wilson, R. & Melendez, S. (1985). *Minorities in higher education: Fourth annual status report*. Washington, DC: American Council on Education.

PART II

OCCUPATIONAL MOBILITY, ECONOMICS, AND CULTURAL PLURALISM

7

Sports and Race Relations in American Society

Jomills Henry Braddock II
Center for Social Organization of Schools
The Johns Hopkins University

Recently the underrepresentation of blacks in the top echelons of professional sports management has been scrutinized as a result of racist public statements by a top executive with the Los Angeles Dodgers and a nationally known network television sportscaster. Even so, few Americans are aware of the degree to which black–white relations in sports mirror common patterns of race relations in other major social institutions in our society. In this chapter I will examine some contemporary patterns of American race relations as they are reflected through sports. The main objective of this chapter will be to illustrate how systemic and institutional barriers continue to block equal employment opportunities for blacks, even in sectors of society which are putatively free of racial discrimination. I will use the National Football League as an example.

This chapter consists of three parts: (a) an overview of black participation patterns in sports; (b) an empirical analysis of institutional discrimination in recruitment of managers in professional sports; and (c) a discussion of the implications of this study for public policy regarding equal employment opportunities and for research on inequality and race relations in American society.

BLACK PARTICIPATION IN AMERICAN SPORTS

Observers of American race relations have pointed often to sports as the arena that epitomizes our society's core egalitarian and meritocratic values, perhaps more than any other major social institution. Sport is presumed to be egalitarian because of its accessibility across racial, ethnic, and social class boundaries. Similarly, sport is perceived to be meritocratic because individual accomplishment presumably is unconstrained by social origins. As a prominent United States senator noted nearly three decades ago while assessing the state of employment discrimination, some of the most striking advances in eradicating racial segregation have been made in the field of sports (Javits, 1960).

A cursory examination of blacks' overall participation patterns in some of the major team sports makes such assumptions easily understandable. In professional baseball, basketball, and football, for example, the representation of blacks as players

A version of this chapter appeared as an article in the *Sociological Spectrum*, 1989, *9*, 53–76.

has equaled or surpassed their proportion in the population since the early 1960s (Eitzen & Yetman, 1977). By 1987 blacks constituted approximately two thirds of all players in the National Basketball Association (NBA), one half of all National Football League (NFL) players, and nearly one quarter of all major league baseball players, whereas blacks represent only 12% of the total U.S. population. Similarly, at the intercollegiate levels—which serve as the unofficial training grounds for the professional ranks—black athletes are overrepresented in basketball and football. Yet despite blacks' prominent presence as basketball, football, and baseball players, most organized professional sports in America, including such high-revenue sports as golf, tennis, soccer, hockey, and horse and auto racing, have remained virtually closed to black athletes.

Nevertheless, in those areas where racial barriers have been overcome, blacks have become dominant in several major team sports (as well as in many individual sports, including boxing and track). In professional basketball, football, and baseball, during the past two decades, black players' performances very often have become the benchmarks by which other athletes' achievements are measured. In professional basketball, blacks dominate the list of all-time leaders in nearly every statistical category including scoring, assists, rebounds, steals, and field-goal percentage. In major league baseball, black players have not only become the all-time home run and stolen-base champions but have won a disproportionate share of batting and slugging titles and Gold Glove awards. In professional football, blacks also dominate in almost every statistical category including single-game, season, and career rushing and receiving yardage, touchdowns scored, and defensive interceptions. Similar patterns are common in intercollegiate sports: During the past decade, with few exceptions, black players have won the Heisman Trophy, awarded annually to the "best" player in college football, have earned Player of the Year honors in college basketball, and have been overrepresented among players earning All-American honors in college basketball and football. Because of blacks' disproportionate representation and outstanding accomplishments as players, many people believe that both amateur and professional athletics have provided black males with avenues for status attainment which are largely unavailable elsewhere in American society (see Braddock, 1980, for a critical review of this literature).

On the other hand, a growing body of empirical evidence suggests that professional and amateur athletics in the United States are neither egalitarian nor meritocratic (Braddock, 1978a, 1978b, 1980; Dougherty, 1976; Eitzen & Yetman, 1977; Loy & McElvogue, 1970; Pascal & Rapping, 1972; Rainville & McCormick, 1977; Rosenblatt, 1967; Scully, 1974). These studies have documented positional segregation, salary discrimination, and biased media treatment against black athletes. Even a quarter of a century ago Hubert Blalock (1962), a prominent race relations scholar, noted that in spite of the rapidly rising rate of black participation in professional sport, retired black athletes would face tremendous obstacles in moving into coaching and front office positions. At the same time, Blalock outlined a theory of occupational discrimination which continues to be useful in explaining racial segregation in American sport (see Loy & McElvogue, 1970).

The accumulated evidence on racial discrimination in sports supports Blalock's prediction and reveals that although blacks have become dominant in the last two decades as players in the three major professional sports, they have made few inroads into professional sports management either on or off the playing fields. Since 1948, when the color barrier was broken by Jackie Robinson of the Brooklyn Dodgers in major league baseball and by Bill Willis and Marion Motley of the Cleveland Browns in professional football, and since 1950, when three black players broke the racial barriers in the National Basketball Association, only three blacks have held positions as managers in major league baseball, and approximately a dozen blacks have served as head coaches in professional basketball. The National Football League recently hired its first black head coach, Art Shell.[1]

INSTITUTIONAL DISCRIMINATION IN THE NFL: A CASE EXAMPLE

Because of its egalitarian and meritocratic creed, organized professional sport provides a uniquely appropriate setting in which to study institutional discrimination. Simply stated, institutional racial discrimination refers to any action, policy, ideology, or structure of an institution which works to the disadvantage of blacks in relation to comparable whites, or to the advantage of whites in relation to comparable blacks (see Alvarez & Lutterman, 1979; Knowles & Prewitt, 1969). In this sense, then, institutional discrimination refers to organizational practices and policies and not directly to the attitudes and behaviors of individuals. Thus the most important characteristic of institutional racial discrimination is that its presence is recognized by *effects*, not by *intentions* (Nordlie, 1979, p. 159).

In an article appropriately titled "Institutional Racism: How to Discriminate without Really Trying," Robert Friedman (1975) analyzed four forms of institutional racism: (a) structural racism, (b) procedural racism, (c) systemic racism, and (d) ideological racism. Of greatest direct relevance to the present study is structural discrimination, which conditions and structures the patterns of black participation in the society's major social institutions. Structural discrimination can operate horizontally or hierarchically. The *horizontal* pattern involves the total exclusion of blacks from the society's major white-dominated institutions. In professional sports, for example, horizontal discrimination ended during the mid-1940s and early 1950s, when blacks were allowed to participate as players in the major professional football, baseball, and basketball leagues. Since that time blacks, as players, have not only reached parity but today are overrepresented numerically on the rosters of America's major professional sports teams.

In contrast, *hierarchical* discrimination constrains blacks' movement up the career ladder within organizations even after they have attained access. In this regard the evidence shows that in professional sports blacks and whites are concentrated in different playing positions, with blacks generally occupying positions characterized by less organizational power and less outcome control (Edwards, 1973); blacks as players receive less pay per unit of performance (Scully, 1974); and retired black players do not remain in professional sports in nonplaying positions as often as their white counterparts (Pascal & Rapping, 1972; Scully, 1974). Thus although blacks participate in relatively large numbers as players, they continue to face limited advancement opportunities (hierarchical or vertical discrimination) in professional sports.

Why have horizontal discriminatory barriers against blacks been eliminated or

---

[1]Fritz Pollard was a black player who (along with Paul Robeson) was a charter member of the Akron Pros of the American Professional Football Association (APFA), the forerunner of the National Football League. Later, from 1923 to 1925, Pollard served as the head coach of the Hammond Pros of the APFA (Treat, 1979).

reduced in professional sports while vertical discriminatory barriers seem to remain? Asked differently, why do NFL team owners employ a disproportionately large number of blacks as players but do not appoint them, after retirement, to either field or front office managerial positions?

Blalock's (1962) early theoretical propositions concerning occupational discrimination provide a useful perspective for understanding the apparent paradox in the racial hiring practices of NFL team owners. This framework uses professional athletes to illustrate principles concerning conditions in which previously closed occupations will be opened to minorities. Assuming that minority group members will be hired only into the least desirable positions unless they possess compensatory resources, Blalock distinguished two types of such resources that members of a minority group might have: competitive resources and pressure resources. *Competitive resources* can be measured in terms of performance per unit of cost. For example, members of the minority group may possess certain special skills or may agree to work for lower wages. *Pressure resources*, on the other hand, may involve negative sanctions which might be used to punish the employer. Examples of pressure resources might include threatened boycotts by minority customers (e.g., the National Association for the Advancement of Colored People) or affirmative action pressures exerted by some external source (e.g., the federal government).

The competitive resources in professional sports have been most influential in creating greater opportunities for blacks to gain access as players.[2] Because of the strong pressure to produce winning teams, and because the performance of individual athletes is measurable, the best players are sought. In a disproportionate number of instances in major professional team sports (including football), the outstanding performers have been black.[3] As a result, these sports in America have become the society's most desegregated labor markets, at least at the players' level. The pressures to win are equally strong at the managerial level, if not stronger (i.e., losing teams often find it easier to change coaches or managers than to make wholesale changes of team players), and the coaches' performance is not independent of their players', but players' performance is not difficult to measure and evaluate. To be competitive as a coach, however, one must receive the opportunity to occupy the position and either to succeed or to fail on the basis of one's competence.

For the most part, coaching and managerial opportunities have been rare for blacks in professional sports, especially in the NFL. Some external pressures have been brought to bear; the National Football Players Association, the Congressional Black Caucus, the Southern Christian Leadership Conference, and the National Conference on Black Lawyers have each brought the matter of racial bias in managerial recruitment in the NFL to the attention of the media and/or the Commissioner of the National Football League. Yet these groups appear to have had little effect in creating greater opportunities for black former players to move into either assistant or head coach positions. Thus in a labor market that lacks clearly defined competitive resources to indicate which of a number of potential candidates is likely to become the most successful head coach or assistant head coach, and in which pressure resources

---

[2]It is true, however, that doors opened to blacks in the major professional team sports in the late 1940s, around the same time as the emergence of organized nationwide civil rights protests. The existence of these external pressure groups may have played some role in promoting greater opportunities, but sports were not a major target of protest activities.

[3]For a comprehensive treatment of this issue see "Black Dominance," *Time*, May 9, 1977, pp. 56–60.

have been absent, ineffective, or not applied forcefully, the postretirement career opportunities for black NFL players remain severely constrained.

The present chapter focuses on the racial distribution of former players as assistant coaches and head coaches in the National Football League. Between 1960 and 1979, blacks accounted, on the average, for 1 of every 4 players in the NFL; yet they have been chosen for fewer than 1 of every 10 assistant coaching positions that were filled by former players. During the same period blacks occupied none of the 68 head coaching positions which have been held by former NFL players.

These figures suggest an unequal distribution of career mobility rewards among black and white professional football players. It is not clear, however, whether the observed differences are equitable or justifiable. Following Alvarez and Lutterman (1979), I will infer institutional discrimination when the observed disproportionate distributions of black and white players across positions and levels of the NFL hierarchy are found to be unjustified. Disproportionate distributions will be considered unjustified when they are based on characteristics such as race, rather than on performance or other characteristics which are associated with performing well at a particular position in the National Football League.

Methods

To measure the equitability of the present allocation of black and white former players into field management positions, I employ a twofold strategy. First, I estimate the influence of race as an ascribed characteristic in relation to other relevant achieved characteristics (i.e., education, leadership ability, competence as a player) on the player-to-coach transition, using multiple regression analysis and structural equations models (Duncan, 1975). Second, I use multiple regression techniques to estimate the proportion of black players who, all else being equal (at least according to the present model of managerial recruitment), might have been selected as either head coaches or assistant coaches in the NFL during the past 20 years if race was not a factor in the selection process. Although these statistical techniques do not allow definitive answers to these questions, they do provide important clues about what seems to be important in recruitment to NFL coaching positions.

In studying managerial recruitment in the NFL, as in other formal organizations, one may emphasize either internal recruitment (promotions from within the organization) or external recruitment (filling managerial positions with personnel from outside the organization). This study, however, is restricted to an examination of the internal[4] promotional practices of NFL teams for several reasons: During the two decades

_____

[4]It would be useful in future research to examine further the external recruitment practices of NFL clubs, in which blacks also are underrepresented. The NFL claims that the lack of blacks in head and assistant coaching positions at the major colleges (National College Athletic Association [NCAA] Division I) is a major factor in their underrepresentation in the professional ranks. On the surface, this argument seems to have some validity regarding external recruitment practices. Yet it does little to explain why white nonformer players who gained their coaching experience outside the major colleges (e.g., George Allen of Whittier College; Don Coryell of San Diego State) appear to have greater opportunities than comparable blacks (e.g., John Merritt of Tennessee State; Eddie Robinson of Grambling) to obtain coaching positions in the professional ranks. Robinson is the most winning coach in NCAA history; both he and Merritt not only have impressive coaching credentials but have provided a wealth of talented players to the NFL. Simply stated, the major colleges have not provided the sole or perhaps even the major pool of nonplayer coaching candidates. Even if they had done so, it would be inadequate to blame the historic and current black underrepresentation in the NFL coaching ranks solely on the major colleges.

covered by the study, a sizable majority of NFL assistant and head coaches were hired from the ranks of former players; the available data for empirical study of the internal candidate pool were superior; and the potential for affirmative action by the NFL appeared to be most promising for its internal hiring practices.

The research model presently employed includes the following variables, which have been linked theoretically or empirically to recruitment into NFL field management positions: race, educational attainment, leadership ability (position centrality), professional accomplishments, and (when the dependent variable is head coach) experience in the NFL as an assistant coach. Figure 1 shows the postulated pattern of causal relations in the simplified model of managerial recruitment.[5]

The model contains five causal steps. Players's race and educational attainment, as exogenous variables, begin the sequence and determine assignment to the second step, a central (leadership) position. Several studies (Brower, 1972; Williams & Youssef, 1972, 1975) note that blacks, as compared to whites, are perceived by coaches as being deficient in those personal attributes (e.g., intelligence and poise) which are associated with playing central positions. In turn, perhaps they are excluded systematically from opportunities to perform in positions where their leadership competence could be developed. Educational attainment also is assumed to reflect intellectual or cognitive ability and self-discipline, which are major requirements for assignment to a central (leadership) position. The third step involves a player's professional accomplishments. In this area, black players and brighter (i.e., better-educated) players may tend to fare better. In the fourth step of the model a player becomes an assistant coach in the National Football League, with causal influences from each of the preceding variables. In the final step the former player achieves the status of head coach of a National Football League team; direct and indirect effects are posited from each of the preceding variables.

I used archival statistical and historical data on professional football teams covering a period of two decades (1960–1979) to examine the process of managerial recruitment within sports teams as formal organizations. I employed several statistical and historical reference systems, including *The Encyclopedia of Football* (Treat, 1979); *The Sports Encyclopedia: Pro Football* (Neft, Cohen, & Deutsch, 1978); the *Official National Football League Record Manual* (1970–1979); the "Football Register" (1966–1979) and the "National Football Guide" (1966–1979) published in the *Sporting News*; the National Football League annual team media guides; and *Ebony* magazine (1960–1979). From these sources I identified a total population of 5,127 cases (players or coaches) whose past or current careers in the National Football League as players and/or as coaches occurred partially or entirely in the two decades from 1960 through 1979. The analyses of institutional discrimination in managerial recruitment in the NFL examine the career mobility processes in this group.

---

[5]An additional factor regarded as potentially important in managerial recruitment is longevity as a player. Although this information was readily available from players' records, length of playing career is not included in the present model because its high correlation (.66) with the player accomplishments measure creates problems of multicollinearity (Gordon, 1968). The simultaneous inclusion in the model of career longevity and player accomplishments would make it difficult to interpret the relative unique effects of each measure. In preliminary analyses I performed regression analyses on the research model; I used career longevity and player accomplishments, each singly and in combination. The results suggest that the race effect remains stable in every instance. Players' accomplishments, rather than career longevity, were included here, however, because of their broader substantive significance to the research model.

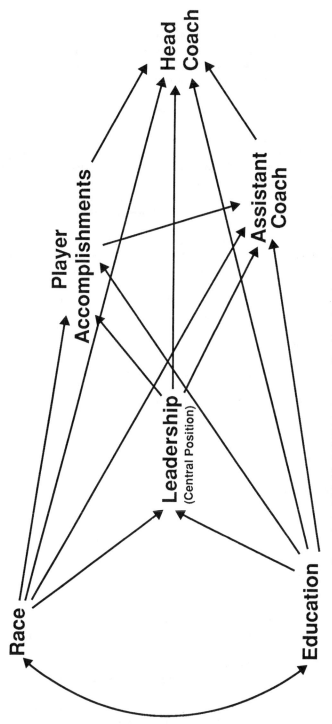

Figure 1 Path Model of Field Management (Coaching) Recruitment in Professional Football.

Findings

The primary question raised in this investigation is as follows: "Other things being equal, does a player's race matter in the recruitment of assistant and head coaches in the National Football League?" If it does matter, two additional important policy-related questions are raised: First, "What is the process through which race operates to limit the opportunities for black players to move into coaching positions after their active playing careers are ended?" and second, "In regard to blacks' opportunities for coaching positions in the NFL, what has been the overall effect of their race as a consideration in team decisions regarding managerial recruitment?

First let us consider whether race exerts a direct effect on coaching opportunities in the NFL. Even after we take into account statistically whatever differences might exist between black and white players in other theoretically relevant areas (educational attainment, leadership position assignment, and professional accomplishments as players), does a player's race help to explain why blacks are less likely than whites to be appointed as assistant and head coaches in the NFL?

First, in respect to the position of assistant head coach, the data provide evidence that the ascribed status—race—operates to the relative disadvantage of black players and to the relative advantage of white players. Table 1 presents the estimated total, direct, and indirect effects of each of the predetermined variables in the model of recruitment of former professional football players to field management (coaching) positions in the National Football League.

Among the predetermined variables in the research model, race ($\beta = -.10$) and players's professional accomplishments ($\beta = .10$) exert the strongest direct effects on becoming an assistant coach in the NFL. The effects of both race and professional accomplishments are nominally statistically significant.[6] The effects of educational attainment ($\beta = .02$) and leadership ability as measured by position centrality ($\beta = .03$) are each considerably weaker than those of race and professional accomplishments; neither reaches statistical significance, although leadership approaches significance at the .05 level. Let me emphasize again that direct effects are net or independent effects. That is, if the model is specified correctly, the findings show that race per se appears to be an important determinant of a professional football player's opportunities to be hired as an assistant coach after his playing career has ended. This relationship holds even after black and white players' differences in educational attainment, leadership position assignment, and professional accomplishments have been equated or controlled statistically. Similarly, we find that a player's professional accomplishments are independently important ($\beta = .10$) determinants of opportunities to obtain an assistant coaching position in the NFL.

The bottom panel of Table 1 shows the results of our analysis of recruitment to head coaching positions in the National Football League. In this case, experience as an assistant coach has been added to the basic model of managerial recruitment. When we examine the direct effects of the predetermined variables on becoming an NFL head coach, we find that assistant coaching experience is a major prerequisite. Among the five predetermined variables in the model, not only does such experience exert the strongest single net or direct effect ($\beta = .41$), but the size of this effect is stronger than that of the combined net effects of the other four predictors. Race also exhibits a statistically significant, though considerably weaker, direct effort

---

[6]Because the standard deviations of the variables exceed the means, it is likely that the assumptions underlying these statistical tests are not met. Tables show "nominal" significance values for the convenience of the readers who may wish to see them. Note: "Metric" coefficients which are twice their standard error are statistically significant ($p < .05$).

Table 1 Total, direct, and indirect effects of predetermined variables in reduced-form structural equations model of recruitment of National Football League players to field management positions (N = 5,127)

Dependent variable	Predetermined variable	Total association	Total effect	Indirect effects			Direct effect	Metric
				Leadership	Achievements	Asst. coach		
(3) Leadership position centrally	(1) Race	-.24	-.24	—	—	—	-.238	-.244[a]
	(2) Education	.06	.06	—	—	—	.066	.063[a]
(4) Player achievements	(1) Race	.05	.07	.00	—	—	.071	.128[a]
	(2) Education	.14	.18	.00	—	—	.177	.281
	(3) Leadership	-.01	-.02	.00	—	—	-.016	-.026[a]
(5) Assistant coach	(1) Race	-.10	-.10	-.01	.01	—	-.103	-.051[a]
	(2) Education	.04	.04	.00	.02	—	.022	.010
	(3) Leadership	.04	.03	—	.00	—	.026	.012
	(4) Achievements	.10	.10	—	—	—	.096	.028[a]
(6) Head coach	(1) Race	-.07	-.07	.00	.00	-.04	-.026	-.007[a]
	(2) Education	.04	.04	.00	.00	.01	.026	.006[a]
	(3) Leadership	.03	.01	—	.00	.00	.010	.002
	(4) Achievements	.07	.03	—	—	.04	-.009	-.001
	(5) Asst. coach	.41	.41	—	—	—	.405	.211[a]

Note. Direct effects are the standardized regression coefficients. Indirect effects are computed from appropriate combinations of paths in the structural equations' solutions for the model. Total effects are the sum of the direct and the indirect effects for each predetermined variable in the model. The analyses presented here are based on the full sample of former and currently active players. To test the possibility that our results were biased by steadily increasing proportions of black players entering the NFL during the 1970s (and who thus would be less likely candidates for managerial positions), we performed parallel analyses only for those players (N = 2,571) who ended their active careers during the 1960s or very early 1970s. The observed race effects for assistant coach (β = -.08) and head coach (β = -.03) for this selected subgroup are virtually identical to those observed for the full sample.
[a]Indicates metric coefficient at least twice its standard error. Suppressor effects in the regression equations are not interpreted.

Table 2 Regression results of revised model of National Football League head coach recruitment
(N = 261)

Predetermined variable	Total association	Standard	Metric
Race	−.153	−.123	−.199[a]
Educational attainment	.110	.158	.133[a]
Leadership	.004	−.035	−.030
Player achievements	−.080	−.084	−.040
Assistant coach experience (number of years)	.202	.184	.015[a]

Note. Standard = standardized regression coefficients; metric = unstandardized regression coefficients.
[a]Size of metric coefficients is twice its standard error. Suppressor effects in the regression equation are not interpreted.

(β = −.03) on recruitment into head coaching positions independent of the effects of educational attainment, leadership positional assignment, player's professional accomplishments, and experience as an assistant coach in the NFL. In contrast to the finding regarding assistant coaching positions, the data show that educational attainment exerts a statistically significant, albeit slight, effect (β = .03) on recruitment to head coaching positions. In the case of head coach recruitment, as with recruitment of assistant coaches, leadership potential (as measured by playing position) surprisingly shows no significant direct or independent effects (β = .01). Although players' professional accomplishments are associated positively at the zero-order level with becoming a head coach, they show no significant direct or independent effects (β = −.01) when the other predetermined variables in the model are taken into account.

Thus, in this model, assistant coaching experience is the main determinant of a former player's recruitment to a head coaching position. In light of that reality, it is important to reestimate the model of head coach recruitment for only the subsample of former players (N = 261) who have had experience as assistant coaches. The reestimated model allows us to take into account the number of years of experience as an assistant coach in the NFL.[7] In professional football as in other occupations, years of experience in a job represent on-the-job training, in some sense. That so many head coaches have been recruited from the assistant coaching ranks attests to the importance of this principle in the NFL. It is also true that blacks have been appointed only recently as assistant coaches; thus, on average, blacks have considerably fewer (M = 3.2) years of experience as assistant coaches than whites (M = 6.8). Thus it might be argued reasonably that the race effect observed earlier is spurious. That is, blacks may receive few opportunities to become head coaches not because of their race, but because they have had less experience at the assistant coach level, which is the main steppingstone to becoming a head coach. Table 2 presents the results for the reestimated model of managerial recruitment.

Among former players who have reached the status of assistant coach, number of years of coaching experience shows the strongest single direct effect (β = .18) on becoming a head coach. Yet even after other relevant factors and length of assistant coaching experience are taken into account statistically, race (β = −.12) continues to act as a significant determinant of retired players' selection for head coaching positions.

[7]Because of the high intercorrelation of years of experience as an assistant coach with ever having held the position, and because of the attendant problems of multicollinearity, it is impractical to include both variables simultaneously when all players are included in the analysis.

Returning briefly to Table 1, we can make some observations regarding how managerial recruitment in the NFL, as depicted by the present research model, operates to the relative disadvantage of black players. The research model employed here, of course, assumes that the process of internal managerial recruitment within the National Football League is based in part on a player's successful progression through several interdependent stages.

On the basis of evidence from prior research, I had assumed that the underrepresentation of black players in leadership positions would be a major reason for their underrepresentation as assistant or head coaches in the NFL. The data suggest otherwise, however. Although a strong and significant effect of race ($\beta = -.24$) on players' position assignments can be observed, one must also note that having played a leadership position has very limited direct influence on becoming either an assistant coach ($\beta = .03$) or a head coach ($\beta = .01$) after other relevant criteria are taken into account.

Assignment to a leadership position mediates only a small portion ($\beta = -.01$) of the effect of a player's race on becoming an assistant coach. This effect, however, is offset by the equal strength of the race effect ($\beta = .01$), which is mediated by player's accomplishments. That is, although black players are placed at a slight disadvantage in becoming assistant coaches by their assignment to noncentral positions, this disadvantage is offset by their superior athletic accomplishments. As a result, the effect of race on becoming an assistant coach appears to be direct rather than indirect. Stated differently, black players, according to the model examined here seem to be chosen as assistant coaches less often than white players not because of differences in objective qualifications but because of racial considerations.

Regarding the process of recruitment to head coaching positions, Table 1 showed that the limited opportunities for black players to become assistant coaches serve in turn to restrict their chances for recruitment into head coaching positions. Specifically, the findings in Table 1 showed that slightly more than half ($\beta = -.04$) of the total effect ($\beta = -.07$) of race on becoming a head coach is mediated by blacks' underrepresentation as assistant coaches. Nevertheless, according to the model, even for those fortunate few who have become assistant coaches, race still appears to be a significant factor in limiting the opportunities to move into head coaching positions (see Table 2).

Finally, let us turn to the hypothetical questions: "What if race didn't matter? Would the resulting distributions of black and white former players in assistant and head coaching positions be different?" To address this issue we must identify a standard against which the actual proposition of black (assistant and head) coaches can be compared. If this standard could be interpreted as the number or the percentage of blacks that one would expect to occupy the positions in question in the absence of differential treatment on the basis of race, we would have grounds for saying how much the actual number differs from the standard and for developing appropriate policy responses as needed.

The idea of an expected number is based on statistical principles. Essentially it is the number of blacks one would expect to find in a given category (e.g., coaching) if skin color were a random variable with respect to membership in that category. If the persons selected for a particular category were drawn randomly from an eligible population, the number of blacks selected would tend to be proportional to the number of blacks in the eligible population. In the present case one might argue that because blacks made up 26% of the total population of players during the 20-year period covered by this study, theoretically, if race were a random variable, they should make up roughly 26% of the 261 assistant coaches and 26% of the 68 head

Table 3 Comparisons of actual and predicted number of blacks (former players) in head and assistant
coaching positions in the National Football League (NFL), 1960–1979

Position	Total no. former NFL players	Actual no. white	Actual no. black	Predicted no. black
Assistant coach	261	241	20	92
Head coach	68	68	0	10

Note. Predicted number = (*y* predicted proportion blacks in position/observed proportion whites in
position) × (% black players/% white players) × (total number of positions), where *y* is the solved white
regression equation with black means substituted for white means.

coaches. This conclusion, of course, assumes (incorrectly) that all other potential
qualifications are equal between black players and white players or are distributed
randomly. The data, however, show relatively minor racial differences in educational
attainment and professional accomplishments but large differences in assignment to
leadership positions and assistant coaching experience. For this reason I have calculated an expected number based on multiple regression analysis, used in a predictive
fashion, which allows me to build into the estimation process controls for other
putatively relevant criteria which I have been able to measure.

Table 3 presents comparisons of the actual and the expected number of blacks in
assistant coach and head coach positions. The estimates presented in this table are
roughly equivalent to asking, "If the managerial recruitment process, as measured by
this study, operated in the same manner for black players as for white players, how
many of the 68 head coaches and the 261 assistant coaches who are former players,
and who coached during the past two decades, would one expect to have been
black?" In simpler terms, "In the absence of racial considerations affecting managerial recruitment in the NFL, how many black players might have become assistant
coaches or head coaches?"

The data in Table 3 show that only 20 black former players have been appointed as
assistant coaches, whereas our research model suggests that in the absence of racial
considerations affecting recruitment, one would have expected 92 such appointments,
over four and one half times as many as were actually made. Until recently, no black
head coaches had been appointed, but one would expect, given the present model,
that in the absence of racial considerations in recruitment 10 of the head coaches who
are former professional football players, or roughly 15%, should have been black.

DISCUSSION AND IMPLICATIONS

I believe that the models and the variables used in this study portray the key
elements needed to assess the racial equity of selection processes under sufficient
management control in a multistage sequence that determines the probabilities of
coaching careers for former NFL players. As in many industries, the personal characteristics needed for filling the top management positions successfully can be judged
most legitimately by on-the-job demonstrations of success at the next lower level; and
it is to be expected that specific objective characteristics related to job performance
are used to determine access to these initial proving grounds. Thus racial equity
would require a fair opportunity for access to the lower-level (assistant coach) proving ground: Reasonable measures must be specified and used as objective screening
mechanisms for these initial positions.

At both stages in the sequence, exclusionary processes were indicated in the analyses of NFL managerial recruitment. Opportunities to serve as assistant coaches were found to be significant determinants of attaining head coaching positions, but no blacks who had served as assistant coaches ever became head coaches, prior to the recent appointment of Art Shell. Furthermore, black former players were unable to obtain the same opportunities as whites for the on-the-job exposure and experience as assistant coaches, even when objective personal characteristics such as performance, experience in leadership roles, or winning traditions were taken into account.

Race, the ascriptive status factor, represents a selection criterion which is at odds with the egalitarian and meritocratic image on which the National Football League prides itself. Race is also of questionable justifiability as a selection criterion for coaching. Because there are no obvious reasons why skin pigmentation should be functionally relevant either to the individual's task accomplishment or to organizational goal attainment, we can only speculate about why race was observed to be a factor in allocating or distributing organizational rewards in the National Football League.

Blalock's (1962) theoretical proportions, discussed earlier, suggest some potential explanations. Those propositions imply that blacks are most likely to suffer discrimination when they seek jobs which have constraining influences (power) over others in the organization and when high levels of interpersonal interaction are required. Assistant coaches exercise power over players; head coaches exercise power over players and assistant coaches. Both assistant and head coach positions require high rates of interaction and thus demand appropriate interpersonal skills. The head coach, of course, would require a higher degree of each characteristic and also would be involved more frequently in interactions with owners or top-level team officials, the mass media, and the general public. Thus, perhaps, team officials may discriminate against blacks in filling managerial positions because of resistance to frequent interactions with blacks or because of reluctance to grant a black organizational control over team outcomes and over individual players. Their reluctance may be due to fear of failure or fear of racial insubordination by either blacks or whites.

The foregoing observations may be plausible but are only speculative. They are not offered as justifications for a distribution of rewards based on race. Ultimately, of course, the National Football League teams themselves are responsible for justifying the present disproportionate racial distribution of coaching positions.

One of the most interesting patterns observed in analyzing coaches' and players' biographies for this study, though not reflected in this analysis, is the existence of relatively close-knit social networks among NFL coaches and between coaches and certain players. These networks seem to facilitate the movement of particular players into coaching positions and the transition of particular coaches from one coaching assignment to another. In fact, it may be through such networking processes that the influence of central positions operates. Coaches, for example, typically spend more time working with central position players. In such contexts, more intense relations and closer ties between coaches and players are likely. Thus, greater opportunities for the development of sponsorship networks are likely in these circumstances.

In addition, when a retired player moves into an assistant coaching position, such a move often does not result from the player's own initiative in applying for a vacant position. Typically, certain players are considered as good coaching prospects on the basis of recommendations and sponsorship by current or past coaches, who are regarded as key figures in informal networks within the coaching subculture. Because, as Massengale (1976, p. 148) noted, "coaches appear to dislike change and tend to be very conservative politically, socially and attitudinally," these informal networks are usually closed to minorities. Further, a very large proportion of NFL coaches who are former players played both in college and professionally in highly segregated circumstances; as a result, their informal social networks also are likely to be highly segregated. This combination of conservative orientations and closed social networks is likely to be a major additional sponsorship factor which helps to explain the existing racial distributions in recruitment to field management positions.

Friendship patterns among NFL players might operate in a similar fashion. Although official team policies may dictate otherwise, often it is stated that black and white players, who themselves are products of largely segregated social backgrounds, seldom interact socially in informal settings; instead they engage in self-segregation of various sorts. As a result, black and white players seldom know each other well enough off the playing field to asses one another's competence, loyalty, or reliability. In these circumstances, professionally functional interracial social networks which could facilitate the career development of black as well as white players are unlikely to emerge.

Thus, in addition to the objective criteria that I have examined here, other subjective (attitudinal) and structural (network) factors may play an important part in managerial recruitment in professional football. These data account for slightly less than one fifth (17%) of the variance in managerial recruitment in the full model; thus it is clear that factors other than those examined here are important in the selection process. Although measurement error and the relatively small amount of variation in the dependent variable are partial sources of the unexplained variation in managerial recruitment, it is also quite probable that latent (unmeasured) sponsorship variables account for a major portion of the residual. As a result, the findings presented in this report represent only an *incomplete* picture of the managerial recruitment process in the National Football League. Nevertheless I do not expect that the basic pattern of relationships observed here would have differed drastically if other relevant criteria had been available and had been incorporated into the research model. The model used here implies that race operates both directly and indirectly; that is, blacks do not become head coaches both because of their race and because they do not enter the queue from which most head coaches are selected. Including additional measures of sponsorship in the recruitment model, for example, probably would tend to increase the indirect or mediated effects of race and to reduce the direct effects rather than "washing away" the overall importance of race in the recruitment process.

These interpretations are consistent with other recent studies of employers' practices that inhibit minority access to equal employment opportunities. For example, data from a recent national survey of employers revealed that in higher-level jobs, the chances are significantly greater that an opening will be filled by a white when employers use social networks as a major recruitment method (Braddock & McPartland, 1987). In the NFL, the old buddy referral system appears to be the major recruitment mechanism. As Philadelphia Eagles General Manager Jim Murray (1981) noted, "There just aren't that many opportunities. These (NFL) jobs are so precious, so coveted, that they're usually filled before anyone knows they're open" (p. 104). Irv Cross, a former player, assistant coach, and sports commentator, goes even further. According to Cross:

The NFL coaching staff is like a men's social club. It develops that way because of the long hours the coaches work, all the time they spend together at training camp, then during the season. So what happens quite often is that the (head) coach puts together his staff the way he'd put together a fishing trip. All the guys he likes to have around, all the guys he likes to drink with. . . . I have no objection to a white being hired ahead of a black, if it's for the right reasons. But to pass up a black because you don't want to drink with him, or your wife doesn't want to swap bon-bons with his wife, well, that's not right. ("The Last Color Line," 1981, p. 72)

The NFL is neither a citadel of racism nor a paragon of social justice. Like most institutions in American society, egalitarian and meritocratic values predominate in some areas and fail in others. On the one hand, as noted above, the large representation of blacks as players reflects, to some degree, equality of access. On the other hand, blacks gross underrepresentation in field and front office management positions reflects, to some degree, inequality of advancement opportunities. The findings of the NFL managerial recruitment study suggest that the National Football League contains deeply embedded and institutionalized processes which operate to restrict blacks' opportunities for advancement.

Opportunity is the key issue. If black coaches are hired, some will succeed and some will fail, as with white coaches. In the National Basketball Association (NBA), for example, where blacks have received somewhat greater opportunities for advancement, the opportunity principle has been demonstrated well. During the past decade four different black head coaches have won NBA championships; others have failed and have been removed from their positions. Until the National Football League is willng to recognize that inequality of opportunity, not lack of qualifications, is the barrier to black advancement in both field and front office management positions, the existing inequities will endure.

Further and more refined research on this topic is needed, but the present evidence suggests that National Football League policymakers should become more highly aware of how "race" may operate to the relative disadvantage of black players and to the relative advantage of white players. Ideally, future deliberations should pay particular attention to organizational policies and practices; ultimately, these are more responsible for the existing racial differences in the distribution of organizational rewards and are more capable of manipulation, in a corrective sense, than are the attitudes and behaviors of individuals. Finally, because racial equality is a widely shared goal, appropriate corrective measures, perhaps including affirmative action strategies, should be adopted and implemented with the highest organizational priority and support.

REFERENCES

Alvarez, R., & Lutterman, K. (Eds.). (1979). *Discrimination in organizations*. San Francisco: Jossey-Bass.

Black dominance. (1977, May 9). *Time*, pp. 56–60.

Blalock, H. M. (1962). Occupational discrimination: Some theoretical propositions. *Social Problems, 9*, 240–247.

Braddock, J. H. (1978a). The sports pages: In black and white. *Arena Review, 2*, 17–25.

Braddock, J. H. (1978b). Television and college football: In black and white. *Journal of Black Studies, 8*, 369–379.

Braddock, J. H. (1980). *Institutional discrimination: A study of managerial recruitment in professional football*. Washington, DC: National Football League Players Association.

Braddock, J. H. & McPartland, J. M. (1987). *How minorities continue to be excluded from equal employment opportunities: Research on labor market and institutional barriers*. Baltimore, MD: Johns Hopkins University.

Brower, J. (1972). *The radical basis of the division of labor among players in the National Football League as a function of racial stereotypes*. Paper presented at the meeting of the Pacific Sociological Association, Portland, Oregon.

Cohen, R. M., Deutsch, J. A., & Neft, D. S. (1979). *The scrapbook history of pro football*. Indianapolis: Bobbs-Merrill.

Cross, I. (1981, November 10). Quoted in *Philadelphia Daily News* (p. 72).

Dougherty, J. (1976). Race and sport: A follow-up study. *Sports Sociology Bulletin, 5,* 1–12.

Duncan, O. D. (1975). *Introduction to structural equations models.* New York: Academic Press.

Ebony magazine. (1960–1979). Chicago: Johnson Publishing.

Edwards, H. (1973). *Sociology of sport.* Homewood, IL: Dorsey.

Eitzen, D. S., & Yetman, N. (1977). Immune from racism? *Civil Rights Digest, 9,* 3–13.

Football Register. (1966–1979). *Sporting News* (St. Louis).

Friedman, R. (1975). Institutional racism: How to discriminate without really trying. In T. Pettigrew (Ed.), *Racial discrimination in the United States* (pp. 384–410). New York: Harper & Row.

Gordon, R. A. (1968). Issues in multiple regression. *American Journal of Sociology, 73,* 592–616.

Javits, J. K. (1960). *Discrimination—USA.* New York: Harcourt, Brace.

Knowles, L., & Prewitt, K. (1969). *Institutional racism in America.* Englewood Cliffs, NJ: Prentice-Hall.

Loy, J. W., & McElvogue, J. F. (1970). Racial segregation in American sport. *International Review of Sport Sociology, 5,* 5–24.

Massengale, J. D. (1976). Coaching as an occupational subculture. In A. Yiannakis et al. (Eds.), *Sport sociology: Contemporary Themes.* Dubuque, IA: Kendall-Hunt. (Reprinted from *Phi Delta Kappan,* 1974, pp. 140–142).

Murray, J. (1981, November 13). Quoted in *Philadelphia Daily News* (p. 104).

National football guide. (1966–1979). *Sporting News* (St. Louis).

Nordlie, P. (1979). Proportion of black and white army officers in command positions. In R. Alvarez & K. Lutterman (Eds.), *Discrimination in organizations* (pp. 158–171). San Francisco: Jossey-Bass.

Official National Football League record manual. (1970–1979). New York: National Football League/Dell.

Pascal, A., & Rapping, L. (1972). The economics of racial discrimination in organized baseball. In A. Pascal (Ed.), *Racial discrimination in economic life* (pp. 119–156). Lexington, MA: Heath.

Rainville, R. E., & McCormick, E. (1977). Extent of covert racial prejudice in pro football announcers' speech. *Journalism Quarterly, 54,* 20–26.

Rosenblatt, A. (1967, September). Negroes in baseball: The failure of success. *Transaction,* pp. 51–52.

Scully, G. W. (1974). Discrimination: The case of baseball. In R. Nott (Ed.), *Government and the sports business* (pp. 221–274). Washington, DC: Brookings Institution.

Treat, R. (1979). *The encyclopedia of football.* Garden City, NY: Doubleday-Dolphin.

Williams, R. & Youssef, Z. (1972). Consistency of football coaches in stereotyping the personality of each position's player. *International Journal of Sport Psychology, 3,* 3–13.

Williams, R. & Youssef, F. (1975). Division of labor in college football along racial lines. *International Journal of Sport Psychology, 6,* 3–13.

8

Race Relations and Sports: Commentary on Braddock

Lodis Rhodes
Lyndon B. Johnson School of Public Affairs
University of Texas at Austin

While race relations as an area of scientific inquiry is rich with a voluminous literature, it rests on a narrow foundation. The contemporary foundation was laid by Robert Park (1950). It has fostered a research tradition that is essentially social-psychological in approach—one that focuses on prejudice, discrimination, and how social groups form and operate. Park proposed that the ordering principles of race relations are competition, conflict, accommodation, and assimilation. The particular concern has been the character and patterns of individual prejudice and institutional discrimination. The research tradition itself is restrictive in at least two important ways. First, as others have pointed out, it does not adequately capture the dynamic quality of race relations. That is, our research models are not particularly good approximations of reality. Second, an assimilationist philosophy undergirds much of the research. To the degree the philosophy shapes the research questions we ask, the research questions, in turn, frame the issues we debate and the policies we choose. The social-psychological tradition has not allowed a full range of policy options to be considered in policy debates . . . especially concerning race relations.

The chapter by Jomills Braddock II reflects the strengths and weaknesses of the social-psychological research tradition. It applies what has served as a sound descriptive approach to explaining race relations for almost three quarters of a century. In a more specific way, Braddock's discussion helps refine important questions about social behavior. However, it leaves unanswered a range of different but important questions about race relations. The limited predictability of Braddock's models reflects the same general limitation found in extant theories of race relations.

Braddock acknowledges progress by citing the increasingly higher rates of participation by black athletes in collegiate and professional football. However, he too concludes that there is a flaw in race relations because blacks have not achieved parity as head coaches in the sport. Braddock's chapter picks up and extends the themes of power, status, sponsored mobility, and a paternalistic system of race relations in his analysis of professional football. He asserts that "black–white relations in sport mirror common patterns of race relations in other major social institutions in our society" (p. 105). He uses the National Football League (NFL) as a case study in an attempt to show how institutional barriers block equal employment opportunities for blacks. He provides data on the rates of participation for blacks and whites as players and coaches. Finally, he suggests his study has implications for public policies related to equal employment opportunity.

There is a core assumption underlying Braddock's analysis: that sport is an egalitarian and meritocratic enterprise. As a society, we value sport for that reason. It is a faulty assumption. Fortunately, it is not his own. The myth is that sport has important symbolic value that is consistent with our democratic ideal—an open, competitive system wherein the rules are known, agreed to, and applied evenhandedly. The reality is that the type of sport Braddock discusses is a multinational corporate enterprise. It has a highly specialized and segmented labor force. As with other corporate enterprises, it is unlikely that a worker will start at the bottom of the organization and by skill and hard work end a career by running the organization. It does not happen at IBM and it does not happen with the Dallas Cowboys.[1]

Braddock uses the theoretical propositions of Hubert Blalock (1962) to set up his own analysis. Because Blalock offered 13 propositions on occupational discrimination, I will not outline them here but instead refer the reader to his article. However, I will note the key aspects of Blalock's discussion. Blalock sought to describe and explain access to and mobility up the occupational ladder for immigrant groups during the first quarter of this century. He was interested in the relative economic and social position of immigrant groups and blacks in an expanding industrial economy. He assumed the industrial economy to be a competitive one wherein different classes of employees had competitive advantages and disadvantages that employers could exploit. His thesis was that members of immigrant groups or blacks who were in low-status and/or skilled occupations could and would be exploited, particularly when there were more jobs than workers in that occupational category. Blalock also suggested that blacks were at risk of becoming a permanent underclass because of job discrimination. Blalock used professional baseball and the entry of black ball players into the white major leagues to illustrate his propositions. In my opinion, Braddock has misused or misunderstood Blalock's propositions. Braddock thus weakens his own analysis of discrimination in professional football and of the occupational mobility of black athletes within the industry.

Blalock was more interested in discrimination as it affects entry into an occupation of an industry than in upward mobility within that industry. He viewed all professional ball players as workers in one undifferentiated occupation—on-field performers. He also drew a distinction between on-field performers as one occupational category and front-office workers (managers and coaches). The distinction is important because Blalock offered his propositions with a qualification. Blalock stated that the prestige level of the job and the general market conditions must not vary or the propositions would not hold. That is, Blalock cautioned that his propositions on the positive and negative competitive advantages for a class of worker would not hold if (a) one looked across rather than within occupational categories, (b) there was a difference in the status of the occupations, and (c) if one did not take into account the demand for and supply of workers for a particular type of job.

---

[1]The Dallas Cowboys' corporation was sold recently for a reported $140–$150 million. The new owner hired a new head coach for the team. If news reports are accurate, the decisive factor in selecting that new coach was the personal relationship the owner had with the new coach. It was a relationship that began in college when both played on the same segregated football team. I can easily argue that the decision to hire a new coach was not racial whereas the entire context of the hiring illustrates accumulated privilege based on race.

Braddock overlooked this qualification in his own analysis. It is precisely the change in participation rates of black athletes in professional sport documented by Braddock which reduces the utility of Blalock's propositions. The Blalock propositions are helpful in understanding how and why the color barrier to on-field participation was broken in collegiate and professional sports, but as Blalock cautioned, they are not good tools for analyzing white-collar occupations. Braddock, however, has a twofold concern: the absence of black head coaches in professional football and the comparative advantage a former player has in becoming a head coach in the NFL. Because of the highly specialized character of the labor market in the entertainment industry, there is significant variation in the prestige and status attached to different segments of that market. Part of the market, before-the-camera jobs, is quite visible to the public. Another part of that market is all but invisible to the public. It includes corporate management. More important, the on-field playing jobs held by athletes are part of a different labor market than that represented by the jobs held by a largely invisible corporate management. It would make more sense to apply Blalock's propositions to corporate management (owners, general managers, legal counsel, and head coaches) than to players.

If one uses Blalock's work to justify an assumption that professional football is an industry, then one cannot argue with a characterization of that professional sport as a large-scale, corporate enterprise with different occupational categories. Within the industry, corporate management is a white-collar category; on-field performers can be thought of as performing a skilled, blue-collar occupation. The industry has relatively few jobs in the white- and blue-collar occupational categories and an oversupply of qualified workers despite the highly specialized, skilled character of the jobs. The position of head coach is one job classification which straddles the white- and blue-collar categories. While it is easy to assume that the position of head coach is the next rung on the occupational ladder for a player, this has not been true for either white or black players. It is more accurate to view it as a mid-level executive position in corporate management. As with the on-field job market, jobs within corporate management vary widely in status and prestige. One could argue that many of the star professional athletes, who are usually more visible and better paid than their head coaches, have higher social prestige with the public than do coaches. It could also be argued that players, whether black or white, are not viewed as executives in the corporate boardrooms of professional sports teams. In this context, they have lower status and power than head coaches, some of whom are also involved in business operations. One should make no mistake in understanding that institutional discrimination is at work in both the white- and blue-collar labor markets of professional football. However, Braddock's analysis would have to tell us more about the labor market for corporate executives to give us useful information about the selection of head coaches in professional football and why blacks have been locked out of the position.

Race relations is really concerned with two broad categories of phenomena. One is the unseen. It is represented by ideals, myths, perceptions, and attitudes we hold about ourselves, others, and our environment. Change can occur in one or all of these areas without necessarily showing up in observable individual or institutional behavior. The other broad category of phenomena is that which is seen—the specific patterns of interaction or lack of same between blacks and whites. It is this category that has been addressed by public policies related to education and other visible realms. Further, the degree of interaction itself has become the standard by which we measure progress in race relations. In a sense, we have reduced the study of race relations to counting contacts between blacks and whites. This approach is a methodological black hole. It is easy to get sucked into it and not easy to get out. That is, the theoretical approaches we use allow us to measure "progress" while requiring us to conclude that the progress is producing the same old symptoms of segregation and isolation. Braddock partially ends up in this black hole. He reports a change in black–white interaction and to some extent acknowledges the change as a form of progress. But he is forced to conclude there has been limited progress in race relations because parity does not exist between blacks and whites in assuming head coaching positions in the NFL.

I agree with the basic conclusion drawn by Braddock—namely, there are still flaws in race relations. The major flaw is in the ideal and its underlying assimilationist philosophy. Both are abstractions for too many blacks. Segregation, and its new variation of isolation, is the norm and very much a concrete reality for many blacks. More important, accumulated group privilege and burden become increasingly difficult for public policies to unravel. The social-psychological approach cannot capture the structural context in which race relations occur. However, it is precisely this inability that illustrates the importance of context when questions of public policy and leadership regarding race relations in sports and other major institutions in society loom in the background, as they usually do.

Contemporary race relations express our differing and contested views of right and privilege. Our views, in turn, emerge from how we value freedom, justice, and equality. One expects good theory to accurately describe, explain, and predict events within the dynamic arena of race relations. On the one hand, a good theory should help answer the questions of how and why we express our individual and institutional views on freedom, justice, and equality as we do. On the other hand, it should recognize the essential character of those expressions as incremental and cumulative. That is, our individual and institutional expressions of right and privilege are not abstractions. We exhibit them daily through our actions and decisions. It is often the context of these actions and decisions that tells us most about race relations. The social-psychological research approach is also very much a part of the larger cultural milieu of American society. That is, the focus on prejudice, discrimination, and the formation and operation of social groups reflects a specific, dominating view of the American political and economic order—democratic idealism. The democratic ideal has individualism as its centerpiece and the democratic process as the preferred procedure for redress of grievances. The ideal was fashioned by Anglo-European males. Although seldom acknowledged, this dominating view of individualism and democratic idealism is ironic and contradictory. The irony is that white males acted to protect as a class their own whiteness, maleness, and status as property owners. They did so by establishing individualism as the standard for protection and privilege and by denying women, blacks, and other racial groups access to the legal and administrative machinery of redress. The contradiction, of course, is that you cannot build individualism on a foundation of class membership that has color, gender, and property ownership as its central operating principles. As a framework for policy the standard of individualism and democratic idealism has always been exclusionary. It set up two classes. The first, white males, was protected and allowed to accumulate privilege; the second, those defined as other, was outside the protection of the law.

Observation tells us that the Anglo-European standard of individualism and democratic idealism was exclusionary in intent, practice, and effect. The standard incorporates a lot of psychological baggage. The ability to exclude carries a stigma for those doing the excluding as well as for those excluded. The stigma has been and continues to be explored in its negative impact on blacks. It has not been explored as either a pathological aspect of American culture or as a positive energizing feature of activist movements. The standard is important as regards the development of public policy because it easily accommodates assimilationism and dependence on legal-administrative remedies for race problems. The democratic process suggests that changes in policy come about through redress of grievances by legal means. Of course, the irony in this is that those groups omitted from or specifically penalized by the Constitution nonetheless have become accustomed to relying, first and foremost, on its legal machinery. They press for inclusion through a system that began with the basic, fundamental flaw of excluding them. Since the system itself excludes, it should not be surprising that the same system would be constrained by that flaw in offering a full range of options to solve race-related problems.

From a social-psychological perspective, the stigma of exclusion is significant. It set an I-They dichotomy wherein the standard for protection and privilege was the Anglo-European male—the I. Whiteness, maleness, and property ownership were traits assumed valid and superior. They required no test or justification. Further, the same standard assumed that other classes of individuals, such as blacks, Native Americans, women, or poor whites without property, possessed no distinguishing characteristics despite obvious and important differences among them. This simplistic and faulty logic embodied in the protected and privileged status that Anglo-European males accorded themselves in the name of individualism and the democratic ideal has extracted a heavy toll. For example, it creates the psychology that leads whites to question affirmative action as reverse discrimination and to overlook their own accumulated privilege and how it was accumulated. It is the interplay of irony and contradiction that so easily permits the focus of research on race relations to shift to the behavior, attitudes, status, and activities of the excluded classes. We have focused almost no attention on whites in general and white males in particular because that focus might include the legal principles of torts, fault, and compensation for intentional and unintentional injury. In this vein, it is entirely appropriate to ask as a matter of law and policy that those who have gained advantage unfairly or illegally "pay" for their accumulated privilege by compensating the injured party.

It is this interplay of individualism and democratic idealism that largely predetermines how researchers interpret their findings—more assimilation is better than less. It also guides researchers away from exploring what I call the pathology of exclusion—the major defining characteristic of the Anglo-European experience. Finally, it nudges researchers away from studying the long-term impact of accumulated privilege—the tendency to willingly accept illegal or unfairly obtained advantage. While we readily accept the concept of competitive advantage in some spheres of economic activity, we have not extended the concept to the arena of race relations. Privilege does accumulate over time to the point at which it creates a distinct and measurable advantage for individuals and groups—a competitive, often unfair, edge. It is this unfair competitive edge, in my opinion, that is a far more appropriate focus for research on race relations than the continuing focus on the disadvantages of people of color. The change in research focus is subtle but important. It shifts one from looking at blacks and other minorities as the victims of racism to looking at individual whites and whites as a class as the beneficiaries of unfair and often immoral competitive practices.

REFERENCES

Blalock, H. M., Jr. (1962). Occupational discrimination: Some theoretical propositions. *Social Problems*, *9*, 240–247.
Park, R. E. (1950). *Race and culture* (p. 150). Glencoe, IL: Free Press.

9

E Pluribus Unum: The Impossible Dream?

Charles B. Keely
Department of Demography
Georgetown University

The motto of the United States, *e pluribus unum*, applies to the formation of the union from the several states. Metaphorically, the motto has been applied to the formation of the nation from a variety of immigrants and their descendants.

National unity with ethnic diversity has always been a source of tension in American life; the responses throughout the history of the Republic have varied. In the *Federalist Papers* (No. 2) John Jay wrote, "Providence has been pleased to give this one connected country to one united people—a people descended from the same ancestors, speaking the same language, professing the same religion, attached to the same principles of government, very similar in their manners and customs" (p. 94). This description was not true, however. It overlooked the Germans, Dutch, and Swedes concentrated in the northern colonies; it glossed over the religious variety among Protestants, not to mention Catholic and Jewish groups; it did not give even a passing nod to the black, predominantly slave, population or to American Indians. Nevertheless, the quotation illustrates nicely the ideal of a white, Anglo-Saxon, Protestant nation that underlies the emphasis on conformity by immigrants. Whether expressed as 100% Americanism, as opposition to hyphenated Americans, or in "Love It or Leave It" bumper stickers, the conformity ideal has been a continuous response to the tension. The majority did not always demand total assimilation, a complete casting-off of the old self. Certain things are unalterable; ancestry cannot be changed. In other spheres, such as religion, tolerance increased over time. Yet in civic culture (principles and underlying values of government) conformity has been expected and demanded continuously.

A second response to the tension emphasized the contribution of various groups to building the American character and nation. Israel Zangwill's play of 1908, *The Melting Pot*, was anticipated in 1782 by J. Hector St. John Crevecoeur's description of America in his *Letters from an American Farmer*: "Here individuals of all nations are melted into a new race of men, whose labours and posterity will one day cause great changes in the world" (p. 55). The melting pot image is vague. Is it a stew in which everything that is thrown into the pot willy-nilly emerges as part of the meal, or is the image more like that of a smelter, where only the useful metal is retained in the new alloy and the dross is eliminated? The melting pot idea is valuable: It calls attention to the actual and potential contributions of people from many backgrounds, and it indicates a greater tolerance of diversity as a source of enrichment. As ideology and as description, however, the melting pot idea is as incomplete as the notion of conformity.

Horace Kallen, in his 1915 articles in *The Nation* (later published as a book), made the argument that true Americanism lay not in destruction of minority cultures but in their conservation. Kallen's argument, however, made little impact on the United States' immigration debate at the time; his conceptualization of pluralism took hold slowly. Yet pluralism assumed a set of values about government and a set of institutions for conducting public business that was in large part a descendant of English tradition, made over in the course of American history. Pluralism has been the dominant ideology of the last quarter century.

THE PROBLEM WITH PLURALISM

The nation today is undergoing a reevaluation of the meaning of pluralism. To question pluralism also means to question what it is that holds us together as a nation, the *unum*. Both the civil rights movement and the 1965 policy changes in immigration law have contributed to this reevaluation. The main purpose of the immigration reforms in the 1965 legislation was the abolition of the national-origins quota system, the mechanism used to reserve immigrant visas for the natives of certain countries, primarily in northern and western Europe. The impetus of the reform had roots in long-standing opposition to quotas, an opposition based on principle, on experience in refugee resettlement after World War II, and on such human problems as family separations under the quota system.

Immigration reform in the mid-1960s and the civil rights movement proceeded on two separate tracks and hardly affected one another, even though they were going on simultaneously and often were represented by the same champions in Congress. Only in their aftermath have people sought to analyze and evaluate the relationships between these two major changes in American policies. The change in immigrants' ethnic origin under the 1965 law (from European to Latin and Asian dominance), the phenomenon of illegal immigration (which was caused partly by the 1965 immigration reforms and which has dominated the immigration debate since the 1970s), and the refugee flows from Cuba, from Indochina, and more recently from Central America have created a link between immigration and civil rights policies.

Pluralism assumes a civil culture: the beliefs, institutions, rituals, heroes, and symbols that provide the basis for a common national identity. Civic culture is at the public end of the continuum between the private and public domains. It is not difficult to construct a list of basic values related to civic culture, but it is more difficult to agree on which values are at the core. I suggest three values of importance: individual freedom, equality of opportunity, and pluralism itself. A basic theme of the founding of the republic was freedom from unreasonable actions of government and the right of the people to govern themselves. This value continues today in calls for minimalist approaches to government. Equality of opportunity emphasizes the right of individuals to pursue their goals on the basis of ability—a downplaying of privilege which, like the freedom value, focuses on the individual. Pluralism has been added to the array of civic values since World War II. Freedom and equality have come to be seen not only as compatible with cultural and ethnic diversity but as requiring tolerance and even respect for those qualities.

It is true that these ideals have never been, and are not now, put into practice as well as everyone would like. Nor do I suggest that the interpretation or meaning of these basic values is unchanging. The addition or at least the formal recognition of pluralism as a basic American value illustrates a potential for flexibility in the civic culture. The ideals of freedom and equality of opportunity, however, are of long standing, and defenders of pluralism refer to the historical facts of religious, racial, and ethnic variety in cultural and social structures to legitimate the recognition of pluralism as a basic ingredient of the American experiment. As American as apple pie, pizza, tacos, and egg rolls, and about time we recognized it, goes the line of argument.

What has caused the current redefinition of pluralism, and what is different from past history, is the role of government not only in promoting and maintaining individual freedom but also regarding equality of opportunity—including the movement toward ensuring this equality by requiring certain measures of equality of achievement—and in fostering pluralism. A list of actions such as support of ethnic heritage studies and bilingual education indicates an active government involvement in fostering pluralism. Programs for equality of opportunity, from affirmative action to minority contractors' set-asides, illustrate the government's activism and the controversial emphasis on equality of achievement. In both cases there is tension with individual freedom, for the spotlight of law and programs is no longer focused on the individual; instead, groups seem to have acquired, and group membership seems to confer, quasi-property rights.

The abolition of national-origins quotas in 1965 could be accommodated in civic culture as a long-overdue end (a) to government discrimination on the basis of nationality, (b) to an aspersion on the ethnic groups who helped to build the country, and (c) to unfair treatment of American citizens in terms of their ability to sponsor relatives simply because they belonged to a particular ethnic group. The problem of immigration policy reform was not so much the question of eliminating quotas. The problem was the result of that legislative change—namely, numerical dominance by immigrants from Asian and Latin countries and an increase in illegal migration. Many of the new immigrants are eligible for programs that seek to bolster equality of access as measured by equality of achievement. The conflicts come quickly to the surface. If affirmative action is intended to right past wrongs, why should a recent immigrant qualify? Moreover, many of the recent immigrants are skilled and professional people. Over 25% of the immigrants under the 1965 Act who stated an occupation on their visa applications were in professional and technical occupations. What is the justification for categorizing a new immigrant professional or his or her child as belonging to a disadvantaged minority solely because of ancestry?

The influx of recent immigrants from Latin and Asian countries, which are also the sources of most illegal migrants and most refugees, has raised a second issue, the absorptive capacity of American society. Questioning the absorptive capacity of society is a long-established and predictable response to each new wave of immigrants in the American experience. Americans have always been ambivalent about immigrants. Unlike past experience, however, the very groups designated by policies to foster equality are augmented in considerable numbers by new residents in an atmosphere of government-sponsored emphasis on ethnicity. If group membership confers benefits, not to mention the political power acquired by group leaders and other "professional ethnics," will these benefits not retard the process of assimilation to the civic culture?

The worst-case scenario from this perspective is a breakdown of civic culture itself: a loss of agreement on basic values and a contest of interests that cannot be accommodated within the political system. The image of Quebec is often conjured, but the situation in the United States is quite different. The variety, dispersion, and lack of a territorial base for Hispanics makes a comparison with Quebec not particularly useful. Yet the threat to system maintenance is also greater because territory provides a basis of accommodation and problem management in Canada; this basis is absent in the United States in view of the wide variety and dispersion of Hispanic groups in this country.

It is easy to be carried away by rhetoric. Pondering ethnic origins, large numbers, and comparisons with events in other places of the globe can lead easily to a vision of Armageddon. Perhaps we should stand back for a moment and consider the basic question: What is the glue, the *unum*, that holds this society together? Whenever a central element of civic culture is questioned—slavery in the nineteenth century or segregation beginning in the 1950s—the coherence of the system is tested. The nation is being tested now, probably not as severely as in the examples mentioned, but tested nevertheless. One way of characterizing the test is to say that pluralism is being redefined. Its reverberations are felt in the law, in education, in housing, in social policy about language, even in the impact on the souls of men and women concerned about what kind of people we are and what kind of people we want to be. It is not clear how the issues of *pluribus* and *unum* will be decided during this round of the making of America, but to ignore the importance of either element is to tempt fate.

WHAT IS "OUT OF CONTROL"?

It was said recently as an editorial and political truism that immigration was "out of control." Members of Congress, cabinet secretaries, and editorial writers told us constantly that our immigration policy was out of hand. Apparently we did not control our borders; we could not limit the number of people coming into the country; nor were we able to choose those whom we wished to welcome as immigrants. Whether we spoke of legal permanent settlement, workers' illegal migration, or the movement of people seeking a safe haven in the United States, it seemed that our borders were not our own.

Something in the human psyche must exist to make us regard every difficulty and every challenge as a crisis, and immigration surely presents a challenge. To a nation as ambivalent about immigration as we have always been, a change in the size, composition, and origin of immigration on the scale that has occurred since the 1965 reform certainly causes hesitancy and doubt about our ability to weather such changes. It is in this context that we heard that our borders were out of control.

The suggested remedies to our immigration "problem" are contained in the Immigration Control and Reform Act of 1986, also known as the Simpson-Rodino Act. The centerpiece of the Simpson-Rodino Act is an attempt to "demagnetize" the workplace so that illegal migrants will not come to the United States because they will not be able to get work here. The provisions for demagnetization, known as employer sanctions, basically make it illegal for an American employer to hire people to work in the United States without authorization. It should be noted that the Simpson-Rodino Act probably will not reduce the number of temporary workers coming to the United States. The law provides for a number of temporary labor procedures and programs that probably will result in as many workers entering as before. What will change is that the law will allow them to enter and work legally rather than illegally. Apparently what was out of control was not the number of people entering the labor force but that they entered without governmental controls. Many people in the country think (and the rhetoric of borders out of control certainly suggests) that too many workers are coming to the United States, whether legally or illegally. To the framers of the 1986 immigration act, however, and to their supporters in the executive branch, the issue was not one of numbers. As the title of the law states, it was an issue of control.

In order to enforce employer sanctions and to avoid any taint of discrimination, employers must now ask new employees to document their right to take employment in the United States. To accomplish this, every individual entitled to work in the United States, citizen and alien alike, must show identification documenting who he or she is and the right to take employment. Passports, immigrant cards, driver's licenses, birth certificates, and a variety of other documents can be shown to the employer. The employer must keep records and show forms certifying that documents were reviewed by the hiring official.

A second aspect of controlling immigration and our borders is an attempt to deal with what the government calls illegal migrants from Central America. In their own eyes and in those of their supporters, these individuals are seeking refuge or safe haven and should be given asylum in the United States. Whatever one thinks about the legitimacy of the Central Americans' claims to refugee status in the United States, the executive branch proposed in the last session of Congress new and broad powers for specially trained asylum officers. These officers would be able to make decisions, with limited access to review by United States courts, on applications by would-be refugees to the United States. Many people claim that decisions about refugees in the United States are made not on universal criteria but to fit the foreign policy objectives of the particular administration making the decisions.

Whether the decisions are to permit entry (as, for example, by Mariel Cubans or Haitian boat people) or to deny entrance (as with Central Americans currently), decisions seem to be dominated by foreign policy and political interests rather than by the needs of refugee applicants. This situation prompted the Moakley-DeConcini bill now pending in Congress, which would require the government not to deport Central American refugee claimants. In the not-too-distant past the Reagan administration also mandated a reevaluation of asylum claims by Cambodians in Thailand, even suggesting that individuals who fled from Cambodia into Thailand need not prove that they were singled out for persecution as a condition of obtaining refugee status for admittance to the United States. This very criterion of individual persecution and of an individual decision based on each claimant's history of persecution, which was waived for Cambodians, is now applied universally by the current administration in Central American cases. One can only wish the Cambodians well in their efforts to obtain a safer haven than they could find in their own country if they were forced to return; yet the actions of this government raise questions about whether refugee policy is designed primarily for the sake of saving people or for advancing American policy interests. Indeed, one can ask why saving people and American national interests are pitted against one another in the first place as incompatible goals.

In both of these cases—employer sanctions and new asylum officers to make decisions on asylum claims with limited recourse to the courts—immigration "problems" lead to suggestions to increase the power of the government. One aspect missing from the debate about immigration problems in the United States is the idea that the state, qua state, has interests in the debate and in its outcome. Sometimes we think of immigration policy development as a broad range of conflicting and often competing interests and attempts to influence government decisions. The government seems to be an arbiter somewhat about and beyond the fray, listening to and perhaps being affected by the arguments and blandishments of this or that interest group. According to this view, the government truly is above it all, the judge of the competing interests. This image, of course, is untrue; the state is a social institution with interests of its own. No state apparatus willingly relinquishes its authority and control. By its very own nature the state is the controller of power in a society; control and use of that power are accepted as legitimate, however bounded by the traditions and laws of a country. Legitimate power or authority to control the relations between entities within a society is what the state is.

One of the universally accepted characteristics of the state today is that it has the sovereign authority to control who enters its borders. Citizens, at least as recognized in the Declaration of Human Rights, have the right to exit and to return to their own country, but those who are not citizens are not conceded any right to enter another country without the permission of the state holding that territory. If a state admits that it has lost control over its borders, it admits that in fact it does not exercise authority over the territory it claims as its own. This is a dangerous admission in the context of the nation-state system. If for no other reason, pride dictates that a state would both feel in control and actually exercise control over its borders. Therefore when officials of the state admit that they have lost control of their borders, it is not surprising that the state, and other important institutions in a society that work symbiotically with the state to maintain and enhance that society, should support measures which promise that the state apparatus again will obtain control over the borders.

All of these abstract words about the state mean that when government spokespersons say they have lost control of the border, it should be no surprise that they will propose laws which would increase the government's power over individuals in order to regain apparent control. In the area of employment, employer sanctions will extend government control over individual citizen and alien alike. Employers must make inspections, keep records, and make them available for government scrutiny. As for refugees, the state will propose new powers (not yet and perhaps never to be granted) to make decisions about giving asylum; it will do so while attenuating an independent judiciary's right to review whether such decisions were capricious, arbitrary, or made within the law. This action would increase the power of the state over individuals because the protection of the courts is lessened. Due process is an early victim of a siege mentality.

In most people's minds, the debate over immigration of the 1970s and 1980s centers on the large numbers of people coming in, whether they are taking jobs away from Americans, and how they may upset various balances within American society. Ironically, the legislation passed and signed into law in November 1986 did not address the issue of numbers. If anything, the numbers of people coming to the United States will increase, including those coming temporarily to work and those coming in as relatives of the newly legalized immigrants under the amnesty program. If the numbers of persons coming to work under temporary legal programs can be increased, apparently Congress is convinced that there are some jobs which Americans are not willing to take or are not willing to take under the conditions and at the wages that employers are willing to offer. It seems that those employers have enough influence to have persuaded legislators to agree with their evaluation of those jobs. The people who enter under such temporary programs probably will be from this hemisphere; more specifically, they will be Hispanics from Mexico and the Caribbean. It would be dishonest to deny that those who worry about immigration and ethnic issues in the United States are concerned mainly about the high proportion of Hispanic people entering the United States legally and illegally. Whether or not one agrees with those concerns, it is clear that the framers of immigration reform legislation were not concerned about ethnic impact.

On the other hand, we usually do not talk about the interests of the state in the immigration debate. Nevertheless, as things have developed, a major outcome of immigration reform will be to increase the state's influence in governing the lives of individuals in the workplace. Another tool is given to the state in order to make life safe for people, but safety in terms of access to the workplace is bought at the price of state control over access to the workplace.

I hesitate even to ask whether employer sanctions will be successful. Experience in other countries is not encouraging. One can expect an initial phase of voluntary compliance by employers. Yet, like the 55-mile-per-hour speed limit, attention to sanctions may diminish, especially if the economy improves and if labor force growth continues into the 1990s. At that time the fewer children of the "baby bust" resulting from the fertility decline of the 1970s will enter the labor force. Even if employer sanctions suffer from lack of attention and congressional funding, still they are on the books. In the case of recession, we can always turn our attention to foreigners as scapegoats and can reinvigorate enforcement of employer sanctions. Such sanctions may turn out to be an undetonated bomb for social and ethnic relations in America.

THE UNUM

Those who have grave questions about immigration believe essentially that too many immigrants are coming into the United States and that they are concentrated in too few ethnic groups, which are too different from the rest of American society. Furthermore, those groups are encouraged, specifically by government activities, to maintain their separateness and identity and thus not to become part of American society.

Whether the number of immigrants is too large is, above all, a matter of taste. Certainly the social sciences provide no information specifying a number or stating a ratio of immigrants to native-born persons that makes a society operable or inoperable. Different societies have different traditions and norms concerning the acceptance of foreign-born persons into their midsts. As a nation of immigrants, the United States, even with its ambivalence, incorporates foreigners more easily than do many European countries. It is much easier to think of a Turko-American than of a Turko-German. The same number or proportion of people probably would be absorbed more easily into the United States than into Germany.

If we look into history, the number of immigrants in the 1970s and 1980s is far from the historic high in terms of absolute numbers; also declining below historic highs is the proportion of foreign-born persons in the total population. The proportion of foreign-born in the United States today also is lower than that in many European countries, such as Germany, France, and Switzerland; those countries are regarded as ethnically homogeneous or as particularly hostile to absorbing foreign-born persons into the population. We even have a lower proportion of foreign-born persons than do our hemispheric neighbors Venezuela and Argentina, and our 6% foreign-born in 1980 fell well below the 15% + of Canada and the 20% + of Australia. Whether the number of immigrants is too high seems to depend on whether one is optimistic or pessimistic about the absorptive capacity of the United States. Some believe that one immigrant is one too many.

A second concern about recent immigration is related to the concentration of immigrants, legal and illegal, among certain ethnic groups. The major concern focuses on Hispanics; Asians are a secondary concern, particularly the refugees from Indochina who came in large numbers in the 1970s. Often it is pointed out that approximately one half of the current immigrants are Spanish-speaking; probably this proportion is higher if one includes illegal as well as legal immigrants. To consider legal and illegal immigrants together raises difficulties for any kind of calm analysis because of unsubstantiated claims about the annual addition to the population through illegal migration. Claims of one-half million annual net additions to the population through illegal migration have gained some currency in the popular press and in political circles but have no empirical basis. In addition, it is clear that illegal migration is not confined to Spanish-speaking people; it includes many individuals from around the world who enter the United States without documents or who enter legally on temporary visas and stay beyond their time.

The presence of one-half million immigrants from one language group may seem unprecedented, but it is not. The proportion of Germans in this country in the 1850s and 1860s was higher than the proportion of people from Spanish-speaking countries in the 1970s and 1980s. There was a great deal of German-language maintenance in the United States, including the use of German as the language of instruction in public schools in some midwestern counties. (That practice was stopped during the anti-German hysteria during and after World War I). People also seem to be concerned that bilingual education will increase the maintenance of language rather than encouraging the smooth development of English-speaking skill among school children.

Ultimately the resolution of the language issue also is a question of personality, of how optimistic or how pessimistic one is about the ability of society's institutions to enable participation by citizens and other residents. Those who are pessimistic about assimilation are alarmed about the concentrations of Spanish-language groups, about bilingual education, and about the fact that English is not officially the language of the United States. (One organization, USEnglish, advocates a constitutional amendment to make English the official language of the country.) Those who are optimistic point to past history, to the dominance of English in the social institutions of the United States, including schools, business, television, and radio, and to immigrants' common sense and their ambitions for their children. Most immigrants, no matter what their ethnic and linguistic background, want a better life for their children than they were able to create for themselves. This improvement requires faith and sacrifices to provide education for their children. Education brings the ability to compete successfully in business, the professions, or any other desired walk of life. To obtain an education, English-speaking skill and the general ability to operate in American society are absolute necessities.

If anything, we ought to have learned that immigrants are not stupid. If they want a better life for their children, those children probably will be able to participate in American society as well as the children of the native-born. This is not to say that everyone will be successful, but at least people with certain characteristics will not be excluded systematically. Various ethnic groups have been able to join American society throughout our history; it seems that they will continue to do so. It may be an additional benefit to the country if the children of current immigrants are able to negotiate well in American society while retaining a mother tongue other than English. The presence of another language can add to the richness and variety of our population and can help us to deal better with other societies in business and in foreign relations.

A third concern is whether immigrants' cultures are too different from that of the United States. Once again we must ask ourselves whether we are optimists or pessimists. I also wonder whether some of the pessimists are not tinged with a racist approach to immigration. If past immigrant groups were able to acculturate to the United States and if their children have been able to operate in this society as well as anybody else, why would current groups be unable to do so? Larger numbers of immigrants, higher proportions of immigrants in the American population, and greater linguistic and ethnic concentrations are more characteristic of the past than of the present. We accept that acculturation and integration took place among those past immigrant groups—Irish, Germans, Italians, eastern European Jews, and others. Why would people of Spanish culture be different unless we assume that they are genetically incapable of assimilation into American society? Such ideas are patently absurd. In view of immigrants' aspirations for their children, their children's isolation from mainstream America would be the very opposite of their desires.

The final concern is that today's pluralist ideology, particularly as institutionalized in government programs, leads to the maintenance of isolation rather than to integration of immigrants into American life. It is much easier, however, to integrate from a position of strength than from a position of weakness. In the past, ethnic groups maintained a certain amount of isolation in their own communities in order to deal from a position of cultural strength as they and their children tried to integrate, to assimilate, or simply to make it in America. The culture from which a people moves over a generation or two, or (more accurately) the culture that they modify, must be strong enough and resilient enough to provide a framework in which that people can live decently and humanly, even as they and their children adopt new values, different emphases, or other ways of doing things.

Ethnic separatism in community life afforded that possibility in the past; it continues to do so. Language, religion, residential segregation, and a host of other cultural practices helped make that position of strength a launching platform into the American mainstream. Some groups we launched faster than others. Some groups focused on and even dominated some occupations; others were dispersed more broadly into the labor force. The pre-World War II ethnic groups are indistinguishable today from Americans in general in regard to language use, educational achievement, income, occupational distribution, fertility, and other social indicators. Are we to believe that government programs to bolster self-identity will be so effective as to prevent today's immigrant groups from pursuing their interests? Are ethnic heritage programs more isolating than ethnic communities? Will the language of MBA programs and technology suddenly become Spanish rather than English? Perhaps I am too optimistic and trust too much in people's common sense.

We preserve the *unum* by preserving our commitment to individual freedom to pursue goals, to ensuring equality of opportunity rather than of privilege, and to leaving people alone. I doubt that government can plan acculturation and assimilation programs any better than it can plan other social programs. Over the centuries people have integrated well into the United States. Why change things? The sky is not falling. The prophets of doom in this arena always have brought out the worst in us as a people. The *unum* is a democratic spirit. A truly democratic ethos is opposed to meddling (especially by government) and to telling other people what their interests are and what they are to do. Immigrants to this country seem always to have had that spirit; that is why they come. They buy into the American civic culture with gusto. Ironically and disturbingly, native-born people and some past immigrants seem to lose the democratic spirit when new groups enter. Government officials and power brokers in big institutions seem especially prone to a general weakening of trust in people's abilities to act for themselves and for their neighbors without interference; perhaps power corrupts. The irony of integration is that it requires attention less to what immigrants do than to a revitalization by the rest of us, especially a revitalization of our desire to tell everybody else what to do and to have things done our way. The *unum* that holds us together consists of pluralism, the values of individual freedom and opportunities that support it, and a general context that allows people to be themselves and to pursue their interests. Without the *pluribus* and without an environment that allows plurality to flourish, there is no *unum* in America. America cannot be united unless we are free to be different. Nothing will destroy the unity of America as completely as uniformity imposed by some of us on all of us.

REFERENCES

Hamilton, A., Madison, J. & Jay, J. (1961). *The Federalist* (p. 94). Cambridge, MA: Belknap Press.
Kallen, H. (1924). *Culture and democracy in the United States.* New York.
St. John Crevecoeur, J. H. [1782] (1925). *Letter from an American Farmer* (p. 55). Reprint. New York: Albert and Charles Boni.
Zangwill, I. [1908] (1975). *The melting pot. Drama in four acts.* Reprint. New York: Arno Press.

10

Race, Ethnicity, and the Portrait of Inequality: Approaching the 1990s

Marta Tienda
Population Research Center
The University of Chicago

There is ample evidence of minority economic progress since 1960 (Bean & Tienda, 1987; Farley & Allen, 1987; Ross, Danziger, & Smolensky, 1987; Wilson, 1978), yet socioeconomic inequality along racial and ethnic lines remains highly visible and pervasive (Jensen & Tienda, 1987; Sandefur & Tienda, 1988a, 1988b). Because of differing patterns and rates of social and economic progress according to race and national origin, the configuration of color and socioeconomic rank changed during the 1970s (Tienda & Jensen, 1988). For example, between 1960 and 1980 average black–white education differentials all but disappeared, but Hispanics still lag far behind non-Hispanic whites in their average educational attainment.[1] This situation is not likely to improve over the short run because rates of age–grade delay and high school noncompletion remain alarmingly high for Hispanic youth (Bean & Tienda, 1987, chap. 8; Nelson & Tienda, 1985). Thus, as we approach the 1990s, Hispanics rather than blacks are the most educationally disadvantaged minority group.

Color lines assume a different configuration with respect to economic inequities. Black men rank lowest in status and income hierarchies, on average, while Hispanic and Asian men stand intermediate to non-Hispanic whites (Tienda & Lii, 1987). Prestige and income gaps between minority and nonminority women are less pronounced than they are among men, but this reflects the salience of gender over race in the U.S. stratification regime (Smith & Tienda, 1986). More recently, Puerto Ricans have begun to rival blacks as the most economically disadvantaged group (Tienda, 1988; Tienda & Jensen, 1989). However, the reasons for the deteriorating economic status of Puerto Ricans since the mid-1970s are poorly understood. My general objective in this chapter is to illustrate how color lines changed during the 1970s and early

This chapter appeared as an article in the *Sociological Spectrum*, 1989, *9*, 23–52.
[1]This generalization of greater educational convergence for blacks than Hispanics holds despite considerable improvement in the educational attainment of younger cohorts of Latinos. However, the averages conceal important differences in the distribution of education by race and national origin, and these indicators are less optimistic for minorities.

1980s and to think critically about likely scenarios for the 1990s. The first section documents changes in the relative and absolute well-being of black and Hispanic families between 1970 and 1985. The next section illustrates a connection between declining family incomes and the labor market status of minority heads of families. Finally, in the conclusion I speculate about the social underpinnings and political implications of the observed changes in family economic inequality.

MINORITY FAMILY WELL-BEING, 1970–1985

In this section I document the relative economic well-being[2] of minority families through an examination of money income and poverty status. The comparisons focus both on period differentials among families of Mexican, Puerto Rican, Cuban, black, or non-Hispanic white origin and on interperiod changes in the relative positioning of these groups in the income hierarchy.

Definitions

For purposes of analyzing changes and differentials in family income, I use the U.S. Bureau of the Census definition of *family* to include a head and all members related by blood, marriage, or adoption.[3] This definition was consistently measured over the period analyzed. Families were classified by race/ethnicity if one or both family heads were Mexican, Puerto Rican, Cuban, or black; others were classified as non-Hispanic whites.

Current money income refers to the sum of (a) money wages and salaries, (b) net income from self-employment, (c) social security income and cash transfers from other government programs, (d) property income (i.e., interest, dividends, and net rental income), and (e) other forms of cash income, including private pensions and alimony. The current money income concept as measured in Census Bureau data excludes capital gains, imputed rents, and in-kind benefits whether provided by government sources (income transfers) or by private sources (health insurance and other fringes) but includes taxes paid. Thus, while seemingly comprehensive and inclusive, current money income does not precisely measure a family's level of wealth, consumption, and general well-being. However, when adjusted for inflation and minor deviations in reporting procedures, money income measures are the most widely used

---

[2]While seemingly straightforward, the concept of economic well-being is complicated because its meaning hinges on several factors. That is, the socioeconomic significance of a fixed level of money income depends on absolute dollars, on the number of individuals who generate and consume it, and on the relative prices of goods and services. By focusing on family units and adjusting income levels for changes in the consumer price index, I am able to monitor these factors that affect the meaning of relative incomes.

[3]The U.S. Bureau of the Census distinguishes between families and households, noting that the former require relationship by blood, marriage, or adoption among all persons sharing a residence, while the latter do not. As such, households can and do include roomers/boarders and their spouses, as well as resident employees. Because the unrelated members are unlikely to pool their resources with the primary family, I confined my analyses to family income rather than household income. However, auxiliary analyses showed relatively little difference between family and household income because Hispanic extended living arrangements largely involve related individuals.

Table 1 Income distribution (%) and median income of families by Hispanic national origin and race

Income measure	Mexican	Puerto Rican	Cuban	Black	Non-Hispanic white
1969 median income					
Actual $	6,150	5,850	8,150	6,350	10,150
Constant $[a]	5,601	5,328	7,423	5,783	9,244
1969 income shares[b]					
$1–$4,999	39.7	45.2	26.2	43.3	20.1
$5,000–$9,999	40.5	39.2	41.6	35.8	34.7
$10,000–$19,999	18.5	14.2	28.3	19.0	36.2
$20,000–$29,999	1.1	0.9	3.1	1.5	5.8
$30,000+	0.2	0.1	0.7	0.4	3.1
Total	100.0	99.9	99.9	100.0	99.9
1979 median income					
Actual $	14,510	11,168	18,650	13,558	21,235
Constant $[a]	6,674	5,137	8,579	6,236	9,768
1979 income shares[b]					
$1–$4,999	35.0	48.3	24.3	39.8	19.3
$5,000–$9,999	38.0	32.8	35.1	33.5	31.9
$10,000–$19,999	24.0	17.1	34.0	23.0	38.0
$20,000–$29,999	2.3	1.5	4.4	3.1	7.4
$30,000+	0.7	0.4	2.3	0.6	3.3
Total	100.0	100.1	100.1	100.0	9.9
1984 median income					
Actual $	16,592	10,152	19,305	12,823	23,189
Constant $[a]	5,333	3,263	6,205	4,122	7,454
1984 income shares[b]					
$1–$4,999	47.3	64.9	42.7	57.6	33.0
$5,000–$9,999	33.1	22.5	31.4	26.9	32.0
$10,000–$19,999	17.2	11.5	21.0	13.8	27.8
$20,000–$29,999	2.1	0.8	3.2	1.5	5.1
$30,000+	0.2	0.3	1.8	0.2	2.0
Total	99.9	100.0	100.1	100.0	99.9

Note. Source: 1970 and 1980 Public Use Microdata Sample (PUMS) Files; March, 1985 Current Population Survey (CPS).
[a]1969 = $1.098, 1979 = $2.174, 1984 = $3.111.
[b]Based on 1969, 1979, and 1984 income figures, expressed in constant 1967 dollars.

measures to assess economic welfare and thus provide comparable measurement over time[4] and with other studies—hence their use in this study.

Median Family Income

Table 1 displays median family incomes for the three largest Hispanic national origin groups, blacks, and whites for 1969, 1979, and 1984, both in nominal (actual) and constant (1967) dollars. Also presented are the income distributions (in constant dollars) for each year. Nominal median family incomes rose for all groups during the

---

[4]Although the Census Bureau used roughly similar definitions of income between 1970 and 1980, except that the amount of detail on income sources increased over time, one change in reporting procedures did affect my presentation of results. Family incomes were truncated at $50,000 in 1970, compared to $75,000 in 1980. This truncation significantly affected comparisons of mean incomes, but not median incomes. Therefore, I restricted temporal comparisons of family incomes to medians. Furthermore, I expressed incomes in constant dollars to adjust for rising prices over time but also reported nominal incomes to provide a perspective on the current income gaps among the national origin groups.

1970–1980 period, but not uniformly according to national origin and race. This is important for thinking about the racial and ethnic configuration of inequality. In nominal terms, median family incomes of Mexicans and Cubans rose by approximately 130% during the 1970s, while the family incomes of Puerto Ricans rose 91%. For blacks and whites the corresponding increases in median family income were 114% and 109%, respectively.

Rather than representing real gains in relative economic well-being, the virtual doubling of family incomes during the 1970s resulted largely, although not exclusively, from the double-digit inflationary spiral that ensued after 1973. Price-adjusted increases in family incomes are far less impressive, but they provide a more accurate assessment of how the *relative* economic standing of Hispanic, black, and white families changed over the decade. In real terms, median family incomes of whites and blacks increased a scant 6% and 8%, respectively, during the 1970s, while Mexican and Cuban families enjoyed increases ranging from 16% to 19%. However, the median family income of Puerto Ricans *declined* 4% in real terms, and the share of Puerto Rican families with incomes under $5,000 actually increased 3 percentage points during the 1970s. This amounts to a widening of income differences between Puerto Ricans and all other groups. The improvement in the relative economic standing of Mexican and Cuban families can be traced to the larger shares of middle-income families, those with annual median incomes between $10,000 and $20,000.

Owing partly to the recession and stagnation that characterized the early 1980s, nominal incomes rose more slowly for Mexicans, Cubans, and non-Hispanic whites, but they actually *declined* for Puerto Ricans and blacks. These declines are especially evident when expressed in real terms. Although real median family income fell for all groups between 1979 and 1984, the decreases were greatest for Puerto Ricans and blacks (36% and 34%, respectively) followed by Cubans, non-Hispanic whites, and Mexicans (27%, 24%, and 20%, respectively). For Cubans, the influx of a large cohort of new immigrants in 1980 partly explains the decline; but for non-Hispanic whites, the lower economic position largely can be traced to the recession. Note, for example, the sharp increases in the shares of families with constant incomes below $5,000.

Because the changes in money incomes were not uniform over the period, the racial and ethnic configuration of inequality increased. Black median family income exceeded that of Mexican and Puerto Rican families in 1969 but was surpassed by that of Mexicans during the 1970s. In contrast, the median family income gap between blacks and Puerto Ricans widened after 1969, reaching approximately $2,700 in nominal terms by 1984. Throughout the period white families enjoyed the highest median incomes. During the 1970s the real median family income gap narrowed between whites and two Hispanic groups (Mexicans and Cubans), but it widened in real terms for Puerto Ricans. The black–white median family income gap remained constant over the decade.

Part of this tendency toward *greater* rather than lesser differentiation in minority versus nonminority family incomes can be traced to changes in demographic composition. Median family income differentials according to nativity and type of headship (shown in Table 2) illustrate the implications of changing sociodemographic composition for corresponding shifts in the economic well-being of minority families. Two types of messages emerge from Table 2. The first derives from the pattern of differentials according to selected demographic characteristics among (and within) the racial/

Table 2 Differentials in median family income according to nativity and family headship by Hispanic national origin and race

Nativity and family headship	Mexican		Puerto Rican		Cuban		Black		Non-Hispanic white	
	Actual $	Constant $[a]	Actual $	Constant $[a]	Actual $	Constant $[a]	Actual $	Constant $[a]	Actual $	Constant $[a]
Overall median, 1969	6,150	5,601	5,850	5,328	8,150	7,423	6,350	5,783	10,150	9,244
Nativity										
Foreign	5,450	4,964	5,650	5,146	8,150	7,423	8,050	7,332	9,700	8,834
Native	7,050	6,421	7,250	6,603	8,150	7,423	6,150	5,601	10,350	9,426
Type of Headship										
Couples	7,250	6,603	7,050	6,421	9,150	8,333	7,550	6,876	10,550	9,608
Single heads[b]	4,250	3,871	3,750	3,415	5,650	5,146	4,050	3,689	7,450	6,785
Overall median, 1979	14,510	6,674	11,168	5,137	18,650	8,579	13,558	6,236	21,235	9,768
Nativity										
Foreign	13,005	5,982	10,692	4,918	18,470	8,496	15,640	7,194	19,935	9,170
Native	16,010	7,364	11,375	5,232	17,005	7,822	12,908	5,937	21,810	10,032
Type of headship										
Couples	15,905	7,316	14,710	6,766	20,015	9,206	17,762	8,170	22,490	10,345
Single heads[b]	8,900	4,094	5,525	2,541	12,600	5,796	8,678	3,992	13,355	6,143
Overall median, 1984[c]	16,592	5,333	10,152	3,263	19,305	6,205	12,823	4,122	23,189	7,454
Type of headship										
Couples	21,600	6,943	21,954	7,057	26,100	8,390	23,160	7,445	30,417	9,777
Single heads[b]	10,000	3,214	5,760	1,851	9,127	2,934	8,454	2,717	13,725	4,412

Note. Source: 1970 and 1980 Public Use Microdata Sample (PUMS) Files; March, 1985 Current Population Survey (CPS).
[a]1967 = $1.00, 1969 = $1.098, 1979 = $2.174, 1984 = $3.111.
[b]Includes both men and women.
[c]The CPS does not include nativity information.

141

ethnic groups at each point in time, while the second focuses on the ways these relationships changed over time.[5]

With the exception of blacks and Cubans, median incomes of families with foreign-born heads were lower than those of families with native-born heads in both years for which nativity information is available. The black exception reflects the positive selectivity of black immigrants (Bach & Tienda, 1984), while Cubans were an exception because of the recency of their arrival. Also, and largely due to differences in the prevalence of multiple earners within families and the lower average earnings of women, in all 3 years families headed by couples received higher incomes than families headed by single persons.[6]

In constant dollars, family income differentials between units headed by couples and those headed by single persons have widened for all groups, although not uniformly among race and origin groups. To the extent that differentials by headship also differed by race and Hispanic origin, changes in headship composition of minority families contributed to greater income differentiation between minority and nonminority families (see Tienda & Jensen, 1988). In constant terms, the 1969 income differential between families headed by couples and families headed by single persons ranged from a low of $2,700 (Mexicans) to a high of $3,200 (blacks and Cubans). By 1984, the real income differential between families headed by couples and families headed by single persons ranged from a low of $3,700 for Mexicans to a high of $5,400 for Cubans and whites. This provides evidence of greater rather than less diversity in the economic well-being of minority families.

A comparison of changes in family income according to nativity of family heads during the 1970s and early 1980s provides clues about the forces responsible for divergence and convergence in the average relative standing of Hispanic, black, and white families. For example, the average 19% real increase in the median family income of Mexican families reflected slightly faster income growth among the families with foreign-born heads, while for Cubans the rise in median family income during the 1970s was three times faster among families with foreign-born compared to native-born heads. At first blush these results may appear to be inaccurate. That is, since immigrants usually earn less than their native counterparts of like national origin (Borjas, 1982; Chiswick, 1979), their faster income growth during the 1970s appears to be inconsistent with the empirically documented patterns. However, two factors are responsible for this seemingly anomalous outcome: the higher labor supply of immigrant men (Borjas, 1983) and the positive selectivity of Cuban immigrants. The latter was counterbalanced by the influx of a large wave of skilled and semi-skilled immigrants in 1980, but too late to be included in the Census counts. Unfortunately, the Current Population Survey (CPS) data do not allow us to extend the series on nativity through 1984.

Net declines in real median incomes of Puerto Rican families must be interpreted in light of the changing character of migration between the island and the U.S. mainland. However, in many ways, Puerto Ricans are socially and politically distinct from Mexicans or Cubans. Not only did the incomes of families with both mainland-born and island-born heads decline in real terms over the decade—21% and 4%, respectively—but the deterioration in real family income was almost five times

---

[5]The textual discussion focuses on the change in constant dollars, but I report the absolute dollars for purposes of comparison with other cross-sectional sources.

[6]Virtually all of the families headed by single persons were headed by women.

greater among the families whose heads were born on the U.S. mainland compared to families whose heads were born in Puerto Rico. These findings challenge claims that assimilation is a vehicle to improve the income and employment possibilities of Puerto Ricans. Alternative interpretations should consider the importance of labor market conditions and employment discrimination in producing these outcomes, a subject taken up in a later section. That Puerto Ricans are more racially diverse also implicates race as a more salient determinant of their labor market position than birthplace. However, because black median family incomes improved during the 1970s, a racial explanation is overly simplistic; the reasons underlying the deterioration of Puerto Rican family incomes obviously are more complex and require due attention to structural factors (Tienda, 1989).

Uneven rates of change in median incomes according to type of headship are also telling about the dimensions of convergence in minority family incomes. Income differentials by type of headship during the 1970s are especially revealing about the underlying factors contributing to the worsened economic status of Puerto Ricans. In real terms, median family income of Puerto Rican families headed by couples increased 5%, while the median income of families headed by single persons dropped a whopping 34%. This trend extended through the early 1980s, when the median incomes of Puerto Rican families headed by couples rose 4% in real terms while those of families headed by single persons declined 37%. Hence for this group, family headship has become an important axis of economic bifurcation. Moreover, because the share of Puerto Rican families headed by single women increased substantially during the past decade (Tienda & Jensen, 1988), the socioeconomic consequences of this growing income disparity are even more profound for the relative economic well-being of Puerto Ricans as a group. Since families headed by single women experience higher poverty risks, this point is starkly illustrated in the following presentation of changes in poverty experiences of minority families.

Poverty and Program Participation

Poverty rates are among the most revealing indicator of economic well-being. The official guidelines for determining poverty status are based on a set of income cutoffs adjusted for household size, the age of the head, and the number of children under age 18.[7] The official poverty income cutoffs provide an absolute measure of poverty which denotes minimal levels of consumption in dollar terms, and these cutoffs are adjusted annually to account for changes in relative prices. Despite sharp criticism to the concept of absolute poverty,[8] when adjusted for relative prices, poverty cutoffs are comparable over time since they represent constant purchasing power. This section documents changes in the proportion of poor minority families and in their welfare participation behavior.

Figure 1, which shows the shares of minority families with poverty-level incomes

[7]Sex of the family head and farm–nonfarm residence were used through 1980 to determine poverty status but since that time have been discontinued. My tabulations have been adjusted to reflect these changes.

[8]Over the years the absolute poverty concept has been sharply criticized, and its adequacy for representing the nature and extent of economic well-being in the United States has been disputed on several grounds. These include its unrealistically low minimum-income threshold, its use of an emergency food plan as the foundation for determining minimal needs, and its reliance on untested normative assumptions about how poor families allocate their money resources among competing basic needs.

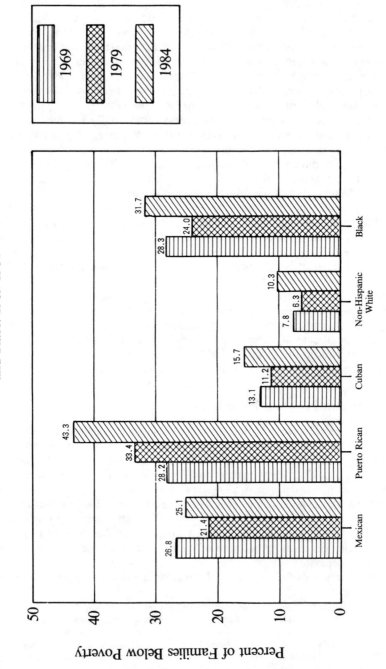

Percent of Families in Poverty by National Origin and Race: 1969-1984

Legend: 1969, 1979, 1984

Percent of Families Below Poverty

National Origin or Race	1969	1979	1984
Mexican	26.8	21.4	25.1
Puerto Rican	28.2	33.4	43.3
Cuban	13.1	11.2	15.7
Non-Hispanic White	7.8	6.3	10.3
Black	28.3	24.0	31.7

National Origin or Race

Figure 1 Percentage of families in poverty by national origin and race: 1969–1984.

Table 3   Nativity and family headship differentials in family poverty rates (%) by race and Hispanic national origin

Nativity and family headship	Mexican	Puerto Rican	Cuban	Black	Non-Hispanic white
Overall rate, 1969	26.8	28.2	13.1	28.3	7.8
Nativity					
Foreign	30.0	29.2	13.5	15.2	9.0
Native	24.4	21.1	3.6	29.5	7.3
Type of headship					
Couples	21.5	18.1	9.4	19.6	6.3
Single heads[a]	41.6	51.7	26.4	47.3	18.9
Overall rate, 1979	21.4	33.4	11.2	24.0	6.3
Nativity					
Foreign	24.0	34.6	11.2	18.3	7.1
Native	19.2	28.4	10.2	25.7	6.0
Type of headship					
Couples	17.1	17.2	8.7	13.0	4.6
Single heads[a]	38.3	59.9	21.5	40.1	17.7
Overall rate, 1984[b]	25.1	43.3	15.7	31.7	10.3
Type of headship					
Couples	20.0	15.3	7.4	13.8	5.6
Single heads[a]	33.8	61.9	30.4	42.0	17.7

Note.   Source: 1970 and 1980 Public Use Microdata Sample (PUMS) Files; March, 1985 Current Population Survey (CPS).
[a]Includes both men and women.
[b]The CPS does not include nativity information.

or below, mimics the picture of increasing heterogeneity in economic well-being based on changing median incomes. During the 1970s, the proportion of families in poverty decreased for Mexicans and Cubans, the two Hispanic groups whose real family income rose. However, poverty rates of Puerto Rican families rose and surpassed those of black families by 1979. To be more specific, while Puerto Rican and black families had virtually identical poverty rates in 1969—approximately 28%—by 1979, the rate of Puerto Rican poverty was 9.4 percentage points higher than the rate for black families. By 1984, the poverty gap between blacks and Puerto Ricans had widened to 11.6 percentage points.

In all three periods, the lowest rates of poverty appeared among non-Hispanic white families. Although the proportion of Mexican families in poverty fell by 5 percentage points during the 1970s, approximately one in five Mexican-origin families had incomes below the official poverty line in 1979. By 1984, this share rose to one in four families. Because poverty rates decreased for Mexican families while they increased for Puerto Rican families, the poverty gap between these two groups increased to 12 percentage points over the 10-year period; and because poverty rose faster for Puerto Ricans than for Mexicans during the 1980s, the poverty gap between them rose to 18 percentage points by 1984.

Table 3 provides additional insight into the correlates of poverty and their changes over the decade. That immigrants confront greater difficulties in earning a livelihood in the United States finds support in the tabulations showing higher rates of poverty among families whose heads were born abroad. Blacks stand as the only exception to this generalization for the selectivity reasons identified earlier. Nativity differentials in poverty converged slightly for all groups during the 1970s despite variation in the magnitudes of the changes. For example, nativity differentials in poverty rates for

Mexicans dropped from 5.6 percentage points in 1969 to 4.8 percentage points in 1979. Even Puerto Ricans, whose poverty rates rose sharply during the 1970s, witnessed smaller nativity differentials in 1979 as compared to 1969. The convergence of nativity differentials in poverty was most pronounced for Cubans, for whom differences in the risk of being poor virtually disappeared during the 1970s. Finally, birthplace differentials in poverty for black families dropped 50% over the decade.

Other noteworthy differentials in minority poverty rates correspond to type of family headship. Not surprisingly, families headed by couples were considerably less likely to be poor in both years compared to families headed by single persons of either sex.[9] However, the familiar theme of extensive differentiation by race and national origin applies to the headship differentials in minority family poverty. For example, in 1969, Mexican and black families headed by single persons were over twice as likely to be poor as those headed by married couples. Cuban and non-Hispanic white families headed by single persons were three times more likely to be poor than their racial/ethnic counterparts headed by married couples, although the absolute level of poverty was lower for these groups.

Puerto Ricans stand apart from the other groups in that, at the start of the period, the absolute differences in poverty rates according to type of family headship were appreciably larger (34 percentage points), and throughout the period they gradually widened. Specifically, 18% of Puerto Rican families headed by couples were poor in 1969 compared to 52% of families headed by single persons. In other words, Puerto Rican families headed by single persons were almost three times (2.8 times) more likely to be poor compared to families headed by a married couple. By 1979 this differential by type of headship *increased* to 3.5 times, and by 1984 to 4 times. Like the data on median family incomes, these results show increasing polarization of Puerto Rican families according to type of headship.

Although couples were less likely to be poor than were single persons throughout the 1970s, for Mexicans the disparity in poverty rates between couples and single persons widened, although to a lesser extent than was true for Puerto Ricans. Cubans presented an opposite pattern of interdecade change in that the amount of differentiation in poverty rates according to type of headship *decreased* by 4 percentage points. For whites and blacks, the headship differential in family poverty remained constant during the 1970s even while the overall poverty rate declined for both groups. Thus, these data also reveal a picture of growing heterogeneity over time.

In its concern to eliminate absolute poverty, the federal government has designed several income maintenance programs to offset the income deficit of the poor. Table 4 reports rates of participation in public assistance programs in 1969 and 1979, which indicate the extent of welfare dependence among minority and nonminority families.[10] Not unexpectedly, Puerto Ricans, who experienced the highest increases in poverty during the 1970s and early 1980s, exhibited the highest rates of welfare dependence.

---

[9]Auxiliary tabulations showed that households headed by single women were more likely to be poor compared to those headed by single men.

[10]The item in the Census which indicates receipt of public-assistance income includes various types of means-tested income programs: Aid to Families with Dependent Children (AFDC); old age assistance; general assistance; aid to the blind; and aid to the permanently and totally disabled. The latter three are grouped under a general heading of Supplementary Security Income (SSI). Unfortunately, it is not possible to separate AFDC and general assistance receipt from the receipt of SSI. Hence, the reported rates of receipt of public assistance are overstatements of the extent of welfare dependence. However, eligibility for these programs is based on economic need, unlike Social Security income or special insurance programs.

Table 4 Nativity and headship differentials in families' receipt of public assistance income by Hispanic national origin and race

Nativity, family headship, and median payment	Mexican	Puerto Rican	Cuban	Black	Non-Hispanic white
Overall rate, 1969 (%)	9.5	21.0	7.4	11.5	2.0
Nativity (%)					
Foreign	11.2	21.7	7.6	4.2	1.8
Native	8.2	16.1	3.6	12.2	2.0
Type of Headship (%)					
Couples	5.5	9.2	4.3	4.1	1.3
Single heads[a]	22.2	48.1	19.7	27.6	7.1
Median payment ($)					
Couples	800	1,500	700	800	750
Single heads[a]	1,200	2,400	900	1,400	1,300
Overall rate, 1979 (%)	8.7	24.4	7.1	14.1	3.2
Nativity (%)					
Foreign	7.4	25.0	7.4	6.3	3.2
Native	9.8	21.9	1.7	16.4	3.2
Type of headship (%)					
Couples	4.5	6.7	4.1	4.0	1.7
Single heads[a]	25.1	53.5	20.1	28.9	13.8
Median payment ($)					
Couples	1,610	3,005	1,875	1,920	2,205
Single heads[a]	2,465	3,785	2,355	2,405	2,835
Overall rate, 1984 (%)	13.2	38.3	17.4	23.5	4.8
Type of headship (%)					
Couples	7.8	14.9	10.9	8.6	2.6
Single heads[a]	22.3	53.9	28.8	32.1	8.1
Median payment ($)					
Couples	2,004	4,200	3,770	2,472	2,410
Single heads[a]	3,000	4,236	3,766	2,856	2,208

Note. Source: 1970 and 1980 Public Use Microdata Sample (PUMS) Files; March, 1985 Current Population Survey (CPS).
[a]Includes both men and women.
[b]The CPS does not include nativity information.

In 1969, 21% of all Puerto Rican families received public assistance payments, and in 1979 a higher share, 24%, did so. By 1984 the welfare recipient population increased to 38%. Non-Hispanic white and black families also increased their participation in public assistance programs during the 1970s, despite the registered improvement in relative economic status portrayed by higher median incomes (Table 1) and lower poverty rates (Table 3).

Mexicans and Cubans, in contrast to the other groups, decreased their reliance on means-tested transfer income during the 1970s, but only marginally (less than 1 percentage point). This situation was reversed during the early 1980s when jobless-ness rose for all groups (Tienda, 1989). As a result, by 1984, the share of Mexican and Cuban families that received transfer income rose to 13% and 17%, respectively. This increase, however, may prove to be temporary when economic conditions im-prove. In short, the picture presented by Table 4 is one of (a) negligible change in welfare dependence for groups whose real family incomes did not deteriorate over the decade, (b) marginally higher welfare utilization for Puerto Ricans, (c) modestly higher welfare participation among blacks and whites during the 1970s, and (d) nota-bly higher welfare participation for all groups in 1984.

Among the most controversial issues considered in recent years with respect to immigration policy is whether immigrants receive welfare income and hence draw more from the public coffers than they contribute. Research and writing on this topic are spotty but consistent with the results of the available studies (Blau, 1984; Simon, 1984; Tienda & Jensen, 1986). The tabulations reported in Table 4 show that in 1969, families with foreign-born heads of Mexican and Cuban origin were slightly more likely than their native counterparts to receive public assistance income.[11] Because of their positive selection, black and white families with foreign heads relied less on public assistance income compared to Hispanic families with immigrant heads.

By 1979 nativity differences in public assistance participation decreased slightly for Mexicans and Puerto Ricans, although the latter increased their participation in income-transfer programs overall. One in four Puerto Rican families with island-born heads received public assistance income in 1979 compared to 22% of families with heads born on the U.S. mainland. Among Mexicans, the public assistance participation rates of families with native-born heads surpassed those of families with foreign-born heads, even though as a group, Mexican immigrant families were less well off than their native counterparts. The increased public assistance participation by black and white families resulted from higher shares of both native and immigrant families receiving transfer income in 1979 compared to 1969.

Given the eligibility rules governing participation in means-tested programs—of which welfare income comprises the largest component—higher shares of families headed by single persons received public assistance income compared to families headed by couples. In 1969 the proportion of families headed by couples who received public assistance income was less than 6% for all groups except Puerto Ricans (who had 9%), while the share of families with single heads receiving public assistance income ranged from a low of 7% for white non-Hispanics to a high of 48% for Puerto Ricans. By 1984 the headship-specific rates of participation in transfer income programs were higher, but the pattern of race and ethnic differentials was similar. Specifically, the share of single-head families receiving public assistance income ranged from a low of 8% for non-Hispanic white families to a high of 54% for Puerto Ricans. This range in public assistance receipt represented no change from 1979 for Puerto Ricans, modest increments for Cubans and blacks, and slight to substantial decreases for Mexicans and non-Hispanic whites.

My final comments on Table 4 pertain to the median payments to families who are eligible for and actually receive public assistance income. That is, of those who received any public assistance income in 1969, the payments were considerably larger for families headed by single persons compared to those headed by couples. This indicates that the former had greater income shortfalls, on average. However, the difference in median payments received by couples and single heads varied appreciably over time and by race and ethnicity. Specifically, in 1969 the payment differential between families headed by singles and families headed by couples ranged from $200 among Cubans to a high of $900 among Puerto Ricans. Blacks and whites fell between those extremes, with a $550–$600 median payment differential between families headed by singles and families headed by couples. By 1984 the differential payment by type of headship was negligible for all groups except Mexicans.

To summarize, the portrait based on trends and differentials in minority family

---

[11]The same pattern obtains for Puerto Ricans, but since they are citizens and automatically entitled to these benefits, the analogy of the island-born with the foreign-born does not apply in this instance.

income and poverty (Tables 1 and 2) shows signs of *increasing* rather than decreasing heterogeneity among and within racial and ethnic groups. That real median family incomes of Mexican and Cuban families increased (although at differing rates) while those of Puerto Rican families decreased in real terms provides the most striking testimony of greater socioeconomic disparities for the Hispanic population. Thus, as we approach the 1990s, it is extremely important to differentiate Hispanics by national origin in studies of economic and social well-being. This is similar to claims made about the black population (Allen & Farley, 1986) and holds for other minority populations as well.

The correlates of poverty and welfare receipt (Tables 3 and 4) also present a complex picture, showing signs of convergence along some sociodemographic dimensions and divergence along others. As with the story on interdecade changes in family income, the general conclusion is one of greater differentiation in poverty rates according to national origin. Equally striking are the interdecade changes in public assistance participation, which increased among all groups except Mexicans and Cubans. Yet Puerto Ricans were the only group to become more impoverished during the 1970s. This indicates either that a higher share of needy families received income-transfer payments or that the tendencies toward economic bifurcation (Tienda & Jensen, 1988; Farley & Allen, 1987) have translated into higher aggregate welfare utilization rates. Unfortunately, cross-sectional data do not permit further scrutiny of these issues, but they are essential to address claims about the emergence of a syndrome of persisting poverty concentrated among minority populations (Tienda, 1989).

Although valuable for documenting the changes in the economic well-being of minority families during the stagnant 1970s, the descriptive statistics raise many questions. Why were Puerto Ricans the only group to experience a deterioration in economic well-being, while blacks, Mexicans, and Cubans—groups with growing shares of immigrants—experienced modest improvements in economic status? My working hypothesis is that the answer resides in the changed employment environment confronted by Puerto Ricans versus the other three minority groups, and that, as a group, Puerto Ricans have not developed the political leverage needed to protect their interests. In the last two sections, I explore these ideas in sequence by examining the changing components of family income during the 1970s, analyzing the labor market behavior of minority heads of household, and speculating about the politics of ethnicity.

INCOME PACKAGING AND LABOR MARKET POSITION

In this section I draw parallels between the economic status of families and the employment status of family heads. First, I examine whether and how the packaging of family income has changed between 1970 and 1980 and whether changes in the share of labor income are responsible for the aggregate changes in median family incomes. Table 5, which decomposes mean family incomes into sources, addresses this question.[12] Subsequently I examine changes in the employment statuses of family

[12]I use mean income for this analysis to illustrate the relative shares of each income source, but because of the skewed income distributions of the groups considered (especially non-Hispanic white families), I also present the median incomes for each group in constant dollars.

Table 5 Components of mean family income by Hispanic national origin and race: 1969–1984

Source	Mexican Constant $[a]	%	Puerto Rican Constant $[a]	%	Cuban Constant $[a]	%	Black Constant $[a]	%	Non-Hispanic white Constant $[a]	%
1969										
Wages and salary	6,406	92.9	5,342	87.8	8,320	95.5	5,790	90.0	9,367	89.6
Social insurance	173	2.5	101	1.7	97	1.1	239	3.7	307	2.9
Public assistance	149	2.2	523	8.6	154	1.8	227	3.5	37	0.4
Other income	170	2.5	120	2.0	143	1.6	175	2.7	743	7.1
Mean total income	6,898	100.1	6,086	100.1	8,714	100.0	6,431	99.9	10,454	100.0
Median total income	6,239		5,510		7,650		5,510		9,153	
Mean total income actual $	7,590		6,701		9,584		7,079		11,469	
1970										
Wages and salary	6,872	89.4	5,021	82.5	8,817	89.8	6,029	84.9	9,239	84.1
Social insurance	210	2.7	157	2.6	301	3.1	344	4.8	493	4.5
Public assistance	182	2.4	548	9.0	201	2.0	304	4.3	69	0.6
Other income	419	5.4	361	5.9	503	5.1	426	6.0	1,182	10.8
Mean total income	7,683	99.9	6,087	100.0	9,822	100.0	7,103	100.0	10,983	100.0
Median total income	6,674		4,834		8,494		5,752		9,962	
Mean total income actual $	16,659		13,148		21,160		15,420		23,705	
1984										
Wages and salary	5,753	87.4	3,832	79.0	6,569	83.3	4,520	81.1	7,088	77.9
Social insurance	476	7.2	335	6.8	524	6.6	631	11.3	1,041	11.4
Public assistance	140	2.1	523	10.7	212	2.7	237	4.2	42	0.5
Other income	213	3.2	169	3.5	578	7.3	187	3.4	932	10.2
Mean total income	6,582	99.9	4,890	100.0	7,883	99.9	5,575	100.0	9,103	100.0
Median total income	5,333		3,263		6,205		4,122		7,454	
Mean total income actual $	20,476		15,212		24,523		17,345		28,319	

heads to draw tighter parallels between the relative economic status of minority families and labor market experiences.

Table 5 reveals that labor income—that is, wages and salaries and income from self-employment—was the major income source for Hispanic, black, and white families throughout the period. Hence, changes in economic status depend heavily on the labor market position of each group. In 1969 labor income comprised from 96% (Cubans) to 88% (Puerto Ricans) of average family income. Over the next 10 years the labor income share of average total family income *decreased* for all groups, with the range from 90% (Cubans) to 82% (Puerto Ricans). By 1984, wage and salary income as a share of total family income fell further still, mostly for non-Hispanic whites.

There are several reasons why these declines have occurred, but two of the most important deserve mention. First, the aging of the population and the trend toward earlier retirement would reduce the average labor share of total family income. Because non-Hispanic whites are older, on average, one would expect higher retirement and hence lower average nonlabor incomes for them, but not necessarily for Puerto Ricans. Second, the labor market standing of minority and nonminority groups has been reconfigured since 1970 (Bean & Tienda, 1987, chap. 9). Not only has the incidence of nonparticipation risen notably, but it has been especially evident for Puerto Ricans and blacks. Both of these distinct forces would lower the average family income shares derived from wages and salary.

As the average share of labor income fell, the mean public-assistance income shares received by families rose, but not by a commensurate amount. For no group did the average increase in public assistance income rise more than 1 percentage point during the 1970s (with blacks experiencing the largest percentage point change). Yet the average declines in labor income shares far exceeded that amount. Public assistance as a share of total family income rose during the early 1980s for Puerto Ricans and Cubans but remained essentially unchanged for the remaining groups. The public assistance component of average family income was highest for Puerto Ricans in all 3 years, comprising nearly 11% of the mean by 1984. Public assistance accounted for 2% to 3% of Mexican and Cuban family income, 3% to 4% of black family income, and less than 1% of non-Hispanic white family income over the 15-year period considered.

Because the relative share of labor income declined more than the proportionate rise in public assistance income, other income sources—namely, social insurance and miscellaneous income sources—permitted the improvements in family incomes during the 1970s (exclusive of Puerto Ricans). From 1959 to 1969, the average share of mean family income comprised by social insurance increased modestly for all groups. This growth partly reflects the older age composition of the population, but the growth in the social insurance payments received by families also results from greater insurance claims by workers who found themselves unemployed for long periods during the economically stagnant 1970s. This is more clearly evident in the sharp increases in social insurance between 1979 and 1984.

As a population ages, a higher proportion of individuals become eligible for social security pensions, survivors benefits, and disability payments. Thus, the average share of family income derived from social insurance should continue to rise over time, but probably very gradually because these demographic changes unfold slowly. Also, the relative contemporary importance of social insurance as a family income source depends in large measure on how well groups fared in the labor market in prior years and on their eligibility for employer-provided unemployment compensation and pension. On the grounds of previous labor market advantages, white families and those with older heads should be most inclined to receive higher levels of social insurance incomes. This partly explains the Hispanic–white average differentials in social insurance payments, but not the black–white differences. Unfortunately, Census data do not permit finer disaggregation to explore this issue further.

Other income sources—rent, dividends, alimony, child support, and the like—also rose over the period and prevented real family incomes from deteriorating as labor income shares fell. For minority families, other income as a share of the average doubled (Mexicans and blacks) or tripled (Cubans and Puerto Ricans) during the 1970s but declined during the early 1980s for all groups except Cubans. Other income sources represented a larger share (approximately 7%) of the total family income for non-Hispanic whites in 1969; hence a percentage point increase of 3.7 during the 1970s—larger than that experienced by most minority groups—represented a rise of 52% for this group. In relative terms, this represents a smaller change than that registered for the minority families.

In sum, these data suggest that unequal labor market experiences were largely responsible for the observed changes in the relative economic standing of minority families during the 1970s. Table 6 further illustrates how the employment configuration of minority and nonminority families evolved between 1970 and 1985. Since this period was characterized by a sharp rise in families headed by single women, the employment status of minority and nonminority families is tabulated separately by type of headship.

In 1970, the share of families with neither head employed (only the head in the case of single-head units) ranged from a high of 27% for blacks to a low of 16% for whites, with blacks and Puerto Ricans hovering around the high level (25% and 24%, respectively). By 1985 the shares of families headed by adults who were not employed (e.g., unemployed or not in the labor force) rose for all groups except Mexicans, but most dramatically for Puerto Rican and black families. Nearly half of Puerto Rican families (46%) and roughly one third of black families reported that neither the head nor the spouse (if present) was employed in 1985. This compares to roughly one in five families of Mexican or non-Hispanic white origin. Clearly the recession of the early 1980s tolled hardest on these two groups.

Two important policy issues emerge from these stark facts. One concerns the economic well-being of the children reared in families with unemployed parents. Unless the rising unemployment and labor force nonparticipation are confined to families who are independently wealthy, these trends signal growing deprivation of minority children. Moreover, children reared in environments where work is not a normative behavior will not internalize normative work behaviors (Wilson, 1985, 1987b), and this will virtually ensure the intergenerational transmission of poverty.

Second, the declining economic status of minority families, but particular Puerto Rican and black families, is intricately tied with the rise in the numbers of families headed by single women. In 1960, the share of families headed by single women ranged from 11% for non-Hispanic whites to 20% and 25% for Puerto Ricans and blacks, respectively (Tienda & Jensen, 1988). This situation changed markedly over the next 25 years when the number of female-headed families jumped 140% for Puerto Ricans—from 20% to 48%—and 96% for blacks (from 25% to 49%). Thus, in 1985, roughly one of every two black and one of every five Puerto Rican families were headed by single adults—virtually all of them women. Among Mexican and

Table 6 Components of change in employment and family headship status by Hispanic national origin and race: 1970–1985

Family headship and employment status	1970	1985	Percentage change
	Mexicans		
Couples			
Both employed	17.1	27.9	63.2
Head employed	43.6	30.3	− 30.5
Spouse employed	3.7	5.7	54.0
Neither employed	16.3	11.8	− 27.6
Single heads			
Head employed	8.3	13.4	61.4
Head not employed	11.0	11.0	0.0
	Puerto Ricans		
Couples			
Both employed	18.3	17.7	− 3.3
Head employed	45.9	17.8	− 61.2
Spouse employed	1.4	5.0	257.0
Neither employed	13.6	11.6	− 14.7
Single heads			
Head employed	10.7	13.5	26.2
Head not employed	10.1	34.4	240.6
	Other Hispanics		
Couples			
Both employed	25.7	34.1	32.7
Head employed	44.2	23.4	− 47.1
Spouse employed	2.2	6.8	209.1
Neither employed	8.2	10.5	28.0
Single heads			
Head employed	9.7	14.4	48.4
Head not employed	9.9	10.8	9.1
	Blacks		
Couples			
Both employed	28.1	24.1	− 14.2
Head employed	26.6	10.7	− 59.8
Spouse employed	4.1	6.7	63.4
Neither employed	8.6	9.8	13.9
Single heads			
Head employed	16.5	23.3	41.2
Head not employed	16.0	25.4	58.8
	Non-Hispanic whites		
Couples			
Both employed	28.7	37.7	31.4
Head employed	44.8	24.6	− 45.1
Spouse employed	3.1	6.0	93.5
Neither employed	11.1	16.5	48.6
Single heads			
Head employed	7.0	9.5	35.7
Head not employed	5.2	5.7	9.6

Note. Source: Adapted from Appendix Table A-1, Tienda & Jensen, 1988.

non-Hispanic white families, the increase in the number of female-headed families between 1960 and 1985 was considerably slower, from 17% to 24% for the former and from 11% to 15% for the latter.

One point bears emphasis in digesting these figures. It is not clear whether the rising incidence of female headship is a cause or a consequence of the deteriorating economic status of black and Puerto Rican families. Declining labor market opportunities for married men and the disillusionment which frequently accompanies long periods of joblessness are a frequent cause of marital disruption, which in turn, contributes to the growth of mother-only families.[13] Moreover, despite the dual burden faced by single mothers who must assume the role of primary breadwinner while also attending to domestic responsibilities, the share of single female heads who worked outside the home also increased throughout the period, although not uniformly by race and ethnicity. This indicates that single mothers are willing to work if their personal circumstances—skills and child responsibilities—so permit them.

For example, among Mexican, other Hispanic, and non-Hispanic white families, the share of single-parent families with employed heads rose faster than the share of single-parent families whose heads did not work—hence the rise of single-head units would not necessarily contribute to declining economic well-being. This situation contrasts sharply with that of Puerto Rican families, for whom the dramatic rise in female headship largely involved the growth in the number of families with no earners who were presumably dependent on public assistance for maintenance. Not surprisingly, during this period, welfare dependency among Puerto Rican families increased over 200% (Tienda & Jensen, 1988). Black families present a third pattern of change in headship and employment status, as the rise in the number of employed, single-parent units was roughly equal to the rise in the number of single-parent units not employed.

Although these data do not establish a causal connection between the changing economic well-being of minority families and the labor market status of minority family heads, there is ample evidence to support claims made by Wilson (1987a, 1987b), Kasarda (1985), and Tienda (1988) that sharply reduced labor market opportunities for minority men hold the key to explaining changes in the economic well-being of families, but especially minority families. Census and CPS data show that the declining economic status of Puerto Rican families can be traced to falling shares of labor income and increasing shares of families without working heads. Further research (Tienda, 1989) indicates that labor market detachment is a major cause of the impoverization of Puerto Ricans, but the reasons for declining labor force activity are far from clear.

Table 6 shows that the share of black and Puerto Rican families headed by employed couples decreased by 14% and 3%, respectively, while this headship arrangement increased for all other racial and ethnic groups. In fact, multiple-earner income strategies have proven to be much more effective hedges against impoverization than income transfers (Tienda & Jensen, 1988). However, this presumes that household heads can obtain employment in the first place, which in the case of blacks and Puerto

---

[13]Marital disruption will not result in female headship if divorced or separated women with children opt to live with parents or other intact families or if disruption occurs among childless couples. To the extent that these practices are pervasive, then the growth of female-headed families will be understated. Moreover, to the extent that these practices are not uniform by race and ethnic origin, then the measured differentials also are likely to be understated.

Ricans remains questionable and highly dependent on the state of the U.S. economy. Hence, the fall in real family incomes of Puerto Ricans and the deteriorating economic position of this minority group are virtually predictable given (a) the dramatic increase in the share of families with single heads who were not employed, (b) the substantial rise in the number of couples with neither member employed, and (c) the appreciable drop in the number of families with employed heads. For other groups, the rise in the share of families headed by employed couples, combined with growing numbers of single-parent families whose heads are not employed, signals intragroup economic bifurcation. Nevertheless, bifurcation can register modest to substantial improvements in relative economic status in the aggregate (as observed among Mexicans, blacks, and non-Hispanic whites). For this reason, it is essential to evaluate changes not only in averages but also in the distribution of economic resources when assessing changes in the economic status of minority populations.

DISCUSSION AND CONCLUSIONS

Contrary to the predictions of postindustrial theorists, the picture of changes in the economic status of minority families is one of *increasing* rather than decreasing diversity. As we approach the 1990s, policymakers can celebrate the modest gains in median family incomes, the declines in aggregate poverty rates, and the narrowing of economic differentials between immigrant and native families and between some minorities—notably Mexicans and Cubans—and non-Hispanic whites. However, growing economic disparities between Puerto Ricans and other minority and majority groups challenge academics to document more fully the dimensions of the growing inequities and, more important, to *explain* them. An equally great challenge, as we approach the 1990s, is to devise innovative political solutions to reduce the inequities that have emerged during the 1970s and continued through the early 1980s.

The persistence of color differentials in the relative economic standing of minority families raises questions about the ascriptive versus the meritocratic assignment of labor market positions, particularly since mainstream social science theories predict the diminishing importance of ascribed characteristics in modern industrial regimes (Featherman & Hauser, 1978). Unfortunately, the importance of examining color in stratifying the U.S. population generally has been related to secondary status. In part this is because a large body of research on racial and ethnic inequality has focused on compositional differences between minority and majority groups (notably in human capital and job experience), and standardization exercises have been used to account for, rather than to *explain*, the origins of wage gaps between people of color and whites (see Reimers, 1985). In these exercises discrimination frequently is invoked as a residual explanation once compositional differences between groups have been standardized (see Hirschman, 1980; Tienda, 1983), but seldom do studies of labor market discrimination elaborate on the social pressures that produce the aggregate differentials.

In very general terms, the patterned differences in the labor market experiences and economic well-being of minority families reflect the operation of many labor market processes, including (a) uneven access to education and other forms of market-enhancing skills; (b) the role of ascription as an allocative mechanism which triggers prejudice and often results in exclusion from full participation in social, economic, and political arenas; and (c) unevenly distributed opportunities for social advancement, which vary across labor markets and over time, depending on the general health of the economy.

But there exists another and profoundly important reason for the persisting racial and ethnic economic inequalities—one not easily studied with Census data: differential control over social and political capital (Tienda & Lii, 1987). As long as power differences between racial and ethnic groups remain pervasive, then the ability of minority groups to exert political leverage to protect their social and economic interests will be limited. Moreover, politically weak groups will remain vulnerable to social dislocations that result when the spatial distribution of opportunities changes (as during the 1970s when job losses were unevenly concentrated in northern industrial cities), when economic growth limits opportunity (as during the 1970s and early 1980s when economic growth was negative), and when the receptiveness of the administration toward social programs dwindles (as occurred during the Reagan years).

Establishing linkages between the economic status of minority families and the labor-force behavior of minority family heads, as I have in this chapter, does not explain *why* some groups have been more successful than others in maintaining or improving their economic status. One set of explanations for the persistence of racial and ethnic differentials in economic well-being is that not all minority groups benefited uniformly from social programs designed to reduce race-linked social inequality (Wilson, 1985, 1987b), especially those programs designed to improve employability and earnings prospects.[14]

Another reason for the widening socioeconomic differentials among minority families is differing access to economic opportunities under conditions of industrial restructuring and sluggish economic growth.[15] This interpretation of differential success, which emphasizes the importance of geographic location in shaping opportunity, acquires special importance for minority populations because of their residential concentration in large central cities and in regions of the country that have experienced uneven growth and decline during the 1970s and 1980s (Bean & Tienda, 1987; Wilson, 1987b). A third and more conventional explanation for the persistence of racial and ethnic economic inequality focuses on the influence of social background in assigning economic rewards.[16] Undoubtedly, there is merit to all three interpretations. However, considerable disagreement exists about the rela-

[14]These arguments are elaborated by Wilson (1987b) in his recent book, *The Truly Disadvantaged: The Inner City, the Underclass, and Public Policy.* For a discussion on the importance of employment policy for reducing racial and ethnic economic inequalities, see also Tienda and Jensen (1988).

[15]William J. Wilson and John Kasarda are identified with this position. Their theses focus on the transformation of the inner city as jobs were relocated from central cities to suburbs and as the most disadvantaged segments of minority populations were left behind. Wilson is quite explicit, as are Farley and Allen (1987), in recognizing that the black population has become economically bifurcated in the process of economic restructuring that has transformed the old industrial cities. However, no parallel evidence has been generated for Puerto Ricans, even though this explanation seems totally appropriate.

[16]Variants of individual interpretations of inequality include labor market discrimination as a reason for unequal social outcomes.

tive importance of individual versus structural factors in determining social and economic outcomes.[17]

Although these debates are not likely to be resolved before 1990, it is essential to come to terms with the political implications of the growing racial and ethnic differentiation documented here. During the 1960s and the early to middle 1970s, a great deal of emphasis was placed on the role of color in allocating social rewards and opportunities. Evidence of narrowed gaps in income and schooling between blacks and whites during the 1960s and into the early 1970s engendered optimism about the prospects for greatly reducing, if not totally eliminating, race-linked economic and social inequities. And, in a bold and assertive statement on this issue, William J. Wilson (1978) declared that the ascriptive significance of race was on the decline and that social class had emerged as a more salient determinant of economic position for blacks.[18]

But the optimism of the early 1970s about the prospects of reducing race-linked social inequities was stymied by the slowdown in worldwide economic growth during the middle to late 1970s. Moreover, other groups, notably Hispanics, emerged as contenders for the political and social benefits of the Great Society programs. As the Hispanic population became more visible demographically and socially, its political clout increased as well, but not uniformly for all national origin groups. That geography and class divisions coincide along national origin lines seems to have mitigated the development of a unified Hispanic political agenda that serves all peoples of Spanish origin. Political coalitions of Hispanic legislators[19] have emerged and are quite effective in gaining concessions for "Hispanic" concerns that cut across national origin lines.[20] However, in general, these coalitions are highly fragile. Hence, if the tendency toward greater rather than lesser socioeconomic differentiation by race and national origin continues, we might expect less rather than more political cohesion among Hispanic groups in the 1990s.

The looming question for the 1990s revolves around the course of political participation of minority groups and the ability of rainbow coalitions to provide economic

[17]This results for several reasons. First, the omission of structural factors from analyses of economic outcomes ignores an important component of variation in experiences and final outcomes. These omissions result in overstating the importance of individual characteristics as factors that explain relative success and failure. Second, variance in findings and conclusions about the labor market experiences of minority workers reflects differing methods and models used to estimate the existence and extent of discrimination. Finally, although most students of racial and ethnic stratification have acknowledged the existence of discrimination in determining the educational and labor market standing of minority workers, data limitations preclude analysts from directly evaluating its impact on educational and employment outcomes. For further discussion of these issues, see Bean and Tienda (1987, chapters 9 and 10).

[18]Wilson was sharply criticized for his statements by others who noted that large socioeconomic differentials persisted between blacks and whites. See the summary of the supporters and critics of Wilson's thesis in Allen and Farley (1986).

[19]The Hispanic Caucus, chaired by Congressman Roybal of California, is the most notable national example, but similar coalitions exist at the state and local level.

[20]Recent examples include the effectiveness of Hispanic lobby groups in influencing the recent immigration legislation and in calling attention to increasing poverty among Hispanic children. Bilingual education programs are a third example, but Cuban legislators appear less concerned with these programs than Mexican legislators.

and social concessions to minority constituencies as well as protect the gains achieved during the 1960s and early 1970s. But in defining and striving for collective economic and social goals through "rainbow" political strategies, it is important to recognize that growing divisions within and between groups, with their deep class and regional underpinnings, almost certainly will undermine the formulation of collective minority agendas—dubbed rainbow coalitions—designed to improve the economic position of *all* people of color.

To be sure, social and economic opportunity is intricately tied to the health of the economy, but it is less clear why minority groups were more adversely affected by the economic recessions of the late 1970s and early 1980s (Tienda & Jensen, 1988). Hence researchers concerned with the dynamics of racial and ethnic inequality must attempt to better understand how the spatial distribution of opportunity and the distribution of political power have shaped the process of economic bifurcation within minority populations. Political actors must be careful not to let secondary issues, such as the filling of affirmative action quotas, deflect attention from the more fundamental issues of economic bifurcation and rising poverty among some minority groups. Similarly, improvements in the economic well-being of some minority groups always must be measured against declines experienced by others because the measurement of inequality is inherently comparative. Failure to take heed of these counterpoised outcomes practically guarantees an increase in economic differentiation by race and national origin during the 1990s. Thus, in the 1990s, it will matter a great deal how the politics of race and ethnicity unfolds.

REFERENCES

Allen, W. R., & Farley, R. (1986). The shifting social and economic tides of black America, 1950–1980. *Annual Review of Sociology, 12*, 227–306.

Bach, R. L., & Tienda, M. (1984). Contemporary immigration and refugee movements and employment adjustment policies. In V. M. Briggs, Jr. & M. Tienda (Eds.), *Immigation: Issues and policy* (pp. 37–82). Salt Lake City, UT: Olympus Press.

Bean, F. D., & Tienda, M. (1987). *The Hispanic population of the United States*. New York: Russell Sage.

Blau, F. D. (1984). The use of transfer payments by immigrants. *Industrial and Labor Relations Review, 32*, 222–239.

Borjas, G. J. (1982). The earnings of male Hispanic immigrants in the United States. *Industrial and Labor Relations Review, 35*, 343–353.

Borjas, G. J. (1983). The labor supply of male Hispanic immigrants in the United States. *International Migration Review, 17*, 653–671.

Chiswick, B. R. (1979). The economic progress of immigrants: Some apparently universal patterns. In William Fellner (Ed.), *Contemporary economic problems* (pp. 357–399). Washington, DC: American Enterprise Institute.

Farley, R., and Allen, W. (1987). *The color line and the quality of life in America*. New York: Russell Sage Foundation.

Featherman, D. L., & Hauser, R. M. (1978). *Opportunity and Change*. New York: Academic Press.

Hirschman, C. (1980). Theories and models of ethnic inequality. In C. Marett (Ed.), *Research in race and ethnic relations* (Vol. 2, pp. 1–20). Greenwich, CT: JAI Press.

Jensen, L., & Tienda, M. (1987). *Rural minority families in the United States. Changes in poverty and economic well-being*. Unpublished manuscript.

Kasarda, J. D. (1985). Urban change and minority opportunities. In P. E. Peterson (Ed.), *The new urban reality* (pp. 33–67). Washington, DC: The Brookings Institute.

Nelson, C., & Tienda, M. (1985). The structuring of Hispanic ethnicity: Historical and contemporary perspectives. *Ethnic and Racial Studies, 8*, 49–74.

Reimers, C. W. (1985). A comparative analysis of the wages of Hispanics, blacks, and non-Hispanic whites. In G. J. Borjas & M. Tienda (Eds.), *Hispanics in the U.S. economy* (pp. 27–75). Orlando, FL: Academic Press.

Ross, C., Danziger, S., & Smolensky, E. (1987). The level and trend of poverty in the United States, 1939–1979. *Demography, 24,* 587–600.

Sandefur, G. D., & Tienda, M. (1988a). Introduction. In G. D. Sandefur & M. Tienda (Eds.), *Minorities, poverty and social policy* (pp. 1–19). New York: Plenum.

Sandefur, G. D., & Tienda, M. (1988b). *Minorities, poverty and social policy.* New York: Plenum.

Simon, J. (1984). Immigrants, taxes and welfare in the United States. *Population and Development Review, 10,* 55–69.

Smith, S. A., & Tienda, M. (1986). The doubly disadvantaged: Women of color in the U.S. labor force. In A. Stromberg & S. Harkness (Eds.), *Working women* (2nd ed., pp. 61–80). Palo Alto, CA: Mayfield.

Tienda, M. (1983). Nationality and income attainment of native and immigrant Hispanic men in the United States. *Sociological Quarterly, 24,* 253–272.

Tienda, M. (1989). Puerto Ricans and the underclass debate: Evidence for a structural interpretation of labor market withdrawal. *Annals of the American Academy of Political and Social Science, 501,* 105–119.

Tienda, M., & Jensen, L. (1986). Immigration and public assistance: Dispelling the myth of dependency. *Social Science Research, 15,* 372–400.

Tienda, M., & Jensen, L. (1988). Poverty and minorities: A quarter century profile of color and socioeconomic disadvantage. In G. D. Sandefur & M. Tienda (Eds.), *Minority, poverty and social policy* (pp. 23–61). New York: Plenum.

Tienda, M., & Lii, D.-T. (1987). Minority concentration and earnings inequality: Blacks, Hispanics and Asians compared. *American Journal of Sociology, 93,* 141–165.

Wilson, W. J. (1978). *The declining significance of race.* Chicago: University of Chicago Press.

Wilson, W. J. (1985). Cycles of deprivation and the underclass debate. *Social Science Review, 59,* 541–559.

Wilson, W. J. (1987a). The hidden agenda: How to help the truly disadvantaged. *The University of Chicago Magazine, 80,* 2–12.

Wilson, W. J. (1987b). *The truly disadvantaged: The inner city, the underclass, and the public policy.* Chicago: University of Chicago Press.

11

Issues in Ethnic Diversity and the Politics of Inequality in the 1990s: Commentary on Keely and Tienda

David Alvirez
Department of Sociology
University of Texas–Pan American

Race and ethnicity will continue to be key factors affecting American human relationships in the 1990s in spite of any progress that has been made by minorities. Problems related to race and ethnicity will continue to plague America and will be especially pronounced among the poor. Although there may be some evidence of overall progress for certain minority groups, such progress is likely to hide the economic bifurcation within specific racial and ethnic groups. Conditions for those at the very bottom are likely to stay the same (the best-case scenario) or to grow worse (the worst-case scenario). Women, especially racial and ethnic minority women, will continue to fare worse than men; this situation is likely to be reflected in an increase in the feminization of poverty.

Any solutions to racial and ethnic problems in the United States will depend in part on what happens in the legal and political arenas. The conservative tone of the American political arena in the 1980s, as evidenced by the election of President Reagan, by some of the legislative actions that reduced benefits for the poor, and by the lessened activity of the Department of Justice concerning the civil rights of minorities, does not bode well for American racial and ethnic minorities. The dominant society may be willing to go so far, and only so far, toward equality. The optimistic side of me hopes for the best; the pessimistic side is concerned that relationships will remain the same or grow worse. Let us consider the two chapters by Keely and Tienda to see whether they provide grounds for optimism or for pessimism.

Charles Keely titled his chapter, "E Pluribus Unum: The Impossible Dream?" The question mark at the end of the title should remain present in our minds as we consider the issue of racial and ethnic relations in the 1990s. The attitudes of the current administration in Washington, together with some surveys of the current thinking of many Americans, seem to indicate that the dream is there for any person to grasp; failure to do so must be laid at the feet of the individual or group that does not achieve it. Keely's chapter provides a good beginning from which to consider the future of racial and ethnic groups in the 1990s.

Keely recognizes clearly that although assimilation (also referred to as Anglo-Saxon conformity) has always been the ideal proclaimed by the media and taught in our public schools, the reality of the American experience is other than this. Equally clear is his understanding that the melting pot concept is also largely inapplicable to the American experience. He raises the valid question, "Is it a stew in which everything that is thrown into the pot willy-nilly emerges as part of the meal, or is the image more like that of a smelter, where only the useful metal is retained in the new alloy and the dross is eliminated?" (p. 125). The apparent explanation for the American experience, with the great variety of groups that have gone into the making of America, is some form of pluralism, although the precise meaning of pluralism is not always clear even for those who strongly advocate it.

As I perceive pluralism in its ideal form, it includes political and economic equality as well as some separation socially. The arguments against pluralism, however, often have been precisely that pluralism goes against our basic values or way of life, especially our "English tradition." I question whether pluralism has been the dominant ideology of the last quarter century, as Keely asserts. It is true that many of the minorities in America have been pushing for pluralism and for the recognition that it expresses the reality of the American experience more clearly, but it has been in constant conflict with the dominant ideology of assimilation, which permeates all of the basic institutions of America, including the legal system and the political arena.

Keely makes an interesting point in telling how the civil rights movement and the changes in the immigration laws in 1965 paralleled each other although people at that time did not make a connection between the two. Both developments led to major changes in the relationship between the dominant society and the more oppressed racial and ethnic minorities. At the same time, both developments seemed to awaken latent racism among many non-Hispanic whites (also referred to as Anglos in much of the literature), who suddenly perceived themselves as threatened by blacks, Hispanics (the term may be used generically or in reference to specific groups such as Mexican-Americans), and Asians. Involved in the racism and the perception of threat is the prejudice of many Americans toward people of color (as defined by the dominant society). The 1990s will continue to see Americans struggling to determine the place of racial and ethnic minorities in our society.

I believe that much of the problem lies with disagreement about the basic values related to civic culture. Keely suggests three such values: individual freedom, equality of opportunity, and pluralism. Keely is too optimistic when he assumes that Americans will be willing to accept pluralism as a value of civic culture on which most of us can agree. American xenophobia resists pluralism rather than endorsing it. Nonetheless, I would agree with Keely's assessment that without pluralism we will never have the *unum* that Americans value so highly.

Keely argues that pluralism is different today because of the "role of government not only in promoting and maintaining individual freedom, but also regarding equality of opportunity . . . and in fostering pluralism" (p. 127). Yet he does not address why the government's role came into being. A reading of history shows that members of the dominant group were and are unwilling to give racial and ethnic minorities the same rights that they take for granted for themselves. Changes such as civil rights legislation and the immigration law of 1965 came about only as a result of pressure, conflict, and the threat of greater conflict from the racial and ethnic groups who were no longer willing to accept America's open racism. Will such pressures emerge again in the 1990s?

The government's role in conferring "quasi-property rights" (p. 127) on certain groups (and on the members of those groups) is an issue that will continue to be defined in the 1990s. Keely raises only one of three related issues concerning group membership. Why should recent immigrants be categorized "as belonging to a disadvantaged minority solely because of ancestry?" (p. 127). Although, as Keely points out, 25% of immigrants under the 1965 Act were in professional and technical occupations, 75% were not. Do the 75% deserve any special treatment? And what about the undocumented immigrants and their characteristics? A second related issue is related more directly to Hispanics, although it also could affect some blacks. The generic term *Hispanic* allows the dominant society to name (say) a Cuban or a Mexican (a recent immigrant from Mexico) to a position that was meant for a Mexican-American. The third related issue has the most serious implications for the more seriously disadvantaged minorities: It concerns the benefits acquired by middle-class members of racial and ethnic groups, benefits that were meant for disadvantaged members of the group. To the degree that this occurs, it contributes to the economic bifurcation within specific groups.

Keely's discussion of the immigration issue as reflected in the Immigration Control and Reform Act of 1986 provides much food for thought. The primary issue, as the government perceives it, is one of government control, not of numbers. Politics seems to be at the forefront in the government's action. First, this preoccupation is reflected in the government's willingness to enforce sanctions against employers who hire undocumented workers while making it easier for employers to bring in temporary workers (a new *bracero* program) regardless of unemployment here. This policy is carried out without ever addressing why Americans are unwilling to do the jobs that the temporary workers (and the undocumented) will take. What the bill does is permit employers to find cheap labor and to keep wages low for the less skilled American workers. Further evidence of this policy is seen in the reluctance of Congress to raise the minimum wage, as well as in past attempts by President Reagan to lower the minimum wage for teenagers.

The second issue concerns how to handle illegal immigrants from Central America. I agree with Keely that "decisions seem to be dominated by foreign policy and political interests rather than by the needs of refugee applicants" (p. 129). Central Americans appear to be pawns in the United States' political games with Central American countries as we strive to keep the Monroe Doctrine alive. In the process, all Americans may find that some of their freedom is being eroded in the name of necessary control to "protect" us. If this sounds extreme, consider the recent release of information concerning FBI surveillance of groups involved in providing assistance and sanctuary to Central American refugees. The only "crime" of which they were found guilty was disagreeing with the Reagan policy on Central America. If the erosion of freedom does occur, minority members will lose more freedom than members of the dominant society if past history is any indication.

In dealing with the *unum* I believe that Keely is on target about the concerns of most Americans, especially non-Hispanic whites, regarding the new immigrants to this country. The numbers are an issue, but the more serious concerns include who the new immigrant groups are, the perception of the dominant society that they are too different from "real" Americans, and the fears that the government's activities serve to keep these groups apart from American society. Less attention is given to the long history of discrimination against Hispanics and Asians, the generic groups that include the new immigrant groups. One must ask whether the Immigration and Naturalization Service is as interested in apprehending undocumented immigrants from the European countries as in apprehending Hispanics and/or Asians. Will Congress pass special legislation to benefit the undocumented Irish? If so, will it do the same for non-European groups? To those who have lived close to the border, as I have, there is no question that one's physical appearance has much bearing on whether one is under suspicion. American xenophobia will affect racial and ethnic minorities in the 1990s.

Keely's primary focus is on the new immigrants and on whether or not they can be absorbed into America's mainstream. Regrettably, very little attention is given to blacks. Although Keely recognizes some of the latent racism that is present in this country, he seems to assume that the new immigrants ultimately will be treated the same as the earlier European immigrants. This European immigrant analogy, I believe, is not applicable to Hispanic or Asian immigrants. One reason for this view concerns racial differences. The experiences of blacks and Mexican-Americans demonstrate that racism is still alive and well; partly because of the closeness of Mexico, that country probably will continue to send the largest number of immigrants to the United States. Another major reason involves continued discrimination, especially institutional discrimination, as well as the unwillingness on the part of many Americans to admit that such discrimination exists. If such denials continue into the 1990s, one might anticipate that little change will occur in the next decade, at least for the more disadvantaged members of certain racial and ethnic groups.

The ties between Charles Keely's and Marta Tienda's chapters are not clear-cut, but the data presented by Tienda confirm my concerns about how much progress racial and ethnic minorities can expect to make in the 1990s. Tienda focuses on Hispanics and blacks and demonstrates that things are not going as well for those groups as Keely's optimism would lead us to believe. Furthermore, by focusing on Mexican-Americans, Puerto Ricans, and Cubans, one can note the important differences that exist among these three groups, which the dominant society often groups together as one. In addition, one can see clearly the differences among the three Hispanic groups, blacks, and non-Hispanic whites. Focusing on differences among and within groups and on changes over time reminds us of the heterogeneity of different minority groups; it shows how changes can occur that benefit one group, harm another, and alter the relative status of both.

Tienda's chapter raises several issues that are relevant to what will happen in the 1990s. Her opening statements about the relative status of blacks, Hispanics, and non-Hispanic whites indicate one of the problems we face in trying to predict what the 1990s will bring. Grouped data indicate that black–white differentials in education have all but disappeared, but a closer analysis raises as many questions as it answers. The median levels may be similar, but the differences in high school completion rates are much greater than the medians would lead us to believe. The completion rate for whites 25 years and older in 1980 was 68.8%, as opposed to 51.2% for blacks. Even among persons 18 to 24 years old, the completion rates are 78.7% and 66.5%, respectively (U.S. Bureau of the Census, 1981). Conditions for Mexican-Americans and Puerto Ricans are much worse than for blacks. Furthermore, the data do not permit us to address the matter of quality of education for blacks and Hispanics, which many indicators demonstrate is inferior to the education provided for whites. If the amount and the quality are inferior, this difference will limit opportunities in the political and legal arenas.

A second issue concerns the policy implications of the positions of Puerto Ricans and of blacks, who are worse off than the Hispanic minorities. If this pattern continues in the 1980s, one would predict less political power for both groups in the 1990s, especially in view of the rapid growth among Hispanics.

Because the relative positions of blacks and of Puerto Ricans are tied to the large number of families with single heads, mostly female, the feminization of poverty must be addressed by policymakers in the 1990s. Increasingly in the 1990s, female-headed families will find themselves among the have-nots, with a greater gap between them and couple-headed families. As Tienda demonstrates clearly, such families will be overrepresented among racial and ethnic minorities. Because of the presence of sexism among both minority and majority people, poor women may find the gap between themselves and others widening more and more. In all probability an increasing gap will signify less political power.

The data presented by Tienda lack breakdowns within groups by geographical area and by socioeconomic indicators. Both types of data may provide needed information showing where the greatest needs lie for different minorities and who may be making satisfactory progress. Specific groups may have different needs in different regions of the country; government programs may need to address the needs of poor minorities more directly. For example, McAllen has been the poorest metropolitan area in Texas for over two decades; yet the state of Texas continues to underfund higher education in that area. Such underfunding, I believe, is tied to a lack of political clout, which is due to a lack of economic power. I do not anticipate major increases in power for Mexican-Americans in south Texas, although the recent suit filed by the Mexican American Legal Defense and Educational Fund (MALDEF) and others against the state of Texas for underfunding higher education in that region, if won, may bring about some needed changes.

Tienda raises the issue of coalitions between the different minorities in the 1990s. Until now such coalitions have been the exception rather than the rule. The minorities continue to lag behind the majority; the increasing heterogeneity among the different minority groups will make it harder, not easier, for such a coalition to develop, especially in view of the increasing economic bifurcation within specific racial and ethnic groups. Even among Hispanics, the differences among the different groups, as well as their concentration in different parts of the country, will make coalitions difficult. Such coalitions will be likely to occur only if minorities recognize the potential advantages.

This point brings us to the last issue considered in Tienda's chapter: the greater political power of the dominant group. Control of the political and legal arenas lies in its hands; one must question how willing members of the dominant group are to give up their power or to share it with minority groups. The structure of society favors those who belong to the dominant group. Although individual minority group members have been incorporated into the mainstream of American society, few changes have occurred that would make it easier for minority members *in general* to enter the mainstream. Gradual progress will be made by some members, but the structural barriers that make it more difficult for minority members to be successful will continue to exist.

What, then, will the 1990s bring? First, class will become increasingly significant within and across racial and ethnic groups. The more successful minority group members will be highly visible and active on the political and legal scenes. More of these minority group members will hold both elected and appointed positions. Minority benefits are more likely to go to these successful persons. The question is this:

Will they identify with the underclass in their own group who haven't made it, or will they forget about their brothers and sisters and identify with the dominant group?

Second, it will be increasingly difficult to speak about a specific racial or ethnic group as if all of its members had something in common. Increasing diversity will be seen not only economically but geographically. The life-styles of middle-class minority-group members will not be the same as those of the underclass. Hispanic groups, whether Mexican-American, Puerto Rican, or Cuban, will demonstrate more and more differences according to the regions of the country in which they live. The growing number of "other Spanish" reported by the U.S. Bureau of the Census (1981) shows that Hispanics are drifting away from a more specific ethnic identification. Many of these persons probably would be considered Mexican-Americans by others. Proximity to the Mexican border will influence the Mexican-American population especially. Immigration, migration, and population growth will contribute to increasing heterogeneity.

Third, I perceive the increasing possibility of an unwillingness among politicians to pass legislation to benefit the underclass in America, especially the minority underclass. This possibility will be affected by the greater number of minority group members who enter the middle class in the 1990s; it is possible that such individuals will join with the majority against the underclass.

Finally, if something is not done for the underclass in the United States, something that will narrow the gap between the haves and the have-nots, there is a growing potential for serious economic and political unrest from the have-nots. The minority underclass has made little, if any, progress in the 1980s; if anything, they have regressed in certain areas (Ogby, 1990; Wilson, 1987). How much longer will the underclass be patient? Whether such unrest (if it occurs) will unite the have-nots across racial and ethnic lines is more problematic because of the long-established patterns of prejudice and distrust among the different racial and ethnic groups and because of the ability of the dominant society to keep minorities fragmented. If the lessons of the past are valid, the underclass minorities are likely to fight among themselves more than against the dominant society, including the members of their own groups who have made it. This conflict will work to the benefit of the dominant society and to the detriment of the minorities, especially the underclass. Only continued pressure from disadvantaged groups will permit positive changes for minorities in the 1990s.

REFERENCES

Ogbu, J. U. (1990). Racial stratification and education: In G. E. Thomas (Ed.), *U.S. race relations in the 1980s and 1990s: Current status and future projections* (pp. 3–34). Washington, DC: Hemisphere.

U.S. Bureau of the Census. (1981). *1980 census of population, general social and economic characteristics, United States summary*. Washington, DC: U.S. Government Printing Office.

Wilson, W. (1987). *The truly disadvantaged*. Chicago: University of Chicago Press.

12

Economic Progress for Black Americans in the Post-Civil-Rights Era

David H. Swinton
School of Business
Jackson State University

Throughout American history the economic status of black, Mexican, Puerto Rican, Native American, and other non-European racial or ethnic groups has been significantly lower than that of white Americans. Their economic disadvantage has been indicated by consistently lower levels of income, wealth, business ownership, occupational status, wage rates, and employment and by higher rates of poverty and unemployment.

The historical economic disadvantage for blacks and others resulted from the fact that the dominant European-American community used its superior economic, political, and social power to exploit, segregate, ignore, discriminate against, and otherwise exclude black and other Americans of non-European descent from equal participation in the American economy. By such means, European-Americans were able to attain and perpetuate an advantaged status in the American society. The economic dominance of European-Americans had the explicit approval and support of the American government for most of American history.

Individual and collective efforts to improve the economic status of black and other nonwhite Americans, at least until World War II, were undertaken largely without official government support and frequently in the face of active governmental opposition. With the implementation of fair employment policies during World War II, however, the civil rights movement began to experience some success in shifting official policy to the promotion of racial equality.

The major success of this movement after World War II is well known. Starting with the Supreme Court's 1954 *Brown v. Board of Education* decision banning official elementary and secondary school segregation, and culminating with the civil rights and social legislation of the 1960s, the civil rights movement was able to elicit the official cooperation of the U.S. government in the struggle to improve the absolute and relative economic status of black and other non-European-American ethnic groups.

By the early 1970s, the civil rights movement had left a legacy of legislation, executive orders, regulations, court rulings, and new or expanded social programs designed to promote the attainment of economic and social equality. The government's official policy had been reversed from one of a at least tacit acceptance of European-American economic domination to the official promotion of racial equality.

The strategy to promote equal opportunity that emerged from the 1960s had three major components. The first was the elimination of segregation and discrimination in public activities. The second was the amelioration of the higher rates of poverty and economic disadvantage found among blacks and others. The third was the elimination of differences in human and nonhuman capital.

Some successes were registered in implementing programs to focus on all three strategic objectives. As a consequence, the 1960s ended amidst widespread optimism that the society was on the verge of eliminating racial inequality in economic life within a reasonable time (Flax, 1971; Freeman, 1973).

Yet, as is now well known, the promise of the late 1960s has not been realized. Today, almost 20 years after the peak of the civil rights movement, racial inequality in economic life persists. Standard economic indicators show that in most respects the economic status of minorities has not improved since the days of a short-lived trend that ended in the early 1970s. Indeed, several indicators show a declining relative economic status for blacks. The evidence is overwhelming that the achievements of the civil rights movement did not usher in the anticipated golden age of racial equality in economic life (Swinton, 1988).

My primary objective in this chapter is to explore the persistence of racial inequality in economic life in the post-civil-rights-movement era. The major focus will be on the unequal economic status of black Americans. There are two primary reasons for restricting my discussion to black Americans. First, blacks are the largest and the most subordinated group. Second, the historical situation of blacks is unique because they were the only major minority group to be subjected to slavery and the formal apartheid of the "Jim Crow" South. In any case I have studied blacks' economic status for nearly 20 years and have much more data, knowledge, and understanding about blacks' economic experiences than about those of the other non-European minority groups.

The simple facts concerning the black experience are clear. Almost 35 years after *Brown v. Board of Education*, 25 years after the passage of the Civil Rights Act of 1964, and about 20 years after the peak period for social legislation to combat poverty and racial inequality, the economic gaps between blacks and whites persist almost unchanged. As surprising as this outcome may seem in view of the high expectations that accompanied the successes of the civil rights movement, the statistical evidence is so overwhelming as to be nearly incontrovertible. In the discussion that follows I will outline this evidence.

The persisting racial disparities in economic life require an explanation. Why did the programs and policies of the last three or four decades have such a minimal impact on the relative economic position of black Americans? This question will be addressed later. I will argue that racial inequality has persisted in the post-civil-rights-movement era because the policies and programs of that period were unable to overcome the economic disadvantages that had accumulated for blacks or to prevent whites from using their superior economic position to maintain their advantaged status. This lack of success will be related to both the magnitude and the nature of the efforts made in that period.

In the final section of the chapter I will discuss the implications of the experience over the last two decades for future efforts to eliminate the unequal economic status of black and other non-European Americans and will comment on the future of race relations in the United States.

TRENDS IN RACIAL INEQUALITY
IN ECONOMIC LIFE

My primary objective in this section is to provide a brief statistical overview of the post-1970 trends in the relative economic status of black Americans. My approach to this task is straightforward: I will examine several basic indicators of blacks' absolute and relative economic status and compare the values of these indicators at the beginning and at the end of the period in question to determine whether any major improvement has occurred in blacks' relative economic status. In general, I will discuss the variation between the two endpoints only when necessary to clarify the interpretation of the longer range trend.

Because the discussion is concerned with the economic status of blacks as a group, the indicators that I use are intended to characterize the position of the whole group. It goes without saying that there will always be variation within the group around any single-valued indicator of group economic status. Some blacks will fare better than the group as a whole; some will fare worse. My main interest, however, is in the relative status of the group as a whole in comparison to the status of Americans of European descent.

The most comprehensive single-valued measures of racial inequality in economic life are based on measures of central tendency for the population as a whole. Thus much of this examination of recent trends will focus on time-series data on the means, medians, proportions, or other measures of central tendency for various indicators of economic status. The evidence from these measures will be supplemented by more extensive discussions of the distribution when this seems useful. I will examine trends separately for subgroups of the population and subregions of the country only when divergent trends exist at the disaggregated level and when an examination of the fuller distribution seems important to understanding the trends in group economic status.

Trends in Income Disparities

Let us begin with a comparison between the current income position of the black population and the position during the early 1970s. As the most comprehensive measure of economic well-being, income is used widely as the standard measure of economic status. Blacks' incomes were substantially less than those of whites in 1970; the differences continued to exist in roughly the same magnitude in 1986. (The discussion below is in terms of 1986 dollars.)

In 1986, the latest year for which income estimates are available, the black population received an aggregate income of about $208 billion (Swinton, 1988; U.S. Department of Commerce, 1987), or about $7,207 for each black person. In absolute terms, this was the highest per-person income ever recorded for blacks. Yet because per-person income generally increases steadily from year to year, records generally are set in nonrecession years. When we compare blacks' income to whites', however, we find that the long-standing inequality in income persisted in 1986: In contrast to the blacks' per-person income of $7,207, whites' per-person income was $12,352. Thus in 1986, black persons on the average received only $583 for each $1,000 received by whites.

Per-person income for both blacks and whites has grown since 1970, when blacks received about $5,278 per person and whites received about $9,471. The degree of racial inequality, however, has not changed much since 1970, as indicated by the fact that the ratio of black per-person income to white per-person income was $557 per $1,000 in 1970. Thus the relative income gap was reduced only by about 6% in the 17 years between 1970 and 1986. At that rate, 283 years would be required to close the gap. Moreover, the absolute gap in per-person income increased from $4,193 in 1970 to $5,145 by 1986, showing that blacks fell almost $1,000 farther behind in absolute terms between 1970 and 1986.

Moreover, the relative per-person income has not followed a constant trend across the period. In fact, it followed an upward trend from 1970 through 1978, fell after 1978 through the recession of the early 1980s, and has recovered slightly since that time. Some of this fluctuation clearly is due to the business cycle. In 1986, however, 4 years into the latest recovery, the racial gap in relative per-person income was still higher than in 1978. The per-person income of blacks relative to that of whites was $594 per $1,000 in 1978 and $583 per $1,000 in 1986. I conclude that by this measure, there clearly has been no significant improvement in the racial income gap during the post-civil-rights era.

The persistence of the high level of racial inequality in income is even more evident in family income statistics. Indeed, racial inequality in family income has worsened in both absolute and relative terms since 1970. In 1986 median black family income was $17,604, versus $30,809 for whites. Thus the median-level black family received only $571 for every $1,000 received by the median-level white family. Both absolute family income and relative family income for blacks have declined since 1970. In 1970, black family income was $17,730 by this measure, compared to $28,904 for whites. Thus the median-level black family received $613 per $1,000 of income available to the typical white family in 1970. The median family income gap grew by about 11% between 1970 and 1986. Moreover, a simple subtraction of the 1970 absolute income gap of $11,174 from the 1986 gap of $13,205 shows that the absolute gap between black and white median family also increased by $2,031 between 1970 and 1986.

As was the case with per-person income, racial inequality in median family income also has increased since the late 1970s. Indeed, even the absolute level of black family income has been significantly lower during the 1980s. In the first 7 years of the 1980s, black median family income averaged about $16,476 in 1986 dollars, compared to $17,765 during the 1970s. Even though 1986 was the peak year for black family income in the 1980s, that level was lower than black family income in 7 of the 10 years of the 1970s.

The aggregate gaps between black and white income are very large in absolute terms. In 1986 aggregate black income was estimated at $208 billion. This income would have to be increased by $148 billion if blacks' per-person incomes were to equal those of whites. This aggregate per-person income gap is $51 billion higher than in 1970 and $25 billion higher than in 1979 (Swinton, 1988).

If we look only at family income, the gap between black and white family income in 1986 (i.e., the amount that would have been required to equalize black and white family incomes in 1986) was about $97 billion (Swinton, 1988). The increased inequality in black family income between 1978 and 1986 cost black families about $4.5 billion. Although the aggregate figures cited in the last two paragraphs are only rough approximations, they reflect accurately the size of the income inequality between blacks and whites that continues to persist.

Although income varies within the black population, blacks' incomes are lower than whites' at corresponding positions throughout the black income distribution.

Blacks in the highest and lowest quintiles of the black income distribution have lower incomes than corresponding whites (Swinton, 1987, 1988). For example, in 1986 the upper limit of the lowest fifth of the black family income distribution equaled only 44.7% of the corresponding position of the white family income distribution. Although the degree of inequality according to this measure declined as black family income increased, the lower limit for the top 5% of the black income distribution still equaled only about 69.7% of the lower limit for whites. Income inequality at intermediate positions on the income distribution lies between these two limits. Thus poor blacks are significantly poorer than poor whites, and higher income blacks have lower incomes than higher income whites.

Moreover, since the late 1970s the degree of inequality has increased for all positions on the income distribution. The increase in income inequality since that time has been relatively sharp for low-income blacks and more modest for higher income blacks.

Distribution of Income Within the Black Community

A particularly disturbing trend since the late 1970s has been a tendency for income distribution to become more unequal for both the black and white populations. This increasing inequality was caused by a fairly sharp rise in the proportion of families who receive extremely low incomes, along with a simultaneous increase in the proportion of high-income families. The trend has been much more pronounced for blacks.

Between 1970 and 1978, for example, the proportion of black families receiving incomes under $5,000 fell from 9.6% to 8.9%. Between 1978 and 1986, however, this proportion rose from 8.9% to 14.0%. The fluctuations were much lower for whites: Between 1970 and 1978 the proportion of white families with incomes of $5,000 or less dropped from 3.1% to 2.6% and rose only to 3.5% between 1978 and 1986. Thus between 1978 and 1986 the increase in the proportion of black families with incomes of $5,000 or less was over five times as great as the corresponding increase for white families. Between these two dates, 362,000 additional black families fell into the below-$5,000 category.

Simultaneously there was an increase in the proportion of black families whose incomes were $50,000 or more. Between 1970 and 1978 this proportion increased from 4.7% to 7.7%. The growth in the proportion of higher income blacks ceased between 1978 and 1983. Growth resumed after 1983, however, and by 1986 the proportion of black families with incomes of at least $50,000 had increased to 8.8%. Of course, the absolute increase in the proportion of higher income whites was larger during this period. The proportion of black families with incomes of at least $50,000 rose 4.1 percentage points between 1970 and 1986, whereas the proportion of higher income white families increased by 7.2 percentage points.

The income distributions for both blacks and whites have become more unequal since 1970. This point is illustrated by the declining share of income received by the poorest 20% of each group and by the increasing share of income received by the richest 20% of each group. The share of aggregate income received by the poorest quintile of the black population dropped from 4.5% to 3.5% between 1970 and 1986. In contrast, the share of income received by the top quintile increased from 43.4% to 46.9%.

The Poverty Level

The poverty level is another indicator of the income status of the black population. By definition, the poverty rate is the proportion of persons who live in spending units with incomes that are too low to achieve minimum standards of consumption. The official poverty statistics released annually by the U.S. Bureau of the Census include transfers of money income in the definition of income and exclude transfers of in-kind income. As a measure of blacks' economic condition, the numbers underestimate poverty from the viewpoint of earnings sufficiency and overestimate poverty from the viewpoint of consumption sufficiency.

In general, poverty status indicators confirm the general finding that racial inequality continues to be quite pronounced. In 1986, for example, 31.1% of black persons were classified officially as poor (Swinton, 1987, 1988). This figure amounted to almost 9 million poor black persons. The proportion of black persons below the official poverty level was lower in 1986 than in 1970, when it was 33.5%, and slightly higher than in 1978, when it stood at 30.6%. Thus very little absolute change in the poverty rate has occurred since the 1970s. This finding is in sharp contrast to the significant decline in black poverty rates that occurred between 1959 and 1970, when the poverty rate fell from 55.1% to 33.5%. Thus although the absolute number of black persons in poverty fell by about 2.8 million between 1959 and 1969, this number increased by about 1.9 million between 1969 and 1986.

In absolute terms, a large gap continues to exist between blacks' and whites' rates of poverty. The black poverty rate of 33.5% in 1970 was 3.4 times greater and 23.4 percentage points higher than the white poverty rate of 9.9%. The poverty gap was slightly lower in 1986, when the black poverty rate of 31.1% was only 20.1 percentage points higher and 2.8 times greater than the white poverty rate of 11.0%. Despite the decline of about 15% in the difference between black and white poverty rates, the rates of poverty for blacks and for whites still differ sharply. In 1986 blacks continued to be roughly three times as likely as whites to be in poverty. Moreover, as I will discuss next, the national trend results from a trend of increasing gaps in the North and decreasing gaps in the South.

Regional Variations in Income and Poverty Trends

Before concluding this discussion of recent trends in income inequality, I should note that income and poverty trends varied in different regions of the country during the period under discussion. In general, absolute and relative income disparities increased in the northern regions and held steady or declined slightly in the South. Income disparities for blacks increased most sharply in the Midwest. For example, black income in the Midwest was almost $5,500 lower in absolute terms in 1986 than in 1978 and 1969 (Swinton, 1987, 1988). The ratio of black to white median family income stood at 56.9% in 1986, compared to 73.4% in 1970. Indeed, relative racial equality in income in the Midwest was much greater during the 1950s and 1960s than it has been during the 1970s and 1980s. A similar pattern is evident in the data for the Northeast, although the last 2 years of the recovery have had a more pronounced effect in improving blacks' relative status in that region. The degree of racial inequality has fluctuated around a steady level in the South.

The absolute and relative rates of black poverty also have followed an upward trend outside the South since 1970. Again, the sharpest upward movements occurred in the Midwest and the Northeast. In the Midwest the black poverty rate rose from 25.7% in 1970 to 34.5% in 1986. The rate in the Northeast increased from 20% to 24% over the same period. In contrast, the poverty rate in the South actually declined from 42.6% to 33.6% between 1970 and 1986.

Although white poverty also increased in the Northeast and the Midwest, the rate of increase was much greater for blacks in both regions; thus the relative gaps increased. For example, the ratio of black to white poverty rates was 2.9 in the Midwest in 1970 and 3.3 in 1986. Again, the racial disparity declined in the South, as the rate of poverty among southern whites actually declined much less than the rate of poverty among southern blacks. Thus, although southern blacks were 3.4 times as likely to be in poverty as southern whites in 1970, they were only 2.8 times as likely in 1986.

Two points must be made about the regional contrast in trends in racial inequality. First, the trends of the post-1970 period have eliminated much of the difference between the income and poverty status of blacks in the South compared to that of blacks in the other regions. This change in the relative position of the South among the regions, however, was caused as much by the decline in the status of blacks in the other regions as by any improvement for blacks in the South. Second, the flatness or stagnation in the trends for the nation as a whole results from diverging trends within the regions. Slight improvement or stability in the South has offset sharper declines in the Midwest and the Northeast. Trends in the West have been much more erratic.

TRENDS IN BLACK PARTICIPATION
IN ECONOMIC ACTIVITY

The income and poverty status of blacks is a consequence of the level and character of black participation in the American economy. Low and unequal black income results from low and unequal participation by blacks as owners and as employees. Blacks traditionally have received relatively small amounts of income from property, such as profits, interest, rent, and dividends, because they have owned relatively few businesses and relatively small amounts of income-producing assets. Blacks also have traditionally experienced relatively low earnings from employment because of high rates of unemployment and limited employment in high-wage, high-status jobs.

Each of these problems was recognized during the civil rights movement; some efforts were initiated to address each of these problems during that era. The persisting high level of racial inequality, however, suggests that the problems of economic participation have not yet been resolved. In this section I will briefly examine the current disparities in black participation in the American economy and comment on trends in these disparities when the data permit.

Business and Wealth Ownership

The latest available evidence, based on the Commerce Department's 1982 Survey of Minority Business Enterprises, suggests that the level of ownership of business enterprises by black Americans is still very small in comparison to the proportion of blacks in the population. Black businesses continue to be small and overconcentrated in a few retail and service-oriented industries.

According to calculations based on various censuses of business, the number of black-owned businesses would have to increase about sixfold if blacks were to own proportionately as many businesses as whites (U.S. Department of Commerce, 1984). Moreover, this fact significantly understates blacks' disadvantage in business ownership because black-owned businesses are not only fewer in number but significantly smaller. Thus the same data sets suggest that the aggregate size of the black business sector, measured by the dollar value of its receipts, would have to be multiplied over 75 times in order for a proportionate share of the receipts of all American businesses to originate in the black-owned sector.

If additional evidence is required regarding the marginal character of black-owned businesses, let us note that not a single black-owned business has made the *Fortune 500* list. In fact, in 1986 the combined sales of the 100 largest black-owned businesses would have placed them at Number 256 on the list (*Fortune*, 1986).

These figures make it clear that black business ownership is marginal at best. In 1982 the total number of paid employees of all the black-owned businesses in the country was only 165,765 persons, according to Census Bureau data (U.S. Department of Commerce, 1984). This level of employment can be contrasted to total private-sector employment of over 70 million persons and to black employment of over 9.2 million persons in 1982 (U.S. Department of Labor, 1985). Employment by black-owned businesses would have to increase more than 50 times in order for those businesses to provide a proportionate share of total private-sector employment.

Moreover, in view of small, marginal status of the black business sector in the latest data, it is apparent that no significant progress has been made in reversing the disparities in business ownership since 1970. In fact, comparisons of the results of the census on black-owned businesses since the first such census was released in 1969 suggest that the place of the black business sector in the American economy has not changed much. Although there is some evidence of a limited increase in the numbers of businesses owned by blacks, this evidence suggests that the relative importance of black-owned businesses may have declined because the share of per-person receipts originating in this sector appears to have declined since 1970.

More complete U.S. Census data on wealth ownership show the limited general participation of blacks as owners of wealth (U.S. Department of Commerce, 1984). According to this report, blacks' wealth holdings were significantly lower than whites' in every category of wealth. This difference is due to blacks' lower likelihoods of holding any particular type of wealth and to lower average holdings among the few blacks who do own wealth. In this report, blacks' overall median net worth was placed at $3,397, in contrast with median wealth holdings of $39,135 among whites. Thus blacks' median wealth holdings were only about 9% of whites' in 1984.

The impact of the differences in wealth ownership can be seen in Census Bureau data that report income receipts by type of income. In 1984, for example, blacks received much lower incomes from sources related to business or to wealth ownership than did whites. Self-employment income is related directly to business ownership; whites received $599 per person from this source, whereas blacks received only $113 per person (U.S. Department of Commerce, 1986). Thus blacks received only about 18.9% of the per-person income received from this source by whites. The disparities in incomes from sources such as interest, dividends, and profits are much larger; these types of income are received as a result of ownership of productive wealth. In 1984 blacks' receipts from this type of property ownership were $119 per person, only 12.6% of whites' receipts of $944.

Lower receipts from property-related income sources are major causes of the racial income and poverty gaps. Moreover, there has been little improvement in the level of receipts from this type of income since 1970 (Swinton, 1987). The ratio of black to white per-person receipts from property income has risen slightly from about 7.9% in 1970 to 12.6% in 1984. The 1984 figure, however, is still too small to be considered significant progress. Moreover, the 1984 ratio of black to white per-person income from nonfarm self-employment—18.9%—is slightly less than the 19.9% ratio calculated for 1970.

In any case, the disparities in wealth and business ownership result in large aggregate income losses for the black population. In 1984, for example, the difference between black and white per-person income from the sources mentioned above was $1,311. This figure implies an aggregate income loss of at least $40 billion, which accounts for about 28% of the gap between black and white income. Thus it is clear that persisting disparities in wealth and business ownership account for a major share of the persistence of lower relative black incomes. The failure to close these ownership gaps significantly during the past two decades accounts in part for the lack of economic progress among blacks during this period. I will return to a discussion of the reasons for the limited progress on this front after a discussion of recent labor market trends.

Labor Market Participation

The importance of working for wages and salaries in determining blacks' relative income and poverty rates is well know. In 1984, for example, blacks received 79.4% of their income from wages and salaries (U.S. Department of Commerce, 1986). This proportion is slightly less than the 84.1% of income originating from this source during 1970 but nonetheless is by far the most important source of income for blacks. Moreover, blacks receive a larger share of their total income than do whites from working for wages and salaries. In 1984 the share of white income originating from this source was only 72.6%, also down from the figure of 78.2% recorded for whites in 1970.

Obviously, because such a large share of their income derives from wages and salaries, blacks' economic status depends crucially on what happens to black workers. In 1984, for example, blacks' earnings from wage and salary employment generated only $4,990 per person, compared to $7,943 for whites. Thus the contribution of black workers to black per-person income was only 62.8% of white workers' contribution to white per-person income. The per-person income gap was $2,953, which generated an $83.1 billion aggregate income deficit. Thus the gap in labor market earnings accounted for 63% of the overall black–white income gap in 1984.

How well blacks fare in the labor market depends on three kinds of factors: demographic factors, an employment factor, and a wage rate factor. The demographic factors determine the size and the characteristics of the population available for work. The employment factor determines the level of employment in the working-age population. The wage rate factor determines how much the employed population earns. I will discuss trends in each of these areas.

The Demographic Factors

Two broad demographic factors have influenced the relative earnings of the black population: the proportion of the black population that is of working age and the relative number of males in the black population. Among blacks, a smaller proportion of the population is generally of working age. Thus there are fewer blacks to earn income. All other things being equal, this fact would cause a reduction in blacks' relative earnings. In 1986 only 72.3% of the black population was of working age, compared to 79.1% percent of the white population (U.S. Department of Labor, 1987).

Blacks also generally have fewer males in their working-age population than do whites. This fact, of course, is part of the reason for the smaller working-age population. In addition, because males earn more than females, relative black earnings are lowered even further. In 1986 there were only 827 black males for every 1,000 black females. These figures suggest that there were about 1,176,000 missing black working-age males in 1986.

Since 1970 these two demographic factors have moved in opposite directions. On the one hand, the proportion of the population that is of working age has increased significantly. In 1970 only 64.6% of the black population was over 15 years old, compared to 72.3% percent in 1986. Moreover, although the proportion of working-age whites also increased, the proportion among blacks increased slightly faster. The gap between the proportion of blacks and whites of working age declined from 7.8 percentage points to 6.8 percentage points between 1970 and 1986.

On the other hand, the proportion of black males in the working-age population actually declined between 1970 and 1986. In 1970 there were 858 black males for every 1,000 females over age 15, compared with 830 males for every 1,000 females in 1986. Moreover, while the ratio of males to females declined among blacks, the ratio among whites increased from 920 to 930 per 1,000 between 1970 and 1986. Thus the problem of missing black males has intensified since 1970.

These two demographic factors have had a significant impact on the inequality of blacks' and whites' earnings. Rough calculations suggest that the missing male factor lowered blacks' wage and salary earnings by about $11.4 billion in 1986. The lower working-age population, excluding the missing males, accounts for roughly another $6.3 billion. Thus these two demographic factors generate roughly 19% of the overall wage and salary gap.

The Employment Factor

The fact that blacks have lower employment levels than whites is the second factor that contributes to lower earnings among blacks. The employment-to-population ratio for blacks in 1986 was only 54.1%, compared to 61.5% for whites (Swinton, 1988). Thus blacks were only about 88% as likely as whites to be employed. The disparity in employment rates was much greater for males than for females. The employment rate for black males was 60.6%, or only about 83.8% of the employment rate for white males, whereas the 48.8% employment rate for black females was 94.4% of the 51.7% white female employment rate.

Since 1970 the relative employment rates for black males and females have decreased. For males the absolute employment-to-population ratio has continued its long-term decline. In 1970, for example, about 62.8% of the black male working-age population was employed, compared to the 60.6% employed in 1986. Black males were 87.5% as likely to be employed as white males in 1970, compared to the 83.8% likelihood for 1986 cited earlier.

Black females were more likely to be employed than white females in 1970, when 43.7% of black females and only 38.6% of white females were employed. Thus black women were 13.2% more likely to be employed than white women in 1970, compared to the 5.6% lower likelihood of employment in 1986. Indeed, since the mid-1970s the historical pattern of greater black female employment, which persisted throughout this century, has been reversed. Thus for both black males and females, relative level of employment has declined since 1970.

The lower employment-to-population ratios result from differences in labor-force participation rates and in unemployment rates. Currently the civilian labor-force participation rate for black males is lower than for white males; and the participation rate for black females is slightly higher than for white females. During 1986, for example, the black male participation rate of 71.2% was only 92.6% of the white male rate of 76.9% (Swinton, 1988). The black female labor-force participation rate of 56.9% was about 3.5% higher than the white female participation rate of 55%.

Since 1970, participation rates for black and white males have declined, but the rate has fallen more for black males than for white males. Thus in 1970, the ratio of black male to white male participation, 95.6%, was slightly higher than the 92.6% ratio noted for 1986. Black females had a 16.2% participation rate advantage in 1970, in contrast to the 3.5% advantage noted for 1986. Thus the relative rate of participation has declined for black women as well since 1970.

Participation trends clearly have contributed to a growing employment disadvantage, but the major factor since 1970 has been increasing unemployment rates (Swinton, 1988). In 1986, for example, the unemployment rate for blacks was 14.5%, or 2.4 times the 6.0% unemployment rate for whites.

Both black males and black females have experienced high absolute and relative unemployment for the past decade. In 1986 black males had a 14.8% unemployment rate, whereas black females had a 14.2% unemployment rate. These rates were, respectively, 2.5 and 2.3 times the corresponding rates for white males and females.

The unemployment rates for both black males and black females have been drifting upward both absolutely and relative to whites since 1970. The black male unemployment rate of 14.8% in 1986 was 7.5 percentage points higher than the 7.3% rate for black males in 1970, whereas the 1986 white male rate of 6.0% was only 2.0 percentage points higher than the 4.0% observed in 1970. Similarly, whereas the black female unemployment rate for 1986 was 4.9 percentage points higher than the rate for 1970, the white female rate was only 0.7 of a percentage point higher. Between 1975 and 1986, black unemployment averaged 15.2%, compared to only 6.7% for whites.

The employment differences between blacks and whites contribute substantially to the earnings gap between these groups. I have estimated elsewhere that black employment levels during 1986 were about 1.6 million jobs lower than they would have been if employment parity had existed between blacks and whites. This figure implies that the earnings for 1986 lost because of lower employment were about $25.6 billion. Thus the employment factor could explain about 30.8% of the overall earnings gap.

The Wage Rate Factor

Employed blacks work for lower wages on the average than do employed whites. In 1986, for example, the usual median weekly earnings of full-time black male workers were only 73% of the earnings for white males; the usual median weekly wage for black females was about 89% of the white female wage (Swinton, 1988). Thus both black male and black female workers usually have lower wage rates than white workers.

The gap in wage rates has persisted since 1970. The 1970 ratio of usual weekly earnings for black and white males—72%—is 1 percentage point lower than the 1986 male earnings ratio. The 1970 female wage ratio of 91% is 2 percentage points higher than the 1970 ratio of usual weekly earnings for black and white females. In general, small increases in the relative earnings of black males and females occurred through the mid-1970s, but since that time a downward trend has occurred in the ratio of blacks' to whites' wages.

The overall ratio of blacks' to whites' median wages in 1986 was 78.6%. If this ratio is taken to approximate the pure wage rate difference factor, then wage rate differences account for about 42.5% of the earnings gap between blacks and whites. In 1986 this gap would have equaled about $40 billion.

Blacks earn lower wages than whites for two basic reasons. First, blacks are more likely to work at low-wage jobs. Second, blacks may earn lower wages than whites on the same job. The available data do not enable us to distinguish these two factors, primarily because there are no data showing the job distribution of blacks and whites. We can come closest by using occupational and industry data. We can gain limited insight into the effect of different job distributions by examining the effect of different occupational and industry distributions. We also may gain limited insight concerning the effect of pay differences within job categories by examining wage differences within occupations.

Black and white workers continue to have slightly different distributions across job class and industry (Swinton, 1988). Blacks are somewhat more likely to work for the government than are whites. Among nongovernment workers blacks are less likely to be self-employed. In major industry sectors blacks have higher probabilities than whites of working for government, services, transportation, communications, public utilities, and nondurable goods manufacturing. They are less likely to work in all of the other sectors. Rough calculations, however, suggest that these differences do not produce any disadvantages for blacks. In fact, blacks probably gain a slight advantage from their industry distribution. I estimate that the industry pattern could reduce the black earnings gap by as much as 5%.

Blacks' occupational distribution, however, apparently does lower blacks' earnings. Blacks continue to be much less likely to be employed in high-wage, high-status occupations. In 1986, for example, only 20% of black males were employed in the four high-wage, white-collar occupations; white males were over twice as likely to be employed in these four occupations, at a level of 40.7%. On the other hand, 51.7% of black male workers were employed as operatives, laborers, and service workers, compared to 28.3% of white workers.

Significant differences in black and white female occupational distributions also exist, although the differences are not as pronounced. In 1986 41.5% of white females worked in the high-prestige, white-collar occupations, compared to 28.5% of black females. In contrast, 30.4% of black females versus 18.4% percent of white females worked in low-prestige, blue-collar occupations.

Since 1970 modest improvement has occurred in the occupational distributions of employed black males and females. Although the occupational classification system changed with the 1980 Census, it is clear that the long-term trend toward white-collar and away from blue-collar occupations has continued both for blacks and for whites.

In 1970 the proportion of black males employed in white-collar occupations was only 19%; by 1986 this figure had increased to 28.6%. However, the proportion of operatives and laborers declined during that period from 45.4% to 34% of employed black male workers.

The racial gaps in occupational distributions also were lower in 1986. Black males, for example, were only 44% as likely as white males to be white-collar workers in 1970 but were 62% as likely in 1986. Similarly, black males were 1.8 times as likely as white males to be operatives or laborers in 1970 but only 1.7 times as likely in 1986. Similar occupational gains were observed for black females. The occupational trend thus has been favorable. The remaining occupational gaps are large, however, and have a major impact on black earnings. My estimates indicate that the occupational differences that existed in 1986 reduced black males' wages relative to white males' wages by roughly 12.2% and reduced black females' wages by about 8.6%. The occupational differences accounted for roughly 46% of the male wage gap and about 82% of the female wage gap.

This finding leads to an estimate of 48% for the overall proportion of the wage gap that is due to occupational differences and implies a total earnings loss of about $19.2 billion due to occupational dissimilarity. Despite the modest improvements since 1970, a less favorable occupational distribution continues to impose a high cost on the black population.

As noted earlier, blacks not only have a less favorable job distribution but also continue to receive lower pay within given job categories. An examination of differences in median wages across broad occupational categories shows that black males in general receive lower median wages within each category. In 1982, for example, while the overall median wage for black males was 76% of the white males' wage, black males' wages in individual categories ranged from 70% to 89% of white males' wages (Swinton, 1983).

Wage differences between black and white females are much smaller. In 1982, in the seven occupational categories for which wage data were available for black and white females, wages were equal in three categories. Blacks' wages were between 88% and 95% of whites' wages in three categories and were 7% higher than whites' wages in the remaining category.

Although the evidence is not overwhelming, indications are that wage differences within broad occupational categories may have decreased until the mid-1970s but probably have increased since that time. For the period as a whole, there was probably very little change in wage differences within occupations.

The average estimate shows that wage differences within occupational categories account for about 57% of the male wage gap and about 8% of the female wage gap. In the aggregate, within-occupation wage differences may account for roughly 43% of the overall wage gap between blacks and whites, or about $17.2 billion in 1986.

EXPLANATIONS FOR THE POST-1970
PERSISTENCE OF RACIAL INEQUALITY

In an earlier section I outlined the dimensions of the persisting racial inequality in economic life. As shown, the relative gaps in income and poverty rates between blacks and whites have not changed much since the early 1970s. Indeed, in some regions, income and poverty gaps have increased since 1970, while in the South there has been modest improvement. In all regions, however, the income and poverty gaps are still large. Blacks still receive less than 60¢ per $1 of income received by whites and are still roughly three times as likely to be poor in every part of the country.

In the previous section I showed that the continuing disparities in income result primarily from persisting inequalities in the character of black American participation in the American economy. Black Americans continue to own and control far fewer businesses than whites. The latest data suggest that the black business sector is at least 50 times smaller than would be required for ownership parity. Total wealth holdings, as measured by the median value of wealth holdings, were over 11 times smaller than would be required for parity. Moreover, there has been no significant amelioration of the disparities in ownership of businesses or wealth since 1970.

Disparities in ownership are at the root of the persistence of economic inequality. As noted, these differences contribute directly to differences in income. They also mean that blacks have much less power and ability to determine their own economic futures. Because of their limited ownership of economic resources, blacks have been dependent on white resource owners for opportunities to participate in the American economy. The degree of black dependency did not decline in the post-1970 period.

Black dependency means that black workers have had to compete for jobs primarily in white-owned or white-controlled businesses and institutions. The outcome for blacks continues to be unfavorable occupational distributions, lower wage rates, and lower levels of employment. Overall, there has been no significant improvement in blacks' labor market status since 1970. Employed workers made small occupational gains, but these were offset by significant absolute and relative losses in employment. Wage inequality has remained about the same or a little higher than in the early 1970s. The net result of these trends is that black workers as a whole have made no significant gain in relative earnings in the post-1970 period. The failure of black workers as a whole to record any significant gains in the labor market explains a major part of the persisting economic disparities in income and poverty rates for the black population.

Thus the persisting income and poverty gaps result from the failure of the black population to make any significant gains in ownership or labor-market status. Why were there so few gains in ownership or labor-market status in the post-1970 period despite the successes of the civil rights movement? Let us turn our attention to this question.

The lowly economic status of blacks at the start of the civil rights movement resulted from the long legacy of racism, segregation, and discrimination that had left the black population with the severe economic disadvantages discussed above: low levels of business ownership and wealth and low levels of education and work experience. Moreover, blacks still were subjected to current market discrimination in gaining equal access to economic opportunities. The lack of amelioration of racial inequality in economic life suggests that the policies and programs implemented by the civil rights movement were insufficient to resolve these underlying causes of inequality.

The civil rights strategy focused on the development of laws, regulations, policies, and programs to eliminate discrimination and differences in human capital. The basic strategic decision implicit in these policies and programs was to ignore differences in wealth and ownership and to focus on the elimination of discrimination and, to a lesser extent, on the improvement of human capital. This strategy contains the assumption that individual black initiative operating through the free market is sufficient to eliminate racial inequality within a reasonable period of time, given a nondiscriminatory environment and improvement in black human capital and despite differences in human capital, business ownership, and wealth.

The decision to focus efforts on nondiscrimination meant that little direct effort was made to eliminate the large gaps in poverty, income, or ownership. Some changes were made in direct income transfer programs, but these were intended primarily to eliminate discrimination in access to benefits. Yet for the most part, the benefit levels in the transfer programs were allowed to remain too low to eliminate poverty or income inequality or to affect it significantly. At best, improvements in benefit levels were designed to ameliorate the worst impacts of poverty in order to facilitate the efforts to improve human capital.

Although some minimal efforts were made to ameliorate disparities in business ownership, these efforts were minimal at best and could not be seen as a major part of the overall civil rights strategy. For the most part, civil rights strategists accepted the extensive inequality in ownership of businesses and wealth and attempted to bring about nondiscrimination without altering the basic distribution of ownership.

The implication of the strategic decision to focus on eliminating discrimination and on improving black human capital was that blacks would continue to be dependent on white-owned or white-controlled businesses and institutions for opportunities to earn income and to improve their human capital. All the blacks' eggs essentially were placed in the integrationist basket. For the 1960s strategy to be successful, the civil rights movement would have had to succeed in implementing policies and programs that could induce whites who controlled access to jobs, education, training, and business opportunities to provide equal opportunities to blacks, despite their long-standing historical preferences for whites and despite the blacks' real disadvantages in wealth, income, and human capital.

The civil rights movement succeeded in causing a broad range of policies and programs to be enacted; these were designed to achieve most of the broad objectives mentioned above. Programs were implemented to improve blacks' relative education. Employment and training programs were developed in order to provide the human capital that blacks lacked because of limited work experience. Laws were passed to make discrimination illegal in employment, education, housing, lending, and most other public activities. In principle, at least, the effort was made to implement the civil rights strategy.

Yet as we have seen, this effort did not produce substantial improvement in blacks' economic status. The primary reason for the failure of the civil rights strategy is related to program design and implementation. The efforts implemented simply were not sufficient to eliminate the inherited differences in human capital or the racial discrimination in the white-dominated system.

Human capital enhancement programs accomplished a great deal but had little success in improving blacks' position in the labor market. In terms of education there was a significant decline in the gap between blacks and whites in years of school completed; hundreds of thousands of blacks also participated in a variety of employment and training programs. Black enrollments in colleges and professional schools rose significantly through the late 1970s.

These changes, however, did not have a major impact on blacks' economic standing for two primary reasons. First, despite the recent efforts, significant gaps in education and training continue to exist. In particular, large disparities remain in the percentages finishing college, the percentages dropping out before completing high school, the quality of education attained, and the quantity and quality of work experience. Indeed, because most of the training and educational programs focused on providing access to entry-level workers, there was no significant possibility of eliminating the racial disparities between experienced workers. Thus the educational and training activities undertaken as a result of the civil rights movement simply proved insufficient to eliminate blacks' accumulated historical advantages.

The second reason why these policies failed to have a major effect on blacks' status is that discriminatory treatment continued even after human capital was enhanced, especially for those who received less than college-level training. The civil rights movement succeeded in causing discrimination to be outlawed. Yet just as the human capital programs failed to eliminate differences in human capital, the antidiscrimination programs failed to eliminate racial discrimination in economic life, especially against average black workers. This outcome is indicated by the wide disparities in employment and earnings between blacks and whites with equal educational attainment.

The principal reason for this failure was white resistance to the development of effective enforcement. The affirmative action strategies promoted by civil rights advocates were never adopted fully and were resisted strenuously by some white workers and employers. Moreover, the federal government increasingly has withdrawn active support of such programs. The enforcement effort was never very effective; it was always engulfed in red tape and confusion.

One fatal flaw in the civil rights strategy was its failure to recognize the necessity of repairing the damages or eliminating the disadvantages that blacks had accumulated because of the history of racism and discrimination. In effect, the programs and policies developed during the civil rights era were designed to end the practice of racism and discrimination, but they paid only minimal attention to the accumulated economic disadvantages. Unfortunately, these disadvantages were real and imposed insurmountable handicaps. Poverty lack of wealth and business ownership, and low levels of human capital made it impossible for blacks to translate nondiscrimination into racial equality.

A second major strategic flaw on the part of the civil rights movement was the failure to recognize the economic importance of unequal opportunity in establishing the white population's advantaged economic status. The distribution game in a market economy is almost zero-sum; whites were relatively advantaged precisely because blacks were relatively disadvantaged. Civil rights thinking tended to ignore the interdependencies in economic status and to commit the fallacy of composition by assuming that the relationship between merit and the determination of a single individual's economic status could be applied without change to all individuals collectively. The primary consequence of this fallacious thinking was the failure to recognize the powerful economic incentives that existed to maintain whites' advantages through discrimination and other means. The civil rights advocates generally underestimated the resistance that whites would offer to the equal opportunity agenda.

Many of the failures of the civil rights strategies resulted from the fact that in making crucial design and implementation decisions, too much consideration was given to the interests of the white population that historically had discriminated against blacks. Consideration of white interests dominated the final decisions about what would be done, how it would be done, and how much would be done. Both human capital and antidiscrimination programs were designed and implemented to have minimal adverse effects on whites.

The desire to minimize these effects has handicapped the effort to improve blacks' relative status in a number of ways. One major effect of this policy has been to restrict most efforts to overcome blacks' historical disadvantages. White conservatives had insisted that no legitimate policies could provide preferential treatment of any kind. This view has made it impossible to tailor programs and policies to overcome the specific economic and social disadvantages that blacks inherited as the legacy of racism and discrimination. Moreover, effective enforcement of antidiscrimination laws and regulations has been handicapped by the promotion of the colorblind principle instead of a results-oriented principle of enforcement. In effect, the principles of nondiscrimination have been employed to block the use of disparate outcomes as evidence of discrimination. Because the intent of discriminators is not visible, this policy makes it extremely difficult to detect discrimination.

Certainly whites' resistance to the design and implementation of an effective program to bring about full equality for blacks was increased further by the economic trends of the post-1970s period. That period has been characterized by a relative shortage of jobs in general and by a shortage of good jobs, especially for males, in particular. In this increasingly competitive environment, racial competition for economic opportunities has increased; it has provided greater incentive for whites to discriminate and has reduced their willingness to support equal opportunity programs. Civil rights advocates had the great misfortune of launching increased efforts to bring about racial equality in economic life at the beginning of a period of economic decline.

In any case, the reason blacks have made little progress despite the efforts of the civil rights movement is straightforward. The efforts of this movement barely addressed the disparities in business ownership and wealth that gave whites the economic power to subordinate blacks. As a result, blacks remained dependent on whites despite the success of the movement. In addition, human capital development programs and antidiscrimination laws were insufficient to induce white-owned and white-controlled businesses and institutions to provide a significantly greater share of economic opportunities to blacks. As a consequence, the labor market and ownership disparities for blacks have not been significantly reduced. In a nutshell, this background explains the persisting economic disadvantage.

CONCLUSIONS AND IMPLICATIONS
FOR FUTURE RACE RELATIONS

The most important lesson to be drawn from the experience of the civil rights movement in the post-1970 period is the difficulty of designing a strategy to eliminate racial inequality in economic life without altering the distribution of economic power or imposing costs on whites. The unwillingness of government officials to impose significant costs on white workers and employers probably accounts for a good share of their failure to design meaningful and effective human capital interventions and for their reluctance to promote equal opportunity. Because of this failure to implement any significant redistribution of wealth or business ownership, blacks were left without the resources for effective internal efforts. As a result, the hopes for the success of the integrationist civil rights strategy in this period received a fatal blow.

In addition, it is very difficult to implement programs to modify white racist or discriminatory behavior and to make a significant reduction in blacks' human capital disadvantages. Whites resist such programs because of their impact on the privileged position that they have attained in the American economy as a direct consequence of the economic subordination of blacks. Moreover, implementation of such efforts is even more difficult in times of economic stringency; this is an often-observed economic fact. When there are no costs or when the pie is growing, it is much easier to convince people to support programs dealing with equity concerns. The cost can be paid out of the growth dividend, and the advantaged classes need not feel the impact. This point implies that future prospects for reducing racial inequality would be aided greatly by establishing a better-performing national economy.

We also should note the lesson that recent experience teaches about the importance of correct strategic thinking. The civil rights movement was a successful self-help movement; it focused on removing external constraints to blacks' progress, particularly those constraints arising from racism and discrimination. Yet the strategy adopted for bringing about racial equality was wrong. Civil rights strategists failed to recognize the importance of changing the distribution of power. They also failed to appreciate fully the necessity and the importance of race-specific policies to overcome historical disparities. Thus although the movement enjoyed a great deal of success in passing legislation and implementing social programs, these results proved ineffective in altering the underlying racial inequality.

Implicit in my argument in this last section is the conclusion that internal inefficiency within the black community played little or no role in blacks' failure to achieve economic equality in the post-1970 period. I suggest that this failure should be attributed entirely to the inadequacy of the ameliorative efforts. Blacks' self-help activities should continue to focus on altering the environmental constraints on black development by redistributing economic power from whites to blacks. Leverage can be applied to limited internal resources by inducing the public sector to assume the cost of reducing racial inequality in economic life.

Today's economic disparities are the result of the historic pattern of racism and discrimination that characterizes American society. The economic legacy of this past is reflected currently in blacks' limited ownership of businesses and wealth and in the accompanying disadvantages in human capital. These factors make blacks a dependent population, subject to discrimination. This situation in turn generates the continuing high level of economic inequality.

The simple logic of economic growth makes it apparent that once such historical differences are in place, it is unreasonable to expect that the disadvantaged group can overcome gaps only through internally directed self-help. Indeed, because the proportion of money saved and invested is generally higher among higher income individuals, it is logical to expect that racial inequality, once established, will continue to grow in the absence of intervention. Even in conditions of complete nondiscrimination, the result will be the same; in the face of discrimination, the gaps will increase.

Ultimately, the only intervention that can guarantee sustainable results in a free-market system is the redistribution of wealth and power. Reparations, seldom discussed in connection with solving the problem of racial inequality, probably are an appropriate approach to the adjustments required to ensure equality in a free-enterprise system. The appropriate amount of reparations would be the amount required to eliminate differences in business ownership, wealth, and human capital. An appropriate strategy for blacks in the 1990s and beyond could be the development of another social movement to obtain such reparations. The only alternative would be to change the economic system so as to break the association between current economic status and prospects for the future.

Although I have not touched explicitly on the subject of race relations in this chapter, it should be apparent that the matters discussed have significant implications for relationships between the races. The persistence of extensive racial inequality in economic life and the attempts by blacks to resolve this problem can be expected to create new tensions and the potential for conflicts. Blacks can be expected to push for new strategies to address the extensive inequality; my analysis suggests that effective solutions will impose unavoidable costs on the white population. Moreover, blacks will seek special race-specific programs as necessary components of any effective strategy to reduce racial inequality.

The persistence of racial inequality and the attempts of blacks to solve the problem will create much interaction between the races. Whether or not this interaction will lead to acrimonious relationships will depend on how both groups react to the situation. Many blacks and many whites have widely differing perspectives on the justification and priority to be given to efforts to improve blacks' relative position; this fact suggests that race relations my deteriorate significantly if this situation is mishandled.

On the other hand, we have a golden opportunity to resolve the race problem by the next century if our society will make a serious commitment to fully recognize what is required to end centuries of racial inequality. The accomplishment of this task will require enlightened and committed white leadership. It is essential that new policies and programs for the 1990s not repeat the serious design and implementation errors of the civil rights era. Policy and program development must be guided by full recognition of the magnitude of required efforts, the unavoidable costs for whites, and the necessity for race-specific remedies. If this situation comes to pass, the prospects for improving race relations will be good. Failure to achieve progress along these lines will lead to increasing deterioration in race relations.

REFERENCES

Brown V. Board of Education of Topeka, Kansas, 347 U.S. 483 (1954).

Flax, M. J. (1971). *Blacks and whites: An experiment in racial indicators.* Washington, DC: The Urban Institute.

Fortune. (1986, April 28). The *Fortune* directory of largest U.S. industrials (pp. 174–232).

Freeman, R. B. (1973). Changes in the labor markets for black Americans, 1948-1972. *Brookings Papers on Economic Activity.*

Swinton, D. H. (1983). The economic status of the black population. In J. D. Williams (Ed.), *The state of black America* (pp. 45–114). New York: National Urban League.

Swinton, D. H. (1986). The economic status of the black population. In J. D. Williams (Ed.), *The state of black America 1986* (pp. 1–27). New York: National Urban League.

Swinton, D. H. (1987). Economic status of blacks 1986. In J. Dewart (Ed.), *The state of black America 1988* (pp. 49–73). New York: National Urban League.

Swinton, D. H. (1988). Economic status of the blacks 1987. In J. Dewart (Ed.), *The state of black America 1988* (pp. 129–152). New York: National Urban League.

U.S. Department of Commerce, Bureau of the Census. (1984). *Survey of minority-owned business enterprises: Minority-owned businesses—black.* Washington, DC: U.S. Government Printing Office.

U.S. Department of Commerce, Bureau of the Census. (1986). *Money income and poverty status of families and persons in the United States: 1984.* Washington, DC: U.S. Government Printing Office.

U.S. Department of Commerce, Bureau of the Census. (1987). *Money income and poverty status of families and persons in the United States: 1986.* Washington, DC: U.S. Government Printing Office.

U.S. Department of Labor, Bureau of Labor Statistics. (1987). *Employment and earnings: January.* Washington, DC: U.S. Government Printing Office.

U.S. Department of Labor, Bureau of Labor Statistics. (1985). *Handbook of labor statistics.* Washington, DC: U.S. Government Printing Office.

Wattenberg, B., and Scammon, R. (1973, April). Black progress and liberal rhetoric. *Commentary, 55,* 35–44.

13

Inequality in America: The Failure of the American System for People of Color

Edna Bonacich
Department of Sociology
University of California, Riverside

Right before Christmas last year—1987—a Chicana was fired from food services on our campus, where she had been working as an assistant cook. She is a single mother with three children.[1] Her own mother suffers from epilepsy. She was making $150 a week and when she was fired she was faced with the prospect of not being able to pay next month's rent, let alone celebrating Christmas.

Food services is subcontracted to Marriott Corporation on our campus. According to university rules, food services has to be self-supporting, but it can't be run profitably on a campus of our size. For years the university lost money on it—around $50,000 a year—so it decided to bail out and subcontract to a private firm.

The decision to subcontract happens to have coincided with a union election victory among service workers in the University of California (UC) system, the first such victory in the system. Whether the union would actually be able to negotiate a pay raise was immaterial. Indeed, the union was exceedingly weak and did not represent the self-organization of the workers. Instead, it operated as a Washington-based bureaucracy that saw the thousands of UC workers as a plum for its own organizational growth. Still, the university administration was quick to preclude any pay raises among the food services staff.

Marriott is managing to turn a losing operation into a profitable one. This miracle is being achieved by paying the workers well below the university wage scale. Most

This chapter appeared as an article in the *Sociological Spectrum*, 1989, *9*, 77–101.

I would like to thank Emily Abel, Lucie Cheng, and Mary Sawyer for their helpful feedback on earlier drafts of the manuscript.

[1] The style of this chapter is more informal than most academic papers. This is purposeful. I am eager to get away from the dry abstraction of academic discourse. As I see it, the style of western academic writing is very much a part of the "white man's civilization," with its dualistic idealism, or division between thought and life. I am seeking a more integrated world view and want my method of communication to match the content. I realize that the imperatives of careerism often force us to speak and write in ways that are not authentic to us, and I am resisting this form of coercion. I hope that you, my readers, will not close your ears to what I say just because my manner of presentation does not meet your preconceptions. Instead, I hope you will listen to its substance and check it against your own experience, against what you know in your hearts to be true.

of their employees, at least on our campus, are women of color. There aren't a lot of other people who are "willing" to work for minimum wage and no benefits. Marriott is, of course, nonunion.

The case against the woman who was fired consisted of latenesses and absences on the job. Perhaps the accusations had some validity. When a person is earning close to minimum wage there isn't a lot of incentive to be a perfectly disciplined, eagerly loyal employee. Besides, her family circumstances made it difficult always to be punctual. There was no give in the situation that could allow for the exigencies of this employee's life. The management of food services claimed that they had given her every break but that they were operating on a tight budget and couldn't afford to hold on to an inefficient worker. The results might be unfortunate for this individual, management claimed, but they weren't a charity. They had a business to run. They had to balance their books.

And so the woman was left without a job right before Christmas. A group of us took her case to the campus administrator in charge of subcontracting. He heard it and rejected it, siding with management that they could not afford to keep an unpunctual worker. After learning of his decision I went back alone one more time to make a humanitarian plea. I tried to draw a parallel to homelessness. Did he sanction it? Did he believe that, if people couldn't pay their rent, they should be thrown out on the streets? Wasn't his action similar in this case? But I was wasting my time. "You can't coddle employees," he said. "We're in business to make money." He wouldn't consider taking her back and giving her another chance. She was "poison" in his eyes, I assume, because she had dared to challenge her firing and had managed to get a group around her to support her case. A politically aroused employee was indeed poison to this man.

Marriott claims it is not making a profit off of food services on our campus, yet it takes out 6% of the gross in "management fees," and the woman who manages the cafeteria for them makes a good salary. Money is certainly being made in this enterprise; it just isn't going to the workers.

I am telling this little story in such detail because it illustrates some of the dynamics of capitalism and its racist manifestations. And it shows that even such seemingly benign institutions as the university are accomplices in the perpetuating of racial oppression in their daily operations. By handing over food services to Marriott, the university has allowed a kind of sweatshop to develop in its midst, a sweatshop that depends on the exploitation of women of color. They save money on the backs of these women. And everyone on the campus benefits by having access to cheaper food.

The university could have decided to subsidize food services. If it feels this is an important service to provide to the campus, it should be willing to pay for it. Other nonacademic services, such as health and counseling centers, are supported by the campus, and their employees are paid the university salary rates. But since food service workers are generally paid low wages, the competitive rates permit the university to save money here. University administrators can and do justify the special treatment of these workers by citing market conditions. If food service workers everywhere are paid poorly, why should the university pay them higher rates? It isn't necessary.

So the poorly paid labor of a group of women of color is used to "subsidize" the mighty University of California. Wealth, as usual, is taken from the poor and transferred to the wealthy and privileged. The pathways of this transfer may be complicated and indirect, but the transfer occurs nonetheless. The university, Marriott, the students, the faculty—all have a little more money in their pockets because these women live so close to the margin.

Jesse Jackson captured this reality eloquently when he said to a group of poor people: "You are not the bottom. You are the foundation." What a profound inversion of the way this society normally looks at itself! And yet, how true are his words. As in the example I have just presented, the whole magnificent edifice of wealth and privilege in this society has been built on the suffering of poor people, large numbers of whom are people of color.

In the remainder of this chapter I shall first present some economic data on inequality, particularly racial inequality, in this country. Then I shall consider some of the ways in which the American system is bound to inequality and show how minor tinkering will never eliminate poverty and oppression. I try to demonstrate that racial oppression is an inherent feature of capitalism and that we will never get rid of it without a profound change in out economic system. Finally, I turn to the 1990s. Rather than attempting to foretell the future, I consider what needs to be done. In particular, I focus on the responsibility of each one of us in making this a more just society.

INEQUALITY IN AMERICA

The United States is an immensely unequal society in terms of the distribution of material wealth, and consequently, in the distribution of all of the benefits and privileges that accrue to wealth, including political power and influence. This inequality is vast, irrespective of race. However, within it, people of color tend to cluster at the bottom so that inequality in this society also becomes racial inequality. I believe that racial inequality is inextricably tied to overall inequality and to an ideology that endorses vast inequality as justified and desirable. I believe we will never get rid of racial disadvantage unless we attack the overall system of inequality in which it is embedded. The special problems of racial inequality require direct attention in the process of attacking inequality in general, but I do not believe that the problem of racial inequality can be eliminated within the context of the tremendous disparities that our society currently tolerates. And even if some kind of racial parity, at the level of averages, could be achieved, the amount of suffering at the bottom would remain undiminished, hence unconscionable.

How unequal is the United States? Typically this question is addressed in terms of occupation and income distribution rather than in terms of the distribution and control of property. By the income criterion the United States is one of the more unequal of the western industrial societies, and it is far more unequal than the countries of the eastern European socialist bloc. The Soviet Union, for instance, has striven to decrease the dicrepancy in earnings between the highest paid professionals and managers and the lowest paid workers, and as a consequence, has a much flatter income distribution than the United States (Szymanski, 1979, pp. 63–69).

To take an extreme example from within the United States: In 1987 the minimum wage was $3.35 an hour, and 6.7 million American workers were paid at that level. That comes to $6,968 a year. In contrast, the highest paid executive, Lee Iacocca, received more than $20 million in 1986, or $9,615 per hour. In other words, the highest paid executive received (I will not say "earned") more in an hour than a vast number of workers received in a year (Sheinkman, 1987).

The excessive differences in income are, of course, given strong ideological justification: They serve, supposedly, as a source of incentive. Who will work hard if there isn't a pot of gold at the end, a pot that can be bigger than anyone else's? People have a need to strive to improve their position both absolutely and relative to their fellows. This competition to be at the top of the heap is deeply embedded in the human psyche. It leads us to greater and greater effort and, consequently, to enhanced achievement. We all benefit from this drive for success. The striving for achievement leads to excellence, and we all are the beneficiaries of the continual improvements and advances that result.

Or are we? I believe a strong case can be made for the opposite. First of all, the presumed benefits of inequality do not trickle down far enough. Those at the bottom of the system rarely see them. The great advances of medical science, for example, are of little use to those people who can't afford even the most elementary of health care. Second, instead of providing incentive, our steep inequalities may engender hopelessness and despair for those who have no chance of winning the big prize. When you have no realistic chance of winning the competition, and when there are no prizes for those who take anything less than fourth place, why should you run all out? Third, one can question how much inequality is neccessary to raise incentives. Surely fairly modest inducements can serve as motivators. Does the person who makes $100,000 a year in any sense work that much harder than the person who makes the $7,000 minimum wage? Altogether, it would seem that the justifications for inequality are more rationalizations to preserve privilege than they are a well-reasoned basis of social organization. The obvious wholesale waste of human capability, let alone life in and for itself, that piles up at the bottom of our system of inequality is testimony to its failure.

Even more fundamental than income inequality is inequality in the ownership of property. Here not only are the extremes much more severe, but the justification of incentives for achievement grows exceedingly thin. First, large amounts of property are simply inherited, and the heirs may never have done a stitch of work in their lives to merit any of it. The property serves as an incentive for nothing other than lavish living, or speculating to get the pot to grow even larger, or throwing wealth around in favor of political causes that keep the wealth intact. Second, and more important, wealth in property expands at the expense of workers. Its growth depends not on the achievements of the owner so much as on his or her ability to exploit other human beings. The owner of rental property, for example, gets richer simply because other people who have to work for a living can't afford to buy their own housing and must sink a substantial proportion of their hard-earned wages into providing shelter. The ownership of property provides interest, rent, or profit simply from the fact of ownership. The owner need put out nothing—no effort, except the capital itself—to have the profits keep rolling in for the rest of his or her life. And the source of those profits lies in the hard labor of other people. You don't really get rich in this society by working hard and achieving. You get rich by owning property and having other people work hard for you. And the more you own, the more you are able to harness the labor of others and the more wealth keeps accruing to you, while the people who work for you get stuck pretty much in the same place, just struggling to make ends meet.

The concentration of property in the United States is rarely studied—I assume because its exposure is politically embarrassing and even dangerous to those in power (who overlap substantially with, or are closely allied to, those who own property).

Only two such studies have been undertaken in the last 25 years, in 1963 and 1983. The 1983 study was commissioned by the Democratic staff of the Congressional Joint Economic Committee (U.S. Congress, 1986). The study may have turned into a political hot potato since shortly after its appearance, a brief 19-line article appeared in the *Los Angeles Times* stating that the Committee withdrew some of its conclusions because of "an error in the figures" ("'Super Rich' Control Misstated," 1986).

That 1983 study found that the top half of one percent (i.e., 0.5%) of families in the United States owned over 35% of the net wealth of this nation. And if equity in personal residences is excluded from consideration, the top 0.5% of households owned more than 45% of the privately held wealth. In other words, if this country consisted of 200 people, 1 individual would own almost half of the property held among all 200. The other 199 would have to divide up the remainder.

The remainder was not equally divided either. The top 10% of the country's households owned 72% of its wealth, leaving only 28% for the remaining 90% of families. If home equity is excluded, the bottom 90% owned only 17% of the wealth.

The super-rich top 0.5% consisted of 420,000 families. These families owned most of the business enterprises in the nation. They owned 58% of unincorporated businesses and 46.5% of all personally owned corporate stock. They also owned 77% of the value of trusts and 62% of state and local bonds. They owned an average of $8.9 million in wealth apiece, ranging from $2.5 million up to hundreds of times that amount.

Forbes magazine publishes an annual list of the 400 richest Americans ("Walton Still Tops *Forbes* List," 1986). In 1986, 26 individuals owned over a billion dollars in assets. The richest owned $4.5 billion. That is a 10-digit figure. The 400th person on the list owned $180 million. So the concentration of wealth at the very top is even more extreme than the 1983 Congressional study revealed. In 1986 for the first time a black man made the *Forbes* list by owning $185 million in assets. The super-rich property owners of this country are generally an all-white club.

By 1987, the number of billionaires in the country as counted by *Forbes* had grown from 26 in 1986 to 49 ("The 400 Richest People," 1987). The average worth of the top 400 had grown to $220 million apiece, a jump of 41% in 1 year. The top individual now owned $8.5 billion. Together, these 400 individuals commanded a net worth of $220 billion, comparable to the entire U.S. mititary budget in 1986 and more than the U.S. budget deficit, or total U.S. investment abroad. The excessively rich are getting even richer.

According to the 1983 Congressional study, the concentration of wealth increased from 1963 to 1983. In 1963, the top 0.5% of households owned a little over 25% of the wealth. This had risen to 35% by 1983. In other words, the top households hold a much higher proportion of the nation's assets now than they did just 25 years ago. Wealth is not only tremendously unevenly distributed but that uneven distribution is becoming ever more extreme. The rich are getting richer and more powerful all the time.

The brief newspaper disclaimer ("'Super Rich' Control Misstated," 1986) that this study was inaccurate stated that the net worth of the top 0.5% was not 35% of the nation's wealth but only 27%. Even if true, this figure still represents an increase over the 1963 figure of 25%. The concentration is still very high and the trend remains ominous.

Table 1   Percentage occupational distribution, 1986

Occupation	White	Black	Hispanic origin[a]
Managerial, professional	25.2	14.7	12.8
Technical, sales, administrative support	31.9	27.0	25.1
Service	12.2	22.9	18.0
(Private household servants)	(0.8)	(2.6)	(1.7)
Precision production, craft, repair	12.6	9.3	14.2
Operators, fabricators, laborers	14.7	23.9	24.9
Farming, forestry, fishing	3.2	2.1	5.0
Total no. employed (in thousands)	95,660	10,814	7,219

Note.   Source: U.S. Department of Labor, Bureau of Labor Statistics (1987, p. 203).
[a]In all tables the titles of groups are the ones used in the original source. Hispanic origin includes people of different "races" and thus overlaps with white and black.

Racial Inequality

The gross inequalities that characterize American society are multiplied when race and ethnicity are entered into the equation. Racial minorities, especially blacks, Latinos, and Native Americans, tend to be seriously overrepresented at the bottom of the scale in terms of any measures of material well-being. Let me present some data to substantiate the point, even though it is so obvious that it doesn't need substantiation.

Table 1 shows the occupational distribution of whites, blacks, and Latinos.[2] Whites are substantially overrepresented in the professional and managerial statum. They are almost twice as likely as blacks (1.71 times) and Latinos (1.97 times) to hold these kinds of jobs. On the other hand, blacks and Latinos are much more concentrated in the lower paid service sector and in the unskilled and semiskilled stratum of operators, fabricators, and laborers. Whereas only 27% of white employees fall into these combined categories, 47% of blacks and 43% of Latinos are so categorized. Finally, even though the numbers are relatively small, blacks are more than three times, and Latinos more than twice, as likely as whites to work as private household servants. This most demeaning of occupations remains mainly a minority preserve.

These general figures mask the degree of detailed occupational segregation along racial and gender lines.[3] For example, Table 2 shows the occupational distribution of the nonacademic staff at UC, Riverside. Perhaps most striking is the high concentration of women in clerical jobs, a tendency that is even more marked for black women and Chicanas. White males predominate in the management and professional fields, followed by white women. (The high concentration of Asians as professionals reflects their high level of employment in the science labs.) Black and Latino men are overrepresented as operatives, whereas black men and women both are more concentrated in services, particularly janitorial services, than other groups. Over a century after the Civil War, black people are still cleaning up after everyone else. (The very small

[2] Note that Latinos are a heterogeneous group. Puerto Ricans and Mexican-Americans are considerably poorer than Cubans, who tilt the averages up.
[3] This point is eloquently documented in *My Troubles Are Going To Have Trouble With Me: Everyday Trials and Triumphs of Women Workers* (Sacks & Remy, 1984).

Table 2   Full-time staff occupations at the University of California, Riverside by race and gender: October 31, 1986

Occupation	Male					Female				
	White	Black	Latino	Asian	Native American	White	Black	Latino	Asian	Native American
Management	8.2%	2.0%	1.2%	2.9%	25.0%	6.9%	0.0%	5.4%	3.3%	0.0%
Professional	39.9	20.4	27.1	62.9	0.0	24.5	15.2	17.8	43.3	0.0
Technical	9.3	10.2	9.4	5.9	0.0	7.0	1.5	0.0	6.7	0.0
Clerical	7.5	8.2	4.7	2.9	0.0	54.4	62.1	69.9	40.0	100.0
Crafts	15.7	8.2	15.3	5.7	50.0	0.8	0.0	0.0	0.0	0.0
Operatives	8.7	16.3	29.4	8.6	0.0	1.0	0.0	0.0	0.0	0.0
Laborers	1.8	6.1	1.2	0.0	0.0	0.8	0.0	0.0	3.3	0.0
Service	8.9	28.6	11.8	2.9	25.0	4.5	21.2	6.8	3.3	0.0
Number	439	49	85	35	4	489	66	73	30	3

Note.   Source: University of California, Riverside Affirmative Action Office.

193

Table 3 Percentage unemployed for persons 16 years or older:
         1986

Racial/ethnic group	Male	Female
White	6.0	6.1
Black	14.8	14.2
Hispanic origin	10.5	10.8

Note. Source: U.S. Department of Labor, Bureau of Labor Statistics (1987, pp. 167, 205).

numbers of Native Americans make their percentages meaningless.) These figures reveal that a race-and-sex caste system clearly persists at UC, Riverside.

Occupational disadvantage translates into wage and salary disadvantage. The median weekly earning of white families in 1986 was $566, compared to $412 for Latino families and $391 for black families. In other words, black and Latino families made about 70% of what white families made. Female-headed households of all groups made substantially less money. Both black and Latino female-headed families made less than half of what the average white family (including married couples) made (U.S. Department of Labor, 1987).

Weekly earnings reflect only the take-home pay of employed people. Table 3 shows the ethnic distribution of unemployment. Clearly, people of color bear the brunt of unemployment in this society. Blacks, in particular, stand out in this regard.

The absence of good jobs or of any jobs at all, and the absence of decent pay for those jobs that are held, translates into poverty. Although the poverty line is a somewhat arbitrary figure, it nevertheless provides some commonly accepted standard for decent living in our society.

Table 4 shows that, as of 1984, over one third of black households lived in poverty. If we include those people who live very close to the poverty line, the near poor, then 41%, or 2 out of 5 blacks, are poor or near poor. For Latinos the figures are only slightly less grim, with over 28% living in poverty and 36%, or well over one third, living in or near poverty.

Female-headed households, as everyone knows, are more likely to live in or near poverty. Over half of black and Latino female-headed families are forced to live under the poverty line, and over 60% of each group live in or near poverty. The figures for white female-headed families are also high, with over one third living in or near poverty. But the levels for people of color are almost twice as bad.

Table 4 Percentage of individuals living below or near the poverty line: 1984

Type of household	White	Black	Spanish origin
Total households	11.5	33.8	28.4
Female-headed households	27.3	52.9	54.3
Households below 125% of poverty level			
Total households	16.1	41.4	36.1
Female-headed households	35.1	61.3	61.5

Note. Source: U.S. Bureau of the Census (1986a, pp. 5, 6, 8, 9).

Table 5 Median net worth of households: 1984

Type of household	White	Black	Spanish origin
Total households	$39,135	$3,397	$4,913
Female-headed households	22,500	671	478
As % of white			
Total households		8.7	12.6
Female-headed households		3.0	2.1
Female-headed minority			
as % of total white		1.7	1.2

Note. Source: U.S. of Bureau of the Census (1986b, p. 5).

As I said earlier, the real inequality of this nation is not fully revealed by employment and take-home pay, but by property ownership. And here the degree of racial inequality is stark—more stark than the income and employment figures. As we see in Table 5, the average white family has a net worth of $39,000, more than 10 times the average net worth of $3,000 of black families, and Latino families are only slightly better off, with an average net worth of about $5,000. The differences are even more marked among female-headed households. The average black and Latino female-headed households have net worths of only $671 and $478, respectively, less than 2% of the net worth of the average white household.

I want to dwell for a moment on the extent of the extremes of wealth and poverty represented in these figures. The richest man in this country owned $8.5 billion in wealth in 1987, and there are a handful of others close behind him. Meanwhile, the average—not the poorest but the average—black and Latino female-headed household commands only a few hundred dollars. How can one even begin to talk about equality of opportunity under such circumstances? What power and control must inevitably accompany the vast holdings of the billionaires, and what scrambling for sheer survival must accompany the dearth of resources at the bottom end? A profound injustice is represented in this gross maldistribution that no talk about equal opportunity can dispel.

Table 6 shows the distribution of assets so that we get a picture of the range. Over half of black and Latino families have less than $5,000 in assets, but only 22% of white families are this propertyless. Almost one quarter of white families own at least $100,000 in assets, whereas for blacks the figure is 4% and for Latinos, 8%.

Disproportionate white control of capital of all sorts is shown in Table 7. Not only are whites much more likely to own their own homes and cars and to have bank accounts and other forms of savings, they also are much more likely to own the business ventures of this nation. To me one of the most signficant figures is the disproportionate white ownership of stocks; whites are three to four times more likely to own stocks than are blacks and Latinos.

While it is certainly true that there are white nonowners, it is also evident that the ownership class in this society is almost exclusively white. Blacks and Latinos, in contrast, are primarily workers. They must sell their labor-power to the owners of capital, who continue to rake in increasing amounts of wealth, leaving poverty in their wake.

As a final piece of evidence on inequality and its devastating effects, Table 8 shows the death rate for persons under 45 years of age. Unfortunately, Latino data were not available, but information on Native Americans was. The table shows the death rate

Table 6 Percentage distribution of household net worth: 1984

Net worth	White	Black	Spanish origin
Zero or negative	8.4	30.5	23.9
$1-$4,999	14.0	23.9	26.3
$5,000-$9,999	6.3	6.8	7.6
$10,000-$24,999	12.2	14.0	11.4
$25,000-$49,999	15.0	11.7	9.5
$50,000-$99,999	20.7	9.3	13.1
$100,000-$249,999	16.9	3.3	5.1
$250,000-$499,999	4.4	0.5	2.1
$500,000+	2.1	0.1	1.0
Number (in thousands)	75,343	9,509	4,162

Note. Source: U.S. Bureau of the Census (1986b, pp.18-19).

for various diseases calculated on a base of white death rates in this age range for the same diseases. Thus, black males are 58.6% more likely than whites to die of cardiovascular disease before 45. For virtually every type of disease, except cancer for the American Indians and injuries for blacks, the minorities show a substantially higher death rate. Perhaps the most shocking statistic is the infant mortality rate, particularly among blacks. Black babies are 1 1/2 times more likely than white babies to die within the first year. Some have commented that the black infant mortality rate resembles the level in some Third World countries. Altogether, by age 45, 147 blacks and about 142 American Indians have died for every 100 whites. Impoverishment in this nation isn't just an unpleasant embarrassment; it has lethal consequences. Inequality is a killer. People of color die as a result of it.

Table 7 Percentage of households owning types of assets: 1984

Type of asset	White	Black	Spanish origin
Interest-earning assets at financial institutions	75.4	43.8	50.8
Other interest-earning assets	9.4	2.1	2.0
Regular checking accounts	56.9	32.0	36.6
Stocks and mutual funds shares	22.0	5.4	7.5
Own business or profession	14.0	4.0	9.6
Motor vehicles	88.5	65.0	74.6
Own home	67.3	43.8	39.9
Rental property	10.1	6.6	6.6
Other real estate	10.9	3.3	5.8
Mortgages	3.3	0.1	1.1
U.S. savings bond	16.1	7.4	6.1
IRA and KEOGH accounts	21.4	5.1	9.1
Other assets	3.9	0.7	1.1
Number (in thousands)	75,343	9,509	4,162

Note. Source: U.S. Bureau of the Census (1986b, pp. 8-9).

Table 8   Percentage of average annual deaths of persons under 45 years of age that are excess deaths: 1979–1981

	Black		Native American	
Cause of death	Male	Female	Male	Female
Cardiovascular disease	58.6	67.8	16.5	29.1
Cancer	24.1	23.7	− 80.0	− 49.0
Cirrhosis	73.0	76.3	83.2	90.9
Infant mortality	48.9	51.6	18.6	24.2
Diabetes	57.2	58.2	50.0	0.0
Injuries	− 1.0	− 4.5	50.9	56.7
Homicide	84.3	76.9	53.5	60.0
Other	45.7	50.1	51.7	42.7
Total	46.7	47.2	43.2	41.1
Number of deaths	31,094	17,232	1,738	872
Excess deaths	14,578	8,134	751	358

Note. "Excess deaths" is the number of observed deaths in excess of the number expected based on white death rates. Source: U.S. Department of Health and Human Services (1985, pp. 71, 80).

CAPITALISM AND RACISM

Now let us turn to a more analytic mode. I want to consider the ways in which the American political-economic system is bound to racism. It is my contention that the racism of this society is linked to capitalism and that, so long as we retain a capitalist system, we will not be able to eliminate racial oppression. This is not to say that racism will automatically disappear if we change the system. If we were to transform to a socialist society, the elimination of racism would have to be given direct attention as a high priority. I am not suggsting that its elimination would be easily achieved within socialism, but its elimination is impossible under capitalism.[4] There is no question that the capitalist system is committed to inequality in general. Its leaders and advocates are opposed to any dangerous "leveling tendencies." They promote hierarchy. They like to see society as a competition, an individualistic race in which

---

[4] I realize that I am entering controversial territory here. There is a major debate around the question of race versus class. See, for example, Alphonso Pinkney's (1984) *The Myth of Black Progress* and Michael Omi and Harold Winant's (1986) *Racial Formation in the United States: From the 1960s to the 1980s.* The question is raised: Which is more important, race or class? Some argue that race cannot be "reduced" to class and that it has independent vitality. A similar argument is made by some feminists regarding gender.

I do not contend that race can be reduced to class, but I do not think that race and class are independent systems that somehow intersect with one another. This imagery is too static. My own view is that race (and gender) are important aspects of capitalist evolution and that one needs to give them full attention. There is indeed a race and gender division of labor within the working class, and these are importantly manipulated by the capitalist class to maintain its rule. Nor can white workers be exonerated from their own participation in the racial order. My point is not to diminish the crushing significance of race in the lives of those who suffer from racial oppression, but rather to show how the whole system depends upon racism. For the poor people at the bottom of the system, it matters little whether you call their oppression "racial" or "class." The pain they suffer is the same; it is one pain, derived from one social system.

Other systems may develop various forms of racial (and gender) oppression. I would not assert that capitalism is the only social form that produces racism. But I will assert that capitalism *does* produce racism in its own way, and understanding the ways that this happens is what concerns me because I live in a capitalist-racist society.

there are winners and losers and in which winners take the big prizes while losers go home empty-handed. This, they believe, is the proper, god-given order of things.

As I suggested before, inequality is justified by the need to provide incentives for people to try their hardest. It is assumed that the benefits of this effort will trickle down to everyone. But, of course, they don't. The truth is, these rationalizations cover up the fundamental need for inequality by the owners of property. Property owners need an impoverished class of people. The employer needs people who have no means of self-support so that they must come to him or her to provide them with work in order for them to make enough for their families to survive. The landlord needs people who can't afford their own housing and must pay rent on the property he or she controls. The banker and money lender need people who have to borrow from them so that they can get back not only the loan but interest as well. These property owners "let their money work for them," which boils down to having other people work for them.

Stripped of all its fancy rationalizations and complexities, the capitalist system depends upon the exploitation of the poor by the rich. We can see this in food services on my campus. And we can see it on a worldwide scale, where, for example, poor Latin American countries sent to American investors and lenders, between 1982 and 1987, $145 billion more than they took in. And these countries still owe a principal of $410 billion in foreign debt and all the billions of dollars of interest payments that will accrue to that ("Hemisphere in Crisis," 1987).

Capitalism depends on inequality. No matter how much the liberals feel sorry for the people who are inevitably thrust to the bottom of such a system, and how much they try to make amends, no real change can be achieved. No poverty programs, no welfare systems, can make a dent in the fundamental commitment to inequality, in the utter dependency of this system on impoverishment of the many to sustain the wealth of the few. The truth is, the idea of equality cannot even be whispered around here. It is too subversive, too completely undermining of the "American way." Liberals, conservatives, Democrats, Republicans—they are all committed to the idea of inequality, and so, no matter how much they yell at each other in Congressional hearings, behind the scenes they shake hands and agree that things are basically fine and as they should be.

They all agree, for example, that Nicaragua is a dangerous threat to American national security. Yes it is, in a sense. Not because the tiny nation of Nicaragua can send troops up through Mexico to attack us. Not even that it can be a beachhead for an assault by the Cubans and the Russians. No, what our leaders fear more than anything else is the infiltration across our border of an IDEA—the idea that the very wealthy do not deserve their wealth and should have it expropriated. What they have stolen for generations should be returned. This idea is so threatening to our national leaders, who are, after all, among the biggest thieves or close friends and allies with them, that they must denounce, drown out, condemn, and utterly destroy that small nation. They must declare it the most evil, ungodly nation on earth and hope that, if they make the accusation stick, no one will hear the idea of equality. It will be silenced.

Perhaps not everyone agrees with my formulation, but I don't think anyone can disagree that there IS a commitment to economic inequality in this system and that no attempt is made to hide it. It is part of the official ideology. However, the same cannot be said for racial inequality today. At least at the *official* level it is stated that race should not be the basis of any social or economic distinction. Thus it should, in theory, be possible to eliminate racial inequality within the system, even if we don't touch overall inequality.

I don't accept this view. Even though an open commitment to racial inequality has been made illegitimate in recent years as a consequence of the civil rights movement and related social movements, I believe that it remains embedded in the capitalist system. The facts that I presented earlier leave no doubt that racial inequality exists and is extreme. I believe this inequality is entrenched in the deep structures of the system and that no amount of lip-service to equality regardless of race, creed, or color will eliminate it.

Before getting into the present dynamics of the system, however, let me point out how deeply racism is embedded in the historical evolution of capitalism. First, one can make the case that without racism, without the racial domination implicit in the early European "voyages of discovery," Europe would never have accumulated the initial wealth for its own capitalist "take off." In other words, capitalism itself is predicated on racism (Williams, 1966).

But let us set aside this somewhat controversial point and note that European capitalist development quickly acquired an expansionist mode and took over the world, spreading a suffocating blanket of white domination over almost all of the other peoples of the globe. The motive was primarily economic, primarily the pursuit of markets, raw materials, cheap labor, and investment oportunities. The business sector of Europe, linked to the state, wanted to increase its profits. Businessmen sought to enhance their wealth.[5]

The belief in the inferiority of peoples of color, the belief that Europeans were bringing a gift of civilization, salvation, and economic development, helped justify the conquest. They were not, Europeans could think to themselves, hurting anyone. They were really benefactors, bringing light to the savages.

The world order that they created was tiered. On the one hand, they exploited the labor of their own peoples, creating from Europe's farmers and craftsmen an owner-less white working class. On the other hand, they created of the conquered nationali-ties a super-exploited work force that produced the raw materials for the rising Euro-pean industries and did the dirtiest and lowest paid support jobs in the world economy. Because they had been conquered and colonized, the peoples of color could be subjected to especially coercive labor systems such as slavery, indentured servi-tude, forced migrant labor, and the like.

Both of these groups of workers were exploited in the sense that surplus was taken from their labor by capitalist owners. But white "free labor" was in a relatively advantaged position, being employed in the technically more advanced and higher paid sectors. To a certain extent, white labor benefited from the super-exploitation of colonized workers. The capital that was drained from the colonies could be invested in industrial development in Europe or the centers of European settlement (such as the United States, Canada, Australia, New Zealand, and South Africa). The white cotton mill workers in Manchester and New England depended on the super-exploitation of cotton workers in India and the U.S. slave South, producing the cheap raw material on which their industrial employment was built.

Although the basic structure of the world economy centered on European capital

---

[5] For a fuller statement of the evolution of capitalist racism, see Lucie Cheng and Edna Bonacich's (1984) *Labor Immigration Under Capitalism: Asian Workers in the United States Before World War II*, especially chapters 1 and 3.

and the exploitation of colonized workers in their own homelands, the expansion of European capitalism led to movements of peoples all over the globe to suit the economic needs of the capitalist class. Internal colonies, the products of various forms of forced and semi-forced migrations, replicated the world system within particular territories. The basic stratification of world capitalism, with workers of color at the foundation, remains in effect today. Women of color, in particular, are the most exploited of workers around the globe.[6] Although race may not be overtly invoked in the exploitation of Third World peoples, the fact is that they *are* peoples of color who suffer external domination and must labor for "white" capitalists. In the case of South Africa, specifically racial oppression is openly endorsed. And the U.S. government's extremely weak response to this reality suggests the degree of their commitment to ending racism. But even if the racist government of South Africa collapses, as it inevitably will, U.S. capital still exploits people of color from Asia to Africa to Latin America, supporting regimes that enforce its ability to suck these nations dry.

Still, we can ask: Is it not possible that within the United States, a redistribution could occur that would eliminate the racial character of inequality? Could we not, with the banning of racial discrimination and even positive policies like affirmative action, restructure our society such that color is no longer correlated with wealth and poverty? Is it not possible to reach a point where, even though overall inequality remains unchanged, the averages of each group will be about the same, and the same proportion of white people will be unemployed and impoverished as people of color? This, I think, is what is meant by racial equality within capitalism. The total amount of human misery would remain unaltered, but its complexion would change.

Setting aside the obvious moral repulsiveness of continuing the impoverishment of millions of people regardless of their color, I want to consider whether such a model would represent the end of racism.

Assimilationism

It seems to me that even if people of color were fully distributed in the capitalist hierarchy like white people, that would not necessarily spell the end of racism. The very idea of such absorption is assimilationist. It claims that people of color must abandon their own cultures and communities and become utilitarian individualists like the white man. They must compete on the white man's terms for the white man's values.

The notion that the American system can be "color blind," a common conservative position, is, of course, predicated on the idea that one is color blind within a system of rules, and those rules are the white man's. Even though he claims they are without cultural content, this is nonsense. They are *his* rules, deriving from *his* cultural heritage, and he can claim that they are universal and culturally neutral only because he has the power to make such a claim stick. There is an implicit arrogance in the notion that the white man's way is the most advanced and that everyone else ought to learn how to get along in it as quickly as possible. All other cultures and value systems are impugned as backward, primitive, or dictatorial. Only western

---

[6] For example, see Annette Fuentes and Barbara Ehrenreich's (1983) *Women in the Global Factory* and Maria Patricia Fernandez-Kelly's (1983) *For We Are Sold, I and My People: Women and Industry in Mexico's Frontier.*

capitalism is seen as the pinnacle of human social organization, the height of perfection.[7]

The ludicrousness of such a position need scarcely be mentioned. The white man's civilization has caused great suffering not only to oppressed nationalities around the globe but also to many of his own peoples. Besides murdering other human beings, he has engaged in wanton destruction of our precious planet to the point that we now seriously question how long human life will be sustainable at all.

Let me give an example of the way in which the white man's seemingly universal rules have been imposed. In 1887 the U.S. government passed the Allotment Act, authored by Senator Henry Dawes. This law terminated communal land ownership among Americans Indians by allotting private parcels of land to individuals. Dawes articulated the philosophy behind this policy by stating that every family in the Cherokee nation had a home of its own, that there were no paupers, and that the nation owed no money to anyone, yet they could not progress because they owned their land in common. In Dawes's view, selfishness lay at the root of civilization. People needed to compete to try to outdo their neighbors. In sum, "until this people consent to give up their lands and divide them among their citizens so that each owns the land he cultivates, they will not make much progress" (Wexler, 1982, p. 64).

Needless to say, the plans to coerce American Indians into participation in the white man's system of private property did not work out according to official plan. Instead, white people came in and bought up Indian land and left the Indians destitute. People who had not been paupers were now pauperized. It is a remarkably familiar story. The workings of an apparently neutral marketplace have a way of leaving swaths of destruction in their path.

The Role of the Middle Class

The growth of a black, a Latino, and a Native American middle class in the last few decades also does not negate the proposition that racial inequality persists in America. In order to understand this, we need to consider the role that the middle class, or the professional-managerial stratum, plays in capitalist society irrespective of race. In my view, middle-class people (including myself) are essentially the sergeants of the system. We professionals and managers are paid by the wealthy and powerful, by the corporations and the state, to keep things in order. Our role is one of maintaining the system of inequality. Our role is essentially that of controlling the poor. We are a semi-elite. We are given higher salaries, higher social status, better jobs, and better life chances as payment for our service to the system. If we weren't useful to the power elite, they would not reward us. Our rewards prove that we serve their interests. Look at who pays us. That will give you a sense of whom we are serving.[8]

Let me take professional educators as an example, since I am one of them. On one level, our role seems to be that of serving the poor, of teaching them what they need to know, of educating them. Surely in the process of educating we are increasing

---

[7] I have elaborated these points in "Racism in the Deep Structure of U.S. Higher Education: When Affirmative Action is Not Enough" (Bonacich, 1989), and "The Limited Social Philosophy of Affirmative Action" (Bonacich, 1987).

[8] For an excellent discussion of the class nature of the professional-managerial stratum, see Ehrenreich and Ehrenreich (1979).

equality? Surely we are enhancing the life chances, the opportunities, of poor people by providing them with the tools for advancement?

Yes, in a sense this is the case. But in another sense we are up to our eyeballs in replicating inequality in this society and providing justifications for it to boot. Our job entails making distinctions among youngsters. We grade them. We place them in a hierarchy that determines who will get the rewards and who will get nothing. We justify this in terms of merit. Those who "do well"in our classrooms will receive the rewards of the society and those who "do poorly" will not. We are the gatekeepers of a meritocratic order in which steep hierarchies of inequality are justified by what we do.

Many individual teachers don't believe in the justice of the unequal social order that they are helping to replicate. Many of them try to help the children in their classes who are obviously slated to be the losers and rejects of the system. And, given the fact that each classroom often represents considerable prior sorting, an individual teacher can feel that his or her distinctions don't really make a lot of difference.

This is true for me. By the time young people arrive at the University of California, considerable sorting has already occurred. I see only the elite. Others have been weeded out along the way. By the time they get to me, the students are pretty much assured of a professional or managerial job of some sort. They can count on a reasonably good salary. Of course, some of them still remain terrified about their prospects in a social system that guarantees no security and where failure spells such a gloomy future. Their terror varies sharply with the business cycle. But on the whole, their class position can more or less be counted on.

So my job is one of fine-tuning the distribution. I help to determine who will get the slightly better jobs in the slightly better companies or law firms or schools and universities. I play a small role, almost small enough that I can ignore it, in determining the last little details of their life chances. Since my grade is only one among many, I can pretend that it doesn't matter, that it won't affect anything important.

But, of course, even at my level, big rewards and punishment accumulate. The "A" students get scholarships that make it easier for them to get their work done. They get into honors programs. They get special attention. Reward accumulates. The already privileged get even more privilege. Advantage accrues. The rich get richer. That is the way the whole system of American inequality works. If you have, you get more. Because if you already have, that proves what an upright citizen you must have been, so you deserve more still.

To sharpen our consciousness of this reality, I tried in my department to establish a "counter honors" program, that is, a program for the sociology majors who were having the most difficulty. I didn't mean it as remedial education with all of the stigma attached to that. I wanted to give *these* students an opportunity, like the opportunity afforded to our honors students, of working one-on-one with a professor of their choice on a project that interested them. I wanted, for instance, to allow some of the black athletes who are struggling academically to develop a research project on the phenomenon of college athletics and the ways in which it exploits black youngsters. I wanted to put into the hands of the most oppressed of our students the research tools that are reserved for the elite and that might enable them to comprehend and challenge their world.

Needless to say, this proposal never got past the department even though I tried to disguise its radical implications. The department members didn't want to do it themselves, and they believed with certainty that the Academic Senate and the University administration would never let such a plan slip through. The elitist structures are firmly entrenched and shall not be challenged.

The point I am trying to make is that we teachers, no matter how liberal and equalitarian our individual ideologies, are caught in a larger system that plays a vital role in reproducing the extreme inequality of American society. Whether we choose to acknowledge it or not, we are part of that system of replication. That is what our jobs, at least in part, are about.

We middle-class people would like to believe that our positions of privilege benefit the less advantaged. We would like to believe that our upward mobility helps others, that the benefits we receive somehow "trickle down." But this is sheer self-delusion. It is capitalist ideology, which claims that the people at the top of the social system are really the great benefactors of the people at the bottom. The poor should be grateful to the beneficent rich elite for its generosity. The poor depend on the wealthy; without the rich elite, where would the poor be? But, of course, this picture stands reality on its head. Dependency really works the other way. It is the rich who depend on the poor for their well-being. And benefit, wealth, and privilege trickle *up*, not down.

So far I have been talking about the middle class in general. The same basic truths apply to the black and Latino middle class but with some added features. People of color are, too often, treated as tokens. Their presence in higher level positions is used to "prove" that the American system is open to anyone with talent and ambition. But the truth is, people of color are allowed to hold more privileged positions if and only if they conform to the party line. Middle-class people of color aren't allowed real authority. They have to play the white man's game by the white man's rules or they lose their good jobs. They have to give up who they are, they have to disown their community and its pressing needs for change, in order to "make it" in this system.

Why do they say Jesse Jackson is unelectable? Because he dares to speak out against some of the social injustices of this system, because he dares to adopt an African-American point of view. The problem, some will tell you, isn't that he is black per se (although some will even admit openly to that). They will claim that some black politicians, like Tom Bradley, would be acceptable on the Democratic ticket, so *they* aren't racist. Yes, so long as black people behave like white men and do everything the white establishment wants of them, they may be acceptable. But heaven help the black politician who speaks with a black voice for the needs of his or her people.

The rising black and Latino middle class is, more often than not, used to control the poor and racially oppressed communities, to crush opposition and prevent needed social change. The same is the case, as I have said, with the white middle class. However, there was an implicit promise that the election of black and Latino political officials and the growth of a black and Latino professional and business stratum would provide benefits that would trickle down to their communities. This has worked as well as trickle-down theory in general. Regardless of the intentions of the black and Latino middle class, the institutional structures and practices of capitalism have prohibited the implementation of any of the needed reforms. Black mayors, for example, coming in with plans of social progress, find themselves trapped in the logic of the private profit system and cannot implement their programs.[9]

This state of affairs is manifest on my campus. There has been a little progress in terms of affirmative action among the staff. However, if you look more closely, you

[9] For an excellent analysis of this process, see Lembcke (1989).

discover that almost all of the black and Chicano staff work under white administrators. Futhermore, those people with professional positions are highy concentrated in minority-oriented programs, such as Student Affirmative Action, Immediate Outreach, Black and Chicano Student Programs, and the like. Even here they are under the direction of white supervisors, who ultimately determine the nature and limits of these programs.

What happens, more often than not, is that professional staff who are people of color become shock-absorbers in the system. They take responsibility for programs without having the authority to shape them. If recruitment or retention of students from racially oppressed communities does not produce results, it is the black, Chicano, and Native American professional staff who are held accountable, even though they could not shape a program that had any chance of succeeding. The staff people of color must accept the individualistic, meritocratic ethic of the institution and cannot push for programs that would enhance community development or community participation in the shaping of the university. They simply have to implement the bankrupt idea of plucking out the "best and brightest" and urging them to forsake their families and communities in the quest to "make it" in America.

These staff people of color have to bear the brunt of the failure of the white administration's programs. They find themselves having to justify the university's poor record as part of their jobs. They become the front line of defense for the university's continued racism. They have no power to implement social change, and so they simply become keepers of the status quo.

Thus, even if there is some upward mobility by individual people of color within the system, they aren't permitted participation as fully autonomous and thinking beings. They aren't allowed to voice their criticisms. They aren't allowed to bring their reality and thoughts to bear on their jobs. The system wants their bodies but not their minds. They aren't allowed to bring honesty to their new positions. They must transform themselves to fit into the white man's system.

Still, even if the ruling class can make use of people of color in middle-class positions, I believe there are real limits to its willingness to allow for enough of a redistribution to occur so that the averages across groups would ever become the same. The powerful and wealthy white capitalist class may be able to tolerate and even endorse "open competition" in the working and middle classes. However, they show no signs whatsoever of being willing to relinquish their own stranglehold on the world economy. They can play the game of supporting a recarving up of the tiny part of the pie left over after they have taken their share. Indeed, it is probably good business to encourage various groups to scrabble over the crumbs. They will be so busy attacking each other that they won't think to join together to challenge the entire edifice.

The white establishment manipulates racial ideology. When it uses the language of colorblindness and equal opportunity, the words need to be stripped of their underlying manipulation. Right now it is useful for that establishment to act appalled by the use of race as a criterion for social allocation. But not too long ago, certainly within my memory, it was happy to use it openly. Has the white establishment suffered a real change of heart? Is a system that was openly built on racial oppression and that still uses it on a world scale, suddenly free from this cancer?

The truth is, a system driven by private profit, by the search for individual gain, can never solve its social problems. The conservatives promise that market forces will wipe out the negative effects of a history of racial discrimination. But this is a mirage. Wealth accrues to the already wealthy. Power and wealth enhance privilege. Nothing in the market system will change the fact that women of color are exploited in food services on my campus. The market system will not iron out this oppression. On the contrary, its operation sustains it. Only political opposition, only a demand for social justice, will turn this situation around.

FACING THE 1990s

The decade ahead seems to me to be filled with the potential for social change. The world capitalist financial system is teetering on the brink of disaster, with the piling up of unrepayable Third World debt. Meanwhile, a massive international restructuring of production is occurring whereby industrial manufacturing is fleeing the United States, leaving behind a poorly paid service sector that provides services for an affluent upper middle class. The United States seems to be moving toward an increasingly class-polarized society and although this polarization is not purely racially defined, the correlation with race is high.

The instabilities of a society divided between the haves and have-nots are obvious. At some point the impoverished will rise up and demand change. They will bring forth leaders, like Malcolm X, who will galvanize their grievances and lead movements for change. I anticipate such movements in the next decade, and even if they don't succeed in producing fundamental change, they will, like the movements of the 1930s and 1960s, batter the fortress of American capitalism with yet another hurricane. Each new wave of storms weakens the foundations of the system further until one day the whole edifice will come crashing down.

You can see the cracks in the structure by the loss of faith in itself that permeates Western civilization. Science, one of the great kingpins of the edifice, is under challenge from several quarters.[10] A widespread cynicism pervades the society; people no longer believe in what they are doing and just do it because of the constraints imposed on them from the outside. There has been a loss of authenticity in this social system, a loss of belief.[11] Not only is there a decadence in social forms the leaves people destitute, but there is a decadence, a hollowness of the spirit, that afflicts even the beneficiaries of the system.

I see this condition all around me. My students, for example, find themselves trapped in life-forms that they despise but see no way out of. They are caught in a system that forces them to pursue their own narrow self-interest, terrified that if they deviate from this path, they will not "make it." But they also recognize, or can easily be aroused to recognize, that some of their most human impulses—to reach out, to love, to create a world that fits what they believe in—are completely thwarted. They feel they must postpone these aspirations until some unspecified future time when they have more security and can pursue what they believe is right, not realizing that such a time never comes because American capitalism is built on perpetual insecurity. They know that their hearts are atrophying as they get caught in the great rat race. They sense that a part of them is dying, and they try to blot that fact out with drugs

---

[10] This challenge to science is coming from all sides, including feminists, Marxists, Afrocentric scholars, and even scientists themselves. For a few examples, see Evelyn Fox Keller's (1982) "Feminism and Science," Marcus G. Raskin and Herbert J. Bernstein's (1987) *New Ways of Knowing,* and Michel Foucault's (1980), *Power and Knowledge.*

[11] The Spanish philosopher, Ortega y Gasset, has written extensively on the issue of modern society's loss of belief in itself in, for example, *The Modern Theme* (1933) and *History as a System* (1941).

and alcohol and TV and spectator sports and consumerism and a host of other escapes.

I believe this condition applies to all of us middle-class people. We are caught up in a colossal contradiction. On the one hand, we feel compelled to focus on our own survival, our own upward mobility in the system. We feel forced to push ourselves and our children to the front of the line. We feel the need to do anything we can to make sure that we and ours get ahead, and the hell with everyone else. The scramble for survival overwhelms us, because the alternatives are too horrible to contemplate.

On the other hand, we recognize (perhaps only at an unconscious level) that in pursuing our own survival, we are participating in the very system that oppresses us. We abandon the collective, political strategies necessary to change the system and, instead, play by the very rules we know are corrupt. Like the students, we are trapped in cynicism. We have fallen for the dominant line that change isn't possible and that therefore one may as well work the system for all one can get out of it.

What we all need to recognize clearly is that the social structure only remains stable so long as we continue to participate in it. The rules of the game are only human-created rules, and their stability inheres in their acceptance by the members of the system. When people decide to disobey the rules, when they collectively challenge them, the system will crumble. Its stability lies in our acquiescence. It cannot withstand our refusal to cooperate. We are the ultimate creators of our social order. Our relationship to it involves a choice. We can either reproduce it by going along with its dictates, or we can struggle toward its transformation by challenging it. In seeking to transform, in seeking to construct a social system that corresponds to the social justice that we want in our hearts, we are fulfilling our most human of capacities.[12]

Now, how do we get from here to there? How do we help to make of the 1990s a revolutionary decade? How do we overcome our own contradictions? How do we survive and struggle at the same time?

I don't have a clear answer to these pressing questions. Each person needs to examine his or her own circumstances and decide on his or her own commitment. But of one thing I am certain. We middle-class people, both whites and people of color, need to recognize with clarity our own participation in the oppression of this society. We cannot fool ourselves into believing that our own upward mobility somehow helps the poor. We cannot blind ourselves to our complicity in the perpetuation of inequality, including racial inequality. We need to see ourselves without blinking. We need to recognize what roles we play in the system, how we help to stabilize it. We need to rid ourselves of our self-delusions that our own advancement and privilege are a step toward greater justice and the amelioration of suffering by the people at the bottom. We need to forswear our own form of trickle-down theory.

It seems to me that there is much that middle-class people like ourselves can do with our positions of privilege. We have skills and resources, we have knowledge and credibility that can be used on behalf of social justice. Those very skills that the people in power pay us to use on their behalf can be used against them. And we can call on some of the espoused principles of the nation, such as freedom of speech, to get our message across. We can, for instance, develop radical pedagogies in our classrooms to awaken the students' consciousness of the absence of democracy in

---

[12] This idea is developed eloquently by Paulo Freire (1981) in *Pedagogy of the Oppressed.* See also Roy Bhaskar's (1979) "On the Possibility of Social Scientific Knowledge and the Limits of Naturalism."

their lives and the need for change. We can expose the elitism of the structures in which we are involved and challenge their obvious antidemocratic implications. We can fight for a say in the running of the university by the excluded communities that it is supposed to serve but doesn't. We can fight for the rights of exploited food service workers. We can, in sum, *take an option for the poor.* The need for change is so vast, the points of necessary challenge so all-encompassing, that it only takes a little imagination to devise a multitude of projects. The key lies in our own consciousness, in a consciousness that keeps asking whose side we are on, whom we are benefiting. If our actions help to stabilize the existing social order, then they need to be questioned.

It is important to recognize that the racism embedded in our institution is not undone by token statements of commitment to affirmative action, nor by the appointment of a few fairly high-level administrators and faculty people of color, nor by the establishment of "multicultural" programs like Black History Month, nor by official condemnation of racial incidents. The truth is that so long as inequality itself is not challenged, so long as the exploitation of women of color in food services remains normal operating procedure, the core of racism remains untouched.

As I look toward the 1990s I see a need for more battles to be fought at the grassroots level, with and on behalf of our fellow community members. I see the need for a demand not so much to reshuffle who is in the middle class as to end the exploitation at the bottom, at the foundation of the system. Political change needs to occur at the top too, of course, and I expect that worldwide financial instabilities will enhance that prospect. However, it is in the lives of people like ourselves, battling the institutions that we participate in every day, that the wellspring of social change really lies. If the fight for democracy is waged by small groups, who don't have large voices, all over the country, the combined sound will be a mighty roar.

We can't sit around and wait for a revolution. We can't just join organizations in our spare time. We need to attack the system right in the middle of where we live in it: *in our places of work.* If we don't do it there, where the heart of the system beats, then we are only playing with change. The risk of such action demonstrates its importance, for it is here that the ruling class will be swift in its retaliation. You can hold all the symbolic Martin Luther King Day celebrations you want, but don't you dare challenge their hierarchies and the profits that derive from them. If you demand greater economic equality, you strike at the core of the capitalist-racist system.

In conclusion, I believe that the fight for racial equality must be coupled with the fight for economic equality. The two cannot be separated. In fighting for economic justice I do not believe that we can treat racism as a secondary issue that will take care of itself. Rather, the unique oppression suffered by people of color, and their special needs today, must be given direct attention. Indeed, I expect that people of color will be the leaders of our movements for change, as they should be. And white people are going to have to learn to accept this leadership because it will be the finest and most far-sighted that the nation will produce. Out of the depths of oppression will arise the leaders who have the greatest understanding of the dynamics of the system, the greatest urgency to bring about change, and the greatest compassion for those who suffer at its hands. They will create a vision of the future that will encompass all of humanity.

We academics like to believe that it is only the educated elite that can rule. We are caught up in the ideology of technocracy. We think that training is the key to wisdom. But, on the contrary, training can often lead to an inability to see the whole picture. We scurry around with our little pieces of expertise, doing our jobs, and failing to hold up our heads to see what is really going on. We need to be led out of our mire.

I believe that the 1990s will bring forth hope from despair, unity out of division, and leadership from the people who are treated as refuse by this system. The 1980s marked a backward movement. But as a result, I hope we will be propelled forward, like a wave, with ever greater vigor, toward a society of equality and justice for all.

REFERENCES

Bhaskar, R. (1979). On the possibility or social scientific knowledge and the limits of naturalism. In J. Mejsham & D.-H. Ruben (Eds.), *Issues in Marxist philosophy* (Vol. 3, pp. 107–139). Brighton, England: Harvester Press.

Bonacich, E. (1987, Winter). The limited social philosophy of affirmative action. *Insurgent Sociologist, 14*, 99–116.

Bonacich, E. (1989). Racism in the deep structure of U.S. higher education: When affirmative action is not enough. In A. Yogev & S. Tomlinson (Eds.), *Affirmative action and positive policies in the education of ethnic minorities* (pp. 3–15). Greenwich, CT: JAI Press.

Cheng, L., & Bonacich, E. (1984). *Labor immigration under capitalism: Asian workers in the United States before World War II.* Berkeley: University of California Press.

Ehrenreich, B., & Ehrenreich, J. (1979). The professional-managerial class. In P. Walker (Ed.), *Between labor and capital* (pp. 5–45). Boston: South End Press.

Fernandez-Kelly, M. P. (1983). *For we are sold, I and my people: Women and industry in Mexico's frontier.* Albany: State University of New York Press.

The 400 richest people in America. (1987, October). *Forbes,* pp. 106–110.

Foucault, M. (1980). *Power and knowledge* (Colin Gordon, Ed., Colin Gordon, Leo Marshall, John Mepham, & Kate Soper, Trans.). New York: Pantheon.

Freire, P. (1981). *Pedagogy of the oppressed.* New York: Continuum.

Fuentes A., & Ehrenreich, B. (1983). *Women in the global factory.* Boston: South End Press.

Hemisphere in crisis. (1987, December 29). *Los Angeles Times.*

Keller, E. F. (1982). Feminism and science. In Nannerl O. Keohane (Ed.), *Feminist theory: A critique of ideology* (pp. 113–126). Chicago: University of Chicago Press.

Lembcke, J. (1989). *Race, class, and urban change.* Greenwich, CT: JAI Press.

Omi, M., & Winant, H. (1986). *Racial formation in the United States: From the 1960s to the 1980s.* New York: Routledge & Kegan Paul.

Ortega y Gasset, J. (1933). *The modern theme.* New York: W. W. Norton.

Ortega y Gasset, J. (1941). *History as a system.* New York: Continuum.

Pinkney, A. (1984). *The myth of black progress.* Cambridge, England: Cambridge University Press.

Raskin, M. G., & Bernstein, H. J. (1987). *New ways of knowing.* Totowa, NJ: Roman & Littlefield.

Sacks, K. B., & Remy, D. (1984). *My troubles are going to have trouble with me: Everyday trials and triumphs of women workers.* New Brunswick, NJ: Rutgers University Press.

Sheinkman, J. (1987, September 9). Stop exploiting lowest-paid workers. *Los Angeles Times.*

"Super rich" control misstated by study. (1986, August 22). *Los Angeles Times.*

Szymanski, A. (1979). *Is the red flag flying? The political economy of the Soviet Union.* London: Zed Press.

U.S. Bureau of the Census. (1986a). Characteristics of the population below the poverty level: 1984. *Current Population Reports* (Series P-60, No. 152). Washington, DC: U.S. Government Printing Office.

U.S. Bureau of the Census. (1986b). Household wealth and asset ownership: 1984. *Current Population Reports* (Series P-70, No. 7). Washington, DC: U.S. Government Printing Office.

U.S. Congress Joint Economic Committee. (1986, July). *The concentration of wealth in the United States: Trends in the distribution of wealth among American families.* Washington, DC: U.S. Government Printing Office.

U.S. Department of Health and Human Services. (1985, August). *Report of the Secretary's Task Force on Black and Minority Health: Vol. I. Executive summary.* Washington, DC: U.S. Government Printing Office.

U.S. Department of Labor, Bureau of Labor Statistics. (1987, January). *Employment and Earnings, 34,* 212.

Walton still tops Forbes list of 400 richest Americans. (1986, October 14). *Los Angeles Times.*

Wexler, R. (1982). *Blood of the land: The government and corporate war against the American Indian Movement.* New York: Vintage.

Williams, E. (1966). *Capitalism and slavery.* New York: Capricorn.

14

The Significance of Race in U.S. Economic and Occupational Life: Commentary on Bonacich and Swinton

Walter R. Allen
Department of Sociology
University of California at Los Angeles

The chapters by Swinton and Bonacich examine American racial and ethnic relations in the 1990s through the lenses of employment and income. Bonacich outlines an analysis of economic inequality, particularly racial inequality, in this country. She argues that the American system is bound to inequality and depends on inequality for its very survival. In this connection she contends that racial oppression is an inherent feature of capitalism; thus we can never rid ourselves of the problem without effecting profound change in our economic system. In Bonacich's estimation, "The whole magnificent edifice of wealth and privilege in this society has been built on the suffering of poor people, large numbers of whom are people of color" (p. 189).

Swinton's chapter proposes to explore the persistence of racial inequality in economic life in the post-civil-rights-movement era. He focuses on trends in the economic status of black Americans since 1970. His analysis reveals that despite a successful mass-based political movement, an abundance of legislation to combat poverty and racial discrimination, and fundamental changes in race relations in this society, "the economic gaps between blacks and whites persist almost unchanged" (p. 168).

Although Swinton and Bonacich differ in tone and in methodological approach (Bonacich is more polemical, makes use of individual cases, and proposes by far the more radical solutions), there is a striking consistency in the substance and the conclusions of their chapters. Both chapters confront the spectrum of racial inequality in our society. Each author offers important insights into the origins and structure of disproportionate poverty among people of color in the United States. It is instructive at this point to consider the chapters in more detail, beginning with that of Bonacich.

The Bonacich chapter begins with a sobering prologue describing the 1987 firing of a Chicana food service worker just before Christmas. The woman was a single mother with three children; she also supported her ailing mother on her $150-per-week salary. This account could serve as the prototypic "everywoman" story for female workers of color who exist on the margins of the U.S. economy.

In this case, however, the story is set in a university, supposedly one of the few remaining bastions of enlightened thinking in this society. As it turned out, efforts to intervene on behalf of this woman by university faculty (Bonacich included) proved futile; the woman was not reinstated. In the course of this narrative we are told of the university's decision to turn over what had been a money-losing venture to a large multinational corporation, which succeeded in getting the university food service operation out of the red by "balancing the books" on the shoulders of disenfranchised, low-status workers (paying them minimum or below-scale wages and cutting back the labor force).

The power of Bonacich's narrative emerges through its ability to reveal the systemic nature of economic and racial oppression in this society. In simplest terms, the narrative ties high academic professional salaries and plush conventions to the misery of the people at the bottom of U.S. society. Bonacich's chapter compels sober reflection through its lucid demonstration of the link between affluence in one sector of this society and deprivation in another. She reminds us that opulent affluence and grinding poverty are inextricably linked . . . across the world, across nations, and across universities.

Just as a good novelist uses details from a single life to reveal universal truths, Bonacich moves from the account of the Chicana food service worker's economic travails to the analysis of society-wide economic inequality. She provides a battery of statistics, staggering in their demonstration of the extreme concentration of wealth in this society. We are shown that the top one half of one percent (0.5%) of families in the United States own over one third of the nation's net wealth. Since 1963 the trend has been toward greater concentration of the nation's wealth in few hands. It is equally striking to note that Lee Iacocca, the nation's highest-paid executive, received over $25 million a year, or roughly $10,000 an hour. For 3 hours' work, one man made more money than 50% of American families (many with two wage earners) earn for a full year (based on 1986 median family wages of $26,000). This figure provides a dramatic demonstration of the wealth gap in this society.

With the extreme economic inequality of this society as a backdrop, Bonacich proceeds to call for a movement toward a more just society. In particular, she presses academics to become active agents for positive change. This call recognizes the historically passive role of academics in the task of societal change. Indeed, Bonacich characterizes academics not merely as passive agents but in many cases as active protectors and perpetrators. She argues that academics, by virtue of their privileged station, have an investment in the maintenance of the system. In this characterization, academics and other middle-class members of elites are viewed as the "sergeants" of the system, a functional "native elite" whose job it is to serve as intermediaries between the system and the masses of oppressed people. Until academics actively renounce this role, according to Bonacich, they will be caught in the contradiction between essence and action. To break this cycle, and by doing so to reshape the American system of economic and race relations, Bonacich requires that academics assume personal responsibility. They must cease engaging in cynical, self-alienating activities and aim consciously at redefinition.

In her discussion of the connections between the American politico-economic system and racism, Bonacich concludes that the two are inextricably bound. She notes a symbiotic link between the structure of economics and the patterns of racism and racial discrimination. Similarly, she sees the U.S. value system as bound up in fundamental ways with racist viewpoints and with the belief in white superiority. Our economic system feeds on inequality, of which racial inequality is perhaps the most extreme form. In this sense capitalism is tied to racism.

Bonacich asks, "Does capitalism need racism?" and concludes that the answer is uncertain. What is certain in her mind, however, and what arises from the analysis, is the understanding that racial and ethnic inequality in this system cannot be addressed apart from inequality in the society as a whole. At this point Bonacich's analysis parallels that of Dr. Martin Luther King in the later years of his life. After a lifetime of fighting the battle for black equality on the grounds of racial justice, King expanded his focus to fight for a more fair economic agenda. Without economic justice, he said, there could be no racial justice.

Swinton begins his chapter appropriately enough, at the point that signaled a new beginning for black Americans, the civil rights movement. On the heels of the movement and of the victories leading to and following this historic struggle, epic change occurred in American race relations. Indeed, profound changes took place in the status of black people in the United States: Legal segregation was outlawed, black people gained the franchise, and the ranks of the middle class expanded as blacks moved into areas of society that previously had been off limits to them. In the midst of these positive developments, however, many problems persisted.

Swinton's analysis provides a report card for the quarter century after the civil rights movement. His evaluation takes the form of a "good news, bad news" assessment. First, the good news: Swinton's impressive array of statistics offers conclusive proof of substantial economic gains for a select subset of black Americans. Those with appropriate technical skills and advanced educations were able to take advantage of the newly created opportunites and to surge forward onto higher economic ground. The bad news, however, was that these people were in the minority; the majority of blacks continued to lag behind in education and in occupational skills. Thus the larger group of blacks missed the wave of economic good fortune or at best caught only its fringe. The result of this uneven benefit was a widening of the gap between the black haves and have-nots. Although many people have written and commented about the increasing economic disparity among black Americans during this period, few have associated this disparity with trends in the large society. Bonacich, however, informs us of a general trend toward increased economic disparity across the larger society.

Swinton devotes little time to the task of identifying trends within a broader context. Instead he concentrates on providing extensive statistical documentation of observed trends. Swinton's account reveals the economic devastation wrought on black Americans by a series of factors: several economic recessions during the 1970s, America's declining industrial sector, the expulsion of black males from the labor force, and the failure of government to sustain and direct public policies aimed at eliminating poverty and discrimination. Unfortunately, Swinton falls short in clarifying sufficiently the origins of the powerful economic patterns revealed by his analysis.

Swinton does provide one of the soundest available empirical analyses of the structural dimensions of black economic deprivation in this society. Blacks are shown to be disadvantaged in private business ownership, accumulation of wealth, labor-force participation rates, occupational status, and a host of other factors. These factors are related in turn to the historic, systematic practices of race-determined exclusion, deprivation, and debilitation. According to Swinton's analysis, the persistence of these structural barriers to full black participation in the society, combined with blacks' accumulated disadvantages, accounted for the less-than-expected economic gains following the civil rights movement.

Faced with the battery of data provided in Swinton's chapter one wonders how other writers could have arrived empirically at their pronouncements that the battle for black economic equality in this society had been won. Moreover, Swinton provides fresh insights into the economic status of the often-criticized black middle class. He shows that despite tremendous gains over the last 25 years, this group exists in a largely precarious state, unable to guarantee that their status will carry over into the next generation and, indeed, uncertain from paycheck to paycheck of their ability to sustain their status in the present. One realizes that many commentators, in castigating this group for not having done more to assist the black underclass, have failed to grasp the true economic instability of middle-class status for blacks in this society. What is evident in this discussion is black Americans' heavy dependence on the government for economic opportunities, advances, and stability.

To his credit, Swinton examines and charts carefully the role of government in the economic lives of black people. To begin, he points out the long history of government involvement in the economic affairs of black Americans. Unfortunately, the bulk of this early involvement was focused negatively; it concentrated on keeping black people economically insecure, subservient, and powerless. With this background in mind Swinton outlines a joint strategy for addressing the economic problems of black people. One set of strategies would require government intervention. Swinton boldly proposes payment of reparations to black people to counteract the historic government-enforced and supported economic underdevelopment of black Americans. This proposal is reminiscent of the "black liberation" period of the late 1960s and early 1970s, when several black activists called for reparations. They asked for the 40 acres and a mule initially promised to blacks at emancipation; the debt was to be paid to all descendants of slaves . . . with accrued interest. Swinton also calls on the black community to rethink objectives, tactics, and strategies. In his view, civil rights strategists "failed to recognize the importance of changing the distribution of power" (p. 184) in this society. He recommends that black self-help efforts in the future concentrate on altering environmental constraints and on achieving a redistribution of wealth in this society.

Bonacich's and Swinton's chapters complement each other. Together they provide powerful insights into the effects of employment and income on racial and ethnic relations in America. However, both chapters can be challenged on some points. For instance, the tone of the Bonacich chapter leaves the author open to charges of being overly polemical. A more measured tone might help to block such an easy avenue of retreat from the hard questions Bonacich raises for American society. Persons interested in discrediting Bonacich's arguments must not be allowed the easy exit of dismissing her chapter as mere propaganda.

At the same time, one of the strongest and most appealing features of Bonacich's chapter is its passionate invocation of moral issues, its unbending insistence on challenging us to confront injustice. The chapter is notable in providing action alternatives for societal change within a neo-Marxist paradigm. Although Bonacich repeats the often-heard assertion that revolution and the decline of capitalism are inevitable, she suggests concrete strategies for improving the quality of life that are immediately available to socially conscious actors. The chapter ends on an optimistic note, foreseeing positive social-economic change powered by social movement that cuts across racial, ethnic, and economic lines. It remains for the future to confirm or refute such a prediction.

A major drawback of Swinton's chapter is his sparse interpretation of the statistics. One has reason to expect deeper discussion of the plentiful statistics, with interpretation of their meaning and reflection on their implications. Too little of this content emerges from the chapter, however. Swinton leaves the reader with too great a burden (or too much latitude) to draw conclusions consistent with his logic. Those who disagree with his views are likely to use his data selectively to refute the very arguments he attempts to make.

Swinton also tends to be harsh, in my opinion, in his evaluation of the successes of the civil rights movement. Obviously, hindsight is 20–20, so from a vantage point of nearly 30 years it is easy to second-guess the decisions made in this movement. More germane to this point, however, is a reminder that the civil rights movement defined a narrow but powerful set of goals. The intent of the movement was to discard this society's legal barriers to full black participation in economic, social, and political life—to gain full citizenship rights for black people. These goals were achieved. The movement should not be condemned for its failure to achieve full economic equality for black people; that struggle remains to be waged. Rather, the movement deserves to be celebrated for its grand achievements. The Emancipation Proclamation essentially accomplished only one end in blacks' continuing struggle for full citizenship: It abolished chattel slavery. Are we to gainsay the importance of this act because at the same time it did not ensure blacks' proportionate representation among the nation's top corporate executives?

Swinton's critique of human capital theory and policies, aimed at addressing blacks' economic deprivation in this society, is revealing. Most important, Swinton compels us to look at structural features, as opposed to individual details, in search of explanation. The oppression and underdevelopment of black people is not due solely (or even primarily) to failures in character by black people or to their having made bad personal choices. Instead, the depressed status of black Americans is the result of systematic oppression, which all too often received the direct cooperation and active support of the government. Thus Swinton also rejects the view that government has no special obligation to foster and fund affirmative action and other compensatory programs. I would have appreciated more details about the structures and procedures of the proposed reparations program. If the redistribution of wealth and power is indeed the only intervention that can guarantee results in a free-market economy, how can this proposal be reconciled with Frederick Douglas's admonition that power yields nothing without struggle? How exactly is the majority group to be sold on a process that seems to go against its immediate self-interest?

REFLECTIONS AND CONCLUSIONS

Recently I appeared on a televised talk show in Washington, D.C., moderated by WRC news anchor Jim Vance. The topic of this program was economic life in American black communities. The other panelists were Bart Landry, author of *Middle Class Black Families,* and Stewart Butler, co-author of the *Welfare Trap.* My participation in the program was inspired by a book that I co-authored recently with W. Reynolds Farley, titled *The Color Line and the Quality of Life in America.*

During our lively discussion, I was struck by two things. On the one hand, Landry's remarks reminded me of how fragile and uncertain middle-class status is among black Americans. He showed that most black middle-class families depend on two earners and rely wholly on earnings for their status. In other words, these families are no more than one or two paychecks away from a precipitous fall into the working class or, in some cases, the lower class.

On the other hand, Stewart Butler's remarks reminded me of social analysts' ingrained insistence on looking at black people's economic situations in individual terms. As a result, these analysts tend to ignore or dismiss the powerful structural factors that define black Americans' economic status. The result of this restricted view is a failure to view the situations of black Americans in a broader context. For instance, only after being reminded of the horrible economic conditions in the old cities in England's industrial belt (e.g., Birmingham, Liverpool, and Manchester) did Mr. Butler begin to see parallels with the economic crisis in American cities. As a group heavily dependent on the industrial sector, blacks were particularly hard hit. The fact of the matter is that black workers in Cleveland and white workers in Liverpool were not put out of jobs and into poverty because of bad personal decisions or poor values. Workers lost jobs and poverty increased because of shifts in the two countries' respective national economies and in the world economy. These shifts imposed a disproportionate disadvantage on certain groups and sectors in the society.

The dilemma at hand regarding blacks' economic deprivation is part and parcel of American life. Ours is a country with an established norm of competition, where the spoils go to the winner. Kept within prescribed bounds, this orientation is not necessarily problematic. Indeed, this competitive spirit has helped to take the United States to a role of world leadership, second to none in power and resources. The competitive emphasis becomes a problem, however, when it is distorted into a pattern of "big losers." This pattern has produced the vast economic disparities between the haves and the have-nots. On one side are the Georgetowns, the Park Avenues, and the Hollywoods; these are the places inhabited by the "winners." The underside of these exclusive areas, which offer the highest standard of material life available on the planet, is found among the street people who camp on corners in these areas—always after night falls, of course. All too often the "big losers" are children, women, and people of color. They are required to carry most of the burden for the affluence enjoyed by a limited few.

The extreme disparities described above reflect larger disorders in the national and the world system. These disorders persist only because so many of us consent to play in the game of high stakes. In particular, minority members of elites must remember the need to resist the game. We must not fall prey to the lure of riches and sell our souls. We must resist the temptation to engage in debates of relative inequality as we are played off against one another. In a contest to name the "most deprived," American Indian children on reservations would win hands down. In the world contest, the biggest losers are the children in underdeveloped nonwhite regions such as Asia, Africa, and Latin America. These children, to quote a phrase that I find objectionable, are the "truly disadvantaged." Needless to say, the academic exercise of presuming to distinguish the "truly disadvantaged" can deteriorate quickly into a vulgar charade. A more useful enterprise for "truly concerned" social scientists might be a systematic attempt to reveal the economic foundations of this society.

W. E. B. DuBois (1961) rang in the twentieth century with the pronouncement that "the problem of the twentieth century will be the problem of the colorline." The record of conflicts around race and skin color over the last 100 years has proven his prophecy correct. As we look forward into the twenty-first century, it is apparent that problems of color (and of its cousin, ethnicity) will remain with us but will be complicated further by the problem of the money line. Color discrimination has created a legacy in which there is nearly a one-to-one correspondence between wealth deprivation and color. Thus, work to achieve true economic justice cannot proceed without concurrent efforts to achieve true racial justice.

The challenge facing each of us is to write a chapter in the volume that will make a new world. We must reject the old paradigms of structured inequality and must become forceful advocates for a new world order. If we are serious, we first must challenge the elaborate justifications that we, as academics, generate to support the status quo. We are shamed by a history of scholarship which pretends that the explanation of black, Chicana, Cambodian, Indian, and Puerto Rican deprivation derives from their character failings or from institutional forms rather than from the fact that these peoples are players in a game rigged to defeat them.

If academics acknowledge the import and the power of ideology, if we relinquish the myth that "what we do really doesn't matter," we have taken an important initial step toward change. To continue with "business as usual," on the other hand, is to perpetuate an unjust system. In the absence of systematic, sustained countering forces, the system of economic inequality established over centuries will not simply cease to exist of its own accord. Oppression, discrimination, and inequality are systems of our creation; thus they will not simply go away. As these systems were built consciously, they must be dismantled consciously.

In conclusion, I am reminded of a provocative remark by a student applying for a graduate fellowship in sociology. She reminded me of the promise and potential of sociology; she judged sociology to be exciting because it was a discipline with "more questions than answers." Similarly, we have more questions than answers about the connections between race and inequality in this society and in this world, but that is alright. What is important is that we have the courage to pose the questions and the vision to discern answers. What matters most is a willingness to seek new formulations and approaches that might hasten the arrival of a new, more equitable world.

REFERENCES

Butler, S. (1987). *Out of the poverty trap: A conservative strategy for welfare reform.* New York: Free Press.

DuBois, W. E. B. (1961). *The souls of black folk.* New York: Fawcett World Library.

Farley, R., & Allen, W. R. (1987). *The color line and the quality of life in America.* New York: Oxford University Press.

Landry, B. (1987). *The new black middle class.* Berkeley: University of California Press.

Wilson, W. J. (1987). *The truly disadvantaged: The inner city, the underclass and public policy.* Chicago: University of Chicago Press.

PART III

AMERICAN INDIANS: A SPECIAL AND NEGLECTED CASE

15

Wounding the Spirit: Discrimination and Traditional American Indian Belief Systems

Carol Locust
Native American Research and Training Center
College of Medicine
University of Arizona

Discrimination against one's beliefs is the most insidious kind of injustice. Ridicule of one's spiritual beliefs or cultural teachings wounds the spirit, leaving anger and hurt that is usually masked by a proud silence. For American Indians[1] this discrimination exists in the extreme against their traditional beliefs, especially when such beliefs conflict with those of the dominant culture's educational systems.

When Europeans first came to North America their hearts were hungry for one thing—freedom from being discriminated against because of their belief systems. The United States of America was founded on the principle of religious freedom, yet the indigenous peoples whose land was used to establish this country were denied this freedom. Incredibly, American Indians were not granted religious freedom until 1978, when Congress passed the American Indian Religious Freedom Act (Public Law 95-341). The passage of a law, however, cannot bring change quickly after decades of discrimination; racist attitudes toward traditional Indian religions still exist even today.

These attitudes manifest themselves in the U.S. educational system, which was not designed to honor diverse racial and cultural groups. In earlier years Indian children did not have easy access to public schools so they were placed in a military-like educational system of boarding schools established by the Bureau of Indian Affairs in 1819 (Roessel, 1963). Neither the public schools nor the military system was de-

---

This article originally appeared in the *Harvard Educational Review, 58*:3, pp. 315–330. Copyright

[1]As defined in Public Law 93-638, the Indian Self-Determination and Education Assistance Act (1975), an Indian means "a person who is a member of an Indian tribe. An Indian tribe means any Indian tribe, band, nation, or other organized group or community, including any Alaska Native village, regional, or village corporation as defined or established pursuant to the Alaska Native Claims Settlement Act (1971) which is recognized as eligible for the special programs and services provided by the United States to Indians because of their status as Indians. Tribal organization means the recognized governing body of any Indian tribe; any legally established organization of Indians which is controlled, sanctioned, or chartered by such governing body or which is democratically elected by the adult members of the Indian community to be served by such organization and which includes the maximum participation of Indians in all phases of its activities."

signed to accommodate tribal religions, ceremonies, cultural differences, or language differences. Change is very slow in coming to educational systems in the United States; very few public or Bureau schools respect Indian traditions and beliefs.

To change this situation in the schools, teachers and administrators must begin to understand that belief systems among Indian people are sacred and holy; moreover, Indians do not separate the sacred from the secular aspects of life. For example, when a medicine person works with an individual to bring about healing of an illness, it is not just an act of obtaining medical help such as going to see a physician for a cold remedy. Healing and worship cannot be separated, as there is little difference between religious and traditional healing practices of American Indians (Aberle, 1966). Jerrold Levy (1963) has described the social behavior of the Indian as inseparable from the culture, sacred narratives, and religion. Clyde Kluckhohn and Dorothy Leighton (1962) noted that there is no distinct term in the Navajo language for "religion" in the Western sense. While doing a study of Tohono O'odham ceremonies, Marvin Kahn et al. (1975) observed that no distinction was made between healing and worship. Carol Locust (1985) stated that there is little or no difference between religion and medicine, between a church and a hospital in the Indian belief system. Carl Hammerschlag (1985), a friend to Indian people and a former psychiatrist at the Phoenix Indian Medical Center, points out that for Indian people the concept of health is not just a physical state, but a spiritual one as well (p. 2). As these studies show, American Indian beliefs about health may be identified as the core beliefs of the cultures themselves. Educators need to learn more about these concepts since they are fundamental to both the traditional ways of Indian life and to the health and spirituality of tribal members. Without this understanding, there can only be discrimination—discrimination that wounds the spirit of Indian people.

There is a long history of misunderstanding of Indian beliefs on the part of the dominant culture. Early, widely referenced scholars (e.g., Morgan, 1892; Reagan, 1930) seem to have assumed that American Indians were pagans (had no religion) or that they worshiped idols, animals, or devils. Such misunderstandings may have occurred because these scholars did not know the language or the customs of the people, and therefore interpreted Indian ceremonies from the perspectives of their own religious backgrounds. For example, eyewitness accounts of Apache culture and religion written by Thomas Morgan (1892) and Albert Reagan (1930) have serious flaws. Thomas Mails (1974) documented his misgivings about the account of the Apaches written by Reagan: Reagan's comments are based on what he saw in only nine months on the western Apache reservations. He was a captain in the Third Cavalry who was among the Apaches from July 1901 until May of 1902. His interpretations of the real meanings and purposes of some acts he saw performed by the medicine men and the Ghan (Mountain spirit) dancers should not be taken as gospel. More probably, excepting those instances where acts were explained to him, he was not informed or sympathetic enough to make a reliable and profound statement. The fact is that tribal belief systems contain highly structured theological organization, protocol, and ritual, just as other religions do around the world. In most Indian traditions every element of existence and every second of time is perceived as being holy, thereby implying that worship is a constant daily function. The fact that there were no familiar religious objects (no altars, crosses, books) for early observers to see contributed to their conclusion that Indians were "pagan."

One of the reasons non-Indian people do not understand much about Indian beliefs is that they vary from tribe to tribe and from clan to clan. For example, Apaches believe that supernatural spirits seek out an individual to become a medicine person. The Tohono O'Odham, on the other hand, believe that one must be born into a lineage of medicine people or must be a twin in order to become a medicine person. Yet in spite of these differences, most systems are built on a common set of beliefs. In a previous work I have identified ten common beliefs that are basic to most Indian tribes in the United States (Locust, 1985). These beliefs are presented here as general statements and should be taken as indicators or guides for further study, not as universals or absolute truths for any one Indian tribal belief system. An understanding of each will help non-Indians begin to comprehend how educational systems suppress and discriminate against the belief systems of Indians.

Several factors may influence the beliefs of an American Indian: subtribe or clan affiliation, tribal sodality (society) membership, formal education, influence of an outside religion, marriage, and length of time and/or experience off the reservation. A tribal member may or may not know many traditional beliefs, and may or may not identify with those that are known. However, the following statements are applicable to the majority of tribal members:

1. American Indians believe in a Supreme Creator. In this belief system there are lesser beings also.
2. Humans are threefold beings made up of a spirit, mind, and body.
3. Plants and animals, like humans, are part of the spirit world. The spirit world exists side by side with and intermingles with the physical world.
4. The spirit existed before it came into a physical body and will exist after the body dies.
5. Illness affects the mind and spirit as well as the body.
6. Wellness is harmony in spirit, mind, and body.
7. Unwellness is disharmony in spirit, mind, and body.
8. Natural unwellness is caused by the violation of a sacred or tribal taboo.
9. Unnatural unwellness is caused by witchcraft.
10. Each of us is responsible for his or her own wellness.

Educators need to understand the meaning of these beliefs because Indian sociocultural behaviors rooted in these traditional beliefs strongly affect their formal educational experiences. But an understanding of Indian beliefs is not enough for educators; they must also be able to identify how such beliefs manifest themselves in Indian attitudes and behaviors toward formal educational systems. Below I discuss each of these ten common beliefs and outline ways in which U.S. educational practices come in conflict with these beliefs.

1. *American Indians believe in a Supreme Creator. In this belief system there are lesser beings also.* Most tribes identify a Supreme Creator by a name and a personage and usually identify a place of residence for that entity. Although often identified as male, the Supreme Creator is considered both male and female. The name of the Supreme Creator is seldom spoken, for it is sacred. Prayer is usually addressed to the Supreme Creator by a term of reverence and endearment, such as "Grandfather." The Creator is usually perceived as omnipotent, in command of all the elements of existence, and as being anthropomorphic but spiritual rather than physical (Lukert, 1977).

Many tribal groups believe in other spirit beings that are associated with the Supreme Creator, such as a partner, co-creator, mate, or offspring. These lesser beings may or may not be impersonated in ceremony. More frequently they are considered exemplary models after which humans are to pattern their own lives. Most Indian tribes also recognize an assemblage of spirit helpers that assist humans. These beings are not gods, nor do they belong to the hierarchy of sacredness; therefore they are not worshipped or prayed to, but they command respect and thanks as angels and saints do in Western religious traditions. These beneficent spirit helpers may be identified (Locust, 1985) as Kachinas (Hopi), Ghan (Apache), or Yei (Navajo).

2. *Humans are threefold beings made up of a spirit, mind, and body.* "Come into this house that has been prepared for you" is a phrase from a Hopi song welcoming an infant into the world. The "house" is the physical body the parents have prepared for the spirit to inhabit. The "I AM" of each person is the spirit that dwells within the physical body. Of the three elements—spirit, mind, and body—the spirit is the most important, for it is the essence of the being. The instrument by which the spirit may express itself is the body. It can learn spiritual lessons and may progress toward the ultimate goal of being united with the Supreme Creator. The mind is the link between the spirit and body and functions as an interpreter between the two. For example, a person hears a truth by means of the ears of the physical body, and recognizes the truth on a spiritual level. The mind, being aware of the disparity between human desires and spiritual truths, then makes adjustments in the thinking and response systems in the consciousness to incorporate this new truth.

The element of existence that gives vitality to all creation is often called "energy" or "power." The Supreme Creator is all powerful; all things he has created have power. This power (energy) is spiritual, so someone referred to as a "powerful" medicine person is identified as a person who has extremely strong personal energy. A stone (such as a crystal) or a plant (tobacco) may be powerful as well. Eagles have very powerful energy, for they fly closest to the sky, the abode of the Supreme Creator. Animals are sensitive to human energy; they can sense if someone is friendly or not. Humans can sense energies also, but most people are not aware of it. For example, a person may meet a stranger that he or she likes immediately and another person that he or she dislikes immediately. Personal energy is spiritual, and if the personal energy of a newborn infant is extremely strong, medicine people will know that the baby is a medicine person. It is difficult to deceive people who can "see," because energies betray what an individual really is.

Unlike Indian medicine, Western medicine does not incorporate the concept of spiritual illness, which can create problems for Indian children in non-Indian schools. For example, suppose an Indian child is absent from school because of a spiritual sickness. What happens if the school requires a doctor's note to the effect that he or she was seen by a physician, and no note is forthcoming? Non-Indian doctors cannot treat illnesses they do not recognize and were not trained to treat. A spiritual unwellness is frequently more devastating than a physical illness, yet this phenomenon is not recognized by many school nurses. Moreover, the concept of spiritual illness means that an individual's illness can affect the group (family and friends) and that group efforts are required to return all members of the group to wellness. As a result, students who are not ill may be absent from school in order to assist a sick relative in returning to wellness. Although this group effort is of vital importance to tribal, clan, and family members, it becomes a point of antagonism between group membership requirements and school rules, resulting in discriminating actions by school authorities.

Furthermore, many tribal customs revolves around the belief that the body and spirit need not be in the same place at all times. What non-Indians may perceive as inattention, "spacing out," or perhaps a petit mal seizure may be a matter of "spirit traveling" for the Indians. The term "spacing out" implies the act of thinking or seeing things in one's mind, either in recall or in imagination, but confined to creation within the mind. "Spirit traveling" refers to the spirit's traveling to another location, assessing the activities and/or situation there (such as in reconnoitering during warfare), and being able to give an account of the information gathered during the travel. The ability to project the consciousness from the body appears to be common among tribal members, as many people have spoken about it to this researcher. However, it can create conflict in the classroom for students who have not yet learned adequate control of it.

Some tribal groups seem to possess the unique ability to "travel in their spirit bodies," or to manifest themselves in bodily form in another location, as part of the projected consciousness. This ability of bilocation may create frustration for teachers, whose Indian students may leave the physical body sitting at a desk in the classroom while their consciousness and spirit bodies go elsewhere (Locust, 1987).

3. *Plants and animals, like humans, are part of the spirit world. The spirit world exists side by side with and intermingles with the physical world.* Most American Indians believe that all creation has a spiritual component because all things were made by the Supreme Creator. The earth is our mother, the sky our father, and the animals our brothers and sisters. Water is our friend, and every living thing is a relative. Traditionally, thanks and a small gift were given to any animal or plant from which life was taken. No life was taken for sport or fun; hunting, fishing, and harvesting were done to obtain food. Most Indian tribes consider the mutilation of a body to be a direct violation of a brother or sister and believe that what is done to others will be done to them in return. This traditional belief comes in conflict with the practice in high school biology classes of requiring students to dissect animals. When faced with the choice of failing the class or bringing terrible consequences into their own lives or the lives of family members by mutilating an animal's body, most Indian students will fail the class (Locust, 1986a).

The idea that spirit forms inhabit the same living space as humans is not uncommon among Indian people. "My [deceased] father came to see me today" is a common statement, although each tribe may attach a different set of meanings to the visitation. Animals, birds, and fish may also manifest themselves in spirit form without a physical body. When an Indian seeks the meaning of his or her life (this is often called a vision quest), an animal from the spirit world may make itself visible to him or her, thus becoming the symbol for his or her life. Traditionally, American Indian people have been visionaries and have had the ability to see into the spirit world. Tribal members with an extraordinary ability in this area become medicine people.

Indian students are frequently reluctant to express their views about spirit beings because they fear ridicule. Non-Indians tend to think of spirit beings as terrifying specters, or else they scoff at anything that smacks of the supernatural. Indian people who acknowledge the spirit world as a normal part of existence have difficulty with both of these non-Indian views; further, they may refuse to debate the issue because of traditional respect for spirit beings.

4. *The spirit existed before it came into a physical body and will exist after the body dies.* The Indian belief in the immortality of the spirit parallels the non-Indian belief in everlasting life. However, unlike some organized religions that define immortality as beginning with birth and moving forward in a continuum of time, American Indians conceive of immortality as circular in nature, having no beginning and no end. In the Indian belief system, when one physical body is worn out, it is shed like

an old garment and the spirit is free to inhabit another body. When that one is worn out, the cycle is repeated until the spirit reaches perfection and returns to the Supreme Creator. This "returning" is basic to the beliefs of most tribes, and although it is also a central concept for many cultures throughout the world, it is frequently a point of ridicule for those whose beliefs differ.

Traditional Indian belief systems do not incorporate an ultimate place of punishment for individuals who have transgressed in this life. Hell as a place of fire is not part of traditional Indian religion, although a state of torment is identified for departed spirits who have transgressed and who need chastisement to remind them not to repeat the same errors when they return in another body. Conversely, a peaceful land of rest and plenty occupies a place in Indian religion, but as a place where existence is carried on rather than a place of eternal sleep, as in Christian religions. This belief affects burial practices: Indian people provide their deceased with the necessities of life in the next world.

5. *Illness affects the mind and spirit as well as the body.* The concept of spirit, body, and mind interacting in humans is basic to most Indian beliefs and traditional healing methods. When Indians become ill, they often ask themselves why they are ill, since the cause of a sickness is as important as the illness itself. If the spiritual energy around a person is strong, he or she will not become ill, and negative things cannot happen to him or her. If an Indian does become ill or experiences difficulties (family problems, for example), he or she must find out why his or her personal energy is low and take steps to correct the situation; otherwise he or she will continue to have problems. And if the source of a student's spiritual weakness is the school, that student may not attend classes until his or her spiritual energy is strong again.

Modern medicine tends to treat the body for illness without treating the spirit. In the Western approach, bodies are cut open, repaired, put back together, cleaned, medicated, and bandaged; but most Western doctors give no thought to the spirit. If the situation indicates emotional or mental problems, the doctor may refer the patient to another doctor who specializes in such illnesses. The physical—and perhaps mental—side of an illness may be taken care of; the spirit, however, is not treated by Western medicine. For this reason many Indians prefer to see a medicine person at the same time that they are being treated by a physician. For example, an Indian may go to the Indian Health Center to have a broken leg cared for. The physician takes care of the physical injury, but to the Indian the spirit must also be cared for properly. Treating the spirit is the process of finding out why the broken leg occurred, understanding the events in a spiritual rather than a physical sense, and then beginning the process of changing whatever it was in the body, mind, or spirit that was out of harmony enough to warrant a broken leg.

In the schools, misunderstandings frequently arise because of the difference between the school systems' definition of "sickness" and the Indian concept of unwellness. Schools may have a list of physical symptoms for which students are automatically sent home: for instance, fever, upset stomach, headache, vomiting, and other obvious symptoms of distress. These physical symptoms are not cause for alarm, however, in most Indian families, whose members have learned to live with minor discomforts and realize that such suffering is usually transient. As a result, Indian parents may be labeled by the school authorities as uncaring, irresponsible, ignorant, or lazy when they send their children to school with a runny nose or a cough, when in fact those symptoms are so common in their culture that they are not considered evidence of illness. In contrast, a child may be kept home several days for traditional treatments for "ghost sickness," a malady of lethargy, apathy, and general nonspecific unwellness caused by the spirits of dead relatives calling for the child to join them. The child may face punishment for his or her absence upon returning to school, since the school's list of excusable illnesses may not include "ghost sickness," and a note from a traditional medicine person—if it could be obtained—may not be considered adequate. Furthermore, a healing ceremony may call for burning powerful, often pungent herbs and enveloping the ill person in the smoke. This treatment usually includes an admonition not to bathe the afflicted person for several days, a practice that precludes the student's returning to school.

6. *Wellness is harmony in spirit, mind, and body.* Harmony is the peaceful, tranquil state of knowing all is well with one's spirit, mind, and body. To be in harmony is to be at "oneness" with life, eternity, the Supreme Creator, and oneself. Many Indians who are visionaries describe the energy (aura) around an individual who has harmony as a light or radiance of being, to which all life forms react with joy. But harmony is not found within the environment, nor does it come from others; it comes from within and from the Supreme Creator. It is toward this harmony that American Indians strive, despite the poverty and deprivation in their lives and discrimination against them for their belief in harmony itself.

Harmony is wellness, but it is not utopia, as an older Cherokee man explained. When asked about harmony, an elderly Hopi responded that each person has his proper set of relationships for being in harmony and that no two people are alike. John Coulehan (1980) found a similar perspective among the Navajo. A person can be in harmony, Indians believe, despite the condition of the body, the mind, or the environment. One person's harmony may include compensating for failing vision. It is not the events that happen to a person, but his or her responses to those events that create harmony. Every human chooses his responses, and thus chooses harmony or disharmony.

7. *Unwellness is disharmony in spirit, mind, and body.* In contrast to wellness or harmony, unwellness is characterized by disharmony. One cannot be in a state of disharmony that is caused by suppressed anger, frustration, heartache, or fear without sooner or later developing unwellness in the physical body from that disharmony. Disharmony may be a vague feeling of things "not being right" in one's life, and a time of meditation may be needed in which to discover what is not right. One can be affected by terminal cancer, but if the spirit, mind, and body are in harmony the cancer becomes part of the harmony and the person is at peace.

Indian tribes tend to allow each person his or her harmony without forcing absolute conformity to all cultural standards. This custom allows the individuals who are less capable mentally to find a meaningful place in their society in simple physical tasks, such as wood gathering. A beautiful Hopi man once wept when he recounted the story of his friend "Bear," a big, loving, mentally retarded boy who was the village water carrier. The Bureau of Indian Affairs social worker insisted that Bear go to a school in the city. Bear went, but he was terribly homesick and became violent. He spent the next twenty years in the state hospital for the criminally insane and then returned to his village to die. What a tragic waste of human life! Bear was in harmony in his village carrying water. His retardation was part of his harmony; the state hospital was not.

Avoiding disharmony is desirable in Indian cultures; disharmony is negative and pervasive and destroys an individual's harmony. For instance, Indian parents frequently refuse to go to the school when called because they have learned that being called means their child is in trouble. The negative situation that is certain to develop among school officials, the child, and the parents brings disharmony for all concerned and can result in illness if spiritual energy becomes low. Therefore the parents may choose not to be involved with the disharmony at the school and instead to counsel the child at home in a positive manner. Non-Indians, whose culture dictates swift and painful punishment for students who transgress school rules, may view the Indian response as too lenient or as pampering the child, and may become angry because Indian parents do not respond in the manner they think appropriate. The disparity between the cultural expectations of parental responsibilities and control of children may create dissension and hostility between school officials and tribal members.

Students who are faced with a disharmonic situation at school may choose to remove themselves from it in an effort to avoid the possibility of disharmony in their own lives. Physically removing themselves—through leaving school or hiding—is the first defense against disharmony. However, if a student is called before a school official and forced to listen to a tirade full of loud, angry reprimands and accusations, and is therefore endangered by being in close proximity to such negativity, the student may choose to protect his or her spirit by removing it through spirit travel if he or she cannot escape physically. At the first available opportunity, the student may also choose to take the physical body along on the spirit travel and leave an empty chair and a furious school official behind. But to Indians, escaping disharmony does not mean escaping the consequences of an action. Indian children are taught early in life that every thought and every action creates a ripple in their being and that the consequences of those actions are inescapable.

8. *Natural unwellness is caused by the violation of a sacred or tribal taboo.* Most American Indians' tribal beliefs include a distinction between those illnesses that are the result of natural causes and those that result from unnatural causes. Natural unwellness is a consequence of violating a taboo, whether it was done intentionally or unintentionally, and can affect the offender or his or her family. Although the word *taboo* is not a perfect translation of the concept, it is closer than any other word in English to the meaning of the concept. However, taboo, in the Indian sense, carries cultural and religious implications, and to violate a taboo brings spiritual as well as physical consequences.

Each tribe has its own taboos, with specific consequences. In some tribes there is a definite relationship between breaking a certain taboo and experiencing identical consequences. Mutilating an animal's paw or leg, for example, always results in injury to the mutilator's foot or leg. In other tribes, a particular reptile may be seen as a carrier of negative energy, and getting near the reptile may cause a variety of illnesses secondary to "reptile illness."

Most tribes recognize cultural and moral taboos that relate to personal conduct, such as never laughing at a disabled person or at an animal (Gifford, 1940). Religious taboos may concern proper observance of rituals. Some of the prevalent tribal taboos concern death, incest, the female menstrual cycle, witchcraft, certain animals, some types of phenomena such as lightning or an eclipse, particular foods, dead bodies, marrying into one's own clan, and strict observance of religious and ceremonial protocol.

One particular taboo, based on the belief that bodies are sacred to their owners, often creates conflict in schools. For Indians, exposing one's bodily sacredness to the indiscriminate view of others violates the holiness of the being. Thus, violation of the sacredness of the body occurs when students are required to change clothes or shower as part of their physical education classes, since many of the schools do not provide private showers or changing rooms. Rather than commit this sacrilegious act of exposing their bodies, many Indian students fail physical education, because changing clothes and showering are required to pass the course. Non-Indian educational systems have been extremely slow to respond to the Indians' need for privacy in regard to this issue.

9. *Unnatural unwellness is caused by witchcraft.* For almost all tribes, evil is a real and powerful adversary, and one must continually be on guard against it. Evil is seen as a power, and it is also identified as an entity, either human or animal. As part of an attempt to develop a clear definition of evil in Indian belief systems, this writer asked several Indians to explain how they perceived evil. The terms they most often used to identify evil were *bad power, bad energy, negative energy, negative power,* or *dark side.* While non-Indians often personify evil as a red being with horns, a tail, and a pitchfork, some tribes see the bear as a personification of evil, and others see evil as being an owl or a reptile. Most tribes identify a legendary cultural figure associated with evil, but unlike the Christian concept of Satan as an entity that creates evil, traditional cultural figures usually only represent it. Evil may manifest itself in a multitude of shapes and forms, and it can be manipulated by witchcraft.

According to some Indian belief systems, an individual may choose not to walk in the spirit of harmony, and instead choose to walk in the power of malevolent spirits and to do harm to other humans. Indians refer to these individuals as *witches* and to their activities as *witchcraft.* Hopi Indians refer to these individuals as *buaka.* In the Yaqui language it is *yesisivome.* These terms are not synonymous with Western concepts of witches and witchcraft—actually there are no English terms for the Indian concept. The Hopi word *buaka* might be translated as "those who go around at night" or "those from the dark side," as compared with nonwitches, who are "beings of light." The Yaqui word *yesisivome* means "one who is on the bad side" of using supernatural power. The Indian term for witch refers to both males and females. Tribal groups differ on what the terms *witches* and *witchcraft* mean in their language, but most Indian people understand the use of negative energy against one another. But one need not be a witch to cast a spell or to "witch" another person, for most Indians know how to manipulate energy (power), especially mental energy. In intense, destructive cases of witchcraft, however, the witch involved makes skillful, professional use of negative power.

Witching usually follows one of two patterns: It may affect the environment around the victim, which in turn affects the person; or it may affect the person directly. If the intended victim's personal power is so strong that the witchcraft cannot affect him or her, a member of the family who is weak will fall victim. Incidences of witchcraft related by Indian people of various tribes indicate that sudden physical illness, sharp pains, accidents, depression, irrational thinking, and unusual behavior are often suspected as having been caused by witchcraft. Protective objects, such as medicine bags, certain stones, bits of organic material, and symbolic items of a religious or spiritual nature, are frequently worn on the body; their removal (which is often required by school officials) can often create a dangerous vulnerability for the individual.

Keeping one's personal energy strong is the best defense against negative energy. Parents are responsible for the personal protection of their children and of any older, weak family members in their household. When the house is filled with love, caring, and kindness, evil cannot find a weakness by which to enter. If it does enter, therefore, one knows that there is a weakness somewhere and that it must be corrected before more harm is done. Staying away from situations that cause an Indian's personal energy to become weak is a survival behavior that may be frustrating to non-Indians. First, such behavior is not part of their culture, and second, the identification of a harmful situation is culturally determined and frequently causes conflict in school settings and, consequently, discrimination.

Medicine people are on the "good side" of the use of energy and are frequently prevailed upon to counteract the negative energy of witchcraft. If the spell is not strong, the victim, with the help of his or her family, may be able to dissolve it. If the negative energy is strong, however, or if the individual does not know where his or her weakness lies, a medicine person may assist the victim in these areas. (Medicine people never claim to "heal" anyone or to "take off" a spell; properly speaking, they assist other people in healing themselves or in dissolving the negative energy around them.) Medicine people are also healers of the physical body; one may specialize in bones and another in childbirth. The visionaries also work with positive energy to counteract negativity, for they have the ability to perceive spiritual matters. In some tribes, healers dedicate themselves to "light" and therefore can never intentionally harm anyone; in others a medicine person may heal someone today and harm someone else tomorrow, depending on the situation. Traditionally, however, medicine people are warriors for "light," and witches are perpetrators of "darkness."

10. *Each of us is responsible for our own wellness.* Many American Indians believe they are responsible for their own wellness. They can make themselves well and they can make themselves unwell. If an individual allows himself or herself to become upset by something, he or she has allowed disharmony to enter his or her life. This disharmony may create physical symptoms such as a headache or indigestion. Thus, that individual has caused the headache or indigestion by allowing himself or herself to become upset. If an individual's spiritual energy is so low that he or she can be affected by witchcraft, then the individual has allowed the witchcraft to affect him or her. Therefore, keeping one's energy strong and keeping oneself in harmony preclude unwellness.

When an Indian is in harmony, his or her spirit, mind, and body are so attuned to the self, the environment, and the universe that transgressions against moral, religious, or cultural taboos do not occur; further, negative energy from witchcraft cannot find a weakness by which to affect him or her. The idea of this powerful protective shield of harmony is articulated in song by the Navajo: "Beauty is above me, beauty is before me, beauty is all around me."

Most tribes believe that a spirit chooses the body it will inhabit. In the case of a handicapped body, the spirit chooses that body knowing its limitations but choosing to use it for some purpose determined by that spirit and the Supreme Creator. Furthermore, tribal members envision the spirit inside a handicapped body as being whole and perfect and capable of understanding everything that goes on in the environment, even when it appears that the physical body cannot comprehend anything. One might express sympathy for the physical conditions of the body in which a spirit chose to express itself, to learn lessons, and to teach lessons. One might express respect and honor for the spirit that is strong and wise enough to inhabit such a body, and assist it in accomplishing whatever it came to the earth to accomplish. Indians distinguish between a spirit in a handicapped body and the body itself: The causes of a body's being handicapped may lie with the parents (as in the case of fetal alcohol syndrome), and consequently the blame for (prenatal) mutilation of a body falls on the parents; the choice of being in the body, however, remains with the spirit in the body, not the parents.

Consider, though, that the concept of handicaps is culturally determined; what may be a handicap to a non-Indian may not be considered a handicap to an Indian. Many Navajo, for instance, are born with a congenital hip deformity, but the condition does not disable them and therefore they are not handicapped. When surgery is performed, however, they become unable to sit on a horse comfortably and therefore become disabled, for riding is still an important mode of transportation in many areas (Rabin, Barnett, Arnold, Freiberger & Brooks, 1967).

In school systems, children may be considered mentally retarded while within their own community they are not retarded but function as contributing members of their society (consider the case of Bear described earlier). Most traditional Indian languages do not have words for retarded, disabled, or handicapped. Dee Brown's (1970) book *Bury My Heart at Wounded Knee* contains many names of individuals that are descriptive of disabilities—No-Eyes, Big-Head, One-Who-Walks-With-a-Limp, Hump, One-Arm—but categories such as "cripples" do not appear in the literature. The Hopi people identify some individuals with the white or snow kachina (albinos), and legends tell them that one deity who was incarnated as a human, the kachina Kokopeli, was humpbacked; neither of these two conditions constitutes a handicap to the Hopi people (Locust, 1986b). A beautiful term for describing a disabled person comes from the Yaquis: *not completed yet* (Locust, 1987).

Obtaining an education has been a necessity for all Indian children. Traditionally, children who learned at a slower pace than others were as normal as children who learned faster than others. Little differences existed in the way they were treated. Only when formal education came to the Indian Nations were labels applied to the differences between children. Public Law 94-142, the Education for All Handicapped Children Act (1975), was a two-edged sword for Indian people. On the one hand, it provided educational opportunities for severely disabled children who were once institutionalized off the reservation by the Bureau of Indian Affairs, but on the other hand, it caused multitudes of children to be labeled mentally retarded or learning disabled who up until that time were not considered handicapped in their cultures (Joe & Miller, 1987). This is because American Indian cultures reinforce nonverbal communication and alternative avenues of communication, including visual/spatial memory, visual/motor skills, and sequential visual memory, but not verbal skills. Psychological evaluations include verbal skills as a large portion of the tests Indian children are given. Tests are conducted in English, a second language to many Indian children. Small wonder, then, that non-Indian tests identify disproportionate numbers of Indian children who score very low in verbal skills.

The formal education process, including standardized achievement and intelligence tests, is designed to assist and measure mental functions desirable in the dominant culture. It is a fact that use of such tests for other cultures is discriminatory; nevertheless, little change has occurred to adjust either the educational or the testing process to accommodate the language or cognition styles of other cultures.

DISCUSSION

Belief systems are integrated into the total being of the American Indian, and discrimination against these beliefs occurs in ways that non-Indians do not easily understand. Indians view immortality and existence as circular rather than linear and appear to learn best when information is presented to them in a circular manner (Emerson, 1987). Traditional ceremonies are based on the concept of circular completion, just as the spirit continues on the medicine wheel until it reaches completion. Formal education, in contrast, is composed of linear lessons, each of which occupies a linear spot on the year's time chart. Completion is from the top to the bottom of the chart, year after year, until the final year has been reached. Traditional education of Indian youth is not linear and frequently not verbal. Indian children learn by watching elders, by having the grandparents identify for them the whole of the task, the complete circle, the perfection of completion.

One of the most blatant issues of discrimination against American Indian belief systems involves traditional ceremonial times. School calendars include holidays based on Christian tradition and on national historical events. Children from other religious backgrounds—those who are Jewish, for instance—typically enjoy the freedom to participate in religious activities without penalty for absences from their classes. In most school systems American Indian children do not enjoy this religious freedom and are penalized for being absent from classes while participating in traditional tribal ceremonies. Consider the case of the Pascua Yaqui Indians near Tucson, Arizona, who attend classes in the Tucson Unified School District. Hundreds of years ago, traditional Yaqui religion was combined with Catholicism, producing a unique belief system with strict religious procedures, ceremonies, and observances in the weeks before the Running of the Gloria (corresponding with Easter Sunday). Each year scores of Yaqui children were absent from school twice a week for several weeks preceding the Lenten season in the spring, and each year the children suffered the humiliation of having to justify their absences. Each year it was the same; excusable absences did not include participation in traditional tribal functions. However, in 1986 the culturally sensitive school board amended its attendance policy so that the observance of traditional Indian ceremonies and feast days became excusable absences. Unfortunately, this bold step toward religious equality in the educational system is an exception, not the norm, for school boards.

The dominant culture's lack of understanding of the tribal concept that the unity of a group is binding also leads to discrimination against Indian people. In years past, it was the unity of the tribe, clan, or even family that enabled its members to survive. This survival instinct is still present in Indian communities, and it dictates behaviors that are frequently misunderstood by non-Indians. For example, the group's survival depends on everyone working together and sharing. All members work together and contribute to the group, supporting each other in times of stress, for they know that they will find the same network of support for themselves should they require it. Children are expected to contribute to their group as soon as they are mature enough, and thus a 4-year-old may have the responsibility of looking after a toddler, and a 6-year-old Navajo may act as a shepherd. With this kind of early responsibility comes an early breaking of the maternal bond; children as young as 9 and 10 "break the apron strings" and are respected as adults since they participate as adults in the group effort. Responsibility, loyalty, and proper codes of behavior are taught to the children by grandparents, who are the traditional teachers in Indian communities. The U.S. educational system has dealt a severe blow to this group bonding behavior by separating children from the home to send them to school, thus removing from the grandparents the opportunity to teach them properly. Frequently, children are still accorded respect as adults at an early age, but too often they have not had the advantage of traditional teachings. This creates freedom without knowledge of how to accept responsibility, and consequently Indian children are called "delinquent," "wild," and "uncontrolled" by a social system that created this situation for them.

Another aspect of the group membership concept often conflicts with educational systems: that of justifying membership in the group through one's contribution and loyalty. Junior high school girls stay home to babysit younger siblings while their parents work, enabling the family to have two incomes without the cost of child care. Young boys, pressed to go to work to help buy food and unable to find employment because of their age, may turn to stealing in order to contribute to the group. So strong is the membership bonding that students go hungry rather than ask their parents for lunch money, for in asking they would be putting their needs in front of the group's needs. For the same reason, Indian students may not participate in group sports that require uniforms or equipment that they must purchase, for money spent on those things means that someone else must go without. In an era when unemployment among American Indians is 62% on and near reservations (Bureau of Indian Affairs, 1987), and the average annual income of all Indian families in the United States consistently runs $6,000 to $7,000 below that of the general population, money is a great concern (Northern Arizona University and the University of Arizona, 1987, p. 6).

Belief systems are the framework upon which cultures and societies function. The belief system is the bond that holds civilizations together, and it is the small voice inside each of us that urges us to be true to what we have been taught. As Native people, we cannot separate our spiritual teachings from our learning, nor can we separate our beliefs about who and what we are from our values and our behaviors. As Indian people, we ask that educational systems recognize our right to religious freedom and our right, as Sovereign Nations, to live in harmony as we were taught. However, non-Indians must be educated about the traditional beliefs that Indian people may have before they can understand what changes may be needed.

Tribal beliefs vary, and the extent to which a tribe embraces its traditional cultural beliefs varies. Each tribal group has distinct and unique beliefs that are basic to that tribe's culture. Most tribes cling to the Old Teachings because they know that, once gone, it means the death of their culture. Educational systems could make it easier to maintain endangered cultures by abandoning the idea that all non-WASPS (White Anglo-Saxon Protestants) wish to become WASP-like and vanish into the melting pot of America. The majority of American Indians wish to maintain their identity as Sovereign Nations under the Constitution of the United States, and they wish to maintain their tribal and cultural belief systems and life-styles. We remain positive that, once understanding has been established between tribal cultures and established educational systems, discrimination will cease.

REFERENCES

Aberle, D. (1966). *The peyote religion among the Navajo.* Chicago: University of Chicago Press.

Alaska Native Claims Settlement Act, 85 Stat. 688 (1971).

American Indian Religious Freedom Act (Public Law 95-341), 42 U.S.C. 1966 (1978).

Brown, D. (1970). *Bury my heart at Wounded Knee.* New York: Holt, Rinehart & Winston.

Bureau of Indian Affairs, Department of the Interior. (1987). *Indian service population and labor estimates.* Washington, DC: Author.

Coulehan, J. (1980). Navajo Indian medicine: Implications for healing. *Journal of Family Practice, 10,* 55–61.

Education For All Handicapped Children Act (Public Law 94-142), 20 U.S.C. 1400–1485 (1975).

Emerson, L. (1987). *Self-determination through culture and thought processes.* Paper presented at the Indigenous People's World Conference, University of British Columbia, Vancouver, British Columbia, Canada.

Indigenous People's World Conference, University of British Columbia, Vancouver, British Columbia, Canada.

Gifford, E. W. (1940). Cultural elements distributions: XII, Apache-Pueblo. *Anthropological Records, 4*(1).

Hammerschlag, C. (1985, April). *The spirit of healing in groups.* Monograph from a modified text of the Presidential address delivered to the Arizona Group Psychotherapy Society, Phoenix Indian Medical Center, Oracle, AZ.

Joe, J., & Miller, D. (1987). *American Indian cultural perspectives on disability* (Monograph). Tucson: Native American Research and Training Center, College of Medicine, University of Arizona.

Kahn, M., Williams, C., Calvez, E., Lujero, L., Conrad, R., & Goldstein, G. (1975). The Papago psychological service: A community mental health program on an American Indian reservation. *American Journal of Community Psychology, 3,* 81–96.

Kluckhohn, C., & Leighton, D. (1962). *The Navajo* (rev. ed.). New York: Anchor Books.

Levy, J. (1963). *Navajo health concepts and behaviors: The role of the Anglo medical man in the Navajo healing process.* (Report to the U.S. Public Health Service, Indian Health Systems). Bethesda, MD: U.S. Public Health Service.

Locust, C. (1985). *American Indian beliefs concerning health and unwellness* (Monograph). Tucson: Native American Research and Training Center, College of Medicine, University of Arizona.

Locust, C. (1986a). *Apache beliefs about unwellness and handicaps* (Monograph). Tucson: Native American Research and Training Center, College of Medicine, University of Arizona.

Locust, C. (1986b). *Hopi Indian beliefs about unwellness and handicaps* (Monograph). Tucson: Native American Research and Training Center, College of Medicine, University of Arizona.

Locust, C. (1987). *Yaqui Indian beliefs about unwellness and handicaps* (Monograph). Tucson: Native American Research and Training Center, College of Medicine, University of Arizona.

Lukert, K. (1977). *Navajo mountain and rainbow bridge religion* (Museum of Northern Arizona series on American Tribal Religions). Flagstaff: Museum of Northern Arizona.

Mails, T. E. (1974). *The people called Apache.* Englewood Cliffs, NJ: Prentice-Hall.

Morgan, T. J. (1892). *Report of Indian commissioners.* Washington, DC: National Archives.

Northern Arizona University and University of Arizona. (1987). *A study of the special problems and needs of American Indians with handicaps both on and off the reservation, Volume II* (Report prepared for the U.S. Department of Education, Office of Special Education and Rehabilitative Services, Rehabilitation Services Administration). Washington, DC: U.S. Department of Education.

Rabin, D. L., Barnett, C. R., Arnold, W. E., Freiberger, R. H., & Brooks, G. (1967). Untreated hip disease. *American Public Health Association Supplement Edition, 55*(2), 1–44.

Reagan, A. (1930). *Notes on the Indians of the Fort Apache region* (Anthropological Publication No. 31). New York: American Museum of Natural History.

Roessel, R. A., Jr. (1963). *San Carlos Apache Indian education* (Monograph). Tempe: Indian Education Center, Arizona State University.

16

Healing the Spirit: Commentary on Locust

Charmaine Bradley
Department of Educational Psychology
Texas A&M University

In reading Locust's chapter I was reminded of a paper, *Song, Poetry and Language—Expression and Perception,* by noted poet and author, Simon Ortiz (1977) in which he reverently described the emotional, cultural, and *spiritual* context of song, poetry, and language inherent in the Native American world. Ortiz noted that "language is more than just a functional mechanism. It is a spiritual energy" (p. 6). He noted that in many instances when we become convinced of the efficiency of our use of language we begin to regard language too casually, to take it for granted, and to forget its sacredness. He also noted that when individuals regard the sacred nature of language, it becomes a part of them and they become a part of the language.

Vocal expression then becomes "an opening from inside of yourself to outside and from outside of yourself to inside . . . there are no separation of parts, no division between that within you and that without you" (Ortiz, 1977, p. 8). In recognizing this "all-inclusiveness" one gains an understanding and an appreciation of one's relationship to *all* things. By perceiving the context, the meaning, and the purpose not as separate parts but as a whole, one learns completeness, wholeness—wellness (as defined by Locust—i.e., harmony in spirit, mind, and body). Language then becomes an expression of one's existence as well as a perception of one's existence.

Locust's chapter reiterates and supports Ortiz's assertions and accurately portrays the discrimination that many Native Americans experience regarding their traditional beliefs and the way they have chosen to express them. Unsatisfied with merely listing beliefs common to many Native American tribes, Locust effectively interprets the fundamental and intrinsic beliefs that define the Native American existence. Locust notes that an understanding of the beliefs fundamental to both the traditional ways of Native American life and the health and spirituality of tribal members is not enough, for "we cannot separate our spiritual teachings [language] from our learning, nor can we separate our beliefs about who and what we are from our values and our behaviors" (p. 231).

Although Locust does not directly describe the spiritualism of language, she does note that several English words cannot be adequately translated into Native American languages. For example, the Hopi term *buaka* and the Yaqui term *yesisivome* are related to *witch* and *witchness* but are not synonymous with the Western concept of *witches* and *witchcraft*. Also, unlike English, many words of Native American languages cannot be broken down or separated into separate elements (Ortiz, 1977). Ortiz noted that English is a very definitive language that prescribes recognition of its parts (letters, sounds, syllables, parts of speech). This limits Native Americans' words and language, which inadvertently limits their perception, knowledge, and understanding. Ortiz (1977) further noted: "Unless you teach and learn language in such a way as to permit it to remain or for it to become all-expansive—and truly visionary—your expressiveness and perceptions will be limited and even divided" (p. 9).

And division, Locust notes, brings about disharmony—disharmony among spirit, mind, and body—and consequently, unwellness. Many non-Native-Americans do not even realize that the requirement of teaching and speaking English in the classroom is discrimination, since it violates Native Americans' most fundamental beliefs in unity, wholeness, and harmony within and without. Teaching the parts of speech, holding spelling bees, and deciphering poems and stories are blatant examples of dividing and separating the language—hence separating the individual from the wholeness of the language.

To Native Americans English is an alien language. It is an alien language of an alien culture that causes much disruption (unwellness) among many tribal members. Many Native Americans themselves do not even realize or recognize the disconnectedness or ambivalence they feel when speaking and learning the English language. For many, all that they know is that they feel "uncomfortable" in the classroom or, as Locust notes, have "a vague feeling of things 'not being right' in one's life" (p. 225). Although they recognize the importance of an education and the significance of English, they continue to feel anomie, depression, confusion, and isolation. Locust notes that suppressed anger, heartache, frustration, or fear sooner or later develops into unwellness in the physical body from the disharmony experienced. It is the individual's responsibility to seek means to regain harmony and to dissolve the negative energy surrounding him or her.

The thrust of Locust's chapter is her accurate perception of the symptoms of disharmony and her description of the prescriptions performed and abided by in the Native American world to restore harmony. Misinterpretation and misunderstanding of the real meanings and purposes of Native American beliefs and the ceremonies conducted affirming these beliefs have plagued the relationship between Native Americans and non-Native-Americans for a long time.

Locust's chapter seeks to remedy this situation by disclosing the meanings and expressions of Native American traditional beliefs that are manifested in the sociocultural behaviors that affect the formal education process of Native Americans. Her emphasis on explaining the prevailing wellness–unwellness duality that surrounds and permeates the ceremonial functions prevalent in the Native American world provides an understanding of the importance and purpose of ceremony. Locust notes that there is no distinction or separation between the sacred or secular aspects of life or between healing and worship. Allen (1983) observed that at the base, ceremonies "restore the psychic unity of the people, reaffirm the terms of their existence in the universe, and validate their sense of reality, order and propriety" (p. 19). Every song, story, and ceremony (whether for purification, vision seeking, healing, hunting, personal power, food, or arts and craft preparation) tells the Native American "that each creature is part of a living whole and that all parts of that whole are related to one another by virtue of their participation in the whole of being . . . [thus] support[ing] the sense of community that is the bedrock of tribal life" (Allen, 1983, pp. 8–10. Reprinted by permission of the Modern Language Association of America).

Locust describes extensively the strong tribal/clan/family orientation that prescribes many tribal members' behavior. Traditionally this orientation has provided Native Americans with a sense of security and a feeling of community. But today, as it comes in conflict with the values of mainstream American society, it is causing feelings of isolation and alienation—disharmony.

LOOKING TO THE FUTURE

Presently, tribal leaders ("Message from the Governor," 1988; Zah, 1983) and elders are advocating that Native American youth get an (American) education and at the same time learn their perspective tribal traditions, ceremonies, and languages. Peterson Zah (1983), Ex-chairman of the Navajo Nation, stated that "some Navajo young adults have *already lost their Navajo language skills,* and are unable to participate in the cultural foundations of our society" (p. 228). He recommended to counteract this disruption that the Navajo language be declared the official language of the Navajo Nation. "No one," he stated, "can fully participate in the affairs of the Navajo people without speaking Navajo" (Zah, 1983, p. 228).

Many tribal leaders continue to conduct cultural, religious, and social ceremonies in their native languages, although a growing number of tribal members do not speak and/or understand their native languages. By actively and persistently using their native language, tribal leaders are hoping that tribal youth will somehow through "osmosis" pick up the language, thus assuring continuance of traditional tribal ways. Navajo youth and other young tribal members who have little or not acquisition of their tribal languages experience feelings of frustration, shame, embarrassment, and anger.

Educators on reservations are told not to ignore the native languages or to replace them with English but to use them. Further, they are instructed to develop comprehensive plans to train and certify teachers proficient in their native languages and cultures. It is believed that teaching the tribal languages in school indicates a respect for the language and for the culture. "Not only does it become OK to *be* [Native American]—but it's OK (as a matter of fact, great) to *talk* 'Indian' too" (Little Soldier, 1985, p. 229).

Bilingual programs on reservations are fairly common today. They serve a variety of meaningful purposes including meeting the objectives of (a) preserving the tribal language, (b) instilling a sensitivity to and an appreciation for Native American culture and heritage, and (c) developing culturally relevant materials. The task of meeting these objectives is not an easy one when we recognize that educators are combating television, video cassette recorders, and rock and country music. Anglo-American values and the English language no longer inhabit only the classroom but are invaders and even welcome guests in many Native American homes on and off reservations.

Greater numbers of Native Americans have migrated from their reservations to urban areas since the mid-1950s, which has resulted in a mixing of tribes and languages. More often than not, English becomes the dominant spoken language in these Native American households. Little Soldier (1985) noted that in urban areas there is much greater social stratification. She contends that the higher an individual rises on the socioeconomic ladder, the greater his or her acculturation, assimilation, and conformity to middle-class norms. A growing number of well-educated, successful professional Native Americans have learned to live in both worlds—the Native American and the non-Native-American—but "may have lost identification with their tribal heritage and have assimilated into the mainstream" (Little Soldier, 1983, p. 228). And "others [who have not totally assimilated] still consider themselves 'Indian' but really know little of their cultural background of the past" (Little Soldier, 1985, p. 228).

Locust notes that Native Americans do not wish to become WASPs (White Anglo-Saxon Protestants) and "vanish into the melting pot of America" (p. 231) but that we want to retain our tribal identities and be allowed to embrace our traditional cultural beliefs, varied as they may be from tribe to tribe. What she fails to relate is that more and more the transmission of these traditional cultural beliefs is being conducted in English, much to the dismay and sadness of elders and tribal leaders. This is especially evident in urban areas, where second- or third-generation Native American city dwellers may have little or no fluency in their tribal languages.

I am not advocating that Native American children not be taught English but instead that an effort be made by American educators to understand the importance and the sacredness of the sounds and words of Native American language in its totality (context, meaning, purpose). *The Sacred: Ways of Knowledge Sources of Life* by Beck and Walters (1977) is an excellent resource for further explanation of and information on the spirituality Locust and Ortiz (1977) speak to and about.

If Native American children *must* be taught in English, tribal leaders, healers, educators, and parents must no longer ignore the feelings surrounding the use of English—the feelings of shame, embarrassment, anger, and guilt. Ignoring them or failing to address them in the core curriculum of Native American education will not make them disappear. These feelings become paramount—especially when a Native American youth seeks to address his or her Native American ethnic identity. To pretend that Native American youth do not have to contend with developing an ethnic identity is ludicrous. Developing an ethnic identity is interdependent with their learning and their academic and social/emotional development (Exum & Colangelo, 1981).

Locust mentions Native American students' reluctance to express their views about spirit beings. This hesitation also extends to their reluctance to discuss or admit their feelings about their inability to "fully participate in tribal affairs" because of their limited tribal language skills and reliance on the English language. Because English is viewed as detracting from tribal cohesiveness, many Native American students "fake" or "weasel" a knowledge and understanding of their native language to avoid disrupting or disturbing the unity of tribe, clan, and family, which has been their survival mechanism. Locust is correct when she refers to this unity as a "survival instinct" (p. 230). In fact, according to Attneave (1982), whenever the needs or goals of a group conflict with individual decisions and preferences, the group will take precedence, whether the group is the tribe, the band, the family, or any other coherent cluster of people (p. 66). However, the indecisiveness, frustration, and fear resulting from this conflict perpetuate low spiritual energy, causing disharmony (unwellness) and inviting witchcraft to affect the individual and thus his or her education. When a Native American experiences disharmony, a traditional healing intervention is required. This ceremony is usually conducted in a native language, with minimal or no English spoken. Thus, it would be accurate to assert that today's Native American youth are caught in a "Catch-22."

The challenges I see for educators and policymakers of the 1990s are to find the ways and means to:

1. Help Native American students develop an ethnic identity with emphasis on group identity development reflective of the Native American world view;
2. Help Native American students fully develop an appreciation of who they are as Native Americans; and
3. Help Native American students attain harmony so they can be contributing citizens to both their tribes and the non-Native-American society.

This will entail developing strong counseling programs that actively incorporate a multicultural curriculum and that train counselors and teachers to acknowledge and utilize the strength of Native American beliefs and tribal teachings. My 7 years' counseling experience with Native American students from kindergarten to post-high-school convinces me that many Native American youth (especially those living in urban areas who do not so readily have opportunities to participate in their perspective tribal religious ceremonies) are experiencing a loss of identity and an emptiness that educators need to alleviate. By providing culturally relevant curriculum materials in the classroom, employing bilingual teachers, and allowing our students to actively participate in Native American cultural events, we can meet the cultural needs of these students.

Outwardly and inwardly many Native American students are questioning their "Indianism," especially in relation to (a) tribal language usage, (b) participation in religious ceremonies, (c) awareness of tribal, clan, and family ancestry, and (d) awareness of their tribal beliefs and value systems. At the base of all this questioning is much pain, which translates into attendance problems, high dropout rates, and apathy toward school and self. Bradley (1989) found that counseling which addresses the maintenance of cultural values and the role of these values in the development of one's social and emotional growth is important. Such counseling could serve as a tool to help Native American youth gain greater insight and self-awareness and resolve their cultural conflicts and identity crises; it could also assist them in becoming more successful and productive contributors to both Native American and American culture.

Essential to the effectiveness of counseling programs for Native American youth is a willingness on the part of tribal leaders, elders, and parents to talk openly and honestly with them about all of the issues that concern them about their Native American identity. Traditional teachings have always been oral. Through advisory sessions, family meetings, clan or kiva gatherings, or tribal council meetings, sacred knowledge has been traditionally disseminated.

Many Native Americans are reluctant or afraid to speak out about the negative effects of the English language on Native American youths' ethnic identity. They will speak about the impact of English, but not the feelings surrounding the use of English. Conversely, Carol Locust takes a daring and bold step in discussing witches and the beliefs in negative powers or energies surrounding them. So deeply ingrained within me is the taboo against talking about witches and witchcraft that Locust's pronouncements about unwellness and its manifestations produced feelings of fear and threat within me. These feelings are akin to the feelings Native American students have expressed to me about their fears of admitting their limited proficiency in their native language and their preference for speaking English. Neither topic readily lends itself to "fireside conversation." Both can be considered part of the "hidden curriculum" of defining "Indianism," wellness, and unwellness.

In conclusion, Locust's article effectively describes the beliefs about the sacred and the holy held among Native American people. It takes us one step closer to bridging the gap of misunderstanding and misinterpretation between Native Americans and non-Native-Americans by disclosing sensitive knowledge surrounding these beliefs. Locust's words are wise and well stated. She knows and effectively conveys the sacredness of language. I hope educators will digest her message and incorporate it into their curricula so that the wounded spirits of Native American youth can be healed.

REFERENCES

Allen, P. G. (Ed.). (1983). *Studies in American Indian literature: Critical essays and course designs.* New York: Modern Language Association of America.

Attneave, C. (1982). American Indians and Alaska Native families: Emigrants in their own homeland. In M. McGoldrick, J. K. Pearce, & J. Giordano (Eds.), *Ethnicity and family therapy* (pp. 55–83). New York: Guilford.

Beck, P. V., & Walters, A. L. (1977). *The sacred: Ways of knowledge sources of life.* Albuquerque, NM: Adobe Press.

Bradley, C. (1989). Give me the bow, I've got the arrow. In C. J. Maker & S. W. Schiever (Eds.), *Critical issues in gifted education: Vol. 2. Defensible programs for cultural and ethnic minorities* (pp. 133–137). Austin, TX: Pro-Ed.

Exum, H. A., & Colangelo, N. (1981). Culturally diverse gifted: The need for ethnic identity development. *Roeper Review, 3*(4), 15–17.

Little Soldier, L. (1985). The whys and wherefores of Native American bilingual education. *The Urban Review, 17*(4), 225–232.

Message from the Governor. (1988, March). *Messenger,* p. 1.

Ortiz, S. (1977). *Song, poetry and language—Expression and perception.* Albuquerque, NM: Adobe Press.

Zah, P. (1983). A blueprint for Navajo education. *Integrateducation, 21,* 227–228.

17

The Foster Children of American Education

Grayson Noley
Education Department Director
The Cherokee Nation of Oklahoma

Although recently, concentrated efforts have been made to tarnish the tradition of American education, most informed people will agree that this institution has served its function well. This statement must be qualified by adding that not all Americans have had the opportunity to enjoy the benefits of education in the same manner as the majority population. American Indians are an example of those whose traditions in education differ from those of other Americans.

The American tradition placed education within the responsibility of individual states, and the concept of local control allows communities to make specific decisions concerning their schools. These decisions are governed by broad but sometimes specific guidelines outlined by state authorities. In exceptional situations the federal government may exert its influence, for example, as a means of eliminating discriminatory actions.

American Indian education under the governance of the United States of America has a tradition which is opposite to that experienced by other Americans. Indian education has been subject to control by the federal government for most of the time during which the United States has been an independent republic. For most American Indian communities, the concept of local control was nonexistent until recently. Even today, approximately 40,000 American Indian school children attend schools operated by the U.S. Bureau of Indian Affairs. The parents of these children have extremely limited influence in the decision-making process in these schools.

Although today approximately 90% of all American Indian school children attend public schools, they are not accepted into these schools with open arms. In this century two major federal assistance programs have been legislated for public schools that enroll Indian students: the Johnson-O'Malley Act and the Indian Education Act. These two acts of Congress, along with other federal programs, provide incentives for public schools to meet the special needs of Indian children. These children might well be characterized by being in situations similar to those of foster children.

The purpose of this chapter is to discuss the needs of American school leaders for information with regard to the Indian children they serve. It also is important to create an awareness of the emergent structures that recently have begun to serve

American Indians. First, however, it will be helpful to provide a short history of American Indian education.

A SHORT HISTORY OF INDIAN EDUCATION

The Beginning of the Relationship

Education was not invented by Europeans. American Indian groups in different areas of North America used methods of education that varied in their degree of formality but that clearly met the needs of their societies. As American Indian societies varied in their complexity, so did their educational structures. These were as formal as the training required of Muskogean physicians and as informal as old men teaching children how to make implements for hunting and fighting (Feiler, 1962; Swanton, 1922). Characteristically, because most American Indian societies were egalitarian, all members of Indian nations were trained in similar fashion. We must believe this because of the evidence that various aspects of Indian culture maintained growth and stability (a condition difficult to claim presently) over what apparently was a long period of time.

When Europeans became established on this continent, their leaders were concerned with finding legitimate means to acquire the land necessary for settlement. Formal agreements began to be made between native nations and the European colonizers; by the time of the American Revolution, treaties had become the principal method by which Indian land was obtained.

Thomas Jefferson was probably the first president to rationalize the relationship between the acquisition of land and the education of American Indian people. In an 1803 letter Jefferson stated that two objectives constituted his principal reasons for keeping agents among Indian people: the preservation of peace and the acquisition of lands. Regarding the latter, he explained that he considered

> leading the Indians to agriculture as the principal means from which we can expect much effect in the future. When they shall cultivate small spots of earth, and see how useless their extensive forests are, they will sell, from time to time, to help out their personal labor in stocking their farms, and procuring clothes and comforts from our trading houses. (Jefferson, 1803/1856, p. 464)

The object of this correspondence clearly was to introduce Euro-American notions of private land ownership as a means of acquiring native land. The "leading" toward this objective would be done by schools.

This intent is brought into focus even more sharply by an 1808 letter. In this letter Jefferson proposed that once native people were situated on small farms, they should be introduced to an "elementary" educational system wherein children would be taught to read and write. In addition, boys would receive instruction in agriculture and mechanical arts, and girls would be taught spinning and weaving (DeRosier, 1970). It appears that Jefferson had established in his own mind that a clear connection between land and education was necessary for the integrity of United States policy regarding native people. Jefferson also seems to have rationalized that his ideas regarding the acquisition of land and the treatment of native people were philanthropic and morally accommodating. Perhaps this point explains why Indians are incredulous when uninformed persons attempt to impress them with a list of things that the federal government does for them.

Treaties and Early Federal Legislation

The impassioned quest of European immigrants to own American soil clearly was the driving force in the young American republic. "Land was the nation's most sought after commodity in the first half century of the republic, and the efforts of men to acquire it were one of the dominant forces of the period" (Land, 1967; Rogin, 1975, pp. 79–81). Those who coveted the land obviously acknowledged its agricultural utility, but the real worth of the land for many people was in its commerical marketability. Land for speculative purposes was sought by many of America's early leaders; in fact, it was the means by which many of the so-called founding fathers were established as members of the American elite. With leaders of the stature of George Washington and Patrick Henry breaking ground for future land speculators, it is not unlikely that a primary purpose of the federal government's activities in acquiring land from native nations was to satisfy the demands created by the politically powerful, who entertained "fantasies of enormous possession" (Rogin, 1975, pp. 81, 102).

As mentioned earlier, the U.S. government used treaties to obtain land, and education was prominent among the treaty-signing incentives offered to native people. The first example of this offer appeared in a treaty negotiated between the United States and the Oneida, Tuscarora, and Stockbridge nations in 1794 (Kappler, 1904, pp. 37–39). After that time, more than 100 treaties were negotiated by the United States with Indian nations, authorizing federal support for educational programs ranging from simple training, such as for the trade of miller or sawyer, to college and university attendance (Kappler, 1904, p. 315).

The earliest federal legislation to provide direct support for the education of Indian children is known as the Civilization Act of 1819, passed during the administration of James Monroe under the guidance of Secretary of War John C. Calhoun. This act provided funds to "benevolent" (i.e., missionary) organizations for the purpose of developing and operating schools for Indians near or within their home areas. The amount of money originally allocated was $10,000 per year. This act was the first effort, other than through treaties, to follow a specific plan providing for the education of American Indians.

This provision of funds, however, has given rise to questions about governmental intent. For example, it is possible that these treaty and congressional stipulations represented federal benevolence arising from a desire, perceived by federal representatives as humanitarian, to bring native people into the Euro-American mainstream. Likewise it is possible that the government, being generously inclined, was simply responding to needs expressed by native people themselves.

Conversely, it might be true that the educational funds were used as treaty-signing incentives on the assumption that native people would find anglicized educational opportunities attractive. Finally, as suggested earlier, it might be reasonable to believe that the federal government intentionally was introducing Euro-American concepts and values to native people as a means of acquiring their land. That is, when native people were taught to accept the Euro-American notion of private land ownership, even Thomas Jefferson assumed that they could be convinced that they could survive on less land than they claimed was necessary. When they were thus convinced, the purchase of native land by the federal government would be facilitated (Jefferson, 1803/1856, p. 464). There appears to be adequate evidence that this last explanation was the most important motive among the federal leaders of the early nineteenth century.

Other important federal activity during the nineteenth century that affected the education of Indian children included what was known as Grant's Peace Policy. Authorized by Congress in 1896, this venture included the appointment of a Board of Indian Commissioners, who were assigned to "stimulate closer cooperation between . . . federal administrators of Indian Affairs . . . and the public" (Priest, 1942, p. 42). The importance of this action to the education of Indian children was that the Board arranged for church organizations to nominate the individuals who were to serve as federal agents among Indian people. Naturally the churches nominated people from within their own ranks; this action was anticipated by the Board members, who assumed that individuals with deep religious convictions would be more likely to carry out federal policy with integrity. This plan eliminated the previous arrangement, by which military men (who often were found to be corrupt administrators) were assigned as agents.

When church groups began to exert their new authority on reservation lands, one of their means of proselytizing was the school. (The vestiges of this activity remain in the form of old mission schools, which exist today on several reservations.) Churches' fighting among themselves contributed to the rapid decay and abandonment of this effort, although it continued to be authorized until the Indian Reorganization Act was passed in 1934.

Another clue to the direction of federal policy for American Indian education is provided by the rapid development of off-reservation boarding schools. Ostensibly these schools followed the example of Richard Pratt, who established the Carlisle Indian School on an abandoned Army post in Carlisle, Pennsylvania. Several other boarding schools for Indians also were founded on abandoned Army posts. Actually, however, the examples for boarding and day schools for Indian children were provided by missionaries of the American Board of Commissioners for Foreign Missions in the schools they established among the Cherokee, Choctaws, Creeks, and Chickasaws in the 1820s.

The Impact of the Nineteenth-Century Federal Actions

By the turn of the century, several kinds of schools were serving or had served American Indian people. Mission schools continued to serve large numbers of children, but their influence and their ability to acquire federal support had diminished. American Indian governments had accumulated nearly 70 years of experience in operating public school systems for their own people. In fact, by 1900 the Choctaw and the Cherokee nations had more experience in this area than did most of the states of the United States. Their system included both neighborhood schools and "academies" designed to serve the more highly motivated and better-qualified students, many of whom continued their training in eastern colleges and universities. Certain Indian nations counted among their members university-trained physicians, seminary-trained ministers, and attorneys of merit. Nearly all of the officials of the Choctaw nation, for example, obtained their early education in Choctaw schools and used the tribe's scholarship funds for their higher education (Debo, 1934, pp. 236–243).

As noted previously, by this time the federal government had developed a system of off-reservation boarding schools, which became infamous for their strict, military-style codes of discipline. These schools uniformly have been condemned for the manner in which they forced Indian children to abandon attachments to their original cultures. Students at these schools were not allowed to speak their own language and suffered severe punishment for disobedience. The schools also were criticized for not providing the academic training necessary to promote students' entry into postsecondary institutions. Instead, they concentrated on the development of vocational skills for boys and homemaking skills for girls.

At the turn of the century, few American Indian students attended American public schools. Oklahoma's public schools were based on the systems organized by the Five Tribes in the eastern half of that state. In other states, however, officials believed that their government had no responsibility for the education of American Indians, even though most Indians had been given U.S. citizenship by that time. The states argued that the federal government should maintain its responsiblity for providing Indian education; hence they refused to admit Indian students to their schools. Unfortunately, some state officials still retain this attitude.

Twentieth-Century Developments

In the 1900s, several developments had an impact on the education available to American Indian children. Federal legislation was required to include sections in appropriation acts to support the commitments made in treaties; this legislation broadened the application of funds to tribes not accommodated otherwise. In effect, the federal government was providing for Ameircan Indian education on a general basis by the 1920s. The Snyder Act of 1921 confirmed this direction by not distinguishing among Indian nations when it asserted

> that the Bureau of Indian Affairs . . . shall direct, supervise, and expand . . . for the benefit, care, and assistance of the Indians throughout the United States for . . . the general support and civilization, including education of Indians. (42 Stat. 596)

Clearly, the United States had affirmed its responsibility for the education of American Indians.

Accusations of corruption in the government administration of Indian affairs culminated in a study known popularly as the Meriam Report (Meriam, 1928). This study documented a variety of ills in several areas of federal responsibility, including education. Congressional debate leading to the passage of the Indian Reorganization Act and the Johnson-O'Malley Act of 1934 included frequent references to the findings of that study.

The Johnson-O'Malley Act, among other things, provided funds to support the entry of Indian students into public school systems. Public schools received per capita aid based on the number of Indian children enrolled. Originally, however, the monitoring of this program was weak or nonexistent; as a result, the schools were not required to convert this aid into direct support for Indian students. This situation was not corrected until the early 1970s.

During Franklin Roosevelt's administration, two federal employees were instrumental in moving toward innovative policies for Indian education: John Collier, Commissioner of the Bureau of Indian Affairs (BIA), and Willard Wolcott Beatty, Director of Education in the Bureau and known as a member of the progressive education movement. Collier and Beatty initiated research and sought to bring about massive changes in the delivery of education to Indian children. Although they were making progress in improving the curriculum and the organization of BIA schools, the onset of World War II drained their resources. After the war a more conservative Congress defeated the system that had begun to take shape, and the momentum was lost. Collier had resigned before the end of the war and Beatty ended nearly 20 years of service several years later.

During the mid-1960s the Johnson administration attempted to make changes in the administration of Indian affairs by proposing to move the BIA from the Department of the Interior to the Department of Health, Education and Welfare. The administration failed to consult Indian leaders, however; the ensuing commotion, when those leaders learned of the plan, effectively ended that effort. From that time to the present, BIA education efforts have never been stable enough to allow for a clearly defined educational direction. The report of the Senate Subcommittee on Indian Affairs (known popularly as the Kennedy Report) offered a promise, which was met to some degree by the passage of the Indian Education Act of 1972. Even so, the results have not lived up to the promise because the legislation received insufficient financial support.

THE PRESENT REALITY

The Status Quo

More than 3,000 American school districts have American Indians in their student populations. Approximately 90% of all American Indian school children now attend public schools. Out of an estimated 450,000 American Indians of school age, the Bureau of Indian Affairs directly serves approximately 40,000 students.

American Indian school childen are generally characterized as low-achieving, with a high potential for dropping out. They also have been characterized as having poor self-concepts and as being disinterested in the schools they attend. Obviously these are broad generalizations, and it should be understood that many outstanding Indian students also attend school. A review of the literature reveals a substantial amount of research (mostly at the dissertation level), but what makes the difference between successful and unsuccessful students remains unknown. Some recent theories suggest that American Indians function differently because of racial characteristics, but these theories have not been studied sufficiently to earn much credibility.[1] Most other studies focus on environmental characteristics, including such factors as socioeconomic status and cultural context, which probably are more credible explanations.

A few students continue to attend off-reservation boarding schools, although they now number only about 3,000. A newer structure for American Indian school children is the tribally controlled contract schoool. Presently there are nearly 60 of these schools. Some originally were operated by the BIA but were taken over by tribal organizations as authorized by the 1975 Indian Self-Determination and Education Assistance Act. The promise of these schools, which receive their operating funds from the Bureau of Indian Affairs on a contract basis, is that they will provide curricula that are more attuned to the cultures from which the students come. This

---

[1] These theories discuss right-brain/left-brain functions and the so-called crossover phenomenon.

recognition of the worth of the cultures is presumed to aid in students' performance in all areas of study, as well as in their self-concepts and interest in school. We still do not know enough about these schools to judge the extent to which they are fulfilling their promise. We do know, however, that the administrative structures of these schools are sufficiently different from previous structures to encourage serious study.

In public schools, nearly 300,000 students are receiving the benefit of the 1972 Indian Education Act. This act, in part, provides assistance to allow local school districts to meet the special culturally related academic needs of Indian children. The recent national evaluation of these programs reveals that much progress is being made in achievement, attendance, self-image, and parents' participation. Yet no one is seeking the answers to serious questions about how this progress is being made.

We do not know the extent to which local grantees have used their funds to learn more about the educational needs of their Indian pupils. They are obligated to develop a certain amount of information about their students as a means of documenting the need for assistance, and they do so with varying degrees of comprehensiveness. Yet these data are not compiled, analyzed, or used for other purposes, nor are they represented in any uniform fashion that would increase their utility for research. If this was accomplished, the federal government and the recipients of Indian Education Act funds would be well served in the development of policy.

Important Needs

The most pressing need in educational research is for a systematic approach to the development of information that will contribute to the emergence of sound and stable policy for the pursuit of excellence in the education of Indian children. Unfortunately, no clearly definable federal policy for research in American Indian education exists in any area. Indeed, many Indian education leaders claim that no sound and stable policy for Indian education exists at either the federal or the state level. This is not necessarily the fault of the administrators of the Bureau of Indian Affairs because they seem merely to be reacting to the demands placed on them by their supervisors in the federal administration. Within the past 15 years, for example, there has been a move to close the off-reservation boarding schools. When pressed for the reasons for these closings, however, the Bureau administrators could only provide the weak explanation that students would be served better by attending public schools. This rationale ignores the fact that many of the students in boarding schools were there precisely because of the public schools' inability to serve their needs adequately. Apparently the reason for the move to close the schools is that their cost, according to federal budget monitors, is unequal to their benefit to the government.

The education of Indian people is a responsibility for both the state and the federal governments. The more than 1 1/2 million American Indian and Native Alaskan people have equal access to public schools, but in many areas of the country the public school systems have had to be complemented by federal schools. The schools serving Indian people apparently provide them with choices, but the effects of these choices are not clear.

In spite of the available choices, American Indians and Native Alaskans suffer from higher dropout rates, lower achievement, much lower job placement after leaving school, and greater alienation from schooling than do non-Indian people in the United States, according to research in Indian education. Indeed, alienation, the clash of native culture with bureaucratized schooling, and the high incidence of behaviors associated with alienation are only a few of the problems that require extensive research in Indian education.

The amount of research on Indian education has increased markedly in recent years as the number of Indian people in graduate schools has increased. However, the amount of educational research conducted at the present time is still far less than is needed if schools for Indian people are to be understood or improved significantly. If the education of Indian people is considered as an area of comparative education, it is one of the least understood and least researched entities. It suffers mainly from lack of attention, understanding, and sustained assistance. Research on Indian education has been poorly supported and often poorly carried out. The findings have been disseminated so poorly that research on education in many foreign countries is more widely known among faculties than research on Indian education. Such research needs regular support so that it can be conducted continually, can address significant issues as identified by Indian people, can attract and hold a core of able researchers, and can be disseminated to users and to other researchers.

At the present time, federal support for research in Indian education comes occasionally from agencies that are concerned about specific problems related to an agency's mission. The Indian Education Programs of the Department of Education and the Bureau of Indian Affairs do not have regular line items for educational research. Evaluation studies of aspects of Indian education have been financed by federal agencies, but the effects of those evaluations have not been followed up rigorously. States have not invested in educational research in Indian education. As a result, few researchers in the United States are able to dedicate themselves completely and continuously to the problems of Indian education.

Because no dedicated amount of money exists for this purpose, the corps of dedicated researchers is small, scattered, and unable to count on either the time or the resources to sustain a research effort. Small but solid effort would have favorable effects on Indian education because the Indian professionals in such groups as the National Indian Education Association and the American Indian special interest group of the American Educational Research Association are actively studying and disseminating research results, in spite of their relatively small numbers. The number of Indian professionals in education has increased greatly in recent years, and the activities of these professionals have increased in scope, level, and quality.

Now that tribes are focusing more attention on the process and technology of education, they are finding a need for access to useful research. In addition, public schools and institutions of higher education are seeking information that will help them better serve the educational needs of American Indian students.

This purpose must guide the future of education for American Indians. No longer can we rely on the intuitive judgments of well-meaning educators. The educational and social status of American Indians in the coming decade must be governed by information that facilitates better teachers for American Indian students at all levels. Only then will American Indians be removed from the "foster care" that presently serves them so inadequately.

REFERENCES

Debo, A. (1934). *The rise and fall of the Choctaw nation.* Norman: University of Oklahoma Press.
DeRosier, A. H., Jr. (1970). *The removal of the Choctaw Indians.* Knoxville: University of Tennessee Press.

Feiler, S. (Ed. and Trans.). (1962). *Jean-Bernard Bosser's travels in the interior of North America, 1751-1762*. Norman: University of Oklahoma Press.

Jefferson, T. (1856). In H. A. Washington (Ed.), *The writings of Thomas Jefferson* (p. 464). New York: Riker. (Original work published 1803.)

Kappler, C. T. (Ed.). (1904). *Indian affairs: Laws and treaties* (Vol. 2). Washington, DC: U.S. Government Printing Office.

Land, A. C. (1967). Economic behavior in a planting society: The eighteenth century Chesapeake. *Journal of Southern History, 33*, 480.

Meriam, L. (1928). *The problem of Indian administration*. Baltimore, MD: Johns Hopkins University Press.

Priest, L. B. (1942). *Uncle Sam's stepchildren: The reformation of United States Indian policy, 1865-1887*. New Brunswick, NJ: Rutgers University Press.

Rogin, M. P. (1975). *Fathers and children*. New York: Vintage.

Swanton, J. R. (1922). *Early history of the Creek Indians and their neighbors*. Washington, DC: U.S. Government Printing Office.

18

American Indians: Education, Demographics, and the 1990s

John W. Tippeconnic III
College of Education
Arizona State University

As we approach the year 2000, it is still difficult to be an American Indian in America. American Indians do not share in the economic wealth and political power and are not part of the higher social levels in America. Generally they are found at the bottom of the economic, social, and educational ladders.

What is it like to be an American Indian? In general, it is to be poor, unemployed, with little formal education, living in substandard housing, and barely managing to survive. It is to be misunderstood, often stereotyped, and viewed as a relic of the past. It is to have experienced racism, prejudice, and discrimination. American Indians' total numbers are small; often they are overlooked or forgotten and are deemed unimportant. They lack confidence, self-esteem, and hope, especially if they live on a reservation, speak their native language, and practice their Indian culture.

The above description is general. Not all American Indians fit this description, but the fact is that too many do. The purpose of this chapter is to present some general demographic and economic data and to discuss briefly the education of Indian people. The intent is not to be inclusive but to increase understanding and interest in the condition of the American Indian.

DEMOGRAPHIC, ECONOMIC, AND SOCIAL DATA

Population Data

Population figures for American Indians differ according to who does the counting and what definition of "Indian" is used. Two common sources of population data are the Bureau of Indian Affairs (BIA) and the Bureau of the Census. As we will see, they reflect different counts based on different ways of identifying American Indians.

The Bureau of Indian Affairs estimates that it provided services to 755,201 American Indians in 1983. The BIA's definition of Indian included persons from one of the 291 federally recognized tribes or 197 Alaskan village communities. Urban Indians generally are not included in the BIA count (U.S. Bureau of Indian Affairs, 1984).

The Bureau of the Census uses self-identification to identify American Indians. The 1980 census reported 1,366,676 American Indians in the United States. An additional 56,367 Eskimos and Aleuts, located primarily in Alaska, also were in-

Table 1 American Indian population, by year

Census year	Population	Percent increase from previous year	States with largest population, by rank
1980	1,366,679	72.4	CA, OK, AZ, NM, NC
1970	792,730	51.4	OK, AZ, CA, NM, AL
1960	523,591	46.5	AZ, OK, NM, AL, CA

Note. Sources: U.S. Bureau of the Census (1973, 1984).

cluded in the 1980 census. The total figure of 1,423,043 represents less than 1% of the total U.S. population of 226,545,805.

As indicated in Table 1, the 1980 total represents a 72% increase over the 1970 census. The rapid growth in 10 years is due to the high birth rate but also can be attributed to the improved methods of counting American Indians used by the Bureau of the Census. Even with this increase, many tribes believe that their populations are greater than shown by the census figures; according to some estimates there are 2 million American Indians in this country.

As also shown in Table 1, California contained more American Indians than any other state in 1980. California (198,275), Oklahoma (169,292), Arizona (152,498), New Mexico (107,338), and North Carolina (64,536) account for 50.6% of the total Indian population.

The 1980 census identified 278 federal and state reservations, with 11 states containing 5 or more reservations. One fourth of all American Indians (339,836) lived on reservations: Arizona had the largest reservation population (113,763), followed by New Mexico (61,876). It is interesting to note that non-Indians constituted about 51% of the total reservation population in the United States. The Navajo have the largest reservation; they also have the largest population (104,517). Five metropolitan areas were identified as having Indian populations of 20,000 or more: the Los Angeles–Long Beach area with 47,234; Tulsa with 38,463; Oklahoma City with 24,695; Phoenix with 22,788; and Albuquerque with 20,721.

The 1980 census also identified the American Indians in the historic areas of Oklahoma, excluding urban areas. The historic areas included reservations that existed in Oklahoma from 1900 to 1907. A total of 121,108 Indians lived in these areas, including the Osage Reservation.

American Indians represent a young population; the median age is 22.9 compared to 30.0 for the total U.S. population.

Economic Data

The 1980 census reported that the unemployment rate for American Indians was twice that of the total U.S. population at 13.0% and 6.5%, respectively. The 1970 rates were 11.1% for American Indians and 4.4% for the general population. The median family income for American Indian families was $13,678, for Eskimo families $13,829, and for Aleut families $20,313. On the Navajo Reservation the median family income was $9,079. The median national family income was $19,917. The poverty rate for American Indians was 27.5%, compared to 12.4% for the total U.S. population. The poverty rates for the Rosebud and the Navajo Reservations were 50.2% and 49.7%, respectively (U.S. Bureau of the Census, 1985).

Table 2 What is the greatest problem facing Indians today?

Problem	Percentage
Alcohol/drug abuse	43.3
Unemployment	36.0
Education	16.4
Cultural loss	14.9
Termination/sovereignty threats	10.9
Health care	10.4
Housing	6.0
Teen pregnancy	1.8
Suicide	1.8
Other problems	3.6
All of the above	12.2

Note. N = 450. Source: *The Arizona Republic,* "Fraud in Indian Country," (October 11, 1987). Reprinted by permission. Permission does not imply endorsement.

As noted previously, the economic situation on reservations is much worse than elsewhere. A recent investigation by the *Arizona Republic* newspaper found the following:

• Indian reservations still lead the nation in indicators of despair. For example, it's not uncommon for a reservation's unemployment rate to exceed 80%. On many reservations, the only Indians with jobs are those who work for the tribe or the federal government ("Fraud in Indian Country," 1987, p. 26).
• The Indian unemployment rate, the highest for any minority in America, is decried by U.S. Senators familiar with Indian issues. Senator Daniel Inouye (D–Hawaii), chairman of the Senate Select Committee on Indian Affairs, calls unemployment on reservations a "national disgrace." Senator John McCain (R–Arizona) compares economic conditions on Indian reservations to those in Third World countries. "The employment that there is—and this is why the statistics lie so much—is provided by the federal government or by the tribal governments themselves. There is no economic enterprise to provide meaningful jobs which make people move up the economic ladder" ("Fraud in Indian Country," 1987, p. 26).

As part of its investigative study, the *Arizona Republic* asked a national sample of 450 American Indians a series of questions. As shown by the results in Table 2, unemployment was considered the second greatest problem facing Indians today. Over 39% of the sample felt that socially and economically, Indians are about the same as 10 years ago; 29.6% felt that Indians are worse off than 10 years ago ("Fraud in Indian Country," 1987, p. 34).

Social Data

The 1980 census (U.S. Bureau of the Census, 1986) presented some interesting social data. For example, 55.8% of the housing units on reservations with an American Indian, Eskimo, or Aleut householder or spouse had no telephone. An amazing 87.3% of the housing units on the Tohono O'Odham Reservation in Arizona and

83.4% of the homes on the San Carlos Apache Reservations in Arizona had no phone. Other data concerning housing units on reservations included the following:

- 15.9% of the housing units were without electric lighting. The percentage was 47.1 on the Hopi Reservation.
- 16.6% did not have a refrigerator. The percentage was 46.9 on the Navajo Reservation.
- 20.8% had an outhouse or privy. The percentages were 55.5 on the Hopi Reservation and 53.5 on the Papago.
- 38.8% had more than 1.01 persons per room. The percentage was 65.0 for the Navajo and 58.8 for the Hopi.

As Table 2 shows, if one were to discuss alcohol and drug abuse, health care, housing, teen pregnancy, suicide, or any other social, economic, or political indicator, the data would probably be the same as those presented above. American Indians are at the bottom; those living on reservations are at the very bottom. Rather than discussing these areas, however, we will turn our attention to education. Education is seen as a critical area and often is identified as the means to change economic and social situations.

THE EDUCATION OF AMERICAN INDIANS

American Indians are unique in that a special relationship exists between Indian nations or tribes and the federal government. No other minority or ethnic group has this kind of legal relationship. It is important to have some knowledge about it in order to understand the complex nature of the education of American Indians today and why the federal government is involved so deeply in the education of Indian people.

The relationship is based on treaties between the federal government and Indian nations that were considered sovereign.[1] Approximately 400 treaties were entered during the period from 1778 to 1871. In general, they granted Indian nations specific services in exchange for land. Education was considered one of these services and is mentioned specifically in 120 treaties (American Indian Policy Review Commission, 1976).

Since 1871, presidential executive orders, acts of Congress, and Supreme Court decisions have further recognized and strengthened this special relationship. It continues to exist today and provides the legal and moral basis for federal responsibility and involvement in the education of Indian people.

A Brief History

History shows that the formal education of American Indians has been "a failure, a national tragedy" (U.S. Senate, 1969).[2] Assimilation, both forced and through

---

[1] The special relationship is treated briefly here. A detailed account of the relationship can be found in Deloria (1975) and in the annual report of the National Advisory Council on Indian Education (1982, pp. 110–124).

[2] My intent here is to present a brief history. A history of Indian education can be found in the report of the American Indian Policy Review Commission (1976), Szasz (1974), and the U.S. Senate (1969) report on Indian education.

persuasion, has been the dominant policy of the federal government toward Indians. During the 1870s the government established boarding schools that often were located at great distances from Indian people. Carlisle Indian School, founded in 1879 in Pennsylvania and remembered because of Jim Thorpe, was such a school. The philosophy of the boarding schools was to assimilate the Indians by separating them from their families, because the Indian culture, including the language, was considered to be a negative influence in the educational process. As we shall see later, boarding schools still exist today.

In the 1930s the federal government changed the educational approach by emphasizing day schools over boarding schools. These day schools, like public schools, were located in communities near pupils' family members. Indian culture was observed in the classroom, although assimilation was still the goal.

In the 1940s, when World War II strained national resources, Indian culture was no longer followed in the classroom. During the 1950s, "termination" became the official policy of the federal government. Termination meant that the government would cease to provide services to Indian tribes; in essence, it was forced assimilation. A few tribes, like the Menominee of Wisconsin and the Klamath of Oregon, actually were terminated. Since that time, however, they have regained federal status, and they continue to receive services from the federal government today. Education during this time reflected the national policy of termination. English was emphasized in the classroom, whereas Indian culture, including Indian languages, was viewed as a barrier in education. The federal government instituted practices such as relocating Indian people from reservations to urban areas, where they would learn a skill and, it was hoped, find employment.

The 1960s brought change as the Great Society programs provided opportunities for economic, community, and educational development. Once again, the education of Indian students included a move toward a relevant curriculum, bilingual and bicultural education, and parental involvement. On the Navajo Reservation in Arizona, Rough Rock Demonstration School was established in 1966 as the first Indian-controlled school in the country. Indian-controlled schools were established as alternatives to public and BIA education; they offered "Indian" approaches to education.

"Self-determination" became the official federal policy during the 1970s, and it continues today. Self-determination means that American Indians will be in control and will make decisions in areas that affect them directly, such as education. The extent to which self-determination works in practice is subject to debate. The bureaucratic nature of governmental agencies, including the federal government, is a limitation that is difficult to overcome.

The Education of American Indians Today

Because of the special relationship, American Indians look primarily to the federal government to support educational programs. At times the responsibility for education is confusing because American Indians, as American citizens, are entitled to all the rights provided by the states, including education. Thus the role and the responsibility of the states and of the federal government in the education of Indian people are not clearly defined. During the 1980s at least two factors made the responsibility even more complex. First, President Reagan's policy of federal fiscal constraints and the move toward states' rights in education resulted in less federal money and more responsibility at the state level. Second, the definition of "American Indian" has

Table 3   American Indian student enrollment by type of school: 1978 and 1987

Type of school	1978	%	1987	%
Public schools	215,000	78	298,107	82
Bureau of Indian Affairs	47,000	17	28,810	8
Contract or tribal schools	2,500	1	11,180	3
Mission/private	9,000	3	25,448	7

Note.   Sources: Havighurst (1981); U.S. Bureau of Indian Affairs (1987).

become a highly political and controversial issue because resources, usually money, depend on the number of American Indians who are eligible for programs.

At the federal level, the BIA and the Department of Education are the agencies that have major responsibility for the education of Indian people. The BIA is housed in the Department of the Interior and has provided education services since 1870. Currently, the BIA operates schools, provides a higher education program and an adult education program, and supports Indian-controlled schools.

The Department of Education administers the provisions of the Indian Education Act of 1972, Title IV, Public Law 92-318, as amended. Title IV, as it is commonly known, provides funds to public schools, Indian-controlled schools, tribes, Indian organizations, and Indian institutions of higher education.

In 1980 the U.S. Department of Education reported 305,730 American Indians attending public elementary and secondary schools. This figure represented 0.8% of the country's total enrollment. Blacks had the largest minority percentage, with 16.1%, Hispanics followed with 8.0%, and Asians accounted for 1.9% (Center for Education Statistics, 1986).

In 1987, 363,545 American Indians attended elementary and secondary schools. Table 3 reports student enrollment by type of school for 1987 and 1978; the majority attend public schools. A comparison of the data for 1987 and for 1978 shows that public school enrollment increased while BIA school enrollment decreased significantly. In 1987 the BIA operated 186 schools, which included 57 boarding schools, 57 day schools, 14 dormitories, and 58 tribal or contract schools.

In higher education, a recent Department of Education report showed that approximately 90,000 American Indians attended colleges and universities in 1986, compared to 76,000 in 1976 (U.S. Department of Education, 1988). The 1986 enrollment figure included 5,000 Indian students at the graduate level and 1,000 in professional schools. In 1976 there were 4,000 graduate students and 1,000 students in professional schools. The report also stated that the majority of American Indians (56.2%) attended public or private 2-year institutions ("Minorities' Share of College Enrollments," 1988). Twenty American Indian Community Colleges enrolled approximately 4,000 students (U.S. Bureau of Indian Affairs, 1985).

The educational data for American Indians are not encouraging. Whether in achievement test results, dropout rates, educational attainment, or other areas, American Indians generally are not doing very well. Consider the following:

American Indians are the most severely disadvantaged of any population within the United States. By adolescence, Indian children show higher rates of suicide, alcoholism, drug abuse, delinquency, and out-of-home placement. School achievement is severely compromised, and many youths drop out before graduation from high school. The Indian child understands the environment through intuitive, visual, and pictorial means, but success in the Anglo school is largely dependent on auditory processing, abstract conceptualization, and language skills. This difference compounds existing problems of poverty, dislocation, alienation, depression and intergenerational conflict and can partially account for the higher rate of emotional and behavioral problems among Indian adolescents. (Yates, 1987, p. 1135)

The following data demonstrate the condition of Indian education today:

• 16.2% of American Indians 25 years old and over and living on reservations completed less than 5 years of school. The figure is even higher (37.4%) for the Navajo (U.S. Bureau of the Census, 1986).

• 56% of American Indians 25 years old and over are high school graduates. The percentage for the total U.S. population is 66% (U.S. Bureau of the Census, 1985). The figure decreases to 43.2% when only reservation Indians are considered (U.S. Bureau of the Census, 1986).

• 8% of American Indians had 4 or more years of college, compared to 16% for the total population (U.S. Bureau of the Census, 1985).

• The dropout rate for 1980 high school sophomores was 29.2% for American Indians and Alaskan Natives, compared to 13.6% for the general public. The dropout rate for Hispanics was 18.0%, for blacks 17.0%, for whites 12.2%, and for Asian-Americans 3.1% (Center for Education Statistics, 1986).

• American Indians and Alaskan Natives represent 0.9% of the children in public schools but only 0.6% of the teachers (American Association of Colleges for Teacher Education, 1987).

• Among American Indians, the college dropout rate ranges from 45% to 62% (Center for Education Statistics, 1987).

During the 1980s, "reform" has been the dominant theme in education in the United States. Governors, federal bureaucrats, business leaders, religious groups, educators, and others have issued reports that recommend ways to bring "quality" and "excellence" to education. A review of the major reports, however, showed that they had little to say about minorities and practically nothing about American Indians. American Indians are not recognized, nor are their educational needs addressed (Tippeconnic, 1988a).

In a related project (Tippeconnic, 1988b), I asked Indian educators what impact the national reform movement had had on the education of American Indians. Forty-five percent of the respondents reported that the reform movement had had little or no such impact. Only 13.3% believed that there had been significant impact. When asked to elaborate, respondents stated that the reform did not address the educational needs of Indian people; that there was a lack of resources, mainly money, to meet the needs of Indian students; and that there was a movement from culturally relevant to academic activities.

OBSERVATIONS: APPROACHING THE 1990s

What general observations can be made from the above data as we approach the 1990s? The American Indian situation in America is difficult and complex. The special relationship of Indian tribes with the federal government has several meanings. First, the relationship continues to exist today, even though many Americans find it difficult to accept; they would just as soon abrogate the treaties and the federal responsibility and involvement in Indian affairs. Second, the relationship causes confusion in roles and responsibilities among governmental agencies that provide services to Indian people. States often look to the federal government to assume responsibility; the federal government may look to the states. Indian tribes, even programs, can be caught in the middle. Finally, the relationship has caused many Indian people to become dependent on the federal government for services. The services, such as education, may not be the best; we become critical of agencies like the Bureau of Indian Affairs and condemn their efforts. Yet in the final analysis, we support the BIA because it represents the relationship.

The special relationship with the federal government will continue into the next century. Given the outcome of the 1988 presidential election, it is likely that the relationship will maintain its current status. It may even grow stronger if the federal government increases resources, mainly money, to support Indian self-determination.

The population data show that American Indians are not a dying relic of the past. Whatever definition of Indian is used, the population is growing at a rapid pace. A recent report stated that "between 1980 and 1984, Indians and Eskimos had a 13 percent increase in births compared to a 2 percent growth for the nation as a whole" ("Indian, Eskimo Births Rising," 1987, p. 10). Also, American Indians are diverse; each tribe has its own culture and often its own language. (Tribes prefer to be called by their tribal name, such as Cherokee, Hopi, or Crow.)

In spite of this growth, however, American Indians make up less than 1% of the total population of the United States. There are more blacks, more Hispanics, and more Asians. American Indians are truly a minority among minorities. This fact has important political, economic, and social consequences when money is allocated, when programs are developed, or when data on minority groups are collected. Often American Indians are forgotten because of their small numbers or are grouped under "Other" when data are collected and analyzed. At times it appears that American Indians are low in priority when compared to other ethnic or special-interest groups.

The 1990 census should reflect another significant increase in the number of American Indians. Even so, the number of American Indians will remain small when compared to the total U.S. population. From a national and state perspective, American Indians will remain low in priority and often will be ignored in the allocation of resources.

The economic data presented here are discouraging, especially in regard to reservations. This situation is difficult to address without economic development and the resources to make it work. Tribes on reservations do not have the resources to address economic reform adequately. It is hoped that the Bush administration will provide the support to tribes and will reverse the harm done by the Reagan administration. The social data reflect the economic situation for many American Indians and also depend on future development.

Education remains the ray of hope for economic self-sufficiency for the American Indian. Yet as noted in the discussion above, the history of formal education for the American Indian has not been impressive. Change comes slowly, especially after years of using education as a means to assimilate the American Indian into mainstream America.

The education reform movement in America since 1983 has created a great deal of awareness and concern about education, especially because the reform is politically and economically motivated. As noted above, however, it is a matter of grave concern that American Indians have hardly been mentioned in reform reports. We fear that unless they are mentioned specifically, the educational needs of American Indian students will go unmet. When American Indians are not mentioned or are grouped under "others," "minorities," or "disadvantaged," they tend to be lost, ignored, or assumed as included. The result is the same; they are forgotten. Thus there is a need to remember American Indians and to include them whenever data are collected, analyzed, reported, and used to develop programs. If this is done, and if the current educational needs of American Indians are taken into consideration before any recommendations are made, "quality" and "excellence" in education for American Indians might be enhanced in the 1990s and beyond.

REFERENCES

American Association of Colleges for Teacher Education. (1987). *Minority teacher recruitment and retention: A call for action.* Washington, DC: Author.

American Indian Policy Review Commission. (1976). *Report on Indian education.* Washington, DC: U.S. Government Printing Office.

Center for Education Statistics. (1986). *The condition of education.* Washington, DC: U.S. Government Printing Office.

Center for Education Statistics. (1987). *The American Indian in higher education, 1975–76 to 1984–85.* Washington, DC: U.S. Government Printing Office.

Deloria, V., Jr. (1975). *Legislative analysis of the federal role in Indian education.* Washington, DC: U.S. Office of Education.

Fraud in Indian country, a billion dollar betrayal. (1987, October 11), *Arizona Republic,* p. 34.

Havighurst, R. J. (1981). Indian education: Accomplishments of the last decade. *Phi Delta Kappan, 62,* 329.

Indian, Eskimo births rising; children's health improving. (1987, September 8). *Scottsdale Progress,* p. 10.

National Advisory Council on Indian Education. (1982). *Indian education: America's unpaid debt.* Washington, DC: U.S. Government Printing Office.

Minorities' share of college enrollments edges up, as number of Asian and Hispanic students soar. (1988, March 9). *Chronical of Higher Education,* pp. A33–A36.

Szasz, M. (1974). *Education and the American Indian: The road to self-determination, 1928–1973.* Albuquerque: University of New Mexico Press.

Tippeconnic, J. W., III. (1988a). *Education reform reports and the American Indian.* Unpublished manuscript.

Tippeconnic, J. W., III. (1988b). [Survey: Education of American Indians]. Unpublished raw data.

U.S. Bureau of the Census. (1973). *Census of population: 1970, American Indians.* Washington, DC: U.S. Government Printing Office.

U.S. Bureau of the Census. (1984). *American Indian areas and Alaskan native villages: 1980.* Washington, DC: U.S. Government Printing Office.

U.S. Bureau of the Census. (1985). *A statistical profile of the American Indian, Eskimo, and Aleut populations for the United States: 1980.* Washington, DC: Author.

U.S. Bureau of the Census. (1986). *1980 Census Supplementary Questionnaire Program. A statistical profile of the American Indian, Eskimo, and Aleut population.* Washington, DC: Author.

U.S. Bureau of Indian Affairs. (1984). *American Indians: U.S. Indian policy, tribes and reservations, BIA: past and present, economic development.* Washington, DC: U.S. Government Printing Office.

U.S. Bureau of Indian Affairs. (1985). *United States Department of the Interior budget justifications, F.Y. 1986.* Washington, DC: Author.

U.S. Bureau of Indian Affairs. (1987). *United States Department of the Interior budget justifications, F.Y. 1988.* Washington, DC: Author.

U.S. Department of Education. (1988). *Trends in minority enrollment in higher education, 1976–1986.* Washington, DC: Author.

U.S. Senate. (1969). *Indian education: A national tragedy—a national challenge.* Washington, DC: U.S. Government Printing Office.

Yates, A. (1987). Current status and future directions of research on the American Indian child. *American Journal of Psychiatry, 144*(9), 1135–1142.

19

Indian Education and the 1990s: Commentary on Noley and Tippeconnic

G. Mike Charleston
American Indian Education Policy Center
Pennsylvania State University

The chapters by Grayson Noley and John Tippeconnic on American Indian education complement one another. Both carry a strong message of inadequate educational services, high unemployment, and poor quality of life for American Indians and express the great need for federal and state efforts to address the issues with adequately funded, culturally relevant programs and increased research. Noley emphasizes the historical perspective of Indian education; Tippeconnic provides an overview of current American Indian demographics and statistical data detailing the ongoing "national tragedy." Both chapters recognize and discuss the special relationship of Indian tribes with the federal government based on treaties. The following is a brief summary of the social, economic, and educational conditions identified and described by Noley and Tippeconnic.

AN OVERVIEW OF THE SOCIOECONOMIC STATUS OF INDIANS

American Indians will enter the twenty-first century at the bottom of the socioeconomic ladder. Although they constitute less than 1% of the total United States population, Indians suffer an unemployment rate twice that of the total population and the highest of all minorities. Concomitant problems are poor housing and facilities and inadequate health care. Teen pregnancy, suicide, and drug and alcohol abuse rates for Indians far exceed the national averages. At the very bottom are Indians living on reservations, where economic conditions have been compared with those in Third World countries.

Although the first treaty negotiating exchange of land for educational services in 1794 authorized support for college and university tuition, the training in the earliest off-reservation boarding schools was vocational rather than academic. In the past, many American Indian students were not prepared for entry into postsecondary schools, and there are still too many Indian students who are not prepared to enter and succeed in higher education. Yet today there is a growth trend in higher education enrollment among Indians, from 76,000 in 1976 to 90,000 in 1986, including 5,000 graduate-level students and 1,000 in professional schools. These figures represent 8%

of American Indians with 4 or more years of college, in contrast to 16% of the total U.S. population.

Currently 90% of all American Indian students attend public schools in more than 3,000 school systems. This figure represents 0.8% of the country's total public school enrollment; blacks account for 16.1%, Hispanics for 8.0%, and Asians for 1.9%. The Bureau of Indian Affairs, given responsibility for Indian education by the Snyder Act of 1921, now serves only one tenth of the school-age Indian population. Off-reservation boarding schools are on the decline; they serve only 3,000 of the 450,000 American Indian students and are being considered for final closing.

The Excellence in Education reform movement of the 1980s has virtually ignored minority groups, especially the American Indian, whose achievement in public schools suffers in part because of failure by those schools to recognize and adapt to Indians' culturally ingrained learning styles. Indian students, with their intuitive, visual, and pictorial orientation, must learn to adapt to white schools, which reward auditory processing, abstract conceptualization, and language skills. Moreover, only 0.6% of the nation's teachers are American Indians. Therefore, it is not surprising that Indian students develop poor self-concepts, become uninterested in school, and are at high risk for dropping out. In fact, the American Indian and Alaskan Native dropout rate is the highest among all minorities: 29.2%, more than twice the national rate of 13.6% and far above the rates of 18.0% for Hispanics, 17.0% for blacks, 12.2% for whites, and 3.1% for Asians.

Although a recent national evaluation of federally funded Indian education programs in public schools shows progress in achievement, attendance, and parental involvement, the factors explaining the difference between successful and unsuccessful students have not been identified. There is a great need for more research in Indian education.

THE FEDERAL RELATIONSHIP

Both Noley and Tippeconnic address the relationship between Indian tribes and the federal government. Unlike other minority or ethnic groups, Indian tribes have a special relationship with the government based on more than 400 treaties enacted between 1778 and 1871. One fourth of the treaties stipulated educational services in exchange for land. Indians are entitled to both federal and state rights to education; the federal responsibilities for Indian education have been established clearly by Supreme Court decisions and federal legislation.

The federal policies regarding implementation of the treaty responsibilities and the overall "Indian problem" have run the gamut from assimilation and termination to the present policy of Indian self-determination. In practice, however, the federal government does not follow a clear policy. Through the Bureau of Indian Affairs, and to a lesser extent through other federal agencies, the government dominates virtually every aspect of the relationship with the tribes. The executive branch of the government continues to practice bureaucratic paternalism coupled with efforts to erode the sovereignty of the tribes.

For example, American Indians were not authorized to control their own schools until 1966, although Indians are experienced educators. Before 1900 they operated public school systems, neighborhood schools, and "academies" for highly motivated well-qualified students and provided the foundation for the public school systems in the state of Oklahoma. The status of Indian education in 1969 prompted a U.S. Senate indictment of it as a "failure and national tragedy."

Entry into the public school systems was encouraged by the Johnson-O'Malley Act of 1934, which authorized per capita aid to schools based on the number of American Indian students enrolled. This act provides funds for public schools on or near reservations and in historic Indian country.

At present a new structure, the tribally controlled contract school authorized by the Indian Self-Determination and Education Assistance Act of 1975, has the potential for improving Indian education with the use of curricula more harmonious with American Indian cultures. Although local control is a new concept for the posttreaty Indian, it can become a vehicle for restoring the excellence in education which was once the hallmark of American Indian school systems. The Bureau of Indian Affairs retains tight control over the operation of the tribally controlled schools, however, by controlling the budgets of the schools and the timeliness of the flow of funds. These schools are extensions of the federal Indian education programs, in which the tribes are allowed to exercise limited authority delegated by the government.

David Adams (1988) argued that the federal government followed a concrete policy in guiding federal Indian education. He identified the Protestant ideology, the civilization–savage paradigm, and the white hunger for Indian land as mutually supporting and defining an education policy aimed at assimilating Indians into white society. The Protestant ideology contributed the definition of civilization to which savage Indians were to be converted through schooling. It also provided the moral justification and the rationale for taking Indian land to accommodate the growth of the young United States. The goal of schooling was to assimilate Indians into the white society as civilized individual citizens who needed only modest amounts of farmland. Tribal organizations, native languages and cultures, and tribal land characterized the savage life-style.

COMMENTS ON PRESENT AND FUTURE
CONDITIONS FOR INDIANS

The historical perspective on Indian education carried to the present day by Noley and the demographic evidence of Indians' present status provided by Tippeconnic suggest that little has changed in the last 100 years. Adams (1988) described Indian education during the period from 1880 to 1900, but I see validity in using the Protestant ideology, the civilization–savage paradigm, and the hunger for control of resources and land to describe the social condition of Indians in the present decade and into the 1990s. The basic Indian education policies being implemented today are quite similar to those in effect a century ago. With few exceptions, the goal of public and federal Indian education is the same today as it was then: to assimilate Indians into white society.

The critical distinction now is made between "ethnicity" and "tribal membership." The continued existence of the special relationship between the federal government and the tribes depends on the existence of the tribes as functioning sovereign governments. The relationship does not exist between individual Indians and the federal government. Thus when an Indian loses the ability or the opportunity to participate as a member of the tribal society and as a citizen of the tribal government, all that remains is classification as a member of an ethnic minority. The identity and the association with the tribal group no longer exist; the Indian outside the tribe is merely an individual assimilated into the group of "other minority," with no special relationship to the government.

White society in general has a difficult time understanding Indians' drive to maintain tribal identity, association, and allegiance. Such an effort by Indians is contradictory to the Protestant ideology; it is considered un-American. Present-day public schools not only ignore the existence of tribal society and government but actively teach Indian children the virtues of shedding tribal membership and joining the mainstream—assimilating into white society as ordinary American citizens with an ethnic heritage. Those who refuse to assimilate and who stubbornly maintain cultural, linguistic, social, and governmental ties with their tribes suffer discrimination. They do not receive the same educational opportunities as other people unless they are willing to conform to the values, learning styles, social behaviors, and cultural expectations of the white society. They must comform to the definition of modern civilization, which generally excludes active membership in a sovereign tribal government and a tribal society.

The stakes are high. If Indian people assimilate by becoming mere members of an ethnic minority, the tribal governments will have no citizens and will cease to exist. The contest for final resolution of the "Indian problem," the existence of Indians, will be won by the federal government. In such a case, justification for funding special Indian education and health programs based on treaty rights and obligations to the tribes could be challenged. The remaining Indian lands and resources held in trust by the federal government would be taken as public property.

Yet Indian people have not relinquished their tribal affiliations and assimilated into white society in spite of the hardships that have resulted from their stubborn determination. It is far better to be at the bottom of the socioeconomic ladder and to exist as a people than to climb the ladder at the expense of one's existence. Many more Indian people are learning to deal with the federal government and the white society in more effective ways. They are obtaining the graduate degrees, the qualifications, and the skills needed to improve the quality of life on reservations and in Indian communities while maintaining allegiance to their tribal governments and tribal societies. Some tribes are establishing relationships between their governments and those of other countries in order to enhance their economic opportunities in the world market.

Education is a critical element in the future existence of tribal life. History has shown that the white society uses education as a means to accomplish the assimilation of Indians. Yet Indians historically have recognized the need for education and fully understand the benefits of an educated population. Education was an important factor in many of the treaties. Now the tribes must exercise control over Indian education.

In Canada the situation existing between the First Nations (Indian tribes) and the federal government and the white society is similar to that in the United States, but the First Nations have conducted and completed their own national review of First Nations' education (Charleston, 1988b). As a result of this review the Assembly of First Nations made a strong "Declaration of First Nations Jurisdiction over Education" (Charleston, 1988a). The Declaration calls for significant reform of the relationship between the First Nations of Canada and the federal government, including repeal of paternalistic laws and elimination of bureaucratic practices and policies that hinder the free exercise of local First Nations' jurisdiction over education. The Declaration proposes the elimination of the Department of Indian Affairs and Northern Development (the Canadian equivalent of the Bureau of Indian Affairs) and the creation of a Ministry of State for First Nations Relations which will deal with the First Nations on a government-to-government basis consistent with the treaties.

The future of Indians as members of tribal societies in the United States rests with the ability of the tribes to exercise their sovereignty and to maintain a population of members. Education continues to be a key factor in the struggle. It can work either for or against the tribe, depending on who controls the educational system and thereby determines whether or not the educational system promotes assimilation of Indians into white society and out of Indian society. In the 1990s, the Indian tribes in the United States must address the issues of jurisdiction and government-to-government relationship with the federal government in a much stronger and more cohesive manner than in this decade. The potentially disastrous effects of the present massive public education of Indian students under the control of the white society must be considered and must be challenged successfully. Our people must be able to climb the socioeconomic ladder to improve the quality of life in our communities while enhancing and developing the strength of our tribal societies.

REFERENCES

Adams, D. W. (1988). Fundamental considerations: The deep meaning of Native American schooling, 1880–1900. *Harvard Educational Review, 58*(1), 1–28.

Charleston, G. M. (1988a). *Tradition and education: Towards a vision of our future. A declaration of First Nations jurisdiction over education*. Ottawa, Canada: Assembly of First Nations.

Charleston, G. M. (Ed.). (1988b). *Tradition and education: Towards a vision of our future* (Vol. 1–3). Ottawa, Canada: Assembly of First Nations.

20

Postscript–The Road Ahead in American Race Relations: Challenges for the 1990s

Gail E. Thomas
Department of Sociology
Texas A&M University

Gauging the nature of American race relations, the significance of race, and the degree of racial progress has a long-standing tradition in the social sciences which can be traced back to the work of Robert Park (1950). The contributors to this volume have extended that tradition by assessing these issues in the 1980s and making projections for the 1990s. In doing so they have focused on a variety of issues from different perspectives and with different styles of presentation. However, despite these differences, the contributors unanimously conveyed the message that *the road ahead in American race relations is long and arduous.*

The contributors have also dispelled the mythology held by some that affirmative action has taken care of minorities to the point that race has little or no significance in contemporary American society. To the contrary, the present findings suggest that racial stratification and racial inequality have changed in nature rather than in significance—from a more overt to a more covert and subtle form of racial isolation and inequality. The findings also indicate that America is regressing in its efforts and success in promoting equality of educational, occupational, and economic opportunity for its citizens of color.

In the 1960s and 1970s relative gains were made in the educational and occupational achievement of blacks, Hispanics, and, to a lesser extent, American Indians. The variety of government-sponsored programs and practices that helped facilitate these gains largely emphasized improving the human-capital stock of minorities. Major studies like James Coleman's (1966) *Equality of Educational Opportunity* formed the basis for government intervention during this time. Coleman's study and subsequent government efforts complemented the human-capital approach and assumed that the major resolution to the problem of racial inequality entailed educationally upgrading and reforming the nation's black and brown citizens. Further, it was held that an investment in the latter would help assimilate these groups more effectively into American society and increase their chances of upward mobility (Kaplan, 1977).

The major conclusions by the authors of this volume pose a serious challenge to proponents of the human-capital and deficit perspectives. The present findings highlight the roles of (a) difference and multicultural theories in explaining racial stratification, (b) structural and technological factors in explaining the relationship of minorities to the means of production and ownership in society, and (c) formal and informal institutional networks in shaping the status attainment and achievement of minorities. Thus, collectively, the dynamic interplay of culture, technology, economics, and normative ideology underlie and explain current U.S. race relations and racial stratification.

In broader terms, the typologies of two social scientists—Lloyd Warner (1936) and Pierre van den Berghe (1978)—provide bases for explaining the structural relationships between the dominant group and American blacks, American Hispanics, and American Indians. Warner proposed that white America has a status hierarchy in which its citizens move from lower to middle to upper status. He noted that blacks also have a status system, which is characterized by clear limitations such that those blacks who reach the highest status in black society cannot attain such status in white America. Warner subsequently concluded that the relationships *within* the white and black communities were relations of *class,* while the relationship *between* them was one of *caste* based on power differentials and on the control of resources, which favored whites.

In a more recent assessment of U.S. race relations, van den Berghe (1978) constructed a typology of race relations that illustrates how race relations in modern industrial societies shifted from a *paternalistic* to a *competitive* mode. Using the United States as an example, van den Berghe noted that race relations between blacks and whites in the agrarian South were based on a master–servant model whereby the division of labor was rigidly ascribed. In addition, racial roles were generally well-defined, understood, accepted, and solidified around paternalistic norms of subservience. Coupled with this model was conspicuous evidence of racial isolation and of legally sanctioned segregation. Thus race relations between blacks and whites were quite paternalistic in pre-industrial America.

By contrast, van den Berghe argued that in post-Civil-War and industrialized America, competitive race relations replaced the previous paternalistic mode. As a result, the master–slave relationship between whites and blacks dissipated under this more modern system with the abolition of slavery and the subsequent ban on legal segregation. van den Berghe noted that this system was a by-product of industrialization and mass modernization. It required that social roles and statuses be assigned more on the basis of competitive and universalistic standards than on the basis of ascriptive and other particularistic criteria.

van den Berghe concluded that his competitive typology characterized the nature of U.S. race relations in postindustrial society. On the surface one might argue that the competitive construct is even more applicable in contemporary high-tech American society. However, the conclusions by David Swinton (Chapter 12), Edna Bonacich (Chapter 13), and John Tippeconnic (Chapter 18) indicate that blacks, Hispanics, and especially American Indians have not achieved "competitive" status relative to whites in terms of political leadership, influence, and economic power. This observation, coupled with the present regression toward social and economic decline for these underrepresented minorities and an increase in racial conservatism and racial isolation (Farley & Allen, 1987; Orfield, 1987; Schuman, Steeh, & Bobo, 1985), suggests that in some respects, current-day U.S. race relations more accurately mirror a modern form of paternalism rather than van den Berghe's competitive model.

Warner's (1936) notion of a caste system is also applicable to present-day U.S. minorities—especially to those who occupy lower and upper-middle class statuses.

William Wilson's (1987) description of the plight of the black "underclass" is an example of the former. Wilson (p. 9) described this class as "the most disadvantaged segment of the black urban community . . . who are outside of the American occupational system." Jomills Braddock's (Chapter 7) portrayal of the limited mobility of blacks to coaching positions in the NFL and Davis and Watson's (1982) description of black life and the lack of mobility of blacks in corporate America are two examples of the color-line and castelike restraints that educated upper class minorities face.[1]

CHALLENGES FOR THE 1990s

Marger (1985) correctly noted that the likelihood is great that race and ethnicity will continue in the future to be the sources of dominant–subordinate relations and societal conflict. Also, while quite engaging, it is unforeseeable—at least in the coming decade—that Bonacich's (Chapter 13) proposal for a redistribution of wealth among the haves and the have-nots will take place. Therefore, the major challenge for the coming decade will be to turn the clock forward in the direction of more progressive and relatively more competitive race relations. I will conclude with a number of alternatives for meeting this challenge.

First, all Americans must view it as in their vested interest to improve race and human relations as well as the social and economic status of underrepresented racial minorities. This is especially true in light of the projected numerical shifts among the races in the coming decades. Between 1990 and the year 2080, approximately 60% of the projected national population growth will come from the black and Hispanic populations (Spencer, 1984). At the same time, the white population is projected to decline by 22%. Eighty percent of the new entrants into the labor force by the end of the 1990s will come from racial minorities, immigrants, and women. Thus, it is clear that the vested interest of society will be better served by maximizing the skills and employment opportunities for these groups. Accepting this fact is an initial step in the right direction. However, it is equally important for Americans (especially those in key authority and leadership positions) to develop a greater sense of moral consciousness regarding the unjust nature and severe consequences of racial inequality and discrimination. Bonacich's paper (Chapter 13) is as much an appeal to Americans to manifest this consciousness as it is a call for major social and economic reform.

Minorities must at the same time assume greater responsibility for their own status and future in American society. More important, it is in the vested interest of these groups to coalesce, sponsor, and support one another. Reich (1981) noted that in the 1930s organized labor and blacks cooperated on an unprecedented scale, to their mutual advantage. As a result, they were successful in making major labor market gains. Similar progress was made for blacks and other minorities during the civil rights movement. However, desegregation of major American institutions, the upward mobility and in some instances cooptation of a segment of the middle class among racial minorities, and the simultaneous expansion of the minority poor have resulted in polarization within and between these groups.

Despite the real or imagined status differentials among underrepresented racial minorities, Bonacich (Chapter 13) vividly makes the point that from the standpoint of a lack of ownership and control of major resources, they [we] *are all in the same*

---

[1]Art Shell, formerly an assistant coach and player for the Los Angeles Raiders, became the first black coach in the history of the NFL on October 3, 1989.

boat. Thus, blacks and other underrepresented minorities might do well to reflect on Bonacich's important observation and adopt a global perspective in doing so. It is also important that the intelligentsia among underrepresented racial minorities develop a broad and adequate knowledge of worldwide systems of racial inequality and establish good communication and working relationships with other disadvantaged minority groups worldwide.

U.S. blacks and Hispanics might also learn from the American Indians' ideology of self-determination. Mike Charleston (Chapter 19) expressed this sentiment on behalf of American Indians by noting that "it is far better to be at the bottom of the socioeconomic ladder and to exist as a people than to climb the ladder at the expense of one's existence" (p. 262). Most of the younger generation of middle-class blacks (and other racial minorities) who were not participants in but were beneficiaries of the civil rights movement especially need to be reminded of Mike Charleston's point.

Many of today's minority YUPPIES (i.e., young urban professionals) lack the knowledge and/or appreciation of their predecessors who risked or sacrificed their lives so that future generations could obtain education, housing, and employment in a desegregated rather than a segregated society. Thus, it is imperative that middle-class minority professionals (a) develop a consciousness and commitment that extends beyond themselves, and (b) demonstrate their appreciation for their cultural heritage and for those who made it possible for them to gain access and some mobility in mainstream American institutions. These individuals must also pool their economic resources, take greater economic risks, make more prudent economic investments, and become more creative and successful entrepreneurs. Self-determination and empowerment for racial minorities are largely contingent upon these latter factors and the confidence of minorities in their ability to become "the masters of their own fate."

Second, Americans must face the reality of the expanding class of the urban poor (which is largely minority) and its implications for all citizens. Prior to improving the human capital of this disadvantaged class, these individuals must be given a chance to live and provided the opportunity to make a meaningful contribution to society. Presently, drugs, alcohol, minority-on-minority crime, poor health, and substandard living conditions negate these possibilities. Thus, meeting the needs of the urban poor must assume a greater national priority if the nation is to more effectively utilize all of its human resources and establish safer and healthier cities for its citizens.

The establishment by the federal government of a national task force on social and economic reform for this specific purpose will be necessary. Racial minorities who qualify as spokespersons for the urban poor, and who have gained the respect and confidence of this disenfranchised population, should be given major leadership roles and adequate representation on such a task force. In addition, national and statewide hearings that will permit the urban poor and grassroots representatives from these communities to articulate their needs should be held systematically and taken seriously.

A third alternative is to further strengthen and expand affirmative action programs. An important prerequisite will be to identify those programs that have been most effective. Also, securing greater support for and greater understanding of affirmative action efforts will be needed. Jenkins and Solomon (1987) and others (Feagin & Feagin, 1978) noted that many white Americans view affirmative action for minorities as a zero-sum game in which they lose and minorities win.[2] Thus, what might be

---

[2]Feagin and Feagin (1978) and Davis and Watson (1982) reported that better educated minorities suffer greater discrimination in job access, promotions, and wages than do less educated blacks.

useful is the formulation in lay terms and the systematic dissemination of a national report card reflecting major indicators of minority and majority group achievement (*with minority groups clearly defined and disaggregated*).

Fourth, individuals who are committed to promoting better race and human relations and racial progress might consider investing more heavily in informal and formal social networks as a method of enhancing communication, understanding, and trust. This approach is more micro and interpersonal relative to the macro and broader-based proposals previously suggested. However, the impact of informal "old boy" networks in the political, educational, and economic arenas cannot be overestimated. In Chapter 7, Jomills Braddock notes the importance of such networks for blacks' gaining access to coaching careers. Similarly, Crain (1970) and Davis and Watson (1982) documented the importance of minorities' being involved in predominantly white informal networks for their overall job attainment and job promotions.

I personally recall the successful networking efforts of one black male—Dr. Will B. Scott—in assisting his leading black undergraduate students in gaining access to the nation's white graduate schools. Dr. Scott is not only committed to his goal but knows the importance of building friendships and referral networks and of gaining the trust and respect of key white administrators and faculty in these institutions. As a result he is more successful than any single individual that I know in facilitating the graduate school access of black undergraduates (myself included) in the social sciences. Thus, efforts to initiate and sustain informal and formal inter- and intraracial networks in the educational as well as the occupational and political arenas should offer high dividends.

Finally, social scientists and students of race relations in the coming decade must meet the challenge of better documenting the newer and more subtle forms of racial stratification and racial inequality and more effectively conveying this information to diverse audiences (i.e., to lay persons, practitioners, and scholars). Ogbu (Chapter 1) argues that in present-day America, expressive forms of racial stratification remain after the more traditional and more instrumental barriers have been removed. Regarding the former, Myrdal (1944, p. 998) argued that the most important prerequisite for progress by American blacks entailed a change in white Americans' attitudes and values to a more favorable disposition toward and more equitable treatment of blacks.

Schuman et al. (1985) reported that although the racial attitudes of whites moved steadily toward favoring racial equality between 1960 and 1980, whites are less supportive of the implementation of targeted programs for minorities. Research is therefore needed to assess the attitudes of whites toward affirmative action and targeted programs for minorities. In addition, research is needed on (a) the experiences of middle-class minorities in predominantly white educational, occupational, and social institutions, and (b) the perceptions and attitudes of minorities and their majority counterparts about the presence and status of minorities in predominantly white settings.

In studying black life in the corporate world, Davis and Watson (1982) found that black employees in these settings experienced psychological strain from subtle forms of racist attitudes and practices. Blacks within these nontraditional settings are compelled to "fit" and "buy into" the norms and life-style of corporate America. Those who do so often encounter great estrangement between themselves, their families, and their communities and derive no corresponding increase in comfort and benefit from their predominantly white work settings (Davis & Watson, 1982, p. 26). Those who are not willing to buy into the folkways and mores of these corporate settings frequently conclude that the price is too high and seek alternative employment.

Future comparative research should address the perceived costs and benefits to members of minority and majority groups in corporate and other highly competitive educational and work settings. In addition, inter- and intraracial forums (like the 1988 conference on Race and Ethnic Relations in the 1990s held at Texas A&M University) to discuss and assess the status and conditions of American race relations should be convened more frequently and more systematically. These forums should extend beyond colleges and universities into the local residential and political communities where race relations and racial policy formulation take place.

A number of additional alternatives, proposals, and challenges for the coming 1990s have been mentioned by some of the contributors to this volume. A number of others could be noted here. Rather than extend the list, it is important to emphasize that *greater commitment* of minorities themselves *and* of the American public will be needed to implement any one or a combination of the proposals described here and elsewhere. Commitment to greater equality of educational and economic opportunity coupled with a commitment of greater resources and more effective minority and majority leadership in all institutions of American society will constitute the major challenges for the coming decade. Also, viewing the long road ahead in American race relations as a *national challenge* rather than as a statewide or a minority challenge might help propel us forward in the 1990s. Finally, viewing the task ahead as an opportunity and an investment rather than as a problem or a liability will be important. In emphasizing the importance of investing and assigning high premium to human resources, Karl Marx (1958) noted that, "if [a thing] be useless, the labor contained in it is useless" (p. 24). Therefore, how we view and invest in underrepresented minorities and human resources in general will certainly chart our course and outcomes in the 1990s and coming decades.

REFERENCES

Coleman, J. (1966). *Equality of educational opportunity.* Washington, DC: U.S. Government Printing Office.

Crain, R. L. (1970). School integration and occupational achievement of Negroes. *American Journal of Sociology, 75,* 563–606.

Davis, G., & Watson, G. (1982). *Black life in corporate America.* Garden City, NY: Anchor Press/Doubleday.

Farley, R., & Allen, W. (1987). *The color line and the quality of life in America.* New York: Russell Sage.

Feagin, J. R., & Feagin, C. B. (1978). *Discrimination American style: Institutional racism and sexism.* Englewood Cliffs, NJ: Prentice-Hall.

Jenkins, R., & Solomos, J. (1987). *Racism and equal opportunity policies in the 1980s.* Cambridge, MA: Cambridge University Press.

Kaplan, R. H. (1977). *American minorities and economic opportunity.* Itasca, IL: Peacock.

Marger, M. N. (1985). *Race and ethnic relations: American and global perspectives.* Belmont, CA: Wadsworth.

Marx, K. (1958). Selected works (Vol. 2). In G. Duncan (Ed.), *Marx and Mill: Two views of social conflict and social harmony* (1973). Cambridge, MA: Cambridge University Press.

Myrdal, G. (1944). *An American dilemma.* New York: Harper & Row.

Orfield, G. (1987). *School segregation in the 1980s: Trends in the states and metropolitan areas.* Report by the National School Desegregation Project to the Joint Center for Political Studies. Chicago: University of Chicago Press.

Park, R. E. (1950). *Race and culture.* Glencoe, IL: Free Press.

Reich, M. (1981). *Racial inequality.* Princeton, NJ: Princeton University Press.

Schuman, H., Steeh, C., & Bobo, L. (1985). *Racial attitudes in America: Trends and interpretations.* Cambridge, MA: Harvard University Press.

Spencer, G. (1984). *Projections of the population of the United States by age, sex, and race: 1983 to 2080.* Washington, DC: U.S. Department of Commerce, Bureau of the Census.

van den Berghe, P. L. (1978). *Race and racism: A comparative perspective.* New York: Wiley.

Warner, W. L. (1936). American class and caste. *American Journal of Sociology, 42,* 234–237.

Wilson, W. J. (1987). *The truly disadvantaged.* Chicago: University of Chicago Press.

Wirth, L. (1945). The problem of minority groups. In R. Linton (Ed.), *The science of man in the world crisis* (pp. 347–372.). New York: Columbia University Press.

Index

Academics (*see* Teachers)
Accommodation, 15
Acculturation programs, 18, 135
Achievement motivation, 23–24
Acting white, 29, 56
Adams v. Richardson/Bennett (1973), 38, 49
Administrators, minority, 61, 81, 83
Admissions criteria, 38, 99
Adolescents:
  oppositional identity and, 28
  poverty and, 71
Affective changes, 59
Affiliation rule, 6
Affirmative action programs, 9, 20, 31, 129, 200, 207,
  enforcement of, 182-183
  expansion of, 268-269
  immigrants and, 129
  minority career options, 83, 129
  mythology of, 265
Alaskan Indians, 245, 249
Allotment Act (1887), 201
Ambivalence, 25–26
American Board of Commissioners for Foreign
  Missions, 242
American College Testing (ACT), 40
American Dilemma, An, (Myrdal), 35
American Educational Research Association, 246
American Indian Movement (AIM), 36
American Indian Religious Freedom Act (1978),
  219
American Indians (*see* Native Americans; *specific
  tribes*)
Amnesty program, 132
Apache Nation, 220–222
Asian-Americans, 35–36
  concentration of, 134
  discrimination and, 163
  population, 79
Asian refugees, 129
Assimilation, 11, 200
  academic success and, 27
  bilingual education and, 134
  denial of, 15
  income and, 143
  Indians and, 253, 262
  reality of, 162

Asylum, for refugees, 131–132
Athletics, black exploitation in, 202

Baccalaureate degrees, 88
  persistence in attaining, 41
  public school teachers without, 69-70
Baseball, 106
Bilingual education, 129, 134, 235
Birthrates (*see specific group*)
Black(s), 152
  alternative career options, 100
  assets, 193, 195
  as assistant coaches, 114
  birthrates, 67, 96
  college attendance rates, 40–41
  corporate world and, 129, 173–175, 180–183,
    211–212, 269–270
  distribution of income, 171
  doctoral degrees, 43–46
  economic progress for, 167–185
  elementary and secondary students, 79, 85–86
  historical disadvantages, 181–185
  in labor market, 175–179
  lesser educational attainment, 53
  median income of, 139–143
  middle class, 203
  migration of, 67
  mobility of professionals, 89
  NFL managerial recruitment, 112, 115
  occupational distribution, 9, 192–193
  oppositional frame of reference, 16–19
  parents' role, 86
  peer culture, 28
  poverty rate for, 74, 97
  public assistance programs, 147
  as racial caste, 6
  status system, 266
  structural barriers, 211–212
  teachers, 46, 69–70, 79–91
  undergraduate degrees, 88
  unemployed, 39, 152, 176–179
  whites' treatment of, 7–19
  (*See also specific issues*)
Black Muslim movement, 16
Boarding schools, American indian, 242–245, 253
Borders, control of, 132
Boundary maintenance devices, 37–38

Boxing, 106
Brown v. Board of Education of Topeka, Kansas
    (1954), 38, 68, 80, 90, 167
Bureau of Indian Affairs (BIA), 219, 225, 229,
    239, 243–244, 246, 249, 256, 261
Bury My Heart at Wounded Knee (Brown), 229
Business ownership, 129, 173–175, 180–183,
    211–212
    (*See also* Capitalism)
Busing, 80

Cambodians, 131
Canada, Department of Indian Affairs, 262
Capital:
    humans as, 180, 183
    white control of, 195
Capitalism, 35
    decline of, 212
    European, 199–200
    racism and, 188, 196–200, 209
Careers, 86, 99
Carlisle Indian School, 242, 252
Caste system, 6, 15, 19, 266
Center for Education Statistics, U.S.
    Department of Education, 74
Central America, illegal migrants from, 131, 163
Certification standards, for teachers, 60, 80–82,
    88, 90
Cherokee Nation, 225, 242
Chickasaw Nation, 242
Choctaw Nation, 242
Cities:
    inner-city poverty, 70–71, 74–75
    in 1980, 71
    in 1967, 67–80
    nonwhite majorities, 66
    resegregation of, 74–75
Civic culture, 128–129, 162
Civilization Act (1819), 241
Civil rights, 30
    enforcement, 182–183
    nondiscrimination focus, 180–181
    retrogressions, 37, 161
    U.S. policies, 9, 96, 98
Civil rights movement, 16, 35–36, 128, 182
    assessment of, 211, 213
    economics and, 168
    immigration laws and, 162
Civil Rights Act (1964) Title VII, 9, 81, 83, 168
Civil War, black education after, 22
Class (*see* Social class)
Classroom segregation, 97
Clientship (Uncle Tomming), 14, 26–27

Coaching, blacks and, 106–119
Collective struggle, 14
Colleges and universities, 85
    admission and selection policies, 48
    attendance rates, 40–42
    blacks and, 9, 20, 49, 58, 106
    campus racism, 49, 89–90, 95
    economic standing and, 181
    historically black (HBCUs), 49
    Indians and, 225, 259
    oppositional identity and, 28
    predominantly white, 87
    teacher education by, 82–83
Colonialism, 35
Color, prejudice toward, 162
Color Line and the Quality of Life in America,
    The (Allen and Farley), 213
Community colleges, 41, 254
Community relations, 86, 89, 97
Competency testing, 80–82, 90, 99
Competition, norm of, 108, 214, 266
Congress for Racial Equality (CORE), 36
Congressional Black Caucus, 108
Contract Schools, Indian, 244–245
Counseling programs, 237
Creek Nation, 242
Crimes, in ghettos, 70
Cubans:
    means-tested transfer income, 147
    median income of, 139–143
    refugees, 128
    rise in median family income, 142
Cultural frame of reference, 15, 27, 56
Cultural inversion, 16–19
Current money income, family's wealth, 138

Dark Ghetto (Clark), 70
Death rate, for persons under 45 years, 195
Decision-making, control of, 37
Declaration of First Nations Jurisdiction over
    Education, 262
Declaration of Human Rights, 132
Democratic ideal, tensions of, 127
Demographic imperatives, 50
Department of the Interior, 254
    (*See also* Bureau of Indian Affairs)
Desegregation, 22, 36, 49, 73, 108
Disabled, Indian vs. Western beliefs, 229
Discrimination, 180–181
    on basis of nationality, 128–129
    disillusionment and, 24–26
    Indian belief systems and, 219–231
    in sports, 106–107

Discrimination (*Cont.*):
    within-school treatment, 23
Disharmony, in Indian cultures, 225–226
Disillusionment, 24–26
Doctoral degrees, minorities and, 43–46, 49, 58–59
Dropout rates, 40, 244–245, 254–255

Economics:
    academic performance and, 98
    antiblack violence and, 12
    attainment and, 76
    black progress, 167–185
    black trends, 173–179
    black-white gaps, 209
    capitalism, 35, 188, 196–200, 209, 212
    commitment to inequality, 198
    disparities in, 39
    family and, 141
    inequities, 137, 168–180, 182, 198
    Native Americans, 250–251, 256
    needs-based equality, 70
    survival strategies, 14
Education, 88
    black-white differentials in, 164
    changes in government policy, 98
    costs of 39, 42–43, 48
    decision makers, 88–89
    demographic imbalances, 79
    denial of equal opportunity, 20–24
    disillusionment and, 24–26
    employment prediction and, 66
    as equalizer, 53
    federal policy since 1967, 96
    history of Indian, 219, 240, 242, 252, 261
    immigrants, 134
    industrial, 22
    inequalities in, 57
    job ceiling and, 9
    linear vs. circular, 230
    local control, 239, 245
    multicultural, 86
    progressive movement, 243–244
    religious equality in, 230
    segregated, 22
    sociology of, 66
    states' rights in, 253
    teacher program, 87–88
    white-oriented, 29–30
    (*See also* Schools)
Education for All Handicapped Children Act
        (1975), 229
Educational reform (*see* Reform movements)
Egalitarianism, ideology of, 3–31

Elementary schools, 69, 79, 85–86
Elitism, 214
Employer sanctions, 132–133
Employment:
    black-owned business, 174
    black vs. white teachers, 80–81
    demographic factors, 175–176
    education and, 22–23
    fair policies, 167
    geographic location and, 156
    illegal immigrants and, 130
    Indian, 251
    job ceilings, 7–9, 14–15, 54
    mainstream, 14
    minority career options, 80, 83
    occupational segregation, 192–193
    power in, 117
    social networks, 269
    status of family heads, 149–155
    training programs, 180
    wage rate factor, 177–179
    (*See also* Labor force)
English language, Indians and, 233–236
Entertainment of, 14
Equal opportunity, 36, 49, 128, 168, 182
Equality of Educational Opportunity (Coleman),
        68, 265
Eskimos, 245, 249, 256
Ethnic heritage programs, 129, 135
Ethnicity, 261
    gross inequalities, 190
    Native American identity, 237
    separatism, 135
    societal conflict, 267
    (*See also specific group*)
Exploitation:
    black responses, 4, 7, 10–20, 54–55
    of colonized workers, 199–200
    of poor by rich, 196–200, 209
    theory, 35
    of women of color, 187–189

Faculty (*see* Teachers)
Family:
    Bureau of the Census definition of, 138
    differentials, 139–141
    headship poverty rates and, 146
Federal legislation (*see specific acts*)
Federal government, as patron, 14
Federalist Papers (Jay), 127
Fellowships, 91
Female-headed families, 61, 143, 152–154, 193
    (*See also* Women)

Financial aid, racial inequalities, 40–43, 48
First Nations, Canada, 262
Football, managerial recruitment in, 105–119
Forbes, 191
Foreign-born persons, in U.S., 133
Foreign policy, refugee status, 131
Freedom, defined, 128

Garvey movement, 16
Gatekeeping methods, 37–38, 82, 99
Gender:
    occupational segregation, 192
    research, 98
    (*See also* Women)
Ghettos, inner-city, 22, 67–68, 70, 96
Graduate education, 41–48, 58, 246, 262
    assistantships, 43, 48
    declines in, 49, 58
    Indian people in, 246
    (*See also specific level*)
Grant's Peace Policy, 242
Great Depression, antiblack violence, 12
Great Society programs, 157, 253
Growing Up Poor (Williams and Kornblum), 71–72

Handicaps, 229
Harmony, Indian beliefs, 225
Healing practices, worship and, 220, 234
Health, American Indian beliefs, 228
Health care, insufficient, 97
High school, completion rates, 40, 255
Higher education (*see* Colleges and universities;
        Teachers)
Hispanics:
    college attendance rates, 40–41
    competency tests and, 82
    concentration of, 134
    dispersion of, 130
    diversity of, 166
    doctoral degrees, 43–46
    educational attainment, 40–41, 137
    expropriation, 35
    as generic term, 163
    political visibility of, 157
    racial isolation, 73
    socioeconomic disparities for, 149
    student population, 79
    unemployment, 39
Historically Black Colleges and Universities,
        (HBCUs), 83, 88, 101
History, revision of, 16

Homelessness, 95–96
Hopi Nation, 222, 225, 227, 252
Housing:
    discimination in, 67–68
    Indian, 252
    inner-city, 71
    public, 96
    substandard, 97
Human capital enhancement programs, 181, 183,
        265
Hustling, 14

Illness, Indian beliefs, 224
Immigrants:
    absorptive capacity of society, 129
    concentration of, 134
    employer sanctions, 131
    European analogy, 164
    minorities, 6
    1965 changes in laws of, 128
    policy reform, 129
    state interests and, 133
    welfare income, 148
Immigration and Naturalization Service, 164
Immigration Control and Reform Act (1986), 130,
        163
Immortality, Indian belief in, 223–224
In-service training programs, 86, 101
Incentives, inequality and, 190, 196–200, 241
Income, 138
    business ownership and, 174
    crime rate and, 70
    demographic characteristics and, 140–142
    differentials by type of headship, 143
    education and, 58
    excessive differences in, 61, 171, 180, 189–
        190
    packaging, 149–155
    trends in disparities, 169–171
    wage rate factor, 177–179
Income maintenance programs, 146
Indentured servitude, 199–200
Indian Education Act (1972), 239, 244–245, 254
Indian Education Programs, BIA, 246
Indians (*see* Native Americans)
Indian Reorganization Act, 243–244
Indian Self-Determination and Education
        Assistance Act (1975), 244, 261
Individualism, mythology of, 3–31
Indochina, refugees, 128
Industrial education, 20, 22, 39, 55
Inequality, racial, 4, 173, 179–183, 189–196, 201
    (*See also specific issue*)

Inner-city schools, 65–76
Institutional racism, 35–50, 164
Integration, 15
Isolation, 97

Japanese American Citizens League (JACL), 36
Job ceilings, 7–9, 14–15, 54
Job training, 39
Johnson-O'Malley Act (1934), 239, 243–244, 260

Kerner Commission (1968), 36, 65–67, 70, 73–76, 95, 98
Klamath Nation, 253

Labor force:
    ascriptive vs. meritocratic, 155
    black participation, 175–181
    economic status, 151
    immigration and, 132–133
    new entrants, 267
    temporary workers and, 163
    rates, 211–212
Land acquisition, Indians and, 201, 240–243, 252, 259–260
Land of the Free, The, 30
Language:
    cultural inversion, 18
    Indian, 253
Latinos:
    assets, 193, 195
    middle class, 203
    occupational distribution, 192–193
    (See also Hispanics)
Learning, black vs. white, 56
Letters from an American Farmer (St. John Crevecoeus), 127
Linear acculturation, 18

Marriott Corporation, 187–188
Means-tested programs, eligibility rules, 148
Median family income, 139–143
Medicine, Indian vs. Western, 222, 224
Meharry Medical College, 49
Melting Pot, The (Zangwill), 127
Melting pot image, 127, 162
Menominee Nation, 253
Mentoring, 85–87
Meriam Report, 243–244
Meritocratic ethic, 155, 204

Mexican-Americans:
    families headed by single persons, 146
    means-tested transfer income, 147
    poverty rates, 145
    median income of, 139–143
    (See also Hispanics)
Mexican American Political Action Committee (MAPA), 36
Middle Class:
    college-educated, 23
    contradictions, 205–206
    instability of, 212
    inequality and, 201
    minorities, 268
Middle Class Black Families (Landry), 213
Migration:
    illegal, 129–130, 134
    Native American, 235
    rural to urban, 96
Minorities:
    business ownership by, 173–175
    caste system, 6, 15, 19, 266
    coalitions, 165
    college-educated, 39–48, 57
    co-optation of, 38
    diversity of, 155
    economic bifurcation within, 163
    economic progress since 1960, 137
    family well-being, 1970-1985, 138–149
    graduate education, 41–48
    human-capital stock, 265
    immigrant vs. involuntary 6, 54
    increasing, 155
    mainstreaming of, 165
    middle class, 201–204, 268
    nonminority family incomes, 140
    population trends for, 74
    political participation of, 157–158
    poverty of, 70–72, 143–149
    reduced labor market for men, 154–155
    school-age population, 61, 79
    screened out of teaching, 60
    socioeconomic differentials among, 156
    stereotypes, 50
    unequal labor market experiences, 152
    work force, 91
    racial stratification and, 6
    welfare dependence, 146
    (See also specific ethnic/racial group)
Minority contractors, set-asides, 129
Minority Mentorship Project, 85–86, 101
Moakley-DeConcini bill, 131

Mobility, limitations on, 39
Monroe Doctrine, 163
Morehouse College, 49
Multicultural education, training in, 86, 88, 237

Nation, The (Kallen), 128
National Advisory Commission on Civil Disorders, 36
National Association for Advancement of Colored Persons (NAACP), 22, 36
National Basketball Association (NBA), 106
National Commission on Excellence in Education (NCEE), 82
National Conference of American Indians (NCAI), 36
National Conference on Black Lawyers, 108
National Education Association, 85
National Football League (NFL), 106, 115
National Football Players Association, 108
National Indian Education Association, 246
National-origin quotas, abolition of, 128-129
National Teacher Examination (NTE), 81, 88
National Urban League (NUL), 36
Nation at Risk, A, (National Commission on Excellence in Education), 82, 100
Nation Prepared, A (Carnegie Forum on Education and the Economy), 83, 100
Nation-state system, border control, 132
Native Americans, 201, 242
    belief systems, 219-231
    death rates, 195, 197
    decimation of, 35
    definition of, 253-254
    education, 239
    future of, 262
    graduate degrees, 262
    group bonding, 230-231, 236
    harmony and, 234
    languages of, 233-235
    loss of identity, 237
    population data, 249-250, 256
    socioeconomic status, 251-252, 259, 261
    student population, 79
    ten common beliefs of, 221-222
Navajo Nation, 220-222, 225, 250, 252-253
Networking, 117-118, 269

Occupational discrimination, 108, 189, 192-193, 211-212
Oneida Nation, 241
Osage Reservation, 250
Other American, The (Harrington), 70

Ownership of property, inequality in, 175, 190-191, 193, 195

Papago Reservation, 251
Passports, 131
Performance assessments, of teachers, 81, 99
Persistence variables, 41, 58
Philadelphia Eagles, 119
Pimping, 14
Plessy v. Ferguson (1896), 80, 99
Pluralism, defined, 128-130, 162
Population, minorities, 97, 249, 267
Poverty, 61
    black, 193
    changes in government policy, 98
    expanding urban, 268
    federal policy since 1967, 96
    feminization of, 98, 143, 146, 161, 165
    Indian, 249
    inner-city, 70-71, 74-75, 95, 268
    minority vs. white, 39
    nativity differentials in, 145
    regional variations, 172-173
    U.S. rates, 74
    and welfare receipt, 149
Power:
    American Indians and, 249
    compliance typology, 57-58
    of dominant group, 165
    pervasive differences in, 37-38, 156
    redistribution of, 184
    theory, 37-38
    (*See also* Whites)
Pressure resources, 108
Private property, ownership of, 175, 190-191, 193, 195, 201, 240-243, 252, 259-260
Professionals, black, 62, 88-89
    (*See also* Middle class)
Property ownership (*see* Private property)
Public assistance income, 146-148
Public school:
    black distrust of, 19
    Indian students, 243-244
    minority percentages, 61
    minority teachers, 50
    (*See also* Education; Schools)
Puerto Ricans, 137
    incomes of, 139-143
    poverty rates, 145
    public assistance and, 151
    single parent families, 152-154
    unemployed, 152
    welfare dependence of, 146-147, 154-155

Puerto Ricans (*Cont.*):
  (*See also* Hispanics)

Race:
  ascriptive significance of, 157
  crime rate and, 70
  psychological research, 98
Race of Manifest Destiny (Horseman), 35
Race relations, competitive mode, 108, 214, 266
Racial isolation in the public schools, 71
Racial stratification, 3–31, 53–54, 155
  blacks' responses to, 55–56
  covert, 192–193, 265
  dimensions of, 4–5
  expressive forms of, 269
  future of, 30
  parallel institutions and, 35–50
  (*See also* Racism; Stratification)
Racism:
  colleges and, 49, 89–90, 95
  immigration, 135
  latent, 162
Rainbow coalitions, 157–158
Reagan administration, 10, 95, 98, 163
Recessions, 152, 158
Recruitment programs, 40–41, 48, 57
  of black students, 85, 87, 100–101
  NFL managerial, 107–119
  old buddy referral system, 119
Reform movements:
  academic achievement, 100
  black teachers and, 90
  education, 80, 82–83, 99
  immigration, 128
  Indians and, 255
  inner-city, 65
  institutional commitment to, 46–50
  negative effects of, 60
  (*See also* Kerner Commission)
Refugee status, 131–132, 163
Regents of the University of California at Petitioner V. Allan Bakke, 38
Religious Freedom, American Indians', 219, 230
Reparations, 184, 212
Republic of New Africa movement, 16
Research:
  American Indian education, 245
  educational, 82–83, 98, 100
  follow-up studies, 75
  of white attitudes, 269
Resegregation, 74, 90, 97

Reservations:
  relocating from, 253
  unemployment rate, 251
  (*See also* Native Americans)
Retardation, Indian vs. Western beliefs, 225, 229
Retention programs, 101
Retirement, 151–152
Riots, 65
Role models, black, 29–80, 84–85, 91, 100
Rough Rock Demonstration School, 253

Sacred: Ways of Knowledge Sources of Life, The (Beck and Walters), 236
Salary disadvantage, 190
  (*See also* Wages)
San Carlos Apache Reservations, 252
Scapegoating, 11, 15
Scholastic Aptitude Test (SAT), 40
Schools:
  admissions criteria, 38
  adoption program, 85
  black isolation in, 68
  black lag in, 3
  black parents' role, 86
  black teacher shortage, 80–91
  community, 97
  distrusting of, 29–30
  Indian beliefs and, 224, 226
  inner-city, 65–76
  local control, 260
  minority enrollment, 73, 97
  resegregation, 65, 74, 90
  segregated, 36, 73–74
  standardized tests, 38
  tribally-controlled, 261
  (*See also* Education)
School boards, 88–89
Segregation, 36
  of nonblack minorities, 97
  residential, 135
  schooling and, 22, 56, 65–76, 90, 95, 167–168
  social networks of sports, 118
  in sports, 106
Self-determination, Indian, 253, 256, 268
Self-employment, black, 174
Self-segregation, 16, 118
Senate Select Committee on Indian Affairs, 251
Separatist strategy, 16
Service sector, 205
Sexism, 116
Simpson-Rodino Act, 130

Single parent families, 142
   minority vs. white, 39
   poverty and, 143, 146
   public assistance, 148
   sharp rise in, 152-154
   (*See also* Women)
Slavery, 199-200
   collective blame and punishment, 18
   oppositional identity and, 15
Snyder Act (1921), 243
Social class:
   economic position and, 157
   significance of, 165
   stratification and, 53
   vs. caste, 266
Social identity:
   black education and, 27
   collective, 15
Social insurance payments, 151-152
Socialism, 197
Social mobility, 10
Social networks (*see* Networking)
Socioeconomic status (*see* Economics)
Souls of Black Folk, The (DuBois), 35
South, resegregation in, 74
South Africa, 200
Southeast Asia, 36
Southern Christian Leadership Conference, 36,
   108
Special education classes, 39, 86
Speech, cultural inversion, 18
Spirit world, of Indians, 223
Sports, black dominance in, 14, 106-119
Standardized tests, schools, 38
Status, sports and, 106
Stereotypes, 88
Stockbridge nations, 241
Strangers Next Door, (Williams), 36
Stratification, 3-31
   color and, 155
   gender over race, 137
   of world capitalism, 199-200
   social class and, 53
Student Nonviolent Coordinating Committee
   (SNCC), 36
Success, folk theories of, 25
Supreme Creator, belief in, 221, 223, 225
Survey of Minority Business Enterprises
   (Commerce Department), 173
Survival strategies:
   black culture and, 12-15
   competing and detracting, 26
Taboos, American Indian, 226

Teachers:
   black, 70-91
   certification standards, 70, 81-82
   as change agents, 210
   commuters, 65
   education programs, 82-83, 87-88, 100
   emergency permits, 82
   exchange programs, 88
   in Indian communities, 230
   in inner-city schools, 69-70
   in-service training programs, 86
   minimally competent, 69-70, 75
   minority declines in, 61, 85-90, 99
   recruitment by, 87
   salaries, 89
   status of, 99
   support of inequality by, 201-204
   transfers of, 70
Teenagers, poverty and, 28, 71, 152
Textbooks, 30
Tohono O'Odham ceremonies, 220-221
Tommorrow's Teachers (The Holmes Group), 83,
   100
Track, 106
Treaties, Indian land control and, 240-243, 252,
   259-260
Tribal Societies (*see* Native Americans)
Trickle-down theory, 203
Truly Disadvantaged, The (Wilson), 71
Tuscarora Nation, 241

University of California, Riverside, 192-204
U.S. Commission on Civil Rights, 68
U.S. Office of Equal Employment Practices, 7
Uncle Toms (*see* Clientship)
Underclass, 4, 31, 166
Unemployment:
   American Indian, 231, 250, 259
   blacks vs. whites, 39
   children and, 152
   compensation and pensions, 151-152
   ethnic distribution of, 192, 195
   temporary workers and, 163
   (*See also* Employment)
United Farm Workers (UFW), 36
United States v. State of South Carolina (1977),
   81
Urban centers (*see* Cities)
Urban growth, changes in government policy, 96,
   98
Urban schools, 65-76

Vested interest thesis, 50
Violence, 12
Vocational education, 20, 22, 39, 55

Wages:
    competency tests and, 81
    disadvantage, 192
    discrimination in, 23, 180
    education and, 22–23
    gap in, 177–179
    minimum, 189
    sports, 106
    teachers', 89
    (*See also* Income)
War on poverty, 70
Wealth, 58, 211–212
    American Indians and, 249
    blacks and, 173–175, 180–184, 189–196
    concentration of, 210
    current family income, 138
    education and, 58
    redistribution of, 212
    studies of, 191
    white vs. minority, 39
    (*see also* Income)
Welfare Trap (Butler), 213

Whites:
    central cities and, 67
    coercive power of, 57–58
    distrust of, 19–20
    educational decision makers, 88–89
    graduate school enrollment, 42
    income of, 39, 139–143, 145, 151, 169–171
    Indian beliefs and, 227–228
    occupational distribution, 192–193
    as ownership class, 193
    public assistance programs, 147
    supremacy doctrine, 35, 91, 182–185
    teachers, 80–81
    treatment of blacks, 7–19
Witchcraft, Indian belief systems, 227–228
Women:
    black employment rates, 176–177
    families headed by, 143, 152–154
    increased poverty of, 161
    wages, 179, 188, 200
Woodrow Wilson Foundation, 88
Working class:
    European, 199–200
    race and gender division, 197

Xenophobia, 164

Yaqui Nation, 227